MW00479603

Oral History
and Public Memories

IN THE SERIES *Critical Perspectives on the Past*
EDITED BY SUSAN PORTER BENSON, STEPHEN BRIER, AND ROY ROSENZWEIG

Tiffany Ruby Patterson, *Zora Neale Hurston and a History of Southern Life*

Lisa M. Fine, *The Story of Reo Joe: Work, Kin, and Community in Autotown, U.S.A.*

Van Gosse and Richard Moser, eds., *The World the Sixties Made: Politics and Culture in Recent America*

Joanne Meyerowitz, ed., *History and September 11th*

John McMillian and Paul Buhle, eds., *The New Left Revisited*

David M. Scobey, *Empire City: The Making and Meaning of the New York City Landscape*

Gerda Lerner, *Fireweed: A Political Autobiography*

Allida M. Black, ed., *Modern American Queer History*

Eric Sandweiss, *St. Louis: The Evolution of an American Urban Landscape*

Sam Wineburg, *Historical Thinking and Other Unnatural Acts: Charting the Future of Teaching the Past*

Sharon Hartman Strom, *Political Woman: Florence Luscomb and the Legacy of Radical Reform*

Michael Adas, ed., *Agricultural and Pastoral Societies in Ancient and Classical History*

Jack Metzgar, *Striking Steel: Solidarity Remembered*

Janis Appier, *Policing Women: The Sexual Politics of Law Enforcement and the LAPD*

Allen Hunter, ed., *Rethinking the Cold War*

Eric Foner, ed., *The New American History*. Revised and Expanded Edition

Collette A. Hyman, *Staging Strikes: Workers' Theatre and the American Labor Movement*

Ellen M. Snyder-Grenier, *Brooklyn! An Illustrated History*

William Eric Perkins, ed., *Droppin' Science: Critical Essays on Rap Music and Hip Hop Culture*

Mike Wallace, *Mickey Mouse History and Other Essays on American Memory*

Thomas Dublin, ed., *Becoming American, Becoming Ethnic: College Students Explore Their Roots*

Susan Levine, *Degrees of Equality: The American Association of University Women and the Challenge of Twentieth-Century Feminism*

Hope Cooke, *Seeing New York: History Walks for Armchair and Footloose Travelers*

George Lipsitz, *A Life in the Struggle: Ivory Perry and the Culture of Opposition*

ORAL HISTORY *and*
PUBLIC MEMORIES

EDITED BY
Paula Hamilton and
Linda Shopes

TEMPLE UNIVERSITY PRESS
Philadelphia

Paula Hamilton is Associate Professor in History at the University of Technology in Sydney, Australia. She is co-director of the Australian Centre for Public History, and co-editor of *Public History Review*.

Linda Shopes is a freelance editor and consultant; and formerly a historian at the Pennsylvania Historical & Museum Commission. She is Past President of the U.S. Oral History Association, and co-editor of the series *Studies in Oral History*.

TEMPLE UNIVERSITY PRESS
1601 North Broad Street
Philadelphia PA 19122
www.temple.edu/tempress

Copyright © 2008 by Temple University Press
All rights reserved
Published 2008
Printed in the United States of America

♾ The paper used in this publication meets the requirements of the American National Standard for Information Sciences—Permanence of Paper for Printed Library Materials, ANSI Z39.48-1992

Library of Congress Cataloging-in-Publication Data

Oral history and public memories / edited by Paula Hamilton and Linda Shopes.
   p. cm. — (Critical perspectives on the past)
Includes bibliographical references and index.
ISBN-13: 978-1-59213-140-2 (hbk. : alk. paper)
ISBN-10: 1-59213-140-9 (hbk. : alk. paper)
ISBN-13: 978-1-59213-141-9 (pbk. : alk. paper)
ISBN-10: 1-59213-141-7 (pbk. : alk. paper)
1. Oral history.   2. Collective memory.   I. Hamilton, Paula.   II. Shopes, Linda.
D16.14.O735 2008
907.2—dc22

2007037073

2   4   6   8   9   7   5   3   1

CONTENTS

PART II

PART III

Introduction: Building Partnerships Between Oral History and Memory Studies

Paula Hamilton and Linda Shopes

When the British oral historian Paul Thompson originally suggested that Linda Shopes from the United States and Paula Hamilton from Australia, who did not then know each other, collaborate on a book about oral history, memory, and the public, he set in train a fruitful and apposite partnership between two women across countries, cultures, and institutions. Both of us had been involved for many years in both public history and oral history, community work, and teaching. We were also in a sense, *more* than oral historians because we had worked in public projects that took us well beyond the archival impulse and engaged us in reflective analysis of oral history's role in the broader community and the more recent scholarship on historical memory. This book represents our individual and shared interests, both enriched by our years of collaboration.

Two observations lie at the core of this book. In the first instance, while there has been extensive scholarship on oral history as a method and practice, too few people take it "out of the house" and past the front door, as Paul Thompson once commented. He was referring to the semiprivatized, marginal nature of the practice and the thousands and thousands of tapes lying unused in drawers and archives—though we note that the people digitizing oral history for the web have taken it "down the street" some way.

Second, we observed that recent scholarship on historical memory in the fields of history, anthropology, sociology, and cultural studies has rarely engaged with oral history as a central practice in many societies where memory and history are inextricably entangled. Quite simply, very little published work examines how oral history, as an established form for actively making memories, both reflects and shapes collective or public memory.

We conceived of this volume as a means of bringing the metaphorically "buried" practice of oral history into the public domain by connecting it with contemporary ideas about how memory works as a social or cultural phenomenon. As the fourteen chapters included here investigate the practice of oral history in a wide range of cultural institutions, sites, and community forums, they demonstrate an understanding of oral history as something more than an archival activity. Oral history, as explicated here, is at heart a deeply social practice connecting past and present and, at times, connecting narrative to action. Together these chapters span the borders of established academic disciplines, contemporary professional practices, and community activism.

Oral History and Historical Memory

As areas of research and writing, oral history and memory studies have had very different historiographic trajectories. This accounts in part for their disconnect. Oral history rose to prominence in a particular context, becoming a mass practice in the climate of the 1960s. The rhetoric used to explain its value has often been framed in terms of "uncovering unknown stories" or "giving voice to the unheard, the secret," making it, in effect, a form of exposé or evidence where no other is available. In the scholarly realm oral history and its variations across disciplines are thus often understood as a source of data, and the focus, particularly in the social sciences, is on method. While lip service is paid to the concept of interdisciplinary approaches to oral history, there is in practice very little real interrogation of its use across different research traditions and the effect this use has on the memories and stories that result. Its widespread and diverse use means that purposes and outcomes range from life history, narrative biography, and both in-depth and unstructured interviews in cultural institutions and forums to the giving of testimony and witnessing in legal and judicial contexts, including those connected to efforts at social justice and restitution. Moreover, while oral history is a well-established field, its origins and diverse practice are responsible for its continued marginalization within the academy, as is its often naïve embrace at the local, grassroots level. All of this serves to cut oral history off from the more recent emergence of memory studies.

Yet there is also a strong awareness, reflected in an extensive and growing theoretical literature, that oral history always operates as an act of interpretation. Initially, the work of the American and Italian scholars Luisa Passerini, Ronald Grele, Michael Frisch, and Alessandro Portelli was particularly useful for oral historians who wanted to move beyond *what* people remember, or the content of the interviews, to *why* they remember, or the meaning of people's recollections. Frisch's work might be taken as representative of this early group. In his influential book *A Shared Authority*, he argued that oral history is

> a powerful tool for discovering, exploring and evaluating the nature of the process of historical memory—how people make sense of their past, how they connect individual experience and its social context and how the past becomes part of the present, and how people use it to interpret their lives and the world around them.[1]

Frisch was concerned to interpret individual stories within a larger frame, but how was this to be done? The title of his book suggested that the meaning of what was produced in an interview is—or could be—negotiated between interviewer and interviewee. While this has proved to be a powerful and persuasive idea for oral historians, few have engaged narrators in a discussion of meaning or have done the sort of close analysis of extant interviews that would give ground to Frisch's suggestion. Similarly, Portelli has written, in what is perhaps the most frequently quoted phrase in the literature, that "errors, inventions, and myths lead us through and beyond facts to their meanings." Although this notion is now invoked in an almost ritualized manner, explication is often quite mechanical—except in the case of Portelli himself, whose most recent work, *The Order Has Been Carried Out: History, Memory, and Meaning of a Nazi Massacre in Rome*, draws upon dozens of interviews to explore the complex ways in which the meaning of this event has operated in public consciousness for over a half-century. "These stories function," he writes, "as the tool that allows us to reconstruct the struggle over memory, to explore the relation between material facts and personal subjectivity, and to perceive the multiple, mutable ways of elaborating on and facing death."[2]

In truth, many people speak of remembering when they write or talk about oral history but are not particularly reflective about the process by which the articulation of memories takes place or how they become public. And this, ironically, is taking place at a time when early practitioners have been joined by a considerable force of oral historians in many countries, along with journals, special publication series, and readers that have helped establish oral history as a global phenomenon with an international association.[3]

Why has the significant body of interdisciplinary work on the construction of social and cultural memory failed to engage directly with oral history? There are numerous reasons. Oral history emerged as a widespread practice in relation to the democratizing of history in the 1960s, fueled by decolonization and the feminist and civil rights movements. In contrast, the "memory turn" in scholarship usually cites as its catalysts the Jewish Holocaust memory "industry" and twentieth-century wars, as well as the end of Communism in eastern Europe, so that it is often associated with "trauma."[4] As a result, much of this work moves beyond the local focus of oral histories to the national stage, played out on a rather larger range of sites than can be encompassed by the memories of individuals. The most notable example here is the monumental three-volume *Realms of Memory: The Construction of the French Past*, written under the direction of Pierre Nora.[5]

In addition, memory scholarship, unlike oral history, has been largely concerned with memory that is sustained beyond the individual lifespan, most often in memorials, monuments, places, or rituals. As it is principally concerned with the memory of groups, it has been distinguished by reference to the adjectives "social," "cultural," "public," "collective." Its genealogy is usually traced to the 1930s and the sociologists Emile Durkheim and especially Maurice Halbwachs. Halbwachs's *Social Frameworks of Memory* and *On Collective Memory* are thought to have been among the first published works that examined how group memory functions as a central element of a group's identity and is continually reworked to adapt to contemporary circumstances.[6] However, the relationship between the individual who does the remembering and the memory of the group has never been successfully resolved. Scholars have been principally concerned not with how individuals produce and make meaning from their memories—a central focus of oral history, which is *de facto* about individual memories—but much more with how a broader cultural memory is created, circulated, mediated, and received.

The field of memory studies has also been concerned with the critique of modernity and has attracted philosophers and phenomenologists, among them Henri Bergson and Paul Ricoeur, who have drawn upon a history of theorizing about the nature of experience and perception.[7] These scholars take a somewhat abstracted approach, a far cry from oral history's more concrete concerns. Media scholars too have found rich possibilities for studying the processes by which various media forms shape public or collective memories across time and space. Barbie Zelizer, for example, has explored the role of journalists in setting the framework within which different groups in the public sphere negotiated the meaning of U.S. President John Kennedy's assassination.[8] Yet all of this work is carried out at quite a remove from oral history, overlooking much of the more reflective work done by oral historians about the dynamic nature of remembering, gaps or silences in the transmission of memory, the collapsing of past and present in individual recall, and people's sense of "living in time" or historical consciousness. Detached from this work, memory theorists have reinvented it in more remote contexts, away from lived experience.

Seeking to explain the disconnect of memory studies from traditional historical scholarship, Katharine Hodgkin and Susannah Radstone, in the introduction to a volume in the recent *Memory and Narrative* series, note that "memory studies itself, despite its interdisciplinary potential . . . is located most firmly in disciplines most accustomed to a concern with representation: literature, film studies, cultural studies." They argue that the new work on memory has had little impact on the historical profession and ironically, for our purposes, tends to be regarded as a "sub-category of oral history."[9] While this may have been the case in English historiography, it was not so across the Atlantic. The American historians David Blight, in *Race and Reunion: The Civil War in American Memory*, and Merrill Peterson, in *Lincoln in American Memory*, among others, have explored the changing representation of a particular public event, person, or experience over time, although the use of oral history is obviated for works that focus on periods beyond living memory. Other work focusing on more recent events, like Emily S. Rosenberg's *A Date Which Will Live: Pearl Harbor in American Memory*, ignores the evidence of oral history; in contrast, Edward Linenthal's *The Unfinished Bombing: Oklahoma City in American Memory*, draws upon oral history unproblematically, as a source of data, rather than interrogating the peculiarities of the source itself.[10]

More importantly, though, historians working within memory studies tend to frame their work differently than oral historians. They ask questions about the broader social and cultural process at work in remembrance, and they are equally concerned with written forms of self-representation, from autobiographies to blogging. Oral historians, on the other hand, privilege the individual narrator and focus necessarily on his/her agency in the world, an approach that too often fetishizes the interview process and fails to understand the interview as but one form of memory-making. Oral history, driven by the passion for the personal story, assumes that every individual's experience can indeed be made into a purposeful story, and so, like autobiography, it tends to offer linear, causal explanations of individuals as the inevitable products of their past experiences. This approach tends to occlude the social and cultural processes that have shaped subjectivity and that are central concerns of historians of memory.

Perhaps, though, recent critiques of memory scholarship open up possibilities for rapprochement with oral history. Those writing in the field have begun to question the usefulness of "memory" as an explanatory framework, particularly when the outcome is a somewhat reified notion of memory as belonging ethereally to a "group." As Barbara Misztal, a sociologist of memory, argues: "In order for the notion of memory to be a useful analytical concept we need to retain a sense of both its individual and collective dimensions."[11]

This is precisely where oral history, with its inevitable focus on the individual, can help right the balance.

Oral History, Memory, and Public History

Although one might expect the field of public history to be an arena where memory studies and oral history meet, that has not necessarily been the case. Oral history and public history were for a time uneasy bedfellows. Oral history has often adopted a populist stance, one that is subversive of conventional history, whereas public history, initially defined as an "alternative" career in the face of a shrinking academic job market, tended to adopt a more conventional professional identity, working for state or federal organizations or carrying out commissions for corporations. Since the 1980s, however, they have found a rapprochement, as oral and public historians have met in community-based projects and developed fruitful partnerships at the local level in a number of countries. Oral history has also been used extensively by public historians as a tool in their work because it is so accessible: it can reach large audiences and present multiple points of view easily and without taking a stand, while providing color and life to the stories public historians seek to present.

Some initiatives by historians have also opened up possibilities for stronger engagement between practitioners in the two fields. Michael Frisch gave his book *A Shared Authority* the subtitle *Essays on the Craft and Meaning of Oral and Public History*, which suggests a much wider conception of authority in historical practice. His ideas were certainly taken up by a range of people employed in public and private cultural institutions over the next few years, but in reality "sharing authority" proved to entail a more complex negotiation over control of interpretation than practitioners imagined, particularly in relation to indigenous peoples.[12]

In *Theatres of Memory*, Raphael Samuel, a British historian with strong roots in the progressive community-history movement as well as a grounding in the new theoretical work on memory, proposed a more scholarly and capacious notion of public history as representation of the past in a variety of public spheres. But it was not until David Glassberg published his programmatic call for linking work in memory studies with public history that American practitioners and scholars alike began to engage seriously with memory studies. Glassberg's "Public History and the Study of Memory" generated wide debate and a roundtable commentary, but its chief value, rather than reducing the gap between oral historians and those working in memory, was to help public historians rethink the nature and purpose of their work and explore the use of memory as an explanatory concept.[13]

Oral History and Public Memories

This book thus represents an effort to link the often highly particular, individualized work of oral history with broader public, civic, or communal memories within the context of recent work in memory studies. Its fourteen chapters roam both geographically and intellectually. Five focus on work in the United States; the remaining nine deal with work that is literally all over the map: Australia, Canada, Colombia, Greece, Kosovo, New Zealand, Singapore, South Africa, and Turkey. We did not impose a specific theoretical framework on our authors, nor did we create a forum for theoretical consistency. Rather, we asked that authors engage in what we have termed an "ethnography of practice," describing specific interviews and specific projects and then reflecting on those interviews and projects as artifacts of memory, variously used "in public" to create, redefine, and subvert a historical past.

Quite serendipitously, the contributions sorted themselves into the three sections around which we have organized this volume: "Creating Heritage," focusing on the use of oral history in official, often state-sanctioned, institutions; "Recreating Identity and Community," addressing less formal, often locally based efforts to sustain memory in the face of multiple challenges; and "Making Change," exploring oral history as an activist practice. Yet these categories need not remain fixed, and readers are invited to recategorize the essays according to their own interests. We asked each author to reflect on the presentational mode in which the (oral) history has been made public, and so, for example, several chapters focus on oral history in museums, together offering a primer on the ways in which these institutions create meaning. Others address the challenges and opportunities of community projects, reflecting on oral history's role not only in documenting individual lives but in making memory social or collective by connecting individual life stories "in public." Some chapters are related thematically: two, for example, in two separate sections, examine the use of oral history to interpret the internment of Japanese Americans during World War II; several deal with oral history in the aftermath of war or other catastrophes. Yet others consider various forms of migration and displacement, exploring the relationship between place and belonging. Many chapters also make explicit how the national context has shaped the local circumstances within which the work under discussion has taken place, allowing for both cross-cultural comparison and an assessment of the relationship between localized studies and the increasingly global context within which public memories are articulated.

Overlaid on this thematic variety is the diversity of analytic modes the authors bring to their work. Some have taken a long view, reflecting broadly on decades of practice, while others discuss particular oral history projects, focusing in varying degrees on the substance, process, and implications of their work. While all understand the relations of power within which cultural work is situated, some authors support an explicitly activist agenda; others offer thoughtful critique, at a slight remove from action. Some write about the subjectivity of a particular practice in an explicitly autobiographical voice; others frame their work in more general terms. We have tried, in the individual sections, to leverage the energy of these diverse voices by arranging the chapters from the general to the particular, from broadly contextualized discussions to richly descriptive ones. Introductions to these sections attempt to make this movement explicit, even as they also forge connections among chapters and identify common themes.

What distinguishes these chapters from much work in oral history is their focus not on the experiences of individual narrators, but on the broader cultural meanings of oral history narratives. What distinguishes them from other work in memory studies is what distinguishes oral history from other forms of cultural practice: a grounding in real events situated in time and place, as well as in human relationships and social processes. As such, we intend for these chapters both to engage with larger discussions about memory and also to inform these often highly abstracted discussions with useful specificity. Collectively, our authors tell us something about the processes—technical, emotional, conceptual, political—by which oral histories move from a interview with and by individuals to the articulation of memories that create a social experience, that have some connection with others.

Such movement always involves some form of representation (re-presentation), which in turn is inevitably a mediation between the original speaker and the intended audience for his or her words. Indeed, the articulation of memory as an act of remembering in either written or oral form always involves mediation. The chapters here—some explicitly, some less so—capture that liminal place between speaking, writing, and representation and the slippery process of making meaning public. We have chosen to use the term "public" in relation to "memories" to signal our understanding of the essentially social nature of this remembering process. But we recognize that even this term can be problematic. Thus it is perhaps useful to conclude with reference to the work of Kendall Phillips, who makes a useful distinction between the "memory of publics" and the "publicness of memory." The former explores "the way that memory affects and is effected by various publics," the latter looks at how and why memories become public. Thus memories in the first category "occur in the open, in front of and with others. . . . These public memories are those about which we can interact, deliberate, share," and they in turn "serve as a horizon within which a public finds itself, constitutes itself, and deliberates its own existence." The "publicness" of memory, on the other hand, opens up questions about why some memories are known and others are forgotten, or emerge in particular ways and are subject to endless repetition in attempts to fix their meaning. These sorts of "public memories" are often shaped by complicated power struggles, ranging from internal discussions about who gets to say what about a given community or experience to instruments of the state authorizing some versions of a story and silencing other ones.[14] Chapters in this volume suggest that oral history helps us understand how intertwined these two notions of public memory are, how an interview can reveal and shape what is known among and by others, even as it can also participate in a broader, often political process of public meaning-making.

Over the many years this book has been under development, we have incurred several debts, most notably to the authors whose work appears herein. Their commitment to their work and to this project and their patience as we have tried to create a volume that is more than a sum of its parts have been exemplary; we are honored to have worked with such a dedicated group of people. Both of us have also enjoyed the intellectual fellowship of oral historians around the world; collectively, their work has informed our own thinking in countless and immeasurable ways. Two individuals, however, deserve particular mention: Paul Thompson and Timothy Ashplant, as editors of Routledge's series *Studies in Memory and Narrative*, encouraged us to develop this volume and helped frame our thinking about it. They also suggested that we work together, thereby initiating a productive collaboration and delightful friendship. The late Roy Rosenzweig, who with Stephen Brier and the late Susan Porter Benson edited Temple University Press's long-running *Critical Perspectives on the Past* series, understood the value of this volume when we first discussed it with him and supported its publication in the series. We are two of the legions of people who owe much to Roy and who mourn his untimely death. At Temple University Press, Janet Francendese, editor-in-chief, and Elena Coler, production manager, maintained a steadying hand through the long process of developing this book. Finally, Paula Hamilton acknowledges the support of the University of Technology, Sydney, particularly her colleague Paul Ashton and her assistant Margaret Malone, who provided wonderful editorial support. Linda Shopes recognizes the Pennsylvania Historical and Museum Commission, her employer during most of the time this book was under development, and especially Paula Heiman, PHMC librarian, who responded to her many requests for research materials with professionalism and good cheer.

Notes

1. Michael Frisch, *A Shared Authority: Essays on the Craft and Meaning of Oral and Public History* (Albany: State University of New York Press, 1990), 188. See also Luisa Passerini, *Fascism in Popular Memory: The Cultural Experience of the Turin Working Class* (Cambridge: Cambridge University Press, 1987), originally published as *Torino operaia e fascismo* (Laterza: Roma-Bari, 1984); and Ronald J. Grele, *Envelopes of Sound: The Art of Oral History,* 2d ed. (New York: Praeger, 1991).

2. Alessandro Portelli, "The Death of Luigi Trastulli: Memory and the Event," in *The Death of Luigi Trastulli and Other Stories: Form and Meaning in Oral History* (Albany: State University of New York Press, 1991), 2; *The Order Has Been Carried Out: History, Memory, and Meaning of a Nazi Massacre in Rome* (New York: Palgrave Macmillan, 2003), 16.

3. Two journals from English-speaking countries are *Oral History*, published by the Oral History Society in Great Britain, and *Oral History Review*, published by the U.S.-based Oral History Association. The Europeans Daniel Bertaux, Selma Leydesdorff, Luisa Passerini, and Paul Thompson set up the *International Yearbook of Oral History and Life Stories* in 1991; it was subsequently replaced by a collective including both oral historians and memory scholars who published the Routledge *Studies in Memory and Narrative.* Transactions Publishers recently replaced Routledge and is republishing some of the earlier volumes in the series. See also Robert Perks and Alistair Thomson, eds., *The Oral History Reader*, 2d ed. (London: Routledge, 2006). The International Oral History Association was formally established in 1996 after several years of biannual meetings.

4. See for example Peter Novick, *The Holocaust and Collective Memory: The American Experience* (London: Bloomsbury, 2001); Oren Baruch Stier, *Committed to Memory: Cultural Mediations of the Holocaust* (Amherst: University of Massachusetts Press, 2003).

5. *Realms of Memory: The Construction of the French Past,* 3 vols., under the direction of Pierre Nora; English-language edition ed. Lawrence D. Kritzman, trans. Arthur Goldhammer (New York: Columbia University Press, 1992–98).

6. See particularly the introduction by Lewis A. Coser to Maurice Halbwachs, *On Collective Memory* (Chicago: University of Chicago Press, 1992).

7. See, for example, Henri Bergson, *Matter and Memory* (1896; reprint ed., New York: Cosimo Classics, 2007); the phenomenological tradition is surveyed in Paul Ricoeur's monumental *Memory, History, Forgetting* (Chicago: University of Chicago Press, 2004). The long tradition of philosophers of memory—originating with Aristotle and Plato and continuing through the early twentieth century with Freud, Nietzsche, and Bergson—has been joined recently by the Israeli philosopher Avishai Margalit, author of *The Ethics of Memory* (Cambridge: Harvard University Press, 2002), and Ricoeur, whose *Memory, History, Forgetting* is cited above.

8. Barbie Zelizer, *Covering the Body: The Kennedy Assassination, the Media and the Shaping of Collective Memory* (Chicago: University of Chicago Press, 1992).

9. Katharine Hodgkin and Susannah Radstone, eds., *Contested Pasts: The Politics of Memory* (London: Routledge, 2003), 2. See also their *Regimes of Memory* (London: Routledge, 2003); Susannah Radstone, ed., *Memory and Methodology* (London: Berg , 2000).

10. David Blight, *Race and Reunion: The Civil War in American Memory* (Cambridge: Harvard University Press, 2001); Merrill D. Peterson, *Lincoln in American Memory* (New York: Oxford University Press, 1995); Emily S. Rosenberg, *A Date Which Will Live: Pearl Harbor in American Memory* (Durham, NC: Duke University Press, 2003); Edward T.

Linenthal, *The Unfinished Bombing: Oklahoma City in American Memory* (New York: Oxford University Press, 2001).

11. Barbara A. Misztal, *Theories of Social Remembering* (Berkshire, England: Open University Press, 2003), 6. For a cogent critique of memory studies, see Wulf Kansteiner, "Finding Meaning in Memory: A Methodological Critique of Collective Memory Studies," *History and Theory* 41 (2002): 179–97.

12. For a discussion of the challenges of "sharing authority," see articles by Daniel Kerr, Wendy Rickard, Alicia J. Rouverol, and Lorraine Sitzia and commentary by Linda Shopes and Michael Frisch in the special section "Shared Authority" in the *Oral History Review* 30 (Winter/Spring 2003): 23–113.

13. Raphael Samuel, *Theatres of Memory: Past and Present in Contemporary Culture* (London: Verso, 1996); David Glassberg, "Public History and the Study of Memory," *Public Historian* 18:2 (1996): 7–23; and "Roundtable Responses to Glassberg," *Public Historian* 19:2 (1997): 31–72, including comments by David Lowenthal, Michael Frisch, Edward Linenthal, Michael Kammen, Linda Shopes, Jo Blatti, Robert Archibald, and Barbara Franco.

14. Kendall R. Phillips, ed., *Framing Public Memory* (Tuscaloosa: University of Alabama Press, 2004), 3–7.

PART I

CREATING HERITAGE

Part I

CREATING HERITAGE

~

The chapters in this section get to the very heart of the volume: each considers the ways in which oral history has informed the creation of cultural heritage, understood broadly as a socially sanctioned, institutionally supported process of producing memories that make certain versions of the past public and render other versions invisible. Within this process, oral history might be understood as culturally neutral: interviews can be conducted and used in ways that support quite conventional views of the past; they can introduce voices that counter those views; they can complicate our understanding of what happened and what it means.

Cultural heritage is often associated with the preservation of landscapes, sites, and structures that have been deemed significant by an official, often state, body. And given oral history's value for, in Alessandro Portelli's resonant phrase, "amplifying the voice" of those who have been historically silenced, it is no accident that interviews are frequently used to expand the scope of preservation initiatives. Thus we begin with David Neufeld's discussion of the way Parks Canada, a federal heritage agency responsible for the preservation of Canada's natural and cultural resources, has used oral history to expand the interpretive reach of heritage sites to include the history of First Nations, as well as to draw upon Native ecological knowledge to inform land management practices. Neufeld's essay is distinguished by the broad intellectual and political context within which he places this discussion. He begins by identifying the hold a progressive, Eurocentric narrative has had over Canadian historiography for more than a half-century, creating a powerful conceptual framework—and informing a network of historic sites—with which new narratives must contend. He then links efforts at developing a more inclusive public history to the broader politics of Native activism for justice, redress, and recognition. At the heart of his chapter are three case studies of cooperative projects between Parks Canada and First Nations. In each case, Parks Canada used oral history in an attempt to get the Indian "side" of the presumably national story it was trying to tell at a national park; Indians, on the other hand, used it to cultivate cultural identity, facilitate intergenerational communication, support prior claims to the land, and, finally, enter into a long-term relationship with Parks Canada in order to alter the dominant narrative. The interviews, often taking the form of traditional, deeply metaphorical stories, did not provide information that could be integrated seamlessly into the existing site interpretation; rather, they offered a parallel narrative, sitting alongside, as opposed to folding into, the dominant story. Neufeld offers no final resolution to this disjunction; he leaves the conclusion open-ended by posing several provocative questions about the ability of official heritage agencies to serve as a middle ground for disparate histories.

In contrast, Kevin Blackburn's chapter shows how Singapore's state-run Oral History Centre has explicitly served the goal of nation building by deliberately excluding voices that challenge—or even complicate—a relentlessly progressive, nationalist narrative. Established in 1978, thirteen years after Singapore became an independent nation-state, the Oral History Centre quite predictably began its work by interviewing the ruling political and business elite; this was followed by projects documenting the experiences of more ordinary Singaporeans. Of particular interest is Blackburn's discussion of the ways in which an oral history project's goals and interviewing methodology—not the social position of the narrator—shape what is said in an interview. While it is perhaps predictable—if regrettable—that interviews with the elite would conform to a nationalist narrative, the fact that interviews with non-elites also do so challenges simplistic notions of oral history as an inherently democratic practice. Similarly, Blackburn's explication of the way exhibits celebrating Singapore's recent history have used highly selective quotations from the Centre's collections to support a nationalist perspective gives a critical edge to the presumed "authenticity" of the first-person voice.

Whereas Chapters 1 and 2 draw upon multiple oral history projects to reflect broadly on the process of heritage production, the next two chapters focus on very particular heritage-oriented projects designed to develop new narratives about old places. Like Neufeld, Maria Nugent discusses the use of oral history to integrate Aboriginal history of the post-European-contact period into the activities of a government heritage agency, in this case the National Parks and Wildlife Service of the Australian state of New South Wales.

Explicating the biases of traditional heritage preservation practices as well as the politics underlying current efforts at a more inclusive cultural practice, Nugent details how interviews with Aboriginal people revealed three layers of their association with the landscape beyond the reserves, or historically segregated settlements: places Aboriginals shared with white settler Australians that nonetheless held different meanings for them than those held by settlers; spaces, often out of doors in what she terms a "backyard zone," where Aboriginals enjoyed activities among themselves; and the spaces in-between—that is, the routes Aboriginal people used as they moved over the landscape, negotiating both social and geographic obstacles. Of particular interest is the method Nugent and her colleagues developed: when they found that explicit questions about "the places that have been significant to you" resulted in awkward silences, they reverted to a life history approach, which seamlessly incorporated references to meaningful places. To make their work useful for heritage preservation, they then used maps to determine the spatial dimensions of everyday life recounted in the interviews, sometimes asking narrators to locate places talked about. Nugent and her colleagues refer to this method as geo-biography, a term that signifies landscape plus life story, as well as, when mapped, the reverse: the biography of a landscape.

Focusing on two specific heritage sites, Işıl Cerem Cenker and Lucienne Thys-Şenocak demonstrate how oral history can open up possibilities for multiple narratives, even about national monuments saturated with a national— and nationalistic—history. They had initially intended to use interviews to supplement what the written record could tell them about the physical features of two seventeenth-century Ottoman fortresses at the entrance to the Dardanelles, currently under development by the Turkish government as national parks. However, like many oral historians, they found that interviewees did not answer the questions they posed, but instead wanted to talk about subjects not part of the original research agenda. So they redirected their inquiry, learning that those living near the forts connected their personal histories to the sites in practical and symbolic ways that both confirmed and countered the dominant historiography. They learned, for example, that twentieth-century immigrants to the region indiscriminately linked their own sacrifices in immigrating to those made by Turkish soldiers during World War I and by the Ottoman queen who used her personal wealth to construct the forts; that narrators made little distinction between the Ottoman empire and the Turkish Republic, a distinction central to Turkish historiography; and that residents displaced from a fort community compared their present circumstances unfavorably with life in the fort village. The authors urge a harmonization of diverse narratives in heritage development; yet, reflecting their informants' concerns about the impact of such development on their current communities,

Cenker and Thys-Şenocak open up questions about the politics of contemporary heritage projects.

Finally, Selma Thomas, anticipating chapters in the next section, broadens our understanding of cultural heritage to include not only landscapes and sites but also museum exhibitions, well recognized as a powerful form for codifying a perspective on the past. Drawing upon more than two decades of experience and recognizing the impact of video technology on museum exhibits, Thomas argues that interviews are not "edited" for inclusion in an exhibit but rather are "curated," much as artifacts are: they must be preceded by careful research, assessed within the context of current historiography, and placed appropriately within the broader intellectual and spatial frame of an exhibit. Much of her chapter is thus given over to a discussion of the decisions she made while curating video interviews for several exhibitions, most notably the Smithsonian Institution's "A More Perfect Union: Japanese Americans and the United States Constitution," which depicts the internment of Japanese Americans during World War II. Thomas understands that museums—and especially the Smithsonian, as the national museum of the United States—confer a certain legitimacy on the particular stories they choose to tell. She further understands that museums' cultural authority derives in large measure from the authenticity of the objects they present, an authenticity that is enhanced—indeed embodied—by the immediacy and intensity of first-person accounts. While Thomas is not critical of the museum's authoritative voice, she does not take it lightly either, recognizing the oral historian's responsibility both to conduct interviews in a manner that allows narrators to tell their stories in depth, in their own way, and to present these stories in ways that do not violate their integrity. Thomas concludes with a thoughtful discussion of the ethics involved in transforming private memories into public accounts.

One might conclude from these chapters that oral history used within the context of cultural heritage programs responds to a broader cultural politics. In Australia and Canada, as elsewhere, the inclusion of Aboriginal voices in heritage activities has become politically imperative. Similarly, in the United States and many other parts of the world, a half-century of social movements and a responsive social history have moved cultural practice toward a more inclusive, less sanguine view of the past. In Turkey, recent immigrants understand national icons in light of their own experiences, undercutting a dominant narrative. In post-colonial Singapore, on the other hand, a new nation's need to create a new identity silences dissenting voices.

1

PARKS CANADA, THE COMMEMORATION OF CANADA, AND NORTHERN ABORIGINAL ORAL HISTORY

~

David Neufeld

Parks Canada, established as a national government agency in 1885, is responsible for the protection and presentation of Canada's natural and cultural heritage through a network of National Parks and National Historic Sites. National Parks, originally selected for their natural beauty and recreational opportunities, are now understood to be a representative sample of the different ecosystems characterizing the country's environmental heritage. National Historic Sites address what are considered to be the significant themes of the country's history. Both parks and sites are powerful images of what Canada is.

The "Story of Canada" represented through these national heritage protected areas is, and remains, a concrete representation of a created place and a created past, both shaped and molded to maintain a unified sense of national identity. The Euro-Canadian vision of common traditions emphasizes the heritage of trans-Atlantic cultural ties to western Europe, the geography of the country, and the political history that established its boundaries, thus both justifying the country's existence and underlining its difference from the United States. This vision was largely drawn from Harold Innis's pioneering analysis of Canada's economic history, written in the 1920s.[1] Innis's work connected the economic exploitation of the country's originally abundant natural resources, including the development of an agricultural frontier, to the importance of trans-Atlantic communication links to the center of the British empire in England. This work focused upon the St. Lawrence River as the core of the Canadian economic and political system. The resulting historiographic direction, described as the "Laurentian thesis," remained the unchallenged analytical framework for the study and understanding of Canada well into the 1970s.

During the 1970s and 1980s, changing appreciations of social justice within the larger society supported increasing political and legal activism among Aboriginal peoples dissatisfied with their position in Canadian society. At the same time, the complexities of environmental issues and the limits of related scientific knowledge were becoming more obvious. These social and environmental pressures affected Parks Canada and served to enhance the profile of Aboriginal peoples in the strategic thinking of the organization's leadership. In 1985 the Historic Sites and Monuments Board of Canada (HSMBC), the federal body mandated to recommend designation of places, events, and persons of national historic significance, acknowledged the cultural imbalance of the country's National Historic Sites and recommended consultations with First Nations to determine their interest in the national commemoration of their history. Within National Parks, consultation with First Nations seemed to offer a possible shortcut to traditional ecological knowledge—that is, to indigenous peoples' deep knowledge about the intricacies of ecosystems. Aboriginal peoples in Canada appeared about to get their due, or at least plenty of attention from well-meaning, if naïve, civil servants such as myself.

In the early 1990s the Tr'ondëk Hwëch'in, a First Nation government, and Parks Canada jointly hosted a Yukon River heritage workshop in Dawson City, Yukon, to advance this work. I hoped the workshop would provide an opportunity to discuss First Nations' cultural values associated with the river and the role that Parks Canada might play in protecting these values and presenting them to Canadians. The program included representatives from a variety of river interest groups, including wilderness protection advocates, several First Nation governments, and both territorial and national government departments, as well as perhaps two dozen community Elders. Parks Canada was represented by Daniel Tlen of the Kluane First Nation, the Yukon Territory's representative on the HSMBC. Tlen described his work on the board and highlighted the importance of national cultural designations. As an example, he described the value of the national commemoration of the archaeological evidence uncovered in Beringia, the unglaciated portion of Ice Age North America linking Asia and America, for telling the story of the peopling of the Americas.

The audience of First Nation Elders and political leaders listened politely. At the conclusion of his presentation, Irene Adamson, an Elder of the Ta'an Kwach'in First Nation, rose and thanked Daniel for his speech. She went on: "I've heard about those people you are talking about. *My grandmother told me stories* about them. She remembered all these strange people walking around, they didn't have any good clothes, didn't know how to hunt, they were just lost and starving—we killed them, those are the people you are talking about."[2] Explicit in her story was the primacy of Aboriginal peoples in North America: "we" were created here, and this is "our" homeland. Implicit was a challenge to the authority of western science: her grandmother's stories versus old bones scrutinized by archaeologists. She thus questioned the "truth" presented by academic perspectives on Canadian history and the authority and power of government agencies relying on this history. Ms. Adamson's use of First Nations oral tradition challenged the assumed distribution of social power inherent in the western understanding of the past and articulated a different vision of how the world was made. She challenged the listeners to consider another way of understanding who we are and where we are going.

These early consultations with Aboriginal peoples, both nationally and regionally, resulted in Parks Canada's recognition of oral history as a key element in the approach to Aboriginal history and commemoration. The recording of oral history was seen as an opportunity to preserve at least some of the knowledge and wisdom from the last generation in the Yukon to have led a largely subsistence lifestyle—a life on the land. As the manager of a Parks Canada cultural research program for National Parks and National Historic Sites in the Yukon Territory, I have worked with a number of different Aboriginal communities over the last twenty years in an attempt to incorporate their stories into what we had assumed was a "shared" national history. The three projects I discuss here were viewed as successful by the host communities. Each project resulted in a collection of transcribed audio- and videotaped interviews with Elders. Each also spawned and supported the production of a variety of useful community-based products and activities, including publications, school curricula, language instruction materials, films, and other art forms; as important, each project enhanced connections between generations. The role of Parks Canada in these projects varied but was generally limited to funding, professional staff support, and some technical resources. To a large extent the projects were organized and completed by community members. In the following paragraphs I trace participants' conscious efforts to shape the public memory of their communities and the efforts of these communities to advance First Nation engagement with the national narrative.[3]

But first I must note that despite these community successes, Parks Canada still faces significant challenges in meeting its own mandate—the protection and presentation of expressed cultural values on a national stage. The passage of discovery we experienced through these projects highlights two continuing issues for Parks Canada. The first is the recognition of a parallel First Nation narrative that attributes meaning and power in the world in a manner different from the dominant narrative. The second is Parks Canada's capacity to extend its mandate to preserve and protect the framework for this narrative as has been done for elements of the Laurentian thesis. That is, how can a national commemorative agency contributing to an existing unified national identity effectively serve the interests of disparate cultural communities included in our national community?

Learning the Ropes: The Chilkoot Trail and the Yukon North Slope

The Chilkoot Trail is a passage connecting two distinct ecosystems: the mild Pacific coast rainforest of southeast Alaska and, separated by the rugged Coastal Mountains of northwestern Canada, the drier but much colder boreal forest of the Yukon interior. Its long use as an Aboriginal trading route is still visible in the family lineages joining communities along the trail. However, in the 1960s the trail was identified as a National Historic Site because of its use during the Klondike Gold Rush of the late 1890s. Tens of thousands of gold-hungry Stampeders, mostly adventurous young men, moved across the trail and left behind a colorful relict landscape of building remains and abandoned piles of what may well be the world's largest collection of early empty tin cans and broken bottles.

Commemorating the Chilkoot Trail was part of a larger effort to recognize the Gold Rush as an important event in Canada's history. Following the Laurentian thesis, this history began with the onset of regional Euro–North American settlement and development, the incorporation of a far-flung corner of the country into the Laurentian network, and its economic contributions to the center. Implicit in the commemorations of the Gold Rush was the recognition of the importance of the economic development of northern Canada. The celebration of the first large-scale exploitation of northern resources thus not only recognized the Gold Rush pioneers; it also gave a stamp of broad public approval to the mining and transportation improvements that opened the frontiers to industrial development in the 1950s and 1960s.[4]

This vision of economic development and settlement as progress had significant implications for Parks Canada's initial understanding of the historic role of the Carcross-Tagish First Nation along the Chilkoot Trail. The three interpretive themes identified for this National Historic Site in the early 1980s were life on the trail, including the experience of the Stampeders, based on their material remains on the trail; transportation technology—that is, the evolutionary progress of freight movement into the north; and national sovereignty, embodied in the role of Canada's Mounted Police in extending social order and establishing the political boundary. Cultural research by archaeologists and historians initially addressed the material culture on the trail and the rich lore found in Stampeders' diaries and letters, as well as the operation of horse packing companies, aerial tramways, and finally the railway; it also explored the differences between stolid Canadian Victorian social values and the wild west of the American republic. The indigenous population of the region had a limited role in this story, recognized only within a transportation subtheme as human pack animals who were contrasted to the white man's more technologically advanced modes of transportation.

As a result of the government's attention to Aboriginal activism in the mid-1980s, however, Parks Canada started to work to make the national story more inclusive, and the "Indian side" of the Chilkoot Trail story was identified as a research priority. Historical research, especially in archival photo collections, offered some limited access to the Aboriginal experience during the Gold Rush, but it was soon clear that the primary source would be the stories and memories of the local First Nation people.

Negotiations for a community oral history project occurred within a context of volatile land claims politics that inevitably shaped the project's outcome. Identification of the Chilkoot historic site had pre-dated the federal government's acknowledgment of Aboriginal claims, and no consideration had been given to Aboriginal interests in the land set aside for the historic site. Parks Canada's first contacts with the Carcross-Tagish First Nation about an oral history project thus coincided with the community's demand for the return of their traditional lands. Recognizing the possibility of misunderstanding, Parks Canada established clear expectations with the First Nation for the oral history project. The goal was to obtain the "Indian side" of the story for presentation at the National Historic Site. Design and control over its products would remain with Parks Canada.

Not surprisingly, the Chilkoot Trail Oral History Project did not fulfill Parks Canada's initial expectations. The attempt simply to throw light on the previously unexplored "Indian side" of the presumed national story was a failure. The Carcross-Tagish were quick to challenge the project's assumptions about the past. In one instance, after an extended set of interviews the project anthropologist and a First Nation Elder were relaxing on a lake shore. The anthropologist found a stone hammer nearby and showed it to the Elder as proof of the long-term Aboriginal presence in the region. The Elder briefly examined the stone and then casually threw it back into the bushes, saying, "What have I been telling you all week?" As the project progressed, we watched the First Nation similarly discard Parks Canada's objectives. It became clear that there was no "Indian side" of the Chilkoot Trail Gold Rush story; the stampede was seen simply as an annoying but brief interruption of their ongoing lives. Community stories instead put forward a parallel historical narrative describing their long use of the area and their connection to it as "home." These stories conveyed a significant message to Parks Canada about how the Carcross-Tagish used their traditional territory to sustain their cultural identity. The First Nation also used the project to make powerful statements about their ownership of this territory, thus returning to the main issue they wished to raise with the federal government.

The Carcross-Tagish effectively used the oral history project as a platform to challenge a national understanding of the historical significance of the Chilkoot Trail, to confirm their interests in the lands of the National Historic Site, and, with some sense of equality, to begin negotiating a relationship with Parks Canada that might benefit both. Today Parks Canada offers a modest public interpretation of the First Nation history for visitors to the trail.[5] It demonstrates respect for the First Nation citizens who live and gain a livelihood in the National Historic Site, and community Elders visit the trail camp annually to meet with Parks Canada staff and orient them to this important piece of their homeland. While efforts to document the "Indian side" of the Gold Rush story proved to be a dead end, the oral history project was an important stepping stone in the development of positive working relationships between the First Nation and Parks Canada.

Ivvavik National Park has a distinctly different origin than the Chilkoot Trail National Historic Site. Plans to develop oil and gas resources in the Beaufort Sea and the Mackenzie River in the Canadian western Arctic stirred up Aboriginal protests in the early 1970s. In response the federal government set up the Mackenzie Valley Pipeline Commission to hear complaints and present recommendations to guide development. To the surprise of both government and industry, one commissioner—Mr. Justice Thomas Berger, who both chaired the commission and prepared its final report to Parliament— recommended a ten-year moratorium on all development to allow settlement of outstanding Aboriginal claims. He also recommended that lands in northern Yukon be set aside for a wilderness park to protect wildlife and allow resident Aboriginal peoples to continue their traditional activities.[6] The Inuvialuit Final Agreement, a treaty settling their claims on Canada, described a new relationship between the national government and the Inuvialuit. And two National Parks, Ivvavik and Vuntut, were ultimately created through the negotiation of final agreements with two Aboriginal groups, the Inuvialuit Regional Corporation (1984) and the Vuntut Gwitchin First Nation (1993).

The Yukon North Slope Oral History Project was initiated in 1990 as a partnership between the Inuvialuit Social Development Program (ISDP), the cultural branch of the Inuvialuit Regional Corporation, the Yukon government's Department of Tourism—Heritage Branch, and Parks Canada.[7] In an arrangement quite different from that which governed the Chilkoot Trail project, the two park partners coordinated their shared interests through a common contractual arrangement with the ISDP, which ran the multiyear project. Although the ISDP contracted with a project anthropologist at the request of the Yukon and Parks Canada partners, there was never any question that the project was run, and the results owned, by the Inuvialuit.

The community's interests became apparent during the course of the project as participating Elders worked to prepare a legacy of traditional teachings. Their primary audience was, as in days past, their children and grandchildren. Recognizing that opportunities to pass stories on to the young at traditional hunting, whaling, and winter camps were increasingly unavailable, Elders were active and eager participants in a process that not only included nostalgic visits to their old camps but also allowed them, through oral and video recordings and texts, to address future generations about the importance of "being Inuvialuit."

Parks Canada had two objectives for the project: to produce an Inuvialuit history of the post-contact period on the Yukon North Slope in order to support public interpretation of the Inuvialuit cultural resources in the park; and to gain access to Inuvialuit traditional ecological knowledge (TEK) to supplement the relatively limited scientific knowledge available for natural resource management. While Parks Canada had a fairly clear understanding of its goals, it only vaguely understood the oral history needed to address them. It had even less comprehension of the community's interests in and intended purposes for the project.

The notion of "being Inuvialuit" did not directly address the Parks Canada interpretive agenda. Although it was expected that traditional life ways would be featured in the park's cultural interpretation, the nature of Inuvialuit identity challenged any simple presentation of Inuvialuit life. During a walk around Herschel Island, Victor Allen, an Inuvialuit Elder (Fig. 1.1), offered me a lengthy first-person narrative describing his social relations with various visitors to the island. It took me some time to realize that he was speaking metaphorically and that "his experiences" had taken place over the course of somewhat more than a century. The passage of real time, the basis of history as a chronological, causal chain of events, was only incidental to his purpose. Rather, Allen's story organized the past as a set of object lessons on relations among family members, places, and neighbors or Newcomers. These relationships all focused on the enhancement of Inuvialuit identity and interests. Many of the narratives collected by the project tended to present this kind of

Fig 1.1 Victor Allen, Inuvialuit Elder, c. 1990. Mr. Allen introduced the author to a nonchronological understanding of the past. *(Photograph by David Neufeld.)*

"life story." Parks Canada's role in the public presentation of this sort of cultural message was questionable, though Inuvialuit appreciated contributions to their own community-building processes.

Expectations for the scientific value of the oral history narratives fared no better. Although Parks Canada wished for specific details about Inuvialuit uses of natural resources and knowledge of animal behavior, these subjects were only obliquely referenced in the interviews. Such information as was available proved to be of limited utility. In an attempt to access this Inuvialuit TEK for the park's computerized geographical information system (GIS), a primary management tool, we combed the interviews to find temporally and geographically delimited data suitable for entry. A detailed study of a single topic—fish—revealed the challenges facing the integration of knowledge sets. Approximately one hundred references to fish, fishing, fish species, and fish as food were identified in the roughly seventy-five project interviews.[8] These references were then analyzed to determine how the Elders incorporated fish into their narratives and what these narratives contributed to the process of cultural reproduction. The results of this analysis indicated first of all that

Inuvialuit Elders knew a lot about both fish species and habitat.[9] In addition to detailed knowledge of most of the fish species identified by science, Inuvialuit stories also noted the periodicity of fish numbers; good times and locations for meeting and harvesting the annual runs, often reflected in place names; the relationships between harvest fish and competing predators, such as seals and killer whales; and, of course, a great deal of detail on effective methods of fishing.

Although they were rich in the expression of traditional knowledge, using the Elders' stories as science presented real problems. Codifying their stories about fish reduced their knowledge to information. That is, the cultural context of the story was discarded. Narrator Lily Lipscombe identified two different species of arctic char.[10] However, when she spoke of their difference, she was not describing fish. *Iqalukpik* (arctic char) were a delicacy to the *Tariuqmiut* (people of the sea). *Iqaluaqpak* (land-locked char) were caught only in springtime, and only the *Nunamuit* (people of the land) would eat them. Lipscombe's story noted her grandparents' preferences for these different species as signs of their different ethnic backgrounds and a key to the social makeup of contemporary Inuvialuit society—a lesson in being Inuvialuit. From the perspective of park scientists, however, the Yukon North Slope Inuvialuit oral history project did not provide the hoped-for bonanza of data to guide management. As in the Chilkoot Trail project, expectations premised on western approaches to the land and culture initially hampered an understanding of the different kind of knowing embedded in the Elders' stories.

Nonetheless, important lessons were learned, and regional Parks Canada staff adapted their working activities to reflect an enhanced awareness of Aboriginal interests. A collaboration between a Parks Canada biologist and a Gwich'in cultural research worker resulted in the joint publication of an ethnobotany book. More recently, Parks Canada completed two interpretive centers in the Inuvialuit region. At the planning stage, these centers were assumed to be for visitors, expected to be few in number. During the course of community consultations, however, this initial assumption was altered to address the communities' interests in also developing the spaces for local exhibits, school projects, and community functions. These activities were all set within a broadening engagement with the Inuvialuit communities to open up the management of the regional National Parks to their expertise (Fig. 1.2).[11]

Thus, in growing cooperation with Parks Canada, the Inuvialuit were able to use the project to advance their own understanding of the greatest need for good management of their territory—the maintenance of an informed and engaged Inuvialuit population. More generally, both the Carcross-Tagish and

Fig 1.2   Renie Arey (L) interviews Sarah Meyook (R) at the place where her cabin used to stand by Ptarmigan Bay. This portion of the Arctic coast of the Yukon is now designated Ivvavik National Park. *(Courtesy of the Inuvialuit Social and Cultural Resource Centre; photograph by Murielle Nagy.)*

the Inuvialuit used the projects to connect with a federal agency managing lands in their traditional territory. They used the power gained by political recognition and the coherence and meanings of their oral history to challenge the assumptions of western historiography and natural science, resulting in Parks Canada's re-evaluation of its understanding of national history and the way First Nations and Inuvialuit might choose to engage with it. The Carcross-Tagish and the Inuvialuit were thus able to bring the government of Canada onto a middle ground where there could be a search for accommodation and the development of shared meanings and practices.[12] Subsequent work with the Tr'ondëk Hwëch'in highlighted an even more important opportunity for Parks Canada to redefine its relationship with Aboriginal communities.

Working on the Middle Ground: The Tr'ondëk Hwëch'in and Tr'ochëk National Historic Site

The ancestors of the Tr'ondëk Hwëch'in, the Hän, were known to early fur traders as the *gens des fous* ("people of passion") because of their exciting dances and pleasing songs. Today their descendants are among the numerous Northern Athapaskan peoples whose lives and culture are shaped by their continuing connection to the landscape of the Yukon River. The spine of the sub-Arctic boreal forest ecosystem characterizing much of the Yukon and central Alaska, the Yukon River rises in the southern lakes of the Yukon and northern British Columbia, arcs northwest to the Arctic Circle in Alaska, then turns southwest to drain into the Bering Sea.[13] It follows a serpentine course through a broad valley of its own making. In some areas the valley floor has been cut down 250 meters in the last five million years, creating a dramatic wooded landscape of rugged cliffs, volcanic basalt flows, and ancient rounded mountains. The regular summertime arrival of spawning salmon moving up the river from the Pacific Ocean and the migration of caribou herds in the fall sustain the Athapaskan communities of the basin. The Tr'ondëk Hwëch'in regard these natural rhythms as part of an established compact among the human, natural, and spiritual inhabitants of the Yukon River lands.

The onset of European contacts in the mid-nineteenth century introduced a set of stressors that, over a century, threatened the cultural identity of the Tr'ondëk Hwëch'in. Fur traders brought new diseases that ravaged Yukon River Aboriginal populations, while the Klondike Gold Rush of the late 1890s brought tens of thousands of Euro-Americans into the heart of their traditional lands. Although displaced by the Newcomers from Tr'ondëk, their seasonal camp at the mouth of the Tr'ondëk (Klondike) River, the Tr'ondëk Hwëch'in managed to relocate to a new camp not far downriver at Moosehide, where they re-established a form of independence and managed their integration with white society. However, in the late 1940s and early 1950s, the collapse of fur prices and a significant increase in government regulation of land use served to redefine the Tr'ondëk Hwëch'in's relationship to the land that had supported them. A concurrent federal program of aggressive cultural assimilation through the establishment of northern Aboriginal residential schools separated them further from the land. Children were removed from their families, and ultimately the community was forced to abandon Moosehide, thus breaking important links between generations and separating the past from the future. Finally, beginning in the mid-1950s and continuing into the 1990s, government and the tourism industry's emphasis on commemorating Klondike Gold Rush history effectively buried the Aboriginal past, hiding it and the people associated with it from the public mind, separating the Tr'ondëk Hwëch'in from their own past, and contributing to the separation of all of Yukon's First Nations from the larger community of Canada. In the course of the first half of the twentieth century, the Aboriginal peoples of the Yukon were transformed into objects of study and wards of the state.

Parks Canada was the agent for the Canadian government's commemoration of the Klondike Gold Rush and thus a player in this objectification of

Aboriginal people. Like the Chilkoot Trail commemorations further south, the work in Dawson, the service town for the Klondike goldfields, was set within the national narrative dominated by the Laurentian thesis. Extensive—and expensive—restoration work on dozens of buildings in town and a mining camp and dredge in the goldfields helped ensure Dawson's survival as a viable Newcomer community and made it a major seasonal tourist destination. One of the tourist highlights is Discovery Day, the annual celebration of the initial discovery of gold in mid-August 1896. The stories told by Parks Canada at Dawson and the town's principal public event thus validated the government's northern development strategies and facilitated the replication of this national vision of Canada in the Yukon.

In the early 1990s, Parks Canada made tentative contacts with the Tr'ondëk Hwëch'in, seeking their participation in the Gold Rush commemorative program. However, the intent of these commemorations offered little of interest to the First Nation. The Tr'ondëk Hwëch'in, already committed to a community program of restoring their history and identity and immersed in negotiation with the government over their final agreement, or treaty, demurred. Understanding the reason for their lack of interest in commemorating the Gold Rush again requires a long view. The call for a final agreement by Yukon First Nations began, surprisingly, as a reaction to the social justice and human rights movements of the 1960s. Aboriginal people in Canada, like indigenous peoples across North America, had participated in the demand for equal treatment. In response, the Canadian government in 1969 issued a White Paper on Indian Affairs that proposed rescinding the special status of Aboriginal people under the Indian Act of 1876 and absorbing them into the mainstream national population.[14] However, First Nations people were not pleased to find that becoming full members of the Canadian community meant that while their common humanity would be recognized, their distinctive cultural identity would not. In the Yukon, First Nations worked together to respond.

Together Today for Our Children Tomorrow: A Statement of Grievances and an Approach to Settlement by Yukon Indian People was the result. A brief document with two messages, it provides an Aboriginal account of recent Yukon history and describes the need for a middle ground between Aboriginal and Newcomer cultures. The first part describes how the original peoples of the Yukon had been left out of history, concluding that "public holidays now have little meaning to the Indian. August 17—Discovery Day means to the Whiteman the day the gold rush started. It means to the Indian the day his way of life began to disappear."[15] The second part describes the need to establish a joint Yukon society. While problems in housing, education, land regulation, and social services are noted, the document sought a framework for a cooperative governance model, inclusive of both cultures in the Yukon, one that would allow First Nations to both regain their humanity and retain their culture. As Roddy Blackjack, an Elder of the Carmacks/Little Salmon First Nation, said, we must become "two cultures side by side."[16] The Parks Canada recognition of this parallel path in the late 1990s provided the middle ground necessary for the eventual recognition of a Tr'ondëk Hwëch'in National Historic Site.

Presented to Prime Minister Pierre Trudeau in 1972, *Together Today for Our Children Tomorrow* was accepted as the foundation for the negotiation of a comprehensive final agreement for Yukon First Nations. Twenty-six years later, in 1998, the Tr'ondëk Hwëch'in signed their agreement with the Canadian government. The negotiations had been long and often confrontational, and the signing was an important symbol of cultural strength for the Tr'ondëk Hwëch'in. It was time to advance their narrative, to challenge the old national narrative that had stripped their lives of meaning. In community meetings to discuss the future of their new heritage site at Tr'ondëk, a site laden with the history of both Aboriginal people and Newcomers, some felt that a clean platform for the representation of the Hän presence was needed and that it was time to take the white history of the place "and throw it all in the river."[17] While this cultural cleansing did not take place, the Tr'ondëk Hwëch'in actively worked to bring the narrative expressed in their oral history and embodied in their continuing use of their traditional lands into the discussions with Parks Canada about their relationship to the national story.

The Tr'ondëk Hwëch'in share the Athapaskan oral tradition, a spoken literature framed by their language and yoked to their land by evocative place names, the whole describing a sophisticated set of relationships to place and their human and nonhuman neighbors. The traditional territory of the Tr'ondëk Hwëch'in is created, understood, described, and explained by their stories; they set a people within an understandable world. Or as Tr'ondëk Hwëch'in Elder Percy Henry puts it: "Our land is our history book."[18] To visit and use places in their lands, even if only in the imagination, is a trigger for the stories and the values and knowledge encapsulated in them. And the catechetical repetition of this place-based spoken literature at camps and on the move throughout the annual round of subsistence activities has been an important part of the transgenerational transmission of cultural identity. This oral tradition incorporates instruction in the practical skills needed to sustain life in the northern boreal forest, provides a moral code for the maintenance of proper relations within their lands, and includes exemplars of wisdom to guide choices made in daily life. They remind listeners that they have both the ability and the responsibility to contribute to the dynamic equilibrium in the world.[19] The stories are also potent statements of an interest in place that western understanding might characterize as ownership.

As explained by these stories, the Yukon River, and time itself, were created by an Athapaskan hero figure, variously known as Smart Beaver Man on the upper river, Tachokaii (the Traveller) in the Dawson area, and K'etetaalkkaan-nee (the One Who Paddled among the People and Animals) among the Koyukon of the lower river. The story cycle describes the mythic Traveller's adventures on a journey from the river's origin to its mouth, adventures that transform the world from chaos, a time of limitless possibilities when humans and animals spoke with each other (and in fact regularly changed from one form to the other), to its present more fixed, more reliable, but still dynamic state. As the Traveller moves down the river, he reworks the landscape by removing obstacles to his journey. He also captures and kills, or tames, bad animals that threaten good relations. Then, at the end of his trip, he vanishes, closing off his influence and transferring responsibility for the world to its inhabitants: "So he went down the Yukon until he got to the ocean. Then he paddle and paddle. Pretty soon he come to a mountain, and there's a channel going through there. That's where he went in. Before he went through, he left a note there that said he was not to be followed."[20]

The Traveller story cycle is one of the most important in the Athapaskan oral tradition. The story not only explains how humans fit into a dynamic world that he has balanced; it also challenges the listeners to be conscious of their specific and detailed responsibility for maintaining this balance. Anthropologist Frederica de Laguna characterizes the Traveller episodes as serious stories that serve "as indirect conveyors of knowledge about the natural (and supernatural) world, of man's place in it, and of how he should behave."[21] Mida Donnessey, an Elder of the Kaska Tribal Council, in her telling of the story episodes said the purpose was to "make the world good for baby."[22]

While the Traveller stories deal with a largely spiritual world, they are also firmly grounded in the familiar riparian landscape of the Athapaskans. Henry's version of the story explicitly links the Traveller's tricking and killing of the monster Ch'ii Choo and the construction of the first birch bark canoe to the sandy flats of the Yukon River as it meanders into the south end of Lake Laberge. Villages along the lake are noted as the scenes of rescues. Another story is set at Old Woman Rock below the confluence of the Fortymile River, while the Traveller's adventures with the *deedaii* (a big bear) in yet another version of the story take place about ten kilometers below Clavath (Calico Rock) at Clavath Mon (Ford's Lake). The geography of the story is explicit as the Traveller moves down past the Ramparts and through the Yukon Flats to the very mouth of the river.[23]

The story cycle also appears to be fixed in time. In Dawson the stories were told in the fall, during the move downriver from the summer fishing camp to the winter hunting grounds to the northwest. As the Tr'ondëk Hwëch'in traveled, stories linked to the places where they camped were repeated, reminding the audience of the moral lessons of the Traveller's experiences in that place and the subsistence knowledge appropriate to that place and time of year. The regular use of particular places for specific purposes at the same time each year reinforces the cultural value of the landscape, and layers of meaning are laminated together by the stories. In this way the world is re-created every year and people are continuously reminded of their ongoing responsibilities in the world.[24]

These intangible cultural constructs—language, oral tradition, practical skills fitted to place, and relationships among both human and nonhuman neighbors—reflect values rising from the long Tr'ondëk Hwëch'in experience in their traditional lands and remain important elements of Aboriginal civilization in the Yukon basin. Thinly veiled stories describe the arrival of the barbarians who so disastrously upset Hän life during the Gold Rush, the character of their contact, and the adjustments the Tr'ondëk Hwëch'in made to maintain their culture over the last century. Stories about Chief Isaac, leader of the Tr'ondëk Hwëch'in during the Gold Rush, and other historic figures remain vital exemplars for youths, remind citizens of their obligations, and guide contemporary leadership. The mythic stories about Tachokaii also remain vibrant, providing a powerful moral framework through which traditional Tr'ondëk Hwëch'in traditional knowledge is transmitted. The Athapaskan oral tradition, rooted in place, thus creates a sense of both personal and community identity, establishes a moral framework binding together the members of that community, evokes a set of ethics describing a responsible approach to the resources of their homeland, provides information on the effective use of those resources, and highlights for others the Tr'ondëk Hwëch'in interest in and rights on these lands. In many ways the visible cultural landscape of the Tr'ondëk Hwëch'in is simply a shadow of the far more vibrant and meaningful parallel intellectual and spiritual landscapes that live in the hearts and minds of these people of the river. This intangible heritage that is passed from one generation to the next contributes to the richness of human existence only as long as the people who continually re-create it through the celebration of their spoken literature retain their traditional relationship with the Yukon River as a cultural landscape.

Parks Canada addressed problems associated with this perplexing parallel narrative through the 1990s. A Royal Commission on Aboriginal Peoples,[25] negotiated treaties, and recognized Aboriginal title to land all pointed to narratives of meaning that were distinctly different from the one carried by the national story. The development of new analytical tools for cultural recognition allowed Parks Canada to engage successfully with Aboriginal peoples.

The HSMBC began discussions to address "the challenge of designating subjects related to Aboriginal Peoples' history which do not conform to the traditional definition of national significance. Parks Canada and Aboriginal Peoples are striving to develop a more positive working relationship at the community level, . . . [including] acceptance for oral history and traditions to explain why these sites are significant to Aboriginal People."[26] In July 1999 the HSMBC accepted the concept of "Aboriginal cultural landscape"[27] as a framework for the national recognition of Aboriginal culture.

At the same time Parks Canada sought to address the erosion of National Park ecosystems through a broader appreciation of both regional and cultural factors affecting the health of the land and animals within them. A national panel reporting in February 2000 on the parks' ecological integrity noted the importance of engaging Aboriginal peoples in the management of National Parks within their traditional lands. With an emphasis on the shared vision to protect these "sacred places," there was also the hope that these examples would inspire other Canadians to acknowledge the country's Aboriginal peoples.[28] As a result of these changes, Tr'ondëk Hwëch'in became more confident that Parks Canada could recognize the existence of a parallel path, and Tr'ochek was designated as one of the first Aboriginal cultural landscapes National Historic Sites in November 2001.

Conclusions

The Laurentian thesis addressed Canada's longtime need for a narrative to affirm its national identity in North America. By reinforcing trans-Atlantic linkages with France and Britain, it acknowledged the "two founding nations" concept that has been the basis of Canadian national politics and has justified the existence of a Canada in North America that is distinct from the United States. The idea also gave meaning and thus distributed social power to the staple industries of the country—fur trade, fishing, agriculture, and mining—by recognizing their role in developing the economic and demographic heart of the country, the St. Lawrence Valley.

By addressing the concerns of Euro-Canadians and affirming the importance of their activities, this national story continues to inspire a vision of Canada's future. However, it also created and perpetuated a vision of a dying indigenous culture that had left an empty land waiting to be developed. The story thus reinforced the social and political structures that developed and implemented policies of Indian assimilation and destruction, thereby confirming the original vision. Broad acceptance of this account of how Canada became a country and a national community within which Aboriginal people did not fit made it possible for Canadian society to minimize individual and national responsibility for the destruction of the distinct cultural identity of Aboriginal peoples. The boundaries of the community did not include those under threat, and there was a sense that those who fell outside the protection of the state or, often, outside the national consciousness could be safely ignored.[29]

In spite of the national story, Aboriginal people and their stories have not disappeared. First Nations remain a vital cultural force within the country, vigorously contesting the national story in which they are rendered powerless. Powerful oral traditions, which give meaning to their lives and advance their vision of the future, direct their political and social actions. In her study of Yukon First Nation storytelling, anthropologist Julie Cruikshank notes Mikhail Bakhtin's recognition of "the transformative power of oral storytelling to destabilize official orthodoxies" and "to challenge conventional ways of thinking."[30] First Nations have used the oral history projects developed with Parks Canada to undermine the constructs of the "Story of Canada," to challenge the authority of western cultural and scientific explanations of the world, and to advance their claims—both to the shadow landscapes of the natural world and the intellectual and spiritual landscapes of meaning directly tied to them. Their history is not rationally understandable within the Laurentian thesis, but it doesn't try to be. All that is required is the acknowledgment that it exists.[31]

The root of our difficulty—reconciling the commemoration of Aboriginal identity with the unified national narrative—thus appears to lie in the different ways that cultures frame meaning. John Gray's notion of "value-pluralism, that ultimate human values are objective but irreducibly diverse, that they are conflicting and often uncombinable, and that sometimes when they come into conflict with one another they are incommensurable; that is, they are not comparable by any rational measure,"[32] suggests the need for a middle ground where these multiple meanings can be acknowledged and accommodated. Rather than attempting to compare or integrate "by any rational measure," perhaps we need to communicate differences and respect alternative visions of the future. For Parks Canada this means a broadened understanding of commemoration (Fig. 1.3).

However, the effects of the Laurentian thesis are not simply limited to the national narrative. The Laurentian thesis was born of a distinct set of political and intellectual conditions that have shaped the entire warp and weave of our broad social understanding of Canada. Innis, his students, their students, and their students' students have sat as members of the HSMBC, which identifies places of national significance; they have been the frontline staff, the managers,

Fig 1.3   Tr'ondëk Hwëch'in dancers celebrate Canada's National Aboriginal Day, 21 June 2004, on the grounds of their Danoja Zho Cultural Centre (Long Time Ago House), Dawson City, Yukon. Events such as this both solidify Native traditions and afford them public recognition and respect. *(Photograph by David Neufeld.)*

and the senior administrators of Parks Canada, myself among them. It is no simple matter to accommodate alternative or parallel narratives. Although Parks Canada's responsibilities are broadly defined as protecting, presenting, celebrating, and serving Canadians using "nationally significant examples of Canada's natural and cultural heritage," the policies, programs, and infrastructure of the agency arise from the fabric of the pervasive unified national perspective.

In his reflections on the tortured history of twentieth-century Europe, Modris Eksteins, a Latvian-Canadian intellectual historian, notes the "thousand deaths [of] history as a progressive vision and imperial dream." Eksteins is not concerned that this loss signals an intellectual crisis; rather, he feels, it signifies escape from totalitarianism, a recognition of diversity, an appeal for humility and respect. "We must accept a variety of histories," he continues, "but we must also accept variety within our history. It is not possible to write history without preconception. It is possible, however, to write history with layers of suggestion, so that history evokes, history conjoins, it involves. History should provoke, not dictate meaning. It should be a vehicle rather than a terminus."[33]

Is it possible for a national agency, responsible for the promotion of a unified Canadian identity, to become a useful tool in the middle ground? Can it assist communities as they negotiate their way into a national narrative of shared meanings? Is there a way it can become a vehicle for the presentation of incommensurable human values? The facile recognition of diversity and multiculturalism does not address the deep-seated concerns of Aboriginal peoples about their participation in Canada. The notion of national identity as a bounded set of meanings has denied participation by others. As the country incorporates the other, it must also accept a more complex, less linear story. As James Clifford suggests, we need to embrace a notion of identity as the "nexus of relations and transactions actively engaging a subject."[34] This approach sets us on the path to a middle ground where diversity is recognized, respectful relations are fostered, and differences are acknowledged. Without discounting the value of existing commemorations for the culture that established them, it is important to recognize both that other cultures have parallel ways of ascribing meaning and that a refusal or determined inability to acknowledge this fact weakens the social fabric that defines our country. To avoid this, Parks Canada must not only continuously re-evaluate its objectives, but craft new analytical tools in an ongoing way to meet the evolving understanding of what is taking place on the middle ground.

Parks Canada celebrates and justifies the distribution of social power in the country by highlighting meanings drawn from the past to explain the present and envision possible futures. These activities establish boundaries for a national community. In the initial approaches to Aboriginal people in the Yukon, Parks Canada struggled to recognize the limits of its own history and its role as an agent of the government of Canada.

A new approach for Parks Canada is the surrender of its role as the steward of the national story, as government negotiator; instead, it looks to become a creature of the middle ground, to serve the articulation and presentation of multiple histories, to be a vehicle for the journey to a more complete recognition of the whole community of Canada. Much of the agency's policy and programming over the last two decades tends in this direction. Parks Canada is being transformed into a broadly accessible cultural tool available to the communities of Canada as the agency begins to recognize identity as the network of relations and actions between peoples. The periphery—the point of contact with the other—is becoming the center; initial concerns over the unity of the national story are being rendered meaningless; and we are instead constructing a national community of cultural accommodation and shared respect. Surely this is the lesson to be gained from the oral tradition of all our Elders.

NOTES

Much of the research for this chapter was completed over the last fifteen years while I worked with the several Yukon Aboriginal communities to preserve and present their cultural heritage. I acknowledge the support of the citizens and governments of these communities and thank all those who guided me through a growing understanding of the Aboriginal oral tradition. The people of the Tr'ondëk Hwëch'in homeland, where the bulk of my work took place, generously and patiently shared their knowledge and celebrated my small advances in understanding. Percy Henry, a Tr'ondëk Hwëch'in leader and Elder, invested much time in my education at his "University of the Bush." Other Elders, notably Ronald Johnson, Julia Morberg, Victor Henry, Peggy Kormendy, Edward Roberts, and Tr'ondëk Hwëch'in citizens Georgette McLeod, Freda Roberts, Ed Kormendy, Edith Fraser, Debbie Nagano, Margie Kormendy, and Angie Joseph Rear, among many others, guided my work and inspired me through their kindness and personal dedication to their community's heritage. Others who deserve thanks for their support and involvement in our joint work with the Tr'ondëk Hwëch'in include Tim Gerberding, Jody Beaumont, Glenda Bolt, Wayne Potoroka, Lue Maxwell, Sue Parsons (all employees of Tr'ondëk Hwëch'in), Helene Dobrowolski, Gary McMillan, TJ Hammer, and Ruth Gotthardt. In the southern Yukon I am indebted to Carcross-Tagish First Nation Elders Winnie and William Atlin and Edna and Walter Helm for their hospitality and stories of Bennett; Clara Schinkel for her guidance during my learning time in Carcross and my continuing work throughout the Yukon; and Doris McLean, who always introduced me as "Parks Canada" in the early stages of the Chilkoot Trail project, ensuring that I remembered who I was and challenging me to figure out what I was supposed to be doing. Sheila Greer's anthropological fieldwork and analysis were indispensable to the project's success.

On the Yukon North Slope, Gloria Allen of the Inuvialuit Social Development Program (ISDP) ensured that the project stayed in touch with the Inuvialuit interests, while Cathy Cockney of Parks Canada provided ongoing grounding in the Inuvialuit communities of the delta. Doug Olynyk, of the Yukon Heritage Branch, made our shared partnership an easy one, while Murielle Nagy worked with grace and diligence to meet our goals.

Parks Canada provides a supportive environment for reflection on its work, and my colleagues within the agency have reviewed and often challenged my own work to make it better. The scholarship and thoughtful personal communications of Dr. Julie Cruikshank and Dr. Patrick Moore, both of the University of British Columbia, Dr. Paul Nadasdy, University of Wisconsin–Madison, Dr. Laura Peers, Oxford University, and Dr. Michael Bravo, University of Cambridge, were much appreciated. Parks Canada and the congenial and stimulating atmosphere of Clare Hall and the Scott Polar Research Institute, Cambridge, are gratefully acknowledged for their support in the preparation of this chapter.

1. Harold Innis was an internationally recognized economic historian whose seminal work is *The Fur Trade in Canada: An Introduction to Canadian Economic History* (London: Yale University Press, 1930). His work spawned a school of Canadian historiography best known for its focus on the nation's staple industries.

2. The italics reflect Ms. Adamson's own emphasis. The story of these killings is recognizable from an Athapaskan myth cycle. A version of a similar story is reproduced in "'K'oyeedenaa Yoo' Little People," in Catherine Attla, K'etetaalkkaannee: The One Who Paddled among the People and Animals (Fairbanks: Yukon Koyukuk School District and Alaska Native Language Centre, 1990), 140–45.

3. Edward W. Said, Culture and Imperialism (New York: Knopf, 1993), xxvi, notes that "narratives of emancipation and enlightenment in their strongest form were also narratives of integration, not separation. . . . [excluded] people fighting for a place [in the main group]."

4. Additional background on this commemoration is available in David Neufeld, "Parks Canada and the Commemoration of the North: History and Heritage," in Kerry Abel and Ken Coates, eds., Northern Visions: New Perspectives on the North in Canadian History (Peterborough, Ontario: Broadview Press, 2001), 45–79.

5. The project and related research produced two publications: David Neufeld and Frank Norris, Chilkoot Trail: Heritage Route to the Klondike (Whitehorse: Lost Moose, 1996), supports the interpretation of the historic trail by Parks Canada and the U.S. National Park Service; Sheila Greer with Carcross-Tagish First Nation, Skookum Stories of the Chilkoot-Dyea Trail (Whitehorse: Parks Canada, 1995), addresses the interests of the Carcross-Tagish First Nation.

6. Thomas Berger, Northern Frontier, Northern Homeland: The Report of the Mackenzie Valley Pipeline Inquiry, vol. 1 (Ottawa: Minister of Supply and Services, 1977), 46–48.

7. Murielle Nagy, Yukon North Slope Inuvialuit Oral History, Occasional Papers in Yukon History 1 (Whitehorse: Yukon Tourism, 1994), xi–xii.

8. Murielle Nagy, Transcripts of the Yukon North Slope Inuvialuit Oral History, vols. 1–2 (Inuvik: Inuvialuit Social Development Program, 1994).

9. David Neufeld, "A Level Playing Field: The Synthesis of Scientific and Traditional Knowledge—A Meeting Ground for Successful Co-management," internal report (Whitehorse: Parks Canada, 1995).

10. Nagy, Transcripts, vol. 2; interview with Lily Lipscombe, Roland Bay, 18/07/1991-25A:10/11.

11. Alestine Andre and Alan Fehr, Gwich'in Ethnobotany: Plants Used by the Gwich'in for Food, Medicine, Shelter and Tools (Inuvik: Gwich'in Social and Cultural Institute and Aurora Research Institute, 2002); Robert Coutts, Parks Canada project manager for Sach's Harbour and Paulatuk Visitor Reception Centres, personal communication, 15 May 2006; and David Neufeld, "Traditional Knowledge as a Contribution to National Park Ecological Integrity," Research Links 9:3 (2001): 17–19.

12. The concept of the middle ground is drawn from Richard White, The Middle Ground: Indians, Empires, and Republics in the Great Lakes Region, 1650–1815 (Cambridge: Cambridge University Press, 1991).

13. The Yukon River, approximately 3,200 kilometers long, drains a basin some 855,000 kilometers square. Major tributaries include the White and Tanana, glacier-fed rivers from the south, and, entering from the northern permafrost taiga flats, the Porcupine and Koyukuk. Timothy P. Brabets, Bronwen Wang, and Robert H. Meade, Environmental and Hydrologic Overview of the Yukon River Basin, Alaska and Canada, Water-Resources Investigations Report 99-4204 (Anchorage: U.S. Geological Survey, 2000).

14. The 1876 Act consolidated legislation on Indian matters dating back to 1850. "History of the Indian Act (Part One)," Saskatchewan Indian 4 (March 1978): 4; reproduced at http://collections.ic.gc.ca/SaskIndian/a78mar04.htm.

15. Council for Yukon Indians, *Together Today for Our Children Tomorrow: A Statement of Grievances and an Approach to Settlement by Yukon Indian People* (Brampton, Ontario: Charters Publishing Co., 1973), 17.

16. Quoted in Amanda Graham, "Spawning Run and Gold Rush: Is a Multicultural History of the Yukon within Our Grasp?" paper presented at Alaska Anthropological Association Conference, Whitehorse, Yukon, 11 April 1997. See also Catharine McClellan, *Part of the Land, Part of the Water: A History of the Yukon Indians* (Vancouver: Douglas and McIntyre, 1987), 95, 101–2.

17. Tr'o ju-wech'in Heritage Site Steering Committee, Minutes, Winter 1999, Parks Canada, Yukon and Western Arctic Historian Collection, Whitehorse, Yukon.

18. Personal communication, field trip, spring 1999.

19. Keith Basso, *Wisdom Sits in Places: Landscape and Language among the Western Apache* (Albuquerque: University of New Mexico Press, 1996), describes this phenomenon among the Athapaskan diaspora in the American Southwest.

20. Joe and Anne Henry, interviewed by Percy Henry, story transcribed by Jackie Worrell, n.d., Tr'ondëk Hwëch'in Heritage Office oral history collection.

21. Frederica de Laguna, *Tales from the Dena: Indian Stories from the Tanana, Koyukuk, and Yukon Rivers* (Seattle: University of Washington Press, 1995), 288. De Laguna recorded Traveller stories in 1935.

22. Donnessey made this comment at the 2003 Yukon International Storytelling Festival in Whitehorse, Yukon.

23. De Laguna, *Tales from the Dena*, 130, 159–60.

24. For examples of similar Traveller stories from the Mackenzie River valley, see Chris Hanks, "Bear Rock, Red Dog Mountain and the Windy Island to Sheldon Lake Trail: Proposals for the Commemoration of the Cultural Heritage of Denedah, and the Cultural History of the Shu'tagot'ine," manuscript (Ottawa: Parks Canada, National Historic Sites Directorate, 1994); George Blondin, *Yamoria—The Lawmaker: Stories of the Dene* (Edmonton: NeWest Press, 1997).

25. *Report of the Royal Commission on Aboriginal Peoples* (Ottawa: Indian and Northern Affairs, Canada, 1996), available at http://www.ainc-inac.gc.ca/ch/rcap/sg/sg1_e.html#0.

26. Historic Sites and Monuments Board of Canada, Minutes, July 1998, Parks Canada Intranet.

27. The HSMBC accepted the following definition at its July 1999 meeting: "An Aboriginal cultural landscape is a place valued by an Aboriginal group (or groups) because of their long and complex relationship with that land. It expresses their unity with the natural and spiritual environment. It embodies their traditional knowledge of spirits, places, land uses and ecology. Material remains of the association may be prominent, but will often be minimal or absent." HSMBC, Minutes, July 1999, Parks Canada. This definition came from Susan Buggey, *An Approach to Aboriginal Cultural Landscapes,* report submitted to HSMBC for that meeting; text available at http://www.pc.gc.ca/docs/r/pca-acl/index_e.asp.

28. Parks Canada Agency, *"Unimpaired for Future Generations"? Protecting Ecological Integrity with Canada's National Parks,* report of the panel on the Ecological Integrity of Canada's National Parks, vol. 1: *A Call to Action;* vol. 2: *Setting a New Direction for Canada's National Parks* (Ottawa: Minister of Public Works and Government Services, 2000). Quotation from vol. 1, p. 15.

29. Victoria Brittain, review of Stanley Cohen, *States of Denial: Knowing about Atrocities and Suffering, Manchester Guardian,* 7 April 2001, at http://books.guardian.co.uk/reviews/politicsphilosophyandsociety/0,,469459,00.html.

30. Julie Cruikshank, *The Social Life of Stories: Narrative and Knowledge in the Yukon Territory* (Vancouver: University of British Columbia Press, 1998), xvii and xiii.

31. Joane Nagel, *American Indian Ethnic Renewal: Red Power and the Resurgence of Identity and Culture* (New York: Oxford University Press, 1996), 27–32.

32. John Banville, review of John Gray, *Heresies: Against Progress and Other Illusions* in *Manchester Guardian,* 9 April 2004, at http://books.guardian.co.uk/review/story/0, ,1295980,00.html.

33. Modris Eksteins, *Walking since Daybreak: A Story of Eastern Europe, World War II, and the Heart of Our Century* (Boston: Houghton Mifflin, 1999), 15–16.

34. James Clifford, *The Predicament of Culture: Twentieth Century Ethnography, Literature and Art* (Cambridge: Harvard University Press, 1988)

2

HISTORY FROM ABOVE: THE USE OF ORAL HISTORY IN SHAPING COLLECTIVE MEMORY IN SINGAPORE

Kevin Blackburn

~

Observers of the practice of oral history and its use in shaping public memory in the postcolonial countries of Southeast Asia have regularly commented that it is used by political elites and state-run institutions to contribute to the goal of nation building. The story of the nation has been fashioned to foster a national identity based on the history of its creation by leaders of its independence movement. This officially constructed narrative is frequently illustrated by selected quotations culled from the collections of the various national repositories of oral history. Lysa Hong, a Singaporean historian of Southeast Asia, has remarked that state-run organizations engaged in pursuing oral history programs in postcolonial Southeast Asia have produced stories of the nation written "from above," and that such "historical research . . . often has the burden of promoting what is perceived to be the 'national interest.'" Paul Thompson has similarly commented that "most of the oral history projects in [Southeast Asia] originated with studies of local political elites: indeed, recording the history of the politicians who achieved national independence from the European colonial powers was a major motive for their initial funding."[1]

The vast oral history collection amassed by Singapore's state-run Oral History Centre provides a good example of the use of oral history to shape public memory in Southeast Asia in the service of nation building. In this chapter, I first discuss the way in which the interview methodology of two major Centre projects supported nationalistic goals and then consider how products developing from these interviews, including exhibitions and publications, supported myth making. I suggest, furthermore, that it is not necessarily the social position of the narrator, but rather the goals and methods of the interview, as well as the way interviews are used, that define the practice of oral history and contribute to its impact on public memory.

The Practice and Use of Oral History in Singapore

Singapore's Oral History Centre, founded informally as the Oral History Programme of the Ministry of Culture in September 1978, was officially established as the Oral History Unit in December 1979.[2] Projects undertaken its early years were largely focused on interviewing former government members and senior civil servants to get their "authoritative" version of the national past.[3] This was in keeping with the ministry's domination of the arts and humanities in Singapore to ensure that versions of the past and artistic impressions of life in that country were acceptable to the government. In 1985 the unit was reorganized as the Oral History Department, a more autonomous body, but one that still saw its goal as collecting material to tell the story of the nation's founding and development. However, many more ordinary people were interviewed in order to illustrate, through the lives of such people, how the nation had been formed and progressed. This type of oral history, as Marcelino Foronda, the director of the Center for Local and Oral History at De La Salle University, Manila, has suggested, can enliven political and economic history with colorful anecdotes and "give a certain immediacy, a sense of recency to the historical narrative—its certain coloring may even make the historical narrative more interesting, and history, for better or for worse, becomes alive."[4]

In 1993 the Oral History Department was renamed the Oral History Centre and became more directly associated with the National Archives of Singapore. After the disbanding of the Ministry of Culture in 1985, later reconstituted as the Ministry of Information and the Arts in 1990, the government exercised less control over the Centre's projects and programs; and after 1993 the Centre collected much more oral history with non-elites.

What is the national narrative that oral history in Singapore has attempted to illustrate? Similar to the national histories of other Southeast Asian countries, it is a story of colonial exploitation leading to an anticolonialist struggle, followed by independence and steady progress. The history of modern Singapore usually begins with its founding as a British colony in 1819 by Sir Thomas Stamford Raffles, who acquired the small island, located at the bottom of the Malay Peninsula, from the Malay Sultan of the Riau-Johor kingdom. Singapore, as a major trading port, extended the interests of the British empire throughout Southeast Asia, particularly into adjacent Malaya, which came under British rule after 1874. While the elites among indigenous Malays and Chinese and Indian immigrant businessmen became wealthy, the vast majority of the local Singaporean population, including Malays, Chinese, and Indians, remained in poverty during colonial rule. The fall of Singapore in 1942 to the Japanese marked a watershed in the history not only of Singapore, but of all the countries of Southeast Asia. The prestige of the white European empires was shattered by their defeat at the hands of the Japanese, who espoused a nationalist rhetoric of "Asia for Asians," although their regime was often brutal and contemptuous of the local population. The Japanese practiced a policy of divide and rule, using Malay police to hunt down mainly Chinese- and Communist-led anti-Japanese guerrillas. Hundreds lost their lives in ethnic conflicts from 1945 to 1946.

During the postwar years, in Singapore as in other Southeast Asian countries, nationalism and Communism were very strong, fed by the poverty and exploitation of colonial rule. In 1959 Singapore achieved self-government under the nationalist, but non-Communist, People's Action Party (hereafter PAP), led by Lee Kuan Yew, who would serve as prime minister until 1990. At the time of independence, the PAP was engaged in a struggle with pro-Communist nationalists. This struggle shaped Singapore's politics until the late 1960s, when the PAP decisively defeated the pro-Communist Barisan Sosialis Party in elections and smashed the pro-Communist trade unions. In a 1962 referendum, the PAP persuaded Singaporeans to vote to join with an independent Malaya to form Malaysia. Among the advantages of this merger for the PAP was the strengthening of the non-Communist bloc, as Malaya was controlled by a strongly anti-Communist Malay-dominated coalition that in 1960 had defeated a Communist insurgency. However, the merger exacerbated tensions dating back to the war and worsened relations between the Malay-dominated politics of Malaya and the Chinese-dominated politics of Singapore. In 1965 Singapore separated from Malaysia to become an independent nation-state. Thereafter, the history of the nation is often presented as a line of unbroken social and economic progress, with government apartments replacing substandard urban areas and rural housing, ethnic tensions fading, and a Singaporean identity growing out of the different ethnic groups.

In December 1979, after the formal establishment of the Oral History Unit, Singapore's PAP rulers commanded this state-run body to collect material in order to tell precisely this story. The Oral History Unit was charged by then Deputy Prime Minister Goh Keng Swee to record the memories of members of the "old guard" of the PAP. As the Ministry of Culture made clear, the goal was "to record the experiences of persons who have participated in the major political, social and economic events in the history of Singapore" so that history could be studied "first hand from the recorded experiences of those who participated in the history forming events of Singapore."[5] Indeed, the decision to form the Oral History Unit had come from the highest level of the government. Prime Minister Lee told the Singapore Parliament that the unit "was the result of discussion I had with the first Deputy Prime Minister."[6]

The Oral History Unit initiated three projects in the 1980s. Two projects—"Political Developments in Singapore 1945–1965" and "Political Developments in Singapore 1965–1975"—focused on politicians and civil servants, while businessmen were the focus in the third, "Pioneers of Singapore." The two "Political Developments" projects, which have been ongoing, have collected well over one hundred interviews. There is no publicly available printed catalogue of these collections indicating who was interviewed, and most interviews remain inaccessible because to listen to them researchers need "official" approval, which is very hard to obtain. However, excerpts have been used for official publications about Singapore's history, most notably Lee Kuan Yew's own memoirs.[7] The "Pioneers" project ran from January 1980 to February 1984 and included interviews with seventy-three prominent businessmen.[8]

Lim How Seng, the coordinator of these projects, later acknowledged that the interviewing instructions handed down to the unit by Singapore's political leaders were flawed. Interviewers were not given the freedom to ask challenging questions, even if they had felt brave enough to do so. Certain areas of inquiry were clearly off limits, such as eliciting criticism of Lee's decisions even when they had patently been mistakes. Following official policy, important archival records were closed and so could not be consulted in preparing questions. The interviewer simply asked a series of nonthreatening questions, and the interviewee responded in a way that put himself or herself in the best possible light or told a story that he or she thought followed the PAP-endorsed version of the past. As Lim noted in 1992, in the testimony of political leaders "we often find some degree of exaggeration and distortion of roles played in a political event, rationalizing a political move and falsification of facts due to deliberate or genuine lapse of memory."[9]

It was precisely the old guard's self-justifying memories that Lee Kuan Yew and the senior cadres of the ruling party wanted the public to see as history. Contrary voices were hard to find. A token number of former members of the opposition Barisan Sosialis Party were interviewed for "balance"; however, these were mainly individuals who had stayed in Singapore and had had to accommodate themselves to a society dominated by the PAP government. Thus, in their interviews they distanced themselves from their former opinions and tended to adopt the PAP's views of their past activities. Members of the opposition who had fled Singapore and feared arrest upon return because they still held the same critical opinions were not interviewed. Moreover, government archival records dating from when the PAP came into power have seldom been opened for use by historians (in other countries official records are released after thirty years). The unwritten rationale for this policy is to prevent anything in the official record from being used to support interpretations of the past that contradict those of the ruling party. For the PAP, then, the most desirable history was based not on the careful study of a variety of sources, but rather on the selective memories of the winners of the battles of history: powerful businessmen, political leaders, and bureaucrats.

Lee himself held a very utilitarian view of what writing history was about. In 1980 he said that "history is not made the way it is written," suggesting that history was essentially what those who lived through it remembered it to be.[10] He did not trust historians, because they tend to see many sides of an issue and rely on written sources and multiple points of view to create a more complicated, less hagiographic, nationalistic history. For Lee, it was the utilitarian purpose of inculcating nationalism and a sense of national identity among the people that gave history its meaning. The practice of doing interviews with old-guard PAP members helped promote this view. Interviews of ordinary people were supposed to make up the chorus, their memories significant only if they added color to the tale of how the elites fashioned the modern nation.

At the same time that the Oral History Unit was recording memories of the PAP, its officers were conducting interviews with wealthy and powerful businessmen for the "Pioneers" project. These interviews were as self-serving as those conducted with the political elites. Lim How Seng, who also coordinated "Pioneers," wrote that "the project is aimed at interviewing and tape-recording the reminiscences of the business pioneers about their 'from rags to riches' success stories and their contributions to Singapore's economic, social, and educational developments."[11] Interviewers did not challenge the interviewees' presentation of themselves as self-made men who owed their success solely to their own hard work and thrift. They did not ask why, if hard work and thrift were the keys to financial success, so many people who worked hard all their lives and saved what little they had nonetheless remained poor.

Popular histories have also drawn uncritically upon the "Pioneers" interviews. In *Stepping Out: The Making of Chinese Entrepreneurs* (1993), Chan Kwok Bun and Claire Chiang not only explained these entrepreneurs' success in terms of the "rags to riches" myth but also ascribed their wealth and success to their Chinese identity—a notion belied by the existence of thousands of poor Chinese coolies throughout most of Singapore's history. Even former Deputy Prime Minister Goh Keng Swee, who had initiated the Oral History Unit's program and has remained an influential adviser, questioned the uncritical use of these interviews in the book's foreword: "Readers of this book will be struck by a theme repeatedly encountered in individual accounts of these pioneering entrepreneurs. This refers to their emphasis on maintaining high moral standards in doing business. How much of this is real? How much is due to a natural desire to project a good image? How much to the oral historian's preconceived ideas?"[12] Nonetheless, Goh affirmed the worth of the "Pioneers of Singapore" project and Chan and Chiang's book because both upheld the "Confucian work ethic," which the government had embraced as the cornerstone of the "Asian values" of hard work and thrift that it was seeking to promote throughout Singapore society in the early 1990s.[13]

The Oral History Unit, like its counterparts in Southeast Asia, gradually moved away from the elite interviews envisaged in 1979 as its *raison d'être*. In the mid-1980s two major projects added the voices of ordinary people to the national history: the "Syonan: Singapore under the Japanese" project, in which 175 people were interviewed, and "Communities of Singapore," which included several hundred interviews with members of Singapore's major ethnic groups, including Chinese, Malays, Indians, and such minority populations as Armenians, Eurasians, Peranakans, Jews, and Vietnamese. Yet officials overseeing the projects maintained that their objectives were not to record the life histories of ordinary people but to "fill in the gaps" or supplement knowledge of "the bigger picture" in order to add color to the story of Singapore's national history.[14] As in "Pioneers" and "Political Developments in Singapore," the interview methodologies employed by these two later projects served nationalistic purposes and constrained interviewees from giving voice to the full complexity of their lives. "Syonan: Singapore under the Japanese" made extensive use of highly structured questionnaires to pose a series of predetermined questions, suggesting a reluctance to let interviewees tell their own stories.[15] The questionnaires demonstrated that it is not *who* is interviewed that necessarily fulfills oral history's democratic potential, but *how* they are interviewed: the assumptions governing the interview, the interview methodology, and the sorts of questions posed can all serve conventional and indeed quite undemocratic ends.

Similarly, interviews in the "Communities of Singapore" project were topically rather than autobiographically organized, focusing on such subjects as social relations, institutions, organizations, identity, multiracialism, and nation building rather than individual, and often idiosyncratic, life histories.[16] Once again structured questionnaires were used, thereby reducing the interviewees' freedom in telling their stories.[17] For project coordinator Daniel Chew, the material collected supported the accepted story of a nation created by different ethnic groups joined by a common political history; as he has written: "A sense of nationhood fostered by political change evolved gradually and defined the national identity for Singapore's various communities."[18] In his view it was not the individual memories that mattered but how they fitted into the national narrative.

Both "Syonan" and "Communities" include interesting examples of how the structured questionnaires operated to subordinate stories of individual lives to a national narrative. The "Syonan" project focused on a single event—the Japanese Occupation—which, though of unquestioned national significance, nonetheless covered only a relatively short period of an individual's life. An interview with Chang Teh Cheok, a well-known war hero born in 1916, extends for more than sixteen hours, but only one half-hour is devoted to the first twenty-five years of his life and little more than an hour to the forty years after the war. Chang's descriptions of the Chinese anti-Japanese resistance forces, their heroes, and their leaders, admittedly an important part of Singapore's history, account for a remarkable fifteen hours of the interview. Interviews with ordinary people less well known than Chang often include just a few minutes of family background and no discussion of the impact of the Japanese Occupation on their postwar lives, or what they did for the four decades after the war ended. They simply recount what they experienced as eyewitnesses to the national event.

"Communities of Singapore" certainly covers more of the lives of ordinary people than the project on the Japanese Occupation. However, those interviewed are led into describing the rituals and cultural practices of their own ethnic community, which are well recorded elsewhere, but they do not seem to have been encouraged to tell their own life stories or recount their views about their family members and community. Narrators are merely eyewitnesses to a certain culture that makes up the national mosaic, not individuals. The interview with Lee Liang Hye, born in 1924, runs for twenty-one hours, during which Lee describes Peranakan life and its place in national history, but rarely discusses his own experiences. Whole parts of his life story that do not reflect Peranakan culture are omitted. The topical approach evident in the interview questionnaire, emphasizing themes of significance to the broader national identity of Singapore, excludes areas of inquiry unrelated to the narrator's particular culture.[19]

Historian Lysa Hong, reviewing the practice of oral history in Singapore and Southeast Asia, has noted that "history from below [does] not automatically come about when ordinary voices are taped," because "more than in the case with elite interviews, the role of the interviewer and the historiographic consciousness of the institut[ion] he represents is [sic] crucial in determining the type of tape [i.e., interview] and hence the nature of the document that results from the interview."[20] Acutely aware of the implications of the interview techniques used by the Oral History Centre, Hong has suggested that the questionnaire used by the interviewer "may unconsciously impose an a priori version of the historical event as obtained from his/her research." She writes that "this happens when the interviews are conducted like debriefing sessions when the interviewees are quizzed on and valued for what they can remember in response to specific questions."[21]

Hong is very critical of this methodology, saying that "the domination of such a fact gathering approach relegates the interviewees as individuals to the background; their role is largely to provide the anecdote, the local color that would give the 'objective picture' flesh and detail and the trappings of 'the voice of the ordinary person.'" For "history from below" to occur, she asserts, oral history should be carried out so that "the tapes carry the story as structured by the narrator himself/herself, and contain what he/she considers to be the most important, feels deepest about, and is most affected by." Drawing upon the work of Michael Frisch, Hong argues that oral history should "tell us less about events than about their meaning. . . . The unique and precious element which oral history forces upon the historian and which no other source possesses in equal measure is the speaker's subjectivity. . . . Oral history tells us not just what people did, but what they wanted to do, what they believed they were doing and what they now think they did."[22]

Using the Collections of the Oral History Centre to Shape Collective Memory

In carrying out its nation-building mission, the Oral History Centre has accumulated a large collection of tapes and transcripts covering numerous aspects of Singapore's history. It is undoubtedly a valuable archive of research material. Yet academic historians have been reluctant to use this material to advance a historical argument. Typically, they have quoted from a few selected interviews to add color to their own work. Paul Kratoska used very brief excerpts from a handful of Centre tapes in his seminal work on the Japanese Occupation of Malaya and Singapore, preferring to rely upon interviews done by his own research students.[23] James Warren's social histories of Singapore make greater use of material from the Centre's collection, but for his major points he relies on written sources and his own interviews.[24]

Given the political context within which the Oral History Centre has conducted interviews, it is no surprise that Singapore's state-run institutions, unlike individual scholars, have regularly drawn upon these interviews to shape public memory, especially for what PAP leaders sometimes call "younger generations who have no experience of the past."[25] Typically, these presentations have taken the form of exhibitions and publications.

The first public exhibition to make use of oral history was the 1984 National Exhibition entitled "25 Years of Nation-Building, 1959–1984," which was organized by the Ministry of National Development and opened by Lee Kuan Yew in Singapore's massive new World Trade Centre Exhibition Halls.

Predictably, the National Exhibition included the memories of the old guard of the PAP interspersed with colorful quotations from ordinary people. The exhibition emphasized the PAP's role in bringing order out of political chaos and economic progress out of widespread poverty. It was the first public representation of the national past, and although Centre collections were not sufficiently developed at the time to inform the exhibit in any substantive way, the exhibition set the precedent for the use of oral history in subsequent exhibitions. Early on, curators decided to present the narrative of nation building by drawing extensively upon quotations from interviews, while keeping their own commentary to a minimum. Their rationale was that the audience would more likely believe the historical "truth" of first-person accounts than an interpretation "fabricated" by curators. Indeed, this technique gave the impression that people from the past were speaking directly to the visitor. However, visitors had little understanding of how selective the choice of quotations had been. Michael Frisch has criticized this approach to using oral history, which suggests that simply being present at a historical event or participating in a historical era automatically confers interpretative authority upon a narrator. This a fallacy, he argues, for one perspective on an event, no matter how close that perspective is to the event in question, does not constitute history; testimony has to be placed in context.[26]

Nonetheless, the National Exhibition faithfully maintained this style of presentation. For example, the Political History Gallery included a recreation of a polling booth from the 1962 referendum on Singapore's merger with the proposed Malaysian federation. In the recreated booth, a mannequin of an election official sat and appeared to be sharpening pencils. A recorded voice explained that the PAP's opposition, the Communists of the Barisan Sosialis Party, had urged voters to deface their ballots and break their pencils to disrupt the democratic process. This protest was indeed led by the Barisan Sosialis Party, but whether it was controlled by Communists has long been a point of debate. The recording also failed to mention that by breaking the pencils, the opposition was registering dissatisfaction with what it believed was an unfair referendum: "no" was not a ballot option; voters had to choose between different forms of merger. The recorded voice itself was that of S. R. Nathan, a senior bureaucrat who had served in the 1970s as permanent secretary of the Ministry of Foreign Affairs and as head of the politically sensitive Security and Intelligence Division of the Ministry of Defence. At the time of the exhibit, he was executive chairman of the government-owned newspaper group that controlled the major English daily, the *Straits Times*, which he had worked to make more amenable to the PAP government's views.[27]

Although Nathan's commentary did not come from the collections at the Oral History Centre, it nonetheless reflected well the pro-PAP point of view found in the interviews from "Political Developments in Singapore 1965–1975." At the time of the 1962 referendum, Nathan was dealing with what the PAP saw as Communist-inspired labor relations problems. His commentary was clearly the perspective of Singapore's political elite, which viewed Singapore's recent history as the PAP's victorious struggle against the opposition party. No voices representing the viewpoint of the opposition party were included in the exhibition scene. As the exhibition handbook noted, scenes such as the recreated 1962 polling booth were designed "to highlight crisis situations that tested the people's determination and will to survive and prosper as a nation and society."[28]

Another section of the National Exhibition attempted to show "what the years of 'nation building' have brought about" by comparing old *attap* huts of the 1960s, roofed with palm tree leaves, with modern government high-rise flats. A reconstructed hut was flanked with quotations from Singaporeans who had lived in such dwellings, describing them as "filthy." Ng Hai San, who moved from a hut to a government flat, said of his new accommodations: "The environment is very clean and quiet, and there's no transport problems for the children who are going to school." His wife recalled "the filth" of the squatter area where their attap hut had been located.[29] Many shared their views, but many also regretted the loss of village life—a perspective not represented in the National Exhibition.

More than forty thousand people a day attended the National Exhibition during its run from 16 November to 30 December 1984. It was popular because it was a large public spectacle that impressed even the skeptical with its visual splendor and many large and interesting exhibits on contemporary life in Singapore. Its success in shaping public memory can be gauged by visitors' responses. Miss J. Tan, a twenty-six-year-old schoolteacher remarked: "I feel much close[r] to Singapore now that I have seen the exhibition. This is a display of our heritage and our achievements."[30] Newspaper columnist Salma Khalik clearly received the message the government wanted to get across, writing that in the exhibits "we see the struggle that forged a nation, and the celebration of a nation that is now poised to take on the future." She continued, "We rejoice in the sense of unity, harmony, hard work, thrift and commitment which has seen Singapore through its tumultuous past—a heritage the younger generation has inherited to help them meet the challenge of preserving and maintaining our hard-earned prosperity."[31] Retiree Lim Ah Tee expressed a less enthusiastic view: "I can't quite remember what I have seen. There is so much to see."[32] Yet Lim's opinion represents about as much dissent as one can find in the pages of the government-controlled press. Members of the Barisan Sosialis Party were scarcely in a position to offer alternative points of view, as many had fled Singapore or had been detained in prison for years, then placed under orders not to speak to the media about their views.

The National Exhibition was but a prelude to the massive blockbuster exhibit "The Singapore Story—Overcoming the Odds," organized by the Prime Minister's Office and held at the Singapore International Convention and Exhibition Centre in the summer of 1998. Drawing extensively upon the oral history collections gathered since 1979, "The Singapore Story," like the earlier exhibit, was motivated by the PAP government's concern about the erosion of nationalistic sentiments, especially among the younger generation, who had been raised in an era of relative stability and prosperity and were ignorant of both the events that led to the development of modern Singapore and the hardships endured by previous generations. As Prime Minister Goh Chok Tong put it at the opening of the exhibition: "Younger Singaporeans have not experienced first hand the tumultuous events of the past 60 years. . . . They were born at a time when things got steadily better year after year, and most families did not have to worry about basic things like food, shelter and jobs."[33]

Quickly dispensing with Singapore's long colonial history, the exhibition focused on the decades following World War II, the Japanese Occupation, and independence. Almost one-fifth of Singapore's entire population of just over three million saw the exhibition, including the entire student population. Like the National Exhibition, "The Singapore Story" used excerpts from oral history interviews to present a seamless, progressive story of the nation's recent past, albeit with considerably more sophisticated technology than the earlier version. As they moved through the exhibit, visitors could read excerpts from transcripts of interviews in the Centre's collection, listen to recorded testimony, and also hear the recorded voices of actors reading from scripts based on oral history transcripts but made more immediate by being turned into drama.

Movable theater seats carried visitors for a thirty-six-minute ride through six chronologically organized galleries, with historical vignettes drawing upon recorded voices as well as moving 3-D images. In the gallery entitled "Political Awakening, 1945–1955," the audience was able to "eavesdrop" on two prerecorded conversations through a mockup of an open window. One simulated Chinese students talking about demonstrations by their Communist classmates. This period of early differences between Communist and non-Communist nationalists was portrayed as a prelude to open conflict between the two sides in the 1960s. The second conversation consisted of two Malay women talking in their attap hut about the 1950 Maria Hertogh racial riots, sparked by British insensitivity toward Muslim beliefs. (Maria Hertogh, a Muslim girl, was separated from her adoptive Muslim parents and placed in a convent after her Dutch Catholic biological parents returned to claim her.) In the last gallery, "The Future in Our Hands," 3-D images of a grandfather passing down his memories of the development of the Singapore nation to his grateful grandchild were projected onto a ten-meter-high screen. "Grandpa" was played by an actor whose "memories" were simply the messages that the PAP government wanted to communicate to the younger generation about the past. These dramatizations were not based on oral history interviews with historical figures; they were merely scripts read by actors. However, juxtaposing this material with actual oral history interviews elsewhere in the exhibit made it hard to distinguish genuine testimony from dramatized recreations.

Once visitors completed their ride through "The Singapore Story," they were free to walk through a formal exhibition that included more than twenty quotations drawn from the collections of the Oral History Centre. The quotations often captioned photographs documenting Singapore's postwar history. To demonstrate the progress the government had made toward creating a peaceful society, "The Singapore Story" emphasized the violent and turbulent aspects of the racial conflict that admittedly existed prior to independence. The testimony of Tay Yen Hoon, a Chinese accounts clerk interviewed for the "Syonan, Singapore under the Japanese" project, provides a good example of the way a selected quotation, stripped of its full context, can skew the story being told: "Before the Japanese surrender . . . a week before they surrendered they sowed discord between Chinese and Malays. . . . They would spread the rumour that the Chinese were assaulting the Malays. . . . The Malays . . . were instigated to hit the Chinese."[34] While major racial clashes like the ones Tay described did occur in parts of Malaya in 1945, in Singapore there were only isolated incidents of racially motivated street fights between small groups of ten or so. In fact, the heavily edited excerpt quoted above leaves out the description of how Tay and his brother prevented one of these street fights and thereby maintained the peace, which was what generally occurred in Singapore. Tay's full testimony suggests that most Chinese and Malays did not support racial violence. Thus, it was not the PAP government's policies alone that eventually brought about peace between the races, as the exhibit narrative suggests. Most citizens did not countenance violence, and many, like Tay and his brother, worked for racial harmony in cooperation with people from other races. However, to suggest this would have diminished the PAP government's claim that it created racial harmony out of chaos.

In addition to exhibitions, numerous publications—both state-sponsored and privately produced—have drawn upon interviews conducted by the Oral History Centre in ways that also support a nation-building, progressive view of Singapore's past—one stripped of nuance, tension, and debate. The Centre itself began in the 1990s to compile selected interview quotations into audiotapes and books focusing primarily on the Japanese Occupation as a watershed in the history of Singapore as a modern nation.[35] Its 1995 publication *Beyond the Empires: Memories Retold*, intended for children and widely circulated in Singapore's schools, described the Japanese Occupation as a time when "we were beginning to lose our previously unwavering faith in the *Great White Man*."[36] The 1942 fall of Singapore to an Asian power and the sight of their former British rulers sweeping the streets as prisoners of war damaged the prestige of the European colonialists. The defeat of the British, who had promised to protect their subjects, also meant that the local population, in particular the Chinese, were left to the mercy of a brutal occupying regime. *Beyond the Empires,* one of several state-sponsored productions on the Japanese Occupation, articulated a nationalistic narrative of "survival"; what was to be remembered about this period in history were the "lessons" and qualities that later helped Singapore survive its challenges.[37] Or as Lily Tan, director of the Singapore National Archives and Oral History Centre, wrote in the book's preface: "I hope this little monograph will serve to remind future generations of Singaporeans to be vigilant, and not to be complacent about our nation's defence even in peace-time." She explicitly linked the oral history interviews included in the book to this purpose: "The oral history interviews of the survivors [of the Occupation] bear testimony to our need to be self-reliant and independent" and show that "we have to be responsible for our own destiny."[38]

In the 1990s, selected quotations from the Centre's collection were included in new history textbooks issued by Singapore's Ministry of Education. Teaching Singapore's national past had commenced in January 1985 as part of the PAP government's desire to educate the younger generations about the progress of the nation, the same impulse that had inspired the 1984 National Exhibition. At that time, the national oral history collection was not large enough to supply quotations for textbooks. By the 1990s, however, the burgeoning Centre collections had sufficient material to pepper the textbooks with quotations to support the government-endorsed nation-building message. For example, the ministry's history texts tended to de-emphasize the ethnic tensions that characterized the Japanese Occupation and highlight the forging of a nation out of the common suffering of all. The well-established fact that the Japanese had favored the Malays and Indians and treated the Chinese harshly was, in effect, erased from this revisionist version of the past. This reinterpretation was possible at least in part because the younger generations, some 80 percent of the population, had no direct experience of the war.[39] *Understanding Our Past: Singapore from Colony to Nation*, introduced by the ministry in 2000, quoted an Oral History Centre interview with Ismail bin Zain: "The Japanese didn't care whether you were a Chinese or a Malay. At road blocks, if you didn't bow to them properly, or if you couldn't answer their question, they would slap you."[40] Throughout his interview, however, Ismail had discussed at great length the differential treatment of Chinese and Malays by the Japanese and, in particular, the reasons why the Malay community was pro-Japanese at the beginning of the Occupation.[41] This material did not find its way into *Understanding Our Past*.

The collection and use of oral history by the state-run Oral History Centre of Singapore offers an instructive example of how national repositories of oral history in developing countries are strongly influenced by the nation-building agenda mandated by the state. Examining how oral history in Singapore has been used to shape collective memory permits an interesting comparison with its practice in developed countries, where there has been less focus on nation building and more on allowing public memory to be influenced by a "history from below" approach. Yet, as I have tried to show, even the presumably more democratic practice of interviewing ordinary people can be subverted by nationalistic agendas and produce "history from above"—that is, oral history shaped by the desire of the state to mold public memory according to the version of history that it endorses.

NOTES

1. Lysa Hong, "Ideology and Oral History Institutions in Southeast Asia," in P. Lim Pui Huen, James Morrison, and Kwa Chong Guan, eds., *Oral History in Southeast Asia: Theory and Method* (Singapore: National Archives of Singapore and Institute of Southeast Asian Studies, 1998), 36; Paul Thompson, "ASEAN Oral History Colloquium 25–28 May 1992, Singapore," *Oral History* 21 (Autumn 1992): 21.

2. "Ministry of Culture Launches Oral History Programme, 13 December 1979," Ministry of Culture Speeches, Statements, Press Conferences, and Interviews 1975–1979, National University of Singapore Library, Singapore.

3. Eva McMahan, *Elite Oral History Discourse: A Study of Cooperation and Coherence* (Tuscaloosa: University of Alabama, 1989).

4. Marcelino A. Foronda, "Notes on Elite Interviewing in the Philippines in ASEAN," paper presented at the Oral History Colloquium: Recording Our ASEAN Heritage, May 1992, Singapore; program organized by Oral History Department, National Museum, National University of Singapore Library.

5. "Ministry of Culture Launches Oral History Programme 13 December 1979."

6. Lee Kuan Yew, *Parliamentary Debates, Republic of Singapore*, March 1981, vol. 40: col. 1202, 25.

7. See the material drawn from interviews with Goh Keng Swee in 1981–1982 in Lee Kuan Yew, *The Singapore Story: Memoirs of Lee Kuan Yew* (Singapore: Singapore Press Holdings, 1998), 569, 601, 656.

8. *Pioneers of Singapore* (Singapore: Archives and Oral History Department, 1984), iii.

9. Lim How Seng, "Interviewing Political Elites: The Singapore Experience," paper presented at the Oral History Colloquium: Recording Our ASEAN Heritage, May 1992, Singapore. See also Tho Meng Choo, "More than Just a Voice: The Development of Oral History in Singapore" (B.A. honors thesis, National University of Singapore, 1992).

10. Lee Kuan Yew, "History Is Not Made the Way It Is Written," *Speeches* 3, no. 8 (February 1980), 3; and see Loh Kah Seng, "Within the Singapore Story: The Use and Narrative of History in Singapore," *Crossroads* 12:2 (1998): 7.

11. *Pioneers of Singapore*, vi.

12. In Chan Kwok Bun and Claire Chiang, *Stepping Out: The Making of Chinese Entrepreneurs* (Singapore: Centre for Advanced Studies, 1993), vii–viii.

13. "Shared Values," pamphlet (Singapore: Government of Singapore, 1991), n.p.

14. Lim Chee Onn, "Foreword," in National Archives of Singapore, *The Japanese Occupation 1942–1945* (Singapore: Times, 1996), 10; see also Daniel Chew, "Oral History in the Republic of Singapore," *International Journal of Oral History* 7 (1986): 206–10; and Tan Beng Luan, "Documenting the Japanese Occupation: The Singapore Experience," paper presented at the Oral History Colloquium: Recording Our ASEAN Heritage, May 1992, Singapore.

15. Oral History Department, *Syonan: Singapore under the Japanese: A Catalogue of Oral History Interviews* (Singapore: Oral History Department, 1986), 202–15.

16. Daniel Chew, "Preface," in Oral History Department, Singapore, *Communities of Singapore Part 1* (Singapore: Oral History Department, 1989), ii.

17. See Oral History Department, Singapore, *Communities of Singapore Part 1*, 104–13. See also comments from Lily Tan, "Archival Strategies for Oral Sources in Southeast Asia—Southeast Asia's Forgotten History," *Comma* 1:2 (2002): 196.

18. Daniel Chew, "Life Story Narratives and Community History," paper presented at the Oral History Colloquium: Recording Our ASEAN Heritage, May 1992, Singapore.

19. See *Syonan: Singapore under the Japanese*, 15–18.

20. Hong, "Ideology and Oral History Institutions in Southeast Asia," in Lim, Morrison, and Kwa, *Oral History in Southeast Asia*, 37.

21. Ibid., 38–39.

22. Ibid.

23. Paul H. Kratoska, *The Japanese Occupation of Malaya: A Social and Economic History* (Sydney: Allen and Unwin, 1998).

24. James Francis Warren, *Rickshaw Coolie: A People's History of Singapore 1880–1940* (Singapore: Oxford University Press, 1986); James Francis Warren, *Ah Ku and Karayuki-San: Prostitution in Singapore, 1870-1940* (Singapore: Oxford University Press, 1993).

25. See Lee Kuan Yew, address at the Opening of the National Exhibition on Thursday, 15 November 1984, at 8:45 P.M. at the World Trade Centre, National University of Singapore Library, Prime Minister's Speeches, Interviews, Statements, Etc., 1984; and report in "A Past Young Didn't Know About," *Straits Times*, 14 July 1998, 1.

26. Michael Frisch, *A Shared Authority: Essays on the Craft and Meaning of Oral and Public History* (Albany: State University of New York Press, 1990), 175–77.

27. Valarie Lee, "Small Tales Behind the Big Story," *Straits Times*, 11 November 1984, 15; and see Mary Turnbull, *Dateline: 150 Years of the Straits Times* (Singapore: Times Editions, 1995), 334–36.

28. Lee, "Small Tales"; see also Ministry of National Development, *National Exhibition: In Celebration of 25 Years of Nation Building, 1959–1965* (Singapore: Ministry of National Development, 1984), 48.

29. "88,000 Visit Big Show in 2 Days," *Straits Times*, 18 November 1984, 3.

30. Salma Khalik, "Significance of the Elements," *Straits Times*, 11 November 1984, 15.

31. "88,000 Visit Big Show."

32. Ngiam Tong Hai, "Look, It's Our Old Home," *Straits Times*, 18 November 1984, 3.

33. "A Past Young Didn't Know About."

34. *Singapore: Journey into Nationhood* (Singapore: National Heritage Board, 1998), 33.

35. National Archives of Singapore, *Oral History Centre* (Singapore: National Archives of Singapore, 2001).

36. Cindy Chou, *Beyond the Empires: Memories Retold* (Singapore: Oral History Centre, 1995), 3.

37. Diana Wong, "War and Memory in Malaysia and Singapore: An Introduction," in P. Lim Pui Huen and Diana Wong, eds., *War and Memory in Malaysia and Singapore* (Singapore: Institute of Southeast Asian Studies, 2000), 1–8; Diana Wong, "Memory Suppression and Memory Production: The Japanese Occupation of Singapore," in T. Fujitani, Geoffrey M. White, and Lisa Yoneyama, eds., *Perilous Memories: The Asia-Pacific War(s)* (Durham, NC: Duke University Press, 2001), 218–38.

38. In Chou, *Beyond the Empires,* n.p.

39. Kevin Blackburn, "Nation Building and Public Representations of History: The Japanese Occupation as a 'Shared Past' in Singapore," *Public History Review* 9 (2001): 8–22; Karl Hack and Kevin Blackburn, *Did Singapore Have to Fall?* (London: RoutledgeCurzon, 2004), chap. 6. See also Kratoska, *Japanese Occupation of Malaya,* 356–58.

40. *Understanding Our Past: Singapore from Colony to Nation* (Singapore: Curriculum Planning and Development Division, 1999), 93.

41. Ismail bin Zain, A 000601/05 Reel 01, Oral History Centre, National Archives of Singapore.

3

MAPPING MEMORIES: ORAL HISTORY FOR ABORIGINAL CULTURAL HERITAGE IN NEW SOUTH WALES, AUSTRALIA

Maria Nugent

In May 2000 I drove five hours north up the coast from Sydney, Australia, to record oral history interviews with Aboriginal people in two communities. This would be the first of many such trips over the following two years, resulting in more than thirty recorded interviews and many more unrecorded ones. My task was not unusual. Since the late 1960s, a historical silence about the racial structure that shaped Australian society from the moment of first European settlement in 1788 has been replaced by an interest in learning about Aborigines and their relations with the colonizers. Aboriginal people's testimony, typically recorded as oral history, has been a critical source in this revisionist history project. In our project, known as "Mapping Attachment: A Spatial Approach to Aboriginal Post-contact Heritage,"[1] we were interested, like other oral historians, in people's lives and their past experiences, but we were especially curious about the spatial dimension of these. This interest in place or, more precisely, in the places that are characteristically embedded in life stories, stemmed from the fact that the project was part of a larger applied research effort aimed at ensuring that the post-contact history of Aboriginal people is properly represented in the state's cultural heritage, or in what might be called its "heritage landscape."[2]

In this chapter I discuss what the oral history interviews revealed about Aboriginal people's experiences of local landscapes. The chapter also considers how these oral histories challenge current cultural heritage practices that divide Aboriginal from non-Aboriginal history by instead drawing attention to the ways in which Aboriginal and non-Aboriginal people have coexisted in the same locales, at times in ways that reinforce the distance between them, at other times in ways that are close, even intimate.[3] As part of the research project, the spatial dimension of the entanglement between Aboriginal and non-Aboriginal people was made visible through a process of "mapping" the oral histories, which I briefly discuss in the final section of this chapter.

A Segregated Cultural Heritage System?

The project was funded by and conducted under the auspices of the New South Wales state government's key natural and cultural heritage conservation agency, the New South Wales National Parks and Wildlife Service.[4] This agency has, since its inception in 1967, been responsible for recording and conserving Aboriginal cultural heritage, but until recently it had done so with only limited reference to the memories of living Aborigines. This was so because since the 1970s the practice of cultural heritage protection in Australia has been a somewhat bifurcated system.[5] Within this system, the period since white settlement in 1788 (termed the "historic period") is defined almost exclusively by structures associated with "settlers" and their descendants, including houses, homesteads, hotels, halls, hospitals, and the like. These buildings, sites, and associated objects, recorded on the historic heritage registers maintained by state and local authorities and deemed of sufficient value to require some form of legislative protection, are a testament to an Australian past characterized by pioneering and progress. Only a small number of buildings and places specifically associated with Aboriginal people are included in the heritage registers for the post-1788 period, and only occasionally do the registers note the significance to Aboriginal people of some of the thousands of other buildings and places listed.[6]

By contrast, the cultural heritage of Aboriginal people has been almost exclusively confined to the pre-contact period and includes such sites as shell-middens, rock art, and stone artifact scatters. These were considered significant—worth recording, preserving, and conserving—because they could be used to tell stories about an "authentic," precolonial, traditional indigenous society and its technology.[7] They had acquired considerable value in the late twentieth century when the field of cultural heritage rapidly expanded as part of a larger nation-building process because they provided evidence of deep time and of a unique indigenous culture, which were highly valued in a comparatively new nation like Australia seeking to strengthen its roots.

As a result of these professional practices, most cultural heritage work in New South Wales has painted a false picture of Aboriginality, of the nature of Aboriginal people's attachment to the post-contact landscape, and of the colonial past more generally. As my co-investigator in this research project, Denis

Byrne, has observed, were one to rely solely on the state's heritage registers for a window onto the historical experience of Aboriginal people since 1788, one could be easily excused for concluding that Aboriginal people had simply left the scene the moment "whites" arrived.[8] But in many parts of New South Wales, as elsewhere in Australia, Aboriginal people have remained a vital local presence, albeit one that has been diminished through frontier violence, disease and starvation, dispossession from land, forced dispersals from one place to another, and the removal of children from families. But despite this, or because of it, the "survivors" identify as a distinct cultural group expressing a strong sense of themselves as different from white Australians, in ways that draw on both notions of indigenousness and shared experiences of oppression as markers of that difference.

That this was indeed the case was shown convincingly through the work of a generation of historians and anthropologists who, beginning in the 1970s, made use of archives, ethnographies, and oral histories.[9] They examined the effects of colonization on Aboriginal people, particularly their dispossession from land; they exposed Aboriginal people's survival within settled Australia; and they conveyed the vitality of what came to be known as Aboriginality.

A strong theme in this historical and ethnographic work was the question of cultural identity. What did it mean, and what was it like, to be an Aboriginal person living in twentieth-century settled Australia? On what basis did Aboriginal people understand themselves as Aboriginal? Some of this research indicated that place, locality, or land played an important role in shaping and expressing identity. For instance, the anthropologist Diane Barwick drew attention to the ways in which Aboriginal people commonly defined and organized themselves in terms of the localities from which they came, as is evident by the fact that Aboriginal people meeting for the first time typically ask each other, "Where you from?"[10] Historians and anthropologists debated among themselves whether or not this identification of Aboriginal people with place ought to be understood as a continuation of a pre-contact relationship to country,[11] or as a result of the experience of dispossession, segregation, and the continual threat of dispersal, or as both enduring tradition and a response to historical change.

For our purposes the point needs to be stressed that place, land, and locality as abstract concepts along with particular places, such as specific Aboriginal reserve settlements or camps on the fringes of rural towns, were clearly evident in the developing literature about Aboriginal people living in this part of the continent after 1788. But despite its obvious spatial themes, the scholarship produced from the 1970s onward was not widely utilized by those working within the field of Aboriginal cultural heritage. The archaeologists who dominated the cultural heritage field tended not to consult the work of historians, sometimes on the basis that historians and anthropologists had not examined Aboriginal people's historical experience with sufficient spatial specificity to make it usable for heritage purposes. For history to inform heritage, it needed to plot its narratives in space as well as in time. A further complicating issue was the absence, or the ambiguity, of the places, objects, and other types of material remains associated with Aboriginal post-contact history.[12] The *absence* of physical traces in places occupied by Aboriginal people reflects their historical experiences of dispossession and dispersal and the seasonal nature of their work patterns.[13] For most of the twentieth century, they have not generally had the means to own land and to build on it; and when they did, the likelihood that structures survived over time is minimal, given settler society's concerted effort to remove Aboriginal people not only from the Australian imagination but also from the Australian landscape.[14] The *ambiguity* of the associations of the material culture that might be found is present because, as Byrne notes:

> The majority of items in their [Aborigines'] post-contact material culture . . . ranging from clothing to cooking utensils, children's toys, building materials, and gardening implements were brought over in unadulterated form (though sometimes radically recontextualized) from the material culture of European colonizers. The objects themselves are likely to be unmarked by their ownership and use by Aborigines, so that this ownership and use has no visibility on or in the objects.[15]

But these difficulties are no justification for ignoring the post-contact period in Aboriginal cultural heritage, or Aboriginal people in Australian historical heritage.

Despite these challenges, by the closing years of the twentieth century some practitioners working within the cultural heritage field began to realize the obvious disjuncture between contemporary Aboriginal people and what the state's heritage registers reflected about Aboriginal people past and present, a disjuncture that allowed settler Australians to continue to perpetuate the myth that "real" Aborigines were remote, in temporal and geographic terms. At the same time, heritage professionals were increasingly dissatisfied with the ways in which the absence of Aboriginal post-contact history from Australian heritage reproduced a view of the past that denied the intertwined lives and histories of Aborigines and non-Aborigines. The 1988 bicentenary of white settlement, which Aboriginal people across Australia had protested with slogans such as "white Australia has a black history," followed by the 1992 Australian High Court's *Mabo* decision, which recognized the continuation of native title rights in some lands, and the inquiry into the separation of Aboriginal children from their families that was initiated in 1995 and reported its findings in 1997, had resulted in a greater public appreciation that there was no Australian history without Aboriginal history.

The growing awareness in Australia of the largely twentieth-century practice of removing Aboriginal children from their families had especially brought this problem home to heritage workers. Some media coverage of these children, known as the "stolen generations," had a strong spatial element to it: the "stolen" traveled back to the places from which they had been taken for emotional reunions with lost kin; and the government-run institutions to which they had been sent became sites for addressing the burden of that past. The politics of reconciliation that had come to dominate public debate in Australia in the 1990s provided further context for a shift to post-contact Aboriginal history in heritage work, particularly because it provided the language for those who had already identified the limitations of current practices to argue for change in the government-funded agencies where they worked. While some agencies responsible for recording and protecting Australia's cultural heritage might have been slow to change their practices, in the current political climate it was difficult for them to continue the fiction that Aboriginal and non-Aboriginal pasts (and indeed presents and futures) were separate. Yet gaining acceptance for changing current practices was only the first step. Models for how best to go about recording and interpreting Aboriginal post-contact heritage were also needed, which explains why I found myself driving north along the highway from Sydney with a tape recorder, large aerial photographs, maps, and a camera beside me.

For the "Mapping Attachment" research project, one of our goals was to show how twentieth-century Aboriginal history—whether based on documentary or oral evidence—could be mapped on the ground. We wanted to show where some of the historical events, processes, and themes recorded in those sources had occurred, or the types of places associated with them. Our other goal was to demonstrate that memories recorded as oral histories, in addition to material remains, were the evidence that cultural heritage workers needed to work with to bring the post-contact period into the field of Aboriginal cultural heritage. Achieving these aims would be the means for integrating into heritage work Aboriginal people's attachment to the landscapes they occupy now, and to places they had occupied in the past.

It is worth noting that our project has proceeded at a time when historians in Australia, Peter Read most prominent among them, have turned their attention to how non-Aboriginal Australians form and express their attachment, or sense of belonging, to place. Read has examined this attachment both in terms of place as an abstract concept that applies to the imagined space of the nation as a colonized territory[16] and in terms of specific places, particularly ones that no longer exist but to which people still feel a strong emotional connection.[17] His work demonstrates the central role that acts of remembrance and other forms of storytelling play in what is sometimes called "place attachment." Read shows how settler Australians have long been telling stories about the country they occupy as part of the process by which they have made a home for themselves in it. In contrast to an earlier twentieth-century historical silence about Aborigines, in recent years some of this storytelling has been attentive to the dispossession of the country's indigenous people. For example, the starting point for Mark McKenna's influential book *Looking for Blackfellas' Point* was his recognition that his own sense of belonging to a piece of land he had recently bought depended upon understanding what had happened to the Aboriginal people who had lived there before him.[18]

But what about the Aboriginal people who today occupy the same local landscapes as "settler" Australians? What stories do they tell about place? Do they focus on dispossession or on other recent historical experiences? If their own narratives are a means for creating and expressing attachment to the locales in which they live, how might they be interpreted, on their own terms and in relation to other public histories about the same places? In the remainder of the chapter I examine some of the oral histories we collected for what they tell us about Aboriginal people's knowledge and experiences of, and attachment to, the post-contact landscape. In so doing I seek to contribute to a broader theorization of "oral history and belonging."[19] But before doing so I briefly outline the approach we developed to record oral histories of place and to extract the geography embedded within them.

People before Place: Notes on Methodology

Quite early on in our research, it became evident that making the immediate physical landscape the focus of the interviews was counterproductive, and that it was more effective to take a life story approach. This was so for a number of reasons, not least of which are the complex ways in which "place" or "landscape" is conceptualized and the almost indefinable quality known as "attachment" is expressed. Aboriginal people rarely talked about places as though they existed "out there," separate from themselves and their memories. For instance, the question "Can you tell me about the places that have been significant to you?" often resulted in a prolonged silence as the interviewee racked his or her brains for a place that might qualify as significant enough to satisfy the interviewer. And, then, having perhaps identified a place that fitted this criterion, he or she faced the next question—equally perplexing: "Why is this place significant to you?" Very few people—other than the especially heritage-minded perhaps—think about places in these rather abstract terms. More typically, expressions of significance, of attachment, of belonging, are embedded in stories and memories of lives lived in particular places.

As we saw it, another drawback of beginning an interview with specific places or "sites" rather than with people's memories of their own pasts was that it risked reproducing the very practices that had marginalized Aboriginal people in the first place. Insofar as much Aboriginal cultural heritage work has privileged material remains from the past over the social experience of Aboriginal people themselves, it seemed to us that a person- rather than place-centered approach to oral history might redress this imbalance.

But while we began with questions about people's lives and memories, we sought to tailor our oral history methodology for cultural heritage work by experimenting with ways to "capture" spatial information. One example was our use of large aerial photographs during the interview process. We would roll these out, usually after an initial interview had been recorded, and ask interviewees, sometimes with the assistance of other local Aboriginal people who had been present at the interview, to plot places and pathways that they had mentioned. Invariably such an activity would produce more spatial information and more stories. We also collected additional spatial detail by visiting places with the narrators who had mentioned them, and sometimes by retracing routes taken across the landscape. As will be briefly discussed in the final section of the chapter, this contributed to our effort to "map memories" and to the production of what we called "geo-biographies."

Oral Histories of Local Places

Many of the Aboriginal people we interviewed for the project lived on, or had lived on, the Purfleet Aboriginal settlement, situated a few kilometers south of, and on the opposite side of the Manning River from, the regional town of Taree. This settlement, like others founded in the same period, had been a product of a late nineteenth-century desire among settler society for racial segregation.[20] With the formation of the New South Wales Aborigines Protection Board in the 1880s, local Aboriginal people, particularly those who had been living in camps in close proximity to white settlements, were removed to reserves, which were small housing settlements for Aboriginal people only, usually located at a short distance from the township but sufficiently distant to be out of sight and to limit contact between blacks and whites. The reserve at Purfleet, which was gazetted in 1900, is *the* place within the local area most closely identified with Aboriginal people. This association is reflected in local histories, and it is reflected in public perception.[21]

Reserves like Purfleet were dotted throughout New South Wales during the twentieth century. Some are still used as Aboriginal settlements, although the reserve era ended in the late 1960s and many are now controlled by local community organizations. But many others were revoked or abandoned during the preceding decades. Current and former Aboriginal reserves are among the few places unambiguously connected with Aboriginal people in the post-contact period for which there are some physical remnants.[22] These places, along with the cemeteries attached to them—Aboriginal people were excluded from interment in the town graveyard[23]— are prime targets for heritage preservation. However, our oral history research found that an emphasis on the reserve settlements, commonly called "missions" because some had resident missionaries, would be somewhat misguided. While such places certainly do feature in the memories of many Aboriginal people, many others spent little or no time on reserves, sometimes by choice, sometimes by circumstance. Moreover, as the oral histories revealed, for those who did live there, the reserve itself, its perimeter usually marked by a fence, is only one element of a much larger landscape that matters. This is because a considerable proportion of their time was spent beyond their settlement's fence.

To convey this, we developed the concept of a "backyard zone" to describe the area that could be encompassed in a day's walk from a government reserve.[24] In Purfleet, where we recorded many of our interviews, the surrounding countryside consists mostly of privately owned farms, some now subdivided for residential and industrial purposes. During the reserve era, Aboriginal people had many reasons to step off their settlement and enter this backyard zone. Some local Aboriginal men worked on a casual basis on neighboring farms. They also fished in nearby creeks and the Manning River. And they hunted in forest reserves that bordered the settlement. Some Aboriginal women worked as "domestics" for local white families in town or on farms. Aboriginal people also sought recreation beyond the confines of the "mission": they went to the river to swim, to the bush to socialize and drink alcohol out of sight of the authorities, and to town for an afternoon's entertainment at the local picture theater. They traveled further afield to visit kin living closer to the coast at a place called Forster or in the hills at Dingo Creek. What is important to note is that the backyard zone is experienced mainly through movement across it, rather than by permanent residence in it. It is a landscape of routes rather than, or at least in addition to, roots.

Once Aboriginal people went beyond the settlement fence, they were on somebody else's land. And on that land they might be welcomed, or simply tolerated, or actively repelled. As some of the oral histories made clear, Aboriginal people's movement through the "occupied" landscape could be a risky affair. Russell Saunders, who grew up at the Purfleet "mission" in the 1950s and 1960s, explained: "All the time you'd be looking over your shoulder, always alert. Because nine out of ten times you'd hear this bang—a shotgun going off. 'Ah you blackfellas, get out of there.' They'd come flying down on a horse, or a car would come flying through. . . . We'd tear up through the bush."[25]

With this in mind, Aboriginal people tended to organize their range of movement according to their quite intimate knowledge of friendly and unfriendly places within the backyard zone. Some local farmers, for instance, were known to be sympathetic to local Aboriginal people; some were even supportive, like the local farmer who grew a vegetable patch for the reserve residents. Others were known to be hostile, which might mean taking a longer route to bypass these properties and avoid confrontation and possible danger.

The oral histories draw attention to the finely calibrated ways in which formal and informal practices of racial segregation structured Aboriginal people's experience of the local landscape. Some geographic features become a "natural" border between "races." Aboriginal narrators who lived on the Purfleet Aboriginal reserve during the 1940s and 1950s typically made reference to the ways in which the southern bank of the Manning River opposite the township of Taree marked the boundaries of their normal range of movement. For instance, Warner Saunders explains a local curfew that required Aboriginal people to be out of town before dark in terms of which side of the river he was allowed to be on:

> We used to have to be out of Taree before dark. We used to have to be home here [at Purfleet] before dark. Yeah. Wasn't allowed, wasn't allowed on the other side of the bridge after dark. . . . We'd just stick to this side of the river or if we went down there fishing, we'd fish this side of the river. We wouldn't go on the other side. More fish on this side of the river.[26]

In a slightly different way, the river has also become an *aide-mémoire* for stories on the theme of racism and segregation. One in particular, told repeatedly by local Aboriginal people, contains a message about the high cost of transgressing racial divides in the segregation era. As we drove across the river, as we often did during our research, we were on occasion told a story about the death of a young Aboriginal man, Cecil Bungie, in the 1950s. He had drowned in the river after fleeing from police for fear that if caught he would be charged with possession of alcohol, which Aboriginal people were prohibited from purchasing until 1963. The story of Cecil Bungie was well known among local Aboriginal people, including the generation born after his death, in part because it had been preserved in print, in a memoir published in the 1970s by Ella Simon, a local Aboriginal woman.[27] But its preservation both in memory and in place can also be explained by its continuing resonance in the present.

In this particular locality, fear for the fate of young Aboriginal men harassed by police remains palpable. Cecil's story condenses a much larger, messy, and indeed continuing past into a memorable incident, the preservation of which is in part enabled by its attachment to a specific place.

In other stories of segregation, the local picture theater becomes the pre-eminent site used to explain the common experience of sharing the same space with whites but in ways that achieve a separation based on race. These theater stories capture the paradoxical experience of closeness and distance that lies at the heart of the logic, or illogic, of racial segregation. As Russell Saunders explained, local Aboriginal people were required to sit in a roped-off section at the front:

> The picture theatre was another case where you paid for the ticket, given them your money at the front office, then you walked around the side. And there was a doorway on either side. And the first three or four rows, there was a chain across the corridor, or hallway, there. You sat in the first four rows with your head like this [demonstrates craned neck], and you watched the pictures. You looked behind you and there was people right up the back up in other seats, and also the top balconies that had a better view. Our view was like this [demonstrates again], looking up at the screen, and when it was finished you went out the side door. Not out the door where everybody else walked. And that was it. And there was a bus, a big red bus waiting for you, the Forster bus, and [you] jumped on that and come home. That was your pictures. Your money was good enough, but your bodily presence wasn't.[28]

Almost all the interviews we recorded with people over fifty years of age included memories of sitting in the roped-off area at the local theater; and indeed such accounts are common in oral histories and published life stories by Aboriginal people across New South Wales. In many towns, the picture theater still stands (at Taree it is now used as a surf shop), and so, for local Aboriginal people, it is a constant physical reminder of past practices of segregation.

The picture theater is also prominent in accounts of Aboriginal people contesting segregation, or of a more generalized process of desegregation. In almost all Aboriginal communities across New South Wales, stories are told about an Aboriginal person or two, often women, who defied the "color bar" imposed at the theater. For instance, a recently published life story of Isabel Flick, an Aboriginal woman from a community some hundreds of kilometers inland from our study area, begins with her account of standing up to the local theater proprietor.[29] Patricia Davis-Hurst, an Aboriginal woman from Pur-fleet, recalls a similar event at Taree involving her mother: "Mum changed the policy at the local picture theatre. Their policy was that all Aboriginals had to sit in the first five rows of the theatre, which was fenced off. She changed this one night by sitting in the back seats and refusing to move, thus making a stand for equality for all."[30]

By drawing attention to the fact that these stories are told by Aboriginal people across New South Wales, my intention is not to discount specific incidents of Aboriginal people contesting the ubiquitous if informal practices of racial segregation. Rather, I want to highlight the way in which various Aboriginal communities tell their own localized version (or versions) of an event centred on a specific site in their local landscape—the picture theater—as a means to explain a general historical process—in this case, desegregation. From this perspective, it is productive to interpret these oral histories both for the information they provide that can be used to tell *new* histories of *old* places and as a mode of storytelling that enables Aboriginal people to represent themselves not only as the subjects of history, but as the makers of it too. Importantly, in this type of remembrance the complex historical process by which explicit forms of racial segregation become a thing of the past get connected to a specific physical place. This helps to localize and ground a broader, delocalized, and at times depersonalized history about Aborigines, whites, and race relations, bringing it home, so to speak. Paradoxically, these oral histories of racial segregation with their attendant geographies provide an argument against (not for) the present practice of separating Aboriginal from non-Aboriginal pasts in the field of cultural heritage. The experience of racial segregation as narrated by Aboriginal people demonstrates precisely how intertwined the lives of Aborigines and non-Aborigines were and how frequently their paths crossed.

While the Aboriginal oral histories I have discussed so far focus on the experience of close contact with, but distance from, non-Aboriginal people, other accounts repeatedly refer to the pleasure of occasions that involved only Aboriginal people in places beyond the gaze of whites. Dotted throughout the landscape are places associated with Aboriginal people coming together to "be Aboriginal." The place that epitomizes this theme in our research is a camping area called Saltwater, located on the coast a few kilometers south east of Purfleet, nestled among a thick littoral rainforest. Each Christmas holiday, which in Australia is a period of six weeks in December and January, families from Purfleet and other regional Aboriginal settlements would decamp to Saltwater for an extended stay. Many Aboriginal reserve settlements had a Christmas camp like this one. Time at such a camp was time away from the government reserve, at a place where Aboriginal people could live without the constant interference of the resident manager monitoring the movements of those under his charge. In oral histories, Saltwater is commonly described as a place where Aboriginal people returned to the old ways of doing things and where they could experience a type of freedom absent from their daily lives on their settlement, in

Taree, and in the backyard zone. This was often expressed in terms of owning Saltwater and feeling strongly that they belonged there. Russell Saunders explained: "Yeah, well you knew that was your place down there. You just knew every little nook and cranny."[31]

Saltwater was a place where families went for extended stays, but there were many other places in the backyard zone where people would go to get away from constant surveillance, including beaches not frequented by whites. These places featured strongly in the memories of the oldest generation of people we interviewed, mainly women now in their seventies and eighties. For instance, Madge Bolt, born in 1922, recalled: "We used to go to the One Mile Beach when I was young. Every Sunday we used to take dinner out there and have dinner on the beach. But they don't do nothing like that now. As I said, it's not like it used to be."[32] The comparison between now and then is common in reminiscences about occasions when Aboriginal people would come together to get away from whites. Fond memories of these places suggest an image of the past in which the social group—whether family or community—was more cohesive than it is perceived to be today.

But these memories need also to be interpreted in the broad context of racial segregation because they are associated with the desire to get away from the strictures imposed on Aboriginal people's freedom. Places where Aboriginal people went to be among themselves are part of the web of places that make up the narrators' landscapes, and without them the most publicly recognized Aboriginal place—the government reserve—makes only partial sense. They exist in the backyard zone and are connected to the reserve by various pathways or tracks. Oral accounts of these places often focus on the experience of *getting* there, rather than or in addition to *being* there, drawing attention to the ways in which it is not only the government reserve as a bounded site, or the temporarily occupied Christmas camps and picnic spots, that matter. The routes between these "sites" and other places frequented by local Aboriginal people are an important part of Aboriginal people's everyday experiences of the landscape, and memories of them detail the ways in which Aboriginal people constantly moved through a landscape owned and occupied by whites—sometimes in a manner that acknowledged that other ownership, sometimes as though they themselves owned it still.

Mapping Aboriginal Memories

Many of the themes that emerged in the oral history interviews were already well known from the extant literature about Aboriginal people, including their employment patterns and experiences, day-to-day life on the government reserve, and racial segregation in the towns. Yet the oral histories we recorded provided detail, especially spatial detail, that would be impossible to gain from other types of historical sources and from published histories and ethnographies. Thus, they are a rich resource for cultural heritage purposes because they make palpable Aboriginal people's attachment to the colonized landscape and explicitly connect remembered historical experience to present physical place, even when material traces on the ground are absent.

To make oral history usable for cultural heritage work, we needed to find ways to geographically locate the stories we heard. It was not enough to say, for instance, that Aboriginal people had been dispossessed from their country and forced to find a place for themselves in the increasingly colonized landscape. We had to show where specifically they found refuge in a landscape that no longer belonged to them. Nor was it sufficient to argue that racial segregation became a defining feature of Aboriginal people's experience during the first half of the twentieth century. We had to illustrate the ways in which formal and informal practices of racial segregation specifically influenced their residence in, movement through, and experience of the local area they occupied.

As the discussion above has demonstrated, many of the themes critical to interpreting the narratives had a quite specific spatial dimension. To reflect this, we produced a series of thematic maps, drawing on a number of oral histories to build up a composite picture. For instance, nostalgia for a time when Aboriginal people pulled together in the face of a general hostility from local whites was often expressed through references to places where they congregated from time to time to get away from whites, such as sites of Sunday picnics at the beach or in the bush. To make these places visible, we produced an overlay on an aerial photograph that plotted some of them in relation to the reserve settlement and included the various routes taken, usually by foot, to get to them (Fig. 3.1). Transit lines radiating out from the settlement show just how diffuse and expansive the Aboriginal presence in the landscape was. Other maps reflect the ways in which Aboriginal people organized the local landscape into friendly and unfriendly zones; the latter, for example, indicated by a route taken across a hostile farmer's land as well as by an escape route into the bush worked out in advance in the event that the farmer chased the "trespassers" off. Others identified those places within the local landscape where Aboriginal and non-Aboriginal people were co-present in a confined (and, in some respects, intimate) space but in ways that emphasized distance between them, such as the picture theater and the local public swimming pool.

To reflect the spatial element of our research, we coined the term "geobiography." Expressing the combination of landscape and life story, "geobiography" conveys that the core of our work lay in transforming autobiographical memory into a textual and visual representation of the landscape, or from a slightly different perspective, in extracting the remembered

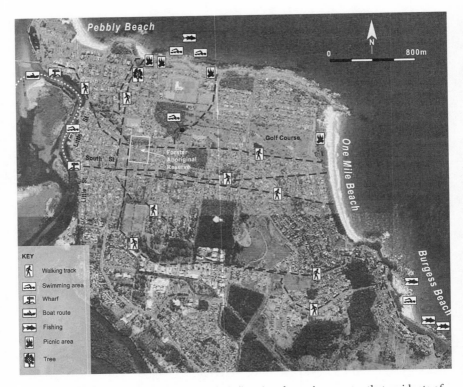

Fig 3.1   An overlay on an aerial photograph showing the various routes that residents of an Aboriginal community in our study used to reach fishing, swimming, and camping spots beyond the bounds of their settlement. *(Photograph copyright of NSW Department of Lands, Panorama Avenue, Bathhurst 2795/www.lands.nsw.gov.au; map copyright NSW Department of Environment and Conservation.)*

landscape embedded in a life story narrative. When interpreted as the geography of a life, geo-biography gives authority to the individual and recognizes the integrity of the autobiographical narrative. This can be important in oral histories with Aboriginal people, who at times, for cultural and political reasons, claim to speak only on their own behalf. Alternatively, the concept of geo-biography can be deployed in collective terms, as the biography of a landscape. Woven mainly from Aboriginal people's memories, the biography of a landscape not only conveys something of a collective vision about the place in which the storytellers live; it also has the potential to disturb public histories of the same landscape that ignore Aboriginal people's memories. It exposes the ways in which parts of these locales are intensely shared, places where the lives and paths of Aboriginal and non-Aboriginal are so inextricably intertwined that it is difficult to disentangle the history and heritage of one from the other. For these reasons, mapped Aboriginal oral histories have the potential to challenge ways non-Aboriginal people think about landscapes or places they imagined they had to themselves, because these histories reveal an intimate local Aboriginal knowledge of—and often presence in—those landscapes. In my mind, this is the flipside to the current practice of settler Australians articulating their relationship to Australia and to the land they own: exposing the historical presence of now-absent Aborigines.

This emphasis on the visibility achieved by mapping memories suggests its potential for various forms of public history, including cultural heritage. But such mapping of memories, especially when aimed directly at cultural heritage work, also poses some challenges. The map as it is used in cultural heritage work pretends to present a fixed reality—these places, *here*, are what matter—and in this context an oral history once mapped threatens to become a relic on the ground—what we have said is *all* that can be said about these places. The oral histories we recorded do tell *new* stories about *old* places, adding more to what we can know about them. But just as often they show the ways in which memories of the past are often only tenuously connected to "real" or "remaining" places on the ground. In the quest to fix memory to physical place, what might get obscured is the very impossibility of the task because the fit between these landscapes in the mind and a "real geography" can be tenuous as well as fluid as it changes over time.

Nonetheless, our purpose in producing these mapped memories was to challenge the ways in which contemporary cultural heritage practice reproduces a separation between the histories of Aboriginal and non-Aboriginal people that was never as complete or as certain as professional practices and bureaucratic processes suggest. Given that purpose, they contribute not simply to recording and preserving new places in the heritage landscape but also to producing new public histories about relations between Aboriginal and non-Aboriginal people. They help to make visible both Aboriginal people's presence in and attachment to the very same landscapes claimed, occupied, and owned by non-Aboriginal people and the entanglement of the pasts and the presences of both. The still-pressing need to make this known, not only at the level of the state, which manages the Australian community's cultural heritage, but also in those local contexts where blacks and whites continue to live side by side, is sufficient to commend the approach and to recommend its further refinement in other contexts in Australia and beyond.

NOTES

This chapter emerges from a much larger research project. Denis Byrne initiated the project and was an inspirational and generous research partner. The project would not have been possible without the support and guidance of Vienna Maslin and Robert Yettica, and the cooperation of the Purfleet-Taree and Forster Aboriginal communities. My special thanks to the people in those communities who shared their stories with us. Finally, my thanks to Paula Hamilton and Linda Shopes for their encouragement and astute editorial advice.

1. Denis Byrne and Maria Nugent, *Mapping Attachment: A Spatial Approach to Aboriginal Post-contact Heritage* (Sydney: Department of Environment and Conservation, 2004), http://www.nationalparks.nsw.gov.au/npws.nsf/Content/mapping_attachment.

2. Throughout this chapter I use the term "place" in two senses: somewhat abstractly to mean "space in general" and much more specifically to refer to particular physical "sites" or geographic locations.

3. For a discussion of "racial intimacies," see Gillian Cowlishaw, *Rednecks, Eggheads and Blackfellas: A Study of Racial Power and Intimacy in Australia* (Sydney: Allen and Unwin, 1999), esp. chap. 5.

4. The New South Wales National Parks and Wildlife Service is subsumed under the Department of Environment and Conservation (NSW).

5. For a discussion of the development of Aboriginal cultural heritage in Australia, see Denis Byrne, "Deep Nation: Australia's Acquisition of an Indigenous Past," *Aboriginal History* 20 (1996): 82–106; Denis Byrne, Helen Brayshaw, and Tracy Ireland, *Social Significance: A Discussion Paper* (Sydney: NSW National Parks and Wildlife Service, 2001).

6. According to Denis Byrne, more than 32,000 Aboriginal pre-contact sites are listed on the Aboriginal Sites Register (now the Aboriginal Heritage Information Management System) maintained by the NSW National Parks and Wildlife Service, but only 200 post-contact sites are listed, mainly cemeteries. The NSW Heritage Office has listed on its State Heritage Inventory a total of 17,500 sites, of which only 7 are Aboriginal post-contact sites. Denis Byrne, "The Ethos of Return: Erasure and Reinstatement of Aboriginal Visibility," *Historical Archaeology* 37:1 (2003): 79.

7. Byrne, "Deep Nation," 92–94.

8. Byrne and Nugent, *Mapping Attachment*, 5.

9. The most notable work in this area for New South Wales includes Gillian Cowlishaw, *Black, White or Brindle: Race in Rural Australia* (Melbourne: Cambridge University Press, 1988); Barry Morris, *Domesticating Resistance: The Dhan-gadi Aborigines and the Australian State* (New York: Berg, 1989); Peter Read, *A Hundred Years War: The Wiradjuri People and the State* (Sydney: Australian National University Press, 1998); Heather Goodall, *Invasion to Embassy: Land in Aboriginal Politics in New South Wales, 1770–1972* (Sydney: Allen and Unwin, 1996), xv. Two important collections of essays about Aboriginality are Jeremy Beckett, ed., *Past and Present: The Construction of Aboriginality* (Canberra: Aboriginal Studies Press, 1988); and Ian Keen, ed., *Being Black: Aboriginal Cultures in 'Settled' Australia* (Canberra: Aboriginal Studies Press, 1988).

10. Diane Barwick, "Writing Aboriginal History," *Canberra Anthropology* 4:2 (1981): 74–86.

11. The word "country," following Heather Goodall, "refers to the area(s) for which Aboriginal people were the owners and custodians." Heather Goodall, *Invasion to Embassy*, xv.

12. Byrne, "The Ethos of Return."

13. Ibid.; Denis Byrne, "Archaeology in Reverse: The Flow of Aboriginal People and Their Remains through the Space of New South Wales," in Nick Merriman, ed., *Public Archaeology* (London: Routledge, 2004), 240–54.

14. For a history of Aboriginal people's efforts to acquire land and repeated phases of dispossession, see Goodall, *Invasion to Embassy*.

15. Byrne, "The Ethos of Return," 80.

16. Peter Read, *Belonging: Australians, Place and Aboriginal Ownership* (Melbourne: Cambridge University Press, 2000).

17. Peter Read, *Returning to Nothing: The Meaning of Lost Places* (Melbourne: Cambridge University Press, 1996).

18. Mark McKenna, *Looking for Blackfellas' Point: An Australian History of Place* (Sydney: UNSW Press, 2002).

19. Read, *Returning to Nothing*, x.

20. Goodall, *Invasion to Embassy*, chap. 7.

21. Byrne and Nugent, *Mapping Attachment*, chap. 10.

22. This is reflected in two current archaeological projects on Aboriginal mission stations: Jane Lydon's study of the Ebenezer Mission, funded by the Australian Research Council, and the "Living Places" project, based in the Cultural Heritage Division, DEC (NSW). On the Ebenezer Mission see Jane Lydon, "Imagining the Moravian Mission: Space and Surveillance at the Former Ebenezer Mission, Victoria, South-eastern Australia," *Historical Archaeology* (forthcoming); and Jane Lydon, with Alasdair Brooks and Zvonkica Stanin, "Archaeological Investigations at the Mission-House, Ebenezer Mission," report (Aboriginal Affairs Victoria and Heritage Victoria, Centre for Australian Indigenous Studies, Monash University: Melbourne, 2004). For "Living Places," see http://www.nationalparks.nsw.gov .au/npws.nsf/Content/aboriginal_living_places. For an earlier project see Peter Kabaila, *Wiradjuri Places: The Murrumbidgee River Basin* (Canberra: Black Mountain Projects, 1995).

23. Heather Goodall, "Mourning, Remembrance and the Politics of Place: A Study of the Significance of Collarenebri Aboriginal Cemetery," *Public History Review* 8 (2002): 72–96; Denis Byrne, *In Sad but Loving Memory* (Sydney: NSW National Parks and Wildlife Service, 1998).

24. Byrne and Nugent, *Mapping Attachment*, chap. 14. Denis Byrne coined the term "backyard zone."

25. Ibid., 82.

26. Ibid., 161.

27. Ella Simon, *Through My Eyes* (Adelaide: Rigby, 1978).

28. Byrne and Nugent, *Mapping Attachment*, 95–96.

29. Isabel Flick and Heather Goodall, *Isabel Flick: The Life Story of a Remarkable Aboriginal Leader* (Sydney: Allen and Unwin, 2003).

30. Patricia Davis-Hurst, *Sunrise Station* (Taree: Sunbird Publications, 1996), 44, cited in Byrne and Nugent, *Mapping Attachment*, 97.

31. Byrne and Nugent, *Mapping Attachment*, 87.

32. Ibid., 147.

4

Moving beyond the Walls: The Oral History of the Ottoman Fortress Villages of Seddülbahir and Kumkale

Işıl Cerem Cenker and Lucienne Thys-Şenocak

It is hoped that all who witness the history of this great munificence will say prayers for the great Valide Sultan [Queen Mother] who had these fortresses built.

ABDI ABDURRAHMAN PASHA, 1659[1]

In the Seddülbahir area, the enemy approached the shore in lifeboats. When they came into range, our men opened fire. Here for years the colour of the sea had always been the same, but now it turned red with the blood of our enemies. . . . In spite of the enemy shelling and machine gun fire, our men continued to hit their targets, and the dead rolled into the sea. The shoreline of Ertuğrul Koyu (V beach) filled with enemy corpses, lined up like rows of broad beans.

MAJOR MAHMUT BEY, 1915[2]

Situated at the entrance to the Dardanelles—the ancient Hellespont—the lands of Seddülbahir and Kumkale abound with many pasts and resonate with a host of contemporary interpretations. Five kilometers from the Ottoman village of Kumkale, the famous archaeological site of Troy dominates the Asian side of the straits. On the opposite shore, just below the fortress at Seddülbahir, one of the most ferocious battles in the Gallipoli campaign of World War I was fought; its Turkish casualties are commemorated by a monument at the entrance to the fortress that is dedicated to the first soldiers who died there. On the shore to the immediate north of the fortress is a larger cemetery for the Royal Dublin Fusiliers, many of whom were killed on 25 April 1915 while trying to reach the beach where they are now buried. On that same morning their comrades from Australia and New Zealand would meet a similar fate below the cliffs at Arıburnu Bay, twenty kilometers to the north of Seddülbahir. For tourists such as the typical Australian backpacker, the journey to Gallipoli has been described as "an international civil religious pilgrimage" where "nationalism and cosmopolitanism could be simultaneously invigorated."[3] For the newly enlisted Turkish soldier or the young primary school student visiting from nearby Çanakkale, the shores of the Dardanelles represent a space where the fierce attachment of the Turk to his or her homeland was made manifest by ordinary soldiers making extraordinary sacrifices, and by the devotion and bravery of the nation's greatest hero, Mustafa Kemal Pasha: Atatürk. (Fig. 4.1)

This chapter examines the results of a three-year oral history project that was initiated in 1999 by Koç University and Istanbul Technical University.[4] The sites for our oral history research were Seddülbahir and Kumkale, two Turkish villages that sit on opposite shores of the Dardanelles in the eastern Aegean.[5] Each village is dominated by a fortress that was built in the seventeenth century by Hadice Turhan Sultan, the concubine mother of the Ottoman Sultan Mehmed IV.[6] The oral history research conducted at these two sites is part of a larger, long-term project that includes the restoration and reuse of the fortress of Seddülbahir and the documentation of the architectural and cultural history of the Ottoman past in the Dardanelles region of Turkey. Within the context of this larger project, oral testimony was used to understand the changes that had been made to the architectural plans and building fabric of the two fortifications during the late nineteenth and early twentieth centuries. However, our research for the oral history project at the fortresses also focused on how the existing Ottoman and European archival records for these two sites, as well as the official Turkish historiography of political events in this region, have shaped the memories of persons currently living among the historical monuments remaining at Seddülbahir and Kumkale. In this chapter we explore, using both textual and oral resources, the kinds of disjunctures that exist among official records, representation, and the local consciousness and identity that have evolved at these two historical sites. Finally, we suggest how divergent meanings and memories that are ascribed to a cultural landscape and historical site can be brought together as enriching rather than competing factors.

What aspects of Seddülbahir and Kumkale's past are remembered by those who now live at these sites? What role has official historiography played in shaping the memories of the inhabitants of these two villages? How do these memories lend meaning to the historical buildings that are currently standing in or adjacent to these villages? With the recent initiative of the

Fig 4.1   The present-day ruins of the lower section of the Seddülbahir fortress, with a view across the entrance to the Dardanelles and the location of Kumkale on the Asian shore. *(Photograph by Işıl Cerem Cenker.)*

Turkish government to reorganize the national parks on either side of the Dardanelles, and to restore and reuse the Ottoman fortress at Seddülbahir as an open-air museum and center for maritime heritage, the questions surrounding local memory, local history, and representation have become increasingly relevant.[7]

The Fortresses of Seddülbahir and Kumkale:
The Built Environment

The fortress of Seddülbahir encompasses an area of 2.5 hectares. Located on a promontory above the Aegean Sea, the grounds are divided into an upper and lower fortress by the uneven topography of the site. On the upper ground, almost 18 meters above sea level, masonry walls 500 meters long enclose an area of 1,300 square meters. The lower section of the fortress rests at sea level; a wall 480 meters long encloses an area of 1,900 square meters. From archival engravings and maps of the fortress from the seventeenth and eighteenth centuries, it is apparent that this basic plan has not changed significantly since the founding of the fortress. However, several sections of the outer walls have been destroyed, as have most of the interior structures.[8] At the present time, only five towers remain at Seddülbahir, but originally there may have been seven. Much of the building has disappeared over the past 350 years as a result of harsh weather, earthquakes, war, and the removal and reuse of the masonry by local residents for the construction of their own homes.

The masonry walls of Ottoman Kumkale enclose 3 hectares. In contrast to the walls at Seddülbahir, which average 8 meters in height, the walls of Kumkale are somewhat shorter at 6.8 meters.[9] Situated on the alluvial shore of the Trojan plain, Turhan's Asian fortress is closer to the sea and presents a less imposing appearance than the fortress at Seddülbahir.[10] Five towers and several sections of the original south wall still remain intact at Kumkale, but there has been a significant amount of change to the original Ottoman plan by the Ottoman and Turkish navies, with the latter still occupying the fortress. Several structures were added in the eighteenth and nineteenth centuries to the original seventeenth-century fortress complex, including a two-story mosque, a second bathhouse, and a fountain.[11] Of particular interest is the large multi-chambered west tower at Kumkale with its large fireplace. There are important remains of the foundations of a small landing where boats such as the sultan's galley, or *kadırga,* could have disembarked during state visits to Kumkale. As at Seddülbahir, the main gate of Kumkale, the *bab-ı kebir,* opened toward the village, which wrapped around the southeast and northeast walls of the fortress in the eighteenth and nineteenth centuries.[12]

In Turhan Sultan's foundation deed of 1665, we learn that the Queen Mother ordered that "inside both fortresses a grand mosque, a fine school, and a clean public bath should be built along with many houses, shops, and markets for the guardians and protectors of the fortresses; these should all surpass those found anywhere else."[13] Ottoman chroniclers writing in the seventeenth century, after the fortresses were completed, and European travelers who saw the fortresses in the late seventeenth century while passing through the Dardanelles, describe

Fig 4.2. The Turhan Sultan fortresses of Seddülbahir (Chateau Neuf d'Europe) and Kumkale (Chateau Neuf d'Asie) are shown in the foreground of this late seventeenth-century map, Veue des Dardanelles de Constantinople, created by Nicholas de Fer. *(Photograph by Lucienne Thys-Şenocak.)*

Seddülbahir and Kumkale as well-inhabited places, with both military and civilian populations (Fig. 4.2). The European traveler William Joseph Grelot remarked upon Turhan Sultan's fortresses shortly after their completion.[14] Although he was not greatly impressed with the village of Seddülbahir, Grelot's account is of interest because he described several structures, such as the water system and mosque, which were part of the infrastructure at the fortress. He informs us that within the walls of Seddülbahir are:

> Certain houses of the Ağa and other officers with a mosque of which the Duomo and Steeple appear very plain to be seen, as well as other edifices, as being generally seated in the highest parts of the fortification, from whence you descend by large steps to the platforms where the guns are planted, which lie equal with the surface of the water. Near to this castle lies a small village, unremarkable for nothing; together with five large pilasters that serve to underprop several conveyances of water to the fort.[15]

Like many European travelers before and after him, Grelot was more interested in the Asian than the Thracian side of the Dardanelles because of its location on the Troad and its proximity to the ancient city of Troy, described in the poems of Homer.[16] Grelot's observations of Kumkale are therefore more detailed than those of Seddülbahir. Of Kumkale, he writes:

> The castle is seated upon a tongue of land pointing out into the sea, upon a square platform composed of four large planes of walls, flanked at the four corners with towers; of which those two next to the sea are square, with a sort of redoubt only on one side; the other two toward the land are quite round. Between these four towers there are five others, of which four are also square and one round, that defend the walls, but neither in thickness, bigness, or distance, one like the other. As for those that are washed by the sea, they are furnished by portholes that are level with the surface of the water as also with their curtains and platforms. I am told above forty of these were provided with cannon, always mounted and continuously charged ready to play upon any enemy that will run the hazard of adventuring in the harbour by force. The way to this castle is from the north (and joins at the end of a street to a very fair mosque which stands at the south side not far from the shore) from whence you may very plainly discern the Duomo and the Tower of the Temple.[17]

Oral Sources: Challenges to Traditional Methodologies

The use of oral sources in historical research challenges traditional assumptions concerning the primacy of the written document and also confronts the historian with a range of methodological issues. The immense collection of archival documents accumulated from centuries of imperial administration that is available to the Ottoman and Turkish historian has shaped an approach to historical inquiry that privileges the written sources. For the majority of historians working on Ottoman or Turkish topics, the archival text is of central importance; only in the past decade has oral history made inroads into the Turkish academy and become accepted by some as a viable approach to use when investigating the past.[18] Once secure in the belief that there was a single truth about an event or a person that could be discovered only in the papers of state archives, historians of the Ottoman and Turkish past, like their counterparts in other countries, now support an examination of the past that allows for a multiplicity of interpretations, an appreciation of how historical knowledge is produced as well as discovered, and a view of "reality as complex and many sided."[19]

Oral testimony can also be extremely valuable in understanding the ways in which local communities identify with and understand historical monuments and the cultural landscapes in which they live. Too often when regions of historical importance are marked for development, the rich local memory that exists at these sites is ignored and ultimately lost, particularly if the indigenous population is displaced. Documentation of this local memory is precisely the task for which oral history is well suited, enriching the meaning of the site for both the local community and the visitor. Today, a more thorough understanding of the complexity of daily life and local history has been achieved through the practice of oral history, particularly in the case of underrepresented groups such as the working class, women, and minorities.[20]

The Ottoman Empire: A Brief Background

The Turkic ancestors of the Ottomans first moved into Anatolia in the eleventh century as part of a great wave of migration from central Asia.[21] Once established as a small principality in the western region of present-day Turkey, the Ottomans began to expand their territories from the early fourteenth century. Within two centuries they had become a world empire. Through religious fervor, sophisticated diplomacy, and military conquest, the Ottomans gradually gained control of the lands that had once been part of the ancient Roman and Byzantine empires, as well as vast territories in the Balkans and many of the lands that make up the contemporary Middle East. From their capital in Istanbul, formerly Byzantine Constantinople, the House of Osman ruled for over seven centuries until the establishment of the Turkish Republic by Mustafa Kemal Pasha, or Atatürk, in 1923.[22] Ottoman historiography is as rich as the history of the dynasty itself, and a thorough study of it is beyond the scope of this chapter. However, three major aspects of this historiography are important for our understanding of the seventeenth-century Ottoman fortress villages of Seddülbahir and Kumkale: the role of Ottoman women, the geo-political significance of the Dardanelles region, and the events in this region that led to the founding of the Turkish Republic.

The Decline Paradigm: Ottoman Women

Until quite recently a central question for Ottoman historians was why the Ottoman empire, after enjoying a particularly brilliant era from the late fifteenth through the sixteenth century, experienced a decline. Several reasons were posited to account for the growing weakness of the state. Frequently cited were the corrupt and inexperienced sultans who, after the sixteenth century, preferred to spend much of their lives sequestered within the confines of the Topkapı Palace in Istanbul. The illegitimate usurpation of power by royal Ottoman women was often presented as another factor. Although the historiography of modern Turkey celebrates the accomplishments of Atatürk and the new Turkish Republic in granting its new female citizens greater freedom and independence, the historiography of imperial Ottoman women did not acknowledge the achievements of royal wives, daughters, mothers, and concubines. Rather, much of this history was shaped by Ahmed Refik, an early twentieth-century historian who drew selectively from the Ottoman chronicles of the sixteenth and seventeenth centuries and described this period (the early modern era) as the *Kadınlar Saltanatı*, "the Sultanate of the Women"; his influential book bears the same title.[23] Working with a paradigm of imperial decline that shaped historical interpretations of the postclassical Ottoman empire, Refik attributed many of the Ottoman government's misfortunes to the backstage machinations of the royal wives and mothers who, he claimed, exercised authority from the confines of the harem. According to Refik, the illegitimate manipulation of power and wealth by self-serving imperial women contributed to the empire's loss of political and economic supremacy after the so-called classical age.

In the past two decades the decline paradigm that has framed so much of the historical discourse about the Ottoman empire has become increasingly suspect. Most current historians recognize it as unable to fully account for the complex transformations that occured in the Ottoman state during the early modern era. As the explanations for the empire's alleged decline came under scrutiny, so too did the various factors that had been held responsible, including imperial Ottoman women. But while many of the previous explanations for changes in the Ottoman state have now lost legitimacy among contemporary historians, the decline discourse is still found in popular historical fiction on Ottoman themes and constitutes the main narrative in the primary, middle, and high school textbooks written for Turkish children.[24] Here, Ottoman women are either absent from the historical narrative or are portrayed as destabilizing causes of political decline.[25] The backwardness of the Ottoman state, represented by its oppression of the female sex, is juxtaposed against the modern vision of Atatürk for the women of the new Republic. The negative portrayal of women in the Ottoman empire in much of traditional history and in official school textbooks is important to consider, since it poses a challenge to those who are living alongside the fortresses of Seddülbahir and Kumkale, both of which were founded by an imperial Ottoman woman, Hadice Turhan Sultan.

The Dardanelles: The Impact of Topography

The second facet of early Ottoman and later Turkish historiography relevant to the interpretation of the past by the residents of Seddülbahir and Kumkale is the geo-political history of the Dardanelles region. For the Ottomans this was strategic territory, for it was on these shores that they gained their first foothold in Europe. In 1352 they crossed the straits and, aided by a fortuitous earthquake that shattered the walls of the Byzantine fortress at Gallipoli, acquired the citadel of Cempe, situated at the northern end of the Gallipoli peninsula. It is no wonder that the Ottomans later set about establishing their own defensive fortresses on either side of the Dardanelles.

Like the Straits of the Bosphorus, through which the waters of the Black Sea pass into the northern end of the Sea of Marmara, the Straits of the Dardanelles channel the southern waters of the Marmara into the Aegean. In Turkish, both straits are called *boğaz* or "the throat," making it difficult to determine whether the Çanakkale or Istanbul straits are being described. Similarly, Ottoman documents composed shortly after the fortresses were completed celebrate them as a pair.[26] Ottoman archival documents, called *tamirat defter,* which record repairs made to the fortresses, as well as descriptions by Ottoman chroniclers and most European travelers' accounts of their visits to the Dardanelles, also describe Seddülbahir and Kumkale as two monuments closely tied to each other at the entrance to the Dardanelles. Indeed, the fortresses were built at the same time, by the same patron, so that they could protect the entrance to the straits with their cross-firing capabilities. Later chronicles and repair documents from the seventeenth and eighteenth centuries also describe them using the single Ottoman word *kal' ateyn,* or the "twin fortresses."[27] Most of the historical documentation, both visual and textual, emphasizes the united purpose and identity of Kumkale and Seddülbahir; in the textual documentation the historical development of the two fortresses is presented as a reflection of their geographic positions.

The Dardanelles: Birthplace of a Nation

The third aspect of Tukish historiography that has shaped the discourse of the region of the Dardanelles and the Gallipoli peninsula is related to the role that this territory played in the official history of modern Turkey. It was in this region that Mustafa Kemal Pasha, who would later become known as Atatürk, fought the Allied forces during the Gallipoli campaign of World War I. This region of the Dardanelles was also where, once the war drew to a close, Atatürk embarked upon a war of independence and the mission of establishing modern-day Turkey. The Gallipoli peninsula and its surrounding areas are thus strongly associated with the birth of the modern nation. Today, on a hill just across from the city of Çanakkale, the words, "Halt traveler! The land upon which you tread unawares is where an era came to end," are emblazoned into the earth, large enough to be read by ships passing through the Dardanelles. Turkish schoolchildren, Rotary and Lions club members, and Turkish soliders visit the region frequently, following a pilgrimage route that highlights the points of the landscape where acts of heroism were undertaken by the nation's founder and his loyal soldiers. There is little room in this official narrative about the birth of the Turkish nation to accommodate the Ottoman past.[28] Rather, the official history emphasizes a clear break between the late Ottoman period and the republican era and rejects any continuity. Defining oneself in opposition to the Ottoman empire became an essential part of the process of becoming a new Turkish citizen. From the rejection of the fez, the Ottoman headwear, to the appropriation of a new Latin alphabet in lieu of the Arabic script, the divisions between the Ottoman empire and the Turks have been made manifest in many real and symbolic ways. Again, the challenges faced by residents of Seddülbahir and Kumkale in reconciling this official history with their Ottoman surroundings have resulted in a rather unique reworking of official history.

The Oral History Project: The Process

During three years of fieldwork, from 1999 to 2002, we conducted a total of thirty-one tape-recorded interviews with residents of Seddülbahir and Kumkale. As our primary objective for the larger architectural documentation and survey project was to gather more information about the immediate pre–World War I physical features of the sites, we first interviewed the older residents. Initially, we assumed that members of this older generation had been eyewitnesses to the villages' histories since, and perhaps even during, World War I, and could therefore provide the most accurate information about the changes that had occurred to the Ottoman structures at Seddülbahir and Kumkale during the twentieth century.

During the preliminary set of interviews in 1999, however, we realized that there were very few residents at either village whose families had lived there prior to World War I. The majority of the residents at Seddülbahir were Turks who had immigrated to the village from Romania in the early 1930s, almost two decades after the end of the war. The majority of the residents at Kumkale had moved to that village on the Asian shore of the Dardanelles from Bulgaria during the same years. We were not discouraged by the low number of eyewitnesses; instead, this new information served to broaden the scope of our oral history inquiries. In addition to the information we were hoping to acquire from this group of older residents concerning the fortresses' architectural changes, the resettlement of these two communities of Balkan Turks into the Dardanelles region became a second avenue of inquiry.

This theme of the 1930s resettlement was not the only new concern that forced us to expand our initial parameters. In many of the interviews we conducted, the residents of Seddülbahir and Kumkale were anxious to voice their concerns about the Turkish government's recent initiatives to establish and re-structure the national parks on the Asian shore of the straits (on the archaeo-logical site of Troy, five kilometers from Kumkale) and on the Gallipoli peninsula. We decided that rather than restrict the project to the immediate needs of our ongoing architectural survey, we would diversify our initial crite-ria for interviewees and explore these new issues that had unexpectedly emerged. By responding quickly to our first set of interviews and enlarging the scope of the project with new sets of queries, we were able to learn about both the architectural changes the two fortresses of Seddülbahir and Kumkale had undergone over time and the ways in which the residents at both sites had in-tegrated the fortresses into narratives about their local histories. It became in-creasingly apparent that while the official Turkish history of the Gallipoli peninsula ignored the pre-republican Ottoman past of the region, there was an acute consciousness of this earlier era among locals. Living among the physical remains of the Ottoman era, residents in Seddülbahir especially, but also in Kumkale, had teased out the threads of earlier local histories of the Dard-anelles and woven them into the rhetoric surrounding the founding of their new country. We explored the degree to which there was divergence as well as convergence in these local and national narratives, and particularly the region's role in the unfolding drama of the foundation of the Turkish Republic. Finally, we were able to elicit various responses to the anticipated impact of the gov-ernment's plans to create a national park project surrounding the archaeologi-cal site of Troy near Kumkale and to redefine the identity of the Gallipoli peninsula as an international peace park.

Diverging Histories

As previously mentioned, when only the archival records of Seddülbahir and Kumkale from the mid-seventeenth to the late nineteenth century are consid-ered, the textual as well as the visual documentation of the two fortresses and their villages has an officially constructed narrative that binds the two sites to-gether. Since the commencement of World War I, however, three major factors served to break apart this unified historical narrative and allow the differing paths of the two sites to emerge: first, the different ways in which Kumkale and Seddülbahir experienced and continue to experience World War I; second, the establishment of a new village for the residents of Kumkale; and third, the move-ment of different communities of immigrants into the two villages in the 1930s.

During World War I, Seddülbahir, because of its physical location on a more elevated promontory overlooking the entrance to the Dardanelles, was in a more strategic position than Kumkale to defend itself and the entrance to the straits against Allied attacks. As the Allied battle plans during the Gallipoli campaign were concentrated on the European side of the straits, the majority of the fighting as well as the casualties occurred on that side of the Dardanelles, particularly at the Arıburnu and Sulva bays, where one of the major Allied offensives occurred at dawn on 25 April 1915. As a result of its strategic location, there are far more monumental structures, sculptures, and cemeteries located in and around Seddülbahir than at the village and fortress environs of Kumkale. In contrast, Kumkale was occupied by French troops for less than one month and did not experience the same degree of Ottoman resistance. With the more prominent commemorative sites of the war drawing pilgrims to the battlefields on the European side of the straits, and the archaeological site of Troy attracting most of the visitors coming to the Asian side, few tourists—national or international—make the effort to come to Kumkale. The war memorials near the village are sparse and neglected; some have even been destroyed. Indeed, anyone attempting to enter the Ottoman fortress of Kumkale is forced to turn around, as it is the site of an operating Turkish naval base and is closed to civilians.

According to Sezai Ercan, a Kumkale resident who is interested in attracting more tourists to his town, one of the monuments built by the French government to commemorate their dead was allegedly destroyed in the 1930s by an irate fisherman.

> Because the French have their martyrs here, they constructed a commemorative monument here. Even today, when they visit the region, they are looking for this monument, which they read about in their guidebooks. Yet there exists no such monument! . . . The construction of the monument was completed together with a similar one on the opposite shore in Seddülbahir. The lieutenant of the military barracks at the place—the Greek village I described to you—told the villagers, "Those who came to conquer your country made a monument here. How can you let them take shelter here?" After these words, a fellow fisherman blew up the monument with two kilos of dynamite. And this was a very big mistake. This region would have been a tourist site. Some people in the village still know its place.[29]

The second important factor that has contributed to the villages' diverging histories was the post–World War I relocation of seaside Kumkale to a site five kilometers inland. Due to the marshy conditions created by the confluence of the Küçük Karamenderes and Dümrek Su (the ancient Scamander and Simois rivers), the village of Kumkale and its fortress were often exposed to malarial conditions. According to Zeki Ulus, a Kumkale resident whose parents were among the first settlers of the new village, these conditions as well as the destruction of the old village's infrastructure during the war were the incentives for the 1926 relocation.[30] By World War II, the Ottoman fortress of Kumkale had been designated a Turkish naval base; the site continues to be inaccessible to the local population.[31] The fact that the present-day residents of Kumkale have no physical access to the Ottoman fortress or the old village is revealed in the degree to which the fortress and its history are absent from their memories. When it is recalled, the memories are about its inaccessibility.

The residents remember the wealth of the old village and cite Old Kumkale's large two-story mosque, two Turkish baths *(hamams)*, a school for instruction in the Islamic religion *(medrese)*, and the existence of a court as proof of the village's prosperity in Ottoman times. Often their accounts contrasted the prosperity of the old village to the poor state of the economy in present-day New Kumkale. Accounts such as the one provided by Nazif Arısan do not contain much detail abut daily life in Old Kumkale; rather, they capture the nostalgia for a life that he believes was idyllic:

> Kumkale was a very developed village known by all in the region. Its fields and lands were fertile and the people were prosperous. Unfortunately, eighty-six years ago, it was razed to the ground during the First World War. Nothing remained from the old village of Kumkale. After the war those who fled returned, but they could not find the place known as Kumkale again. Only the fortress was there. The prewar era was prosperous, as I said before. They were employing Greeks in their fields; they [the Turks] themselves were wealthy. . . . The immigrants from Bulgaria settled in the present-day village of Kumkale. This village is a new one. It does not resemble the old village. It was an entirely different place.[32]

In contrast to the more general feelings of nostalgia expressed by the residents of Kumkale, most of the people interviewed at Seddülbahir recounted specific details about their fortress. They were able to recall stories about the foundation of the fortress and the Ottoman village that once existed there. Seddülbahir villagers frequently repeated a founding legend concerning actions taken by the sultan's mother, or *valide*, in the face of the empire's deteriorating economic circumstances. According to the legend, Queen Mother Turhan Sultan financed the construction of Seddülbahir and Kumkale by selling a pair of her golden slippers. One resident, Ahmet Aydagün recounted:

> Again, the state was weak, because it was around the seventeen hundreds; they [the fortresses] were built in the seventeenth century. You know, the state was weak, I mean the Ottomans, and so the construction took some

time. We heard from our grandparents that the power of the state was insufficient, so the Queen Mother, I do not recall her exact name, but you know there was a period in Ottoman history where the royal women were strong. This was after Hürrem Sultan, one of those Queen Mothers. She had golden slippers . . . she sold one of them for here, the other for Kumkale. You see how strong her feelings were for the country. See the desperate situation they [the Ottomans] were facing, and they finished this building [the fortress] like this.[33]

Ismail Bozkurt, another resident of Seddülbahir, recalled a story about the large numbers of people who were sent from various locations in the Ottoman empire to help with the construction of the fortress. According to Bozkurt, the population of workers was so great that feeding them all was a challenge; indeed, "camel loads of cutlery were brought in for the builders."[34]

Other residents told about life within the walls of the fortress. Most of these more detailed memories of Seddülbahir belonged to Fatma Tuncer, who was ninety-five years old at the time of the interview and whose father had served as a soldier in the village during World War I. The village of Seddülbahir had been crowded and well-to-do before the war, she recalled, its social and economic life comparable to Istanbul's. Seddülbahir, she said, was known as "Little Istanbul" then and had large bazaars and various shops. She recounted her grandmother's descriptions of the interior and exterior of the fortress and how the villagers could move between these worlds on most occasions:

When it got dark, the doors of the fortress were closed. Our people [living outside the fortress] were also going into the fortress, to visit acquaintances, to [visit] relatives, "Oh," they would say, "let us leave before the doors were closed." The doors were closed at eleven P.M. "Let us go," they said, "we have chickens, animals to look after." When they went to the door and saw them closed, the soldiers would say, "That is it, we close at eleven, where were you? Go home in the morning!" They never let them out when they were late. My grandmother used to say that they stayed inside the fortress many times when they were late.[35]

New Immigrants: Merging Local Memory with Official History

While the recent past should provide more documentary evidence for the historian than earlier eras do, the textual sources for the local history of the villages of Seddülbahir and Kumkale are rather limited for the two decades following World War I.[36] The war left much of the region depopulated; a significant proportion of the Greek population had fled the villages in the Dardanelles just before the war broke out. In both Seddülbahir and Kumkale, resettlement started by the early 1930s. Turkish immigrants from Romania were moved to Seddülbahir, while those from Bulgaria were settled in Kumkale. Because these immigrants arrived two decades after the major evacuation of the war-stricken region, there exists a significant gap in the historical memory of the residents of both villages for the period between the Mondros Armistice of 1918 and the 1930s, when these communities began to reestablish themselves. Both groups of immigrants took part in the struggle to survive in their new homeland and, as new citizens, to strengthen the young nation of Turkey. The stories from Seddülbahir in particular strongly emphasize the themes of wartime memories and the appreciation of personal sacrifices made by soldiers to establish the Republic of Turkey. Their recollections reflected the official historiography of the region, which emphasizes the War of Independence as the source of Turkish national identity. Beyond this meta-narrative of devotion to the nation, however, the memories were remarkably different for residents of Kumkale and Seddülbahir, particularly regarding the Ottoman past. The physical removal of the Old Kumkale inhabitants from the lands adjacent to the Ottoman fortress—and from all other areas where there was material evidence of the Ottoman past, such as the large eighteenth-century Ottoman cemetery 100 meters to the southwest of the fortress—has effectively severed these residents from the Ottoman heritage of their homeland.[37] The physical distance between the old village and its new location, the demographic changes experienced in relocated postwar Kumkale, and the continuing military presence at the fortress have limited both the physical and the psychological attachment of Kumkale residents to the old village and its fortress.

The situation at Seddülbahir was remarkably different. Impossible to ignore, the Ottoman ruins were appropriated by the villagers and recast as evidence of the sacrifice that one extraordinary person, the sultan's mother, had made to assist the state. Consequently, the villagers developed a rather different view of Ottoman women than that espoused in official textbooks produced by the Turkish Ministry of Education. Seddülbahir villagers, particularly the women, spoke of the female patron of the fortress, Hadice Turhan Sultan, with admiration. She was remembered and celebrated for her act of benevolence and personal sacrifice and was not perceived as an illegitimate political figure. Rather, the Queen Mother was celebrated as an important historical figure who supported the state when it was in need. According to the public memory at Seddülbahir, the fortress had been constructed at a time when the straits and the Ottoman empire itself were under attack. The patron's vision and her determination to preserve the empire were perceived by many as admirable, considering the deteriorating financial and military conditions of that time. For the residents of Seddülbahir, the two fortresses had come into existence as a result of a personal sacrifice for the country, something that resonated with the sacrifices that they had made in their new homeland after leaving Romania. Many of those interviewed in Seddülbahir spoke of the hardships of resettlement and the dire economic circumstances they faced upon their arrival in the war-torn Gallipoli peninsula. The village is described as having been in ruins at the time of resettlement. Some residents stated that they had to stay in the abandoned military barracks for a while, since the houses of Seddülbahir had been so damaged as to be uninhabitable. Others described fields full of cannons, rifles, bullets, and even skulls that welcomed them to their new homeland. Because of prolonged years of warfare, the soil was not immediately suitable for farming; many of the immigrants survived by selling old ammunition and ordnance for scrap iron and lead. Severely damaged during the bombardments of the Gallipoli campaign, the fortress of Seddülbahir was also in ruins and became a ready source of masonry as the residents began to rebuild their lives and homes. The sacrifices made by the new immigrants to Seddülbahir, the sacrifices made by the soldiers who fought against the Allied forces in the Gallipoli campaign and made the creation of the Republic of Turkey possible, and the sacrifices of the Ottoman Queen Mother who built the fortress are wound into a single narrative in which local and national histories merge. The overarching theme of this narrative is of benevolence and personal sacrifice for the homeland.

The public memory at Seddülbahir does not create a disjuncture between the Ottoman empire and the Turkish Republic. For the residents of Seddülbahir, it was of little consequence whether Hadice Turhan Sultan's act of generosity was intended to support the empire or the republic. Rather, her personal support was interpreted to mean that the sacrifices made in Seddülbahir by individual residents had a long history dating to the seventeenth century. According to many older residents whom we interviewed, putting aside one's own needs for a greater good, whether it was for the Ottoman empire or the Turkish Republic, was what the fortress most clearly represented. The fortress stood as the site where the constructed divide between Ottoman and republican histories dissolved and the two pasts were allowed to coexist.

Oral History and Cultural Heritage

We started our oral history research with the hope of obtaining more information about two monuments from the seventeenth century. By the time we concluded our research, we were listening to the very contemporary concerns of residents from both Kumkale and Seddülbahir about two government-initiated projects to establish and restructure the national park lands near the two Ottoman fortresses: an archaeological park at Troy and the Gallipoli Peace Park on the European peninsula. A desire to increase tourism in the region has led to the establishment of new roads, several visitors' centers, memorials, and museums throughout the Dardanelles region. An essential aspect of the successful development, management, and sustainability of cultural heritage resources like these Ottoman fortresses is a deep understanding of the local community, yet few of the residents in either Kumkale or Seddülbahir have been consulted or informed about the changes that are slated to occur in these regions in the near future.

As the municipal head of the village at Kumkale, Rahmi Şengezer, said: "Now, we do not know what will happen to the village in the master plan of the National Park [of Troy]. The people are anxious. They do not know what to do. Maybe some of them will have to emigrate, but they cannot decide what is to come. Maybe the master plan will be very beneficial to the village, but we do not know this either."[38]

For the foreseeable future the fortress of Kumkale is to remain in the hands of the Turkish navy and will not be incorporated into the national park at Troy. The separation between the residents of New Kumkale and the old fortress and village will therefore persist and undoubtedly become greater as members of the older generation pass away, taking their memories of Old Kumkale with them. A similar source of distress exists in Seddülbahir. All the lands in the peninsula have been under the direction of the National Park Directorate since 1973. In 1997 a new project to restructure the park was initiated, and after a hiatus of eight years, it resumed in 2005. The Gallipoli Peace Park Project intends to present the peninsula's historical importance together with its natural beauties to national and international visitors in a more organized and hospitable way. The fortress at Seddülbahir has been designated in the long-term development plan for the region commissioned by the Forest Ministry as a space that should function as both a peace park and a museum of naval warfare. At Seddülbahir, residents expressed reservations as well as optimism about the inclusion of the village in this project. Their reservations stem from inadequate information about the plans and unsubstantiated rumors of land expropriation. They are, however, optimistic about the new opportunities it could bring to the village. The theme of peace for the park and the fortress struck a positive chord with residents of a landscape that has been remembered to date primarily for war. As Osman Yarış, the lighthouse operator at Seddülbahir, stated:

The peace park . . . it is called the International Peace Park. All people of the world should live peacefully; this is not only for Turkey. Why would we wage war against each other when we can live in peace side by side? Why would we fight? Why would we enter into a weapon race? This life is not long. Yet we often fight rather than trying to live in peace.[39]

Our own journey as historians took us far beyond the walls of our discipline and some of its more traditional methodologies. Initially, oral testimony for us was simply a way to confirm the textual data we had collected in various archives and to supplement our understanding of the history of these two Ottoman fortresses. Yet as we moved into territories and times where there were no written records, we discovered an extraordinary historical richness that forced us to continually reassess and readjust the framework we had first brought to our explorations of these lands, their inhabitants, and their memories. As we begin the process of restoration at the fortress at Seddülbahir and explore its potential for use, it is increasingly clear to us that the oral history research we conducted in the villages of Seddülbahir and Kumkale has been essential in furthering our understanding of the multiple pasts that exist in this region of Turkey. It has been invaluable in shedding light upon the past memories as well as the present concerns of the residents. And it is our hope that through studies such as this one, we can draw attention to the importance of listening to the stories in villages such as Seddülbahir and Kumkale. It is only when the rich histories and memories that live on the shores of these ancient straits are understood that wise decisions can be made about the future of these important cultural heritage resources from the Ottoman past.

NOTES

We would like to thank the people of Seddülbahir and Kumkale for their enthusiasm, interest, and support for our oral history research. We also thank our team members from the KALETAKIMI (see the project website, www.seddulbahir-kumkale.org, for a complete list of names), particularly the project co-director, Professor Rahmi Nurhan Çelik from Istanbul Technical University. For financial support for our research at Seddülbahir we thank the Vehbi Koç Foundation, the Fondation Max van Berchem, the American Research Institute in Turkey, and the Alywin Cotton Foundation for Mediterranean Archaeology.

1. Court chronicler Abdi Abdurrahman Pasha, commemorating in 1659 the royal procession of the Ottoman sultan Mehmed IV and his mother, Hadice Turhan Sultan, to the Dardanelles fortifications of Seddülbahir and Kumkale. Topkapı Saray Museum Archives, Evrak (document) 2477. See also the chronicle of Abdurrahman Abdi Pasha, transliterated by Fahri Çetin Derin, "Abdurrahman Abdi Paşa Vekayi'name'si" (Ph.D. diss., Istanbul University, 1993).

2. Major Mahmut Bey, an Ottoman soldier who participated in the defense of Seddülbahir on 25 April 1915, describing the siege of the Royal Dublin Fusiliers as they moved in to take the Ottoman fortress. Taken from Mehmed Fasih, *Gallipoli 1915: Bloody Ridge (Lone Pine) Diary of Lt. Mehmed Fasih 5th Imperial Ottoman Army: The Campaign as Viewed from the Ottoman Trenches,* ed. Hasan Danışman (Istanbul: Denizler Kitabevi, 1997), 9.

3. Brad West, "Travel, Ritual and Memory: Exploring International Civil Religious Pilgrimage," paper presented to Hawaii International Conference on Social Sciences, 12–15 June 2003, Honolulu, 14.

4. See project website www.seddulbahir-kumkale.org.

5. The GPS coordinates for the sites are as follows: Seddülbahir, latitude: 40° 02' 34", longitude: 26° 11' 17"; Kumkale, latitude: 40° 00' 23", longitude: 26° 11' 55".

6. For a comprehensive study of Turhan Sultan's architectural patronage, see Lucienne Thys-Şenocak, *Ottoman Women Builders: Hadice Turhan Sultan* (Aldershot, UK/Burlington, VT: Ashgate Press, 2007).

7. The park at the Gallipoli peninsula was established in 1973. In 1997 the Forest Ministry sponsored an international competition to restructure and redesign the park and establish it as a peace park. For information about the 1997 competition, see Raci Bademli, *Gallipoli Peace Park International Ideas and Design Competition* (Ankara: Turkish Ministry of Forestry, 1997), and the website: http://vitruvius.arch.metu.edu.tr/gallipoli. The extensive long-term planning document for the Gallipoli peninsula—Raci Bademli, K. Burak Sarı, et al., *Gelibolu Yarımadası Tarihi Milli Parkı(Barış Parkı) Uzun Devreli Gelişme Planı Çalışmaları* [The Working Report of the National Peace Park: Long-Term Development Plan for the Gallipoli Peninsula] (Ankara: Middle Eastern Technical University Press, 2002)—was updated in November 2004 and is currently being used by the Forest Ministry.

8. For a comprehensive analysis of this visual documentation, see Thys-Şenocak, *Ottoman Women Builders,* chap. 4.

9. The highest wall at Kumkale is the south wall of the southwest tower, which reaches 11.29 meters.

10. Evliya Çelebi's *Seyahatnamesi,* documents his travels through the Ottoman world between 1631 and 1670. In it, he gives the circumference of the walls of Kumkale as 1,100 footsteps (*bin yüz adım*) (vol. 5, p. 157); in the *Tarih-i Naima* (422), the chronicler Naima claims it is 300 *zira* long and 300 *zira* wide (*tûlen ve arzen üçer yüz zirâ' olmak üzre*).

11. An earlier double-chambered bath at Kumkale was most probably built in the seventeenth century, as it is mentioned in the foundation charter for the fortress.

12. Mention of the *bab-ı kebir* at Kumkale first appears in the repair records in the Başbakanlık Osmanlı Archives, Istanbul, BOA/MAD 3160, p. 275, from 16 January 1768. By the mid-nineteenth century there may have been an additional entrance to Kumkale. In an unpublished report submitted by the French Chief of the Battalions of the 10th Legion and dated June 1841, the entrance of Kumkale is recorded as accessible through two well-defended posterns that were situated on the east and south façades of the fortress. The report describes the main entrance as located along the south or meridian entrance and protected by a long, covered entryway. ["On entre par deux poternes bien défendues situées sur la face l'Est et Sud. La porte principale établie sur le coté méridional conduit au corps de garde par une longue galerie couverte qu'enfile une pièce de gros calibre."] See Château de Vincennes, Paris, Article 14, Turquie II, Services Historiques de l'Armée de Terre (SHAT), p. 20, Vincennes, France.

13. Süleymaniye Ktp. 150, folio 15a, Süleymaniye Library, Istanbul.

14. The French account is titled *Relation nouvelle et un voyage de Constantinople,* by Guillaume Grelot (Paris, 1681); the English translation was published under the title *A Late Voyage to Constantinople* (London: J. Playford, 1683).

15. Grelot, *A Late Voyage,* 15–16.

16. The Troad is the ancient region of northwestern Turkey, bounded by the Aegean to the west and a mountain range to the east. It is mentioned in both Homer and the Bible.

17. Grelot, *A Late Voyage,* 4–5.

18. The Turkish History Foundation has been particularly active in supporting and presenting oral history studies in Turkey (http://www.tarihvakfi.org.tr/english/). It translated two pioneering books in the field: Paul Thompson, *The Voice of the Past* (London: Oxford University Press, 2000), and Stephen Caunce, *Oral History and the Local Historian* (London: Longmans, 1994). The foundation also publishes books on oral history and memory and was among the hosts of the Eleventh International Oral History Association Conference, held in 1999 at Boğaziçi University, Istanbul. This was an important step in the legitimization of oral history in the Turkish academy.

19. Paul Thompson, "The Voice of the Past," in Robert Perks and Alistair Thomson, eds., *The Oral History Reader* (London: Routledge, 1998), 21–29. A good introduction to the theory and practice of oral history is Ronald J. Grele, ed., *Envelopes of Sound: The Art of Oral History* (Chicago: Precedent Publishing, 1975).

20. See Luisa Passerini, "Work Ideology and Consensus under Italian Fascism," in Perks and Thomson, *The Oral History Reader,* 53–63. For a very good analysis of the relationship between history, memory, and oral history, see Alessandro Portelli, *The Death of Luigi Trastulli and Other Stories: Form and Meaning in Oral History* (Albany: State University of New York Press, 1991).

21. Several recent histories can be consulted for a more detailed discussion of the Ottoman empire's rise to power and rule; these depart from the traditional historiography that is referred to in this chapter. For more contemporary interpretations of the Ottoman past written in English, see Jane Hathaway, "Problems of Periodization in Ottoman History: The Fifteenth through the Eighteenth Centuries," *Turkish Studies Association Bulletin* 20:2 (1996): 25–31; Daniel Goffman, *The Ottoman Empire and Early Modern Europe* (Cambridge: Cambridge University Press, 2002); Caroline Finkel, *Osman's Dream: The Story of the Ottoman Empire 1300–1923* (London: John Murray, 2005).

22. For a thorough analysis of the history of modern Turkey in the English language, see Erik Zürcher, *Turkey: A Modern History* (London: I. B. Tauris, 1997); Andrew Mango, *Ataturk: The Biography of the Founder of Turkey* (New York: Overlook, 2002); William Hale, *Turkish Foreign Policy, 1774–2000* (London: Frank Cass, 2002).

23. Ahmed Refik Altınay, *Kadınlar Saltanatı* [The Sultanate of the Women] (Istanbul: Tarih Vakfı Yurt Yayınları, 2000), 108.

24. In the textbooks for the early years of primary education, the history of the Ottoman empire is not well integrated into the curriculum. Emphasis is placed upon the history of Atatürk and the Turkish War of Independence. The cultural and political transition from the late Ottoman empire to the republican period is presented as a radical break, with two quite distinct and separate histories. See, for example, *İlköğretim Okulu Hayat Bilgisi 3.Sınıf* [Life Information for Primary School, 3rd Grade] (Istanbul: Milli Eğitim Basımevi, 2001), 48–60.

25. In their rare appearances in the pages of these textbooks, Ottoman women are slaves (*cariye*) or self-serving women. See Gürkan Tekin and Yüksel Turhal, *Orta Okullar İçin Milli Tarih 2* [National History for Middle School] (Istanbul, 1993). This 159-page

textbook contains only four references to females in the sections dealing with Ottoman history. An extensive study of Turkish textbooks, initiated in 1993 by the Buca Educational Faculty of Dokuz Eylül University, became the topic of a workshop and symposium held by the Turkish Economic and Social History Foundation from 29 September to 1 October 1994. The publication that resulted from this symposium was Salih Özbaran, *Tarih Öğretimi Ders Kitapları: 1994 Buca Sempozyumu* [Textbooks for Teaching History] (Istanbul: Tarih Vakfı Yurt Yayınları, 1995). Its many useful articles discuss several topics related to Turkish and Ottoman historiography and current pedagogical practices in Turkey. Various paradigms used in the teaching of Ottoman and Turkish history, ethnocentrism, nationalism, and Islam in the primary, high school, and university curricula were investigated in the symposium.

26. The seventeenth-century chronicler Abdi Abdurrahman Pasha's commemorative eulogy, written on the occasion of a visit by the valide and the sultan to the fortresses at the Dardanelles, includes a specific dedication to the history of the fortress of Seddülbahir entitled the *Târîh-i Kal'a-ı Seddü'l-bahr*. Two of the couplets read: "Behold the charitable act she has undertaken; look at these two strong fortresses, / Each of them an honorable guard of the west [the western border of the empire]. / By building these two fortresses on both sides [of the Dardanelles] / The villages of the believers are made secure from the enemies." Topkapı Saray Museum Archives, E. 2477. See also Derin, "Abdurrahman Abdi Paşa Vekayi'name'si."

27. In the contemporary construction records located in the State Ministry Ottoman Archives of Istanbul BOA Maliye Defteri (MMD 1372, p. 18), the name of Seddülbahir appears in an official record for the first time in 1659, and the fortresses are referred to as the "two new fortresses" (*binâ-i kal'ateyn-cedîdeteyn-i mezbûreteyn*).

28. The official history of the early republic was heavily politicized because of the need of the founding elite to create a modern citizenry with a common identity and history. This identity was based on ethnicity and geography—that is, being a Turk and living within the borders of the Turkish Republic. The historical research of this formative period (1919–1937) had two goals: to link the building of the modern Turkish state to the glory and endurance of former Turkic empires, now anachronistically referred to as "states," and to present Anatolia as the legitimate homeland for the Turkish people. Praising the history of a distant past was a deliberate strategy, since the story of a more recent (traditional) and (Islamic) Ottoman empire would undermine the (modern and secular) foundations of the republic. For the development of this official history in the formative years of the republic, see Buşra Ersanlı Behar, *Iktidar ve Tarih* [Power and History] (Istanbul: Afa Yayınları, 1992). In his book *Tarih Ders Kitaplarında (1931–1993) Turk Tarih Tezinden Turk-Islam Sentezine* [The Turkish-Islamic Synthesis in Turkish History in the History Textbooks (1931–1993)] (Istanbul: Tarih Vakfı Yayınları, 2000), Etienne Copeaux mentions the continuity of this historiography over decades, with important modifications on the subject of Islam. His examination reveals that besides the stress on ethnicity and geography, the official history has started to put more emphasis on Islam, largely because of the rising conservatism of the 1980s. The result has been a reformulation of the national identity along the lines of the so-called Turkish-Islamic Synthesis. Both Behar and Copeaux underline the fact that from the early years of the republic until the present, the official history of Turkey has been subjected to political and ideological influences with the help of a nationalistic and exclusionary narrative.

29. Interview with Sezai Ercan, resident of Kumkale, 10 July 2001. Interviews are archived at Koç University, Istanbul, and were translated by Işıl Cerem Cenker and Lucienne Thys-Şenocak.

30. Interview with Zeki Ulus, resident of Kumkale, 14 July 2001.

31. Seddülbahir, on the other hand, was demilitarized in 1997 and was accessible to the public until it was closed again in 2005 for restoration and excavation work by our research team. See www.seddulbahir-kumkale.org for details of the project.

32. Interview with Nazif Arısan, resident of Kumkale, 13 July 2001.

33. Interview with Ahmed Aydagün, resident of Seddülbahir, 13 and 16 July 1999.

34. Interview with Ismail Bozkurt, resident of Seddülbahir, 9 and 16 July 1999.

See also Tulay Duran, ed., *Tarihimizde Vakıf Kuran Kadınlar: Hanım Sultan Vak-fiyyeleri/Deeds of Trust of the Sultans Womenfolk/Actes de Fondation de Sultane Hanım*, (Istanbul: Arastrma Merkezi, 1990), 84, and the original charter document in the Süleymaniye Library Ktp. 150. Information about the resources and personnel sent by the central government is corroborated in the official Ottoman foundation charter of 1665. This document indicates that large numbers of workers were sent from Istanbul to assist with the new fortifications: "Masters, workers, and carpenters of unmatched skill, uncountable quantities of goods and money were sent, and the necessary tools, equipment, and requisites were prepared. Expert architects versed in the business and masters without equal set themselves to the task, and showing more effort and perseverance than can be described in words they completed two castles with big and strong foundations."

35. Interview with Fatma Tuncer, resident of Seddülbahir, 6 and 18 July 1999.

36. J. M. Cook has commented that the ruins at the fortress of Kumkale were accessible in 1959 when he was surveying for his book, but were closed to the public in 1966, after the present-day naval base was built. See J. M. Cook, *The Troad: An Archaeological and Topographical Study* (Cambridge: Clarendon Press, 1973), 151. A series of Turkish censuses after the war document the population of New Kumkale after the village was moved to its present location, five kilometers from the fortress and Old Kumkale. The 1940 census records a population of 391 households in the village of Kum Kale Koy; there were 360 households in 1959. Many of these were Turks from Bulgaria who had been settled in this region of the Troad after World War I. In the 1955 census New Kumkale was also referred to as Mısırlık and Masırlık. See ibid., 67, 419–425, for demographic information on the Troad from the 1940 census and 420 for information on Kum Kale Koy. Halil Inalcık in *The Ottoman Empire: Conquest, Organizations, and Economy* (London: Variorum Reprints, 1978), 227, also reports that in 1945 all property in this region of Turkey over 500 *dönüms* (approximately 125 acres) was nationalized and distributed to the peasantry.

37. An article on the Ottoman cemetery at Kumkale is being prepared by Lucienne Thys-Şenocak, Hasan Karatas, and Caner Guney; see also www.seddülbahir-kumkale.org.

38. Interview with Rahmi Şengezer, resident of Kumkale, 10 July 2001.

39. Interview with Osman Yarış, resident of Seddülbahir, 12 July 2000.

5

PRIVATE MEMORY IN A PUBLIC SPACE: ORAL HISTORY AND MUSEUMS

~

Selma Thomas

Museums are civic and cultural institutions, created for the public good. They are physical manifestations of cultural aspirations—buildings filled with objects collected over time. Some of the objects are uniquely associated with famous individuals (the uniform worn by General George Washington during the American Revolution, the desk on which Thomas Jefferson wrote the Declaration of Independence); some recall the lives of ordinary people (a woman's dress, a farm tool). The reason for collecting, preserving, and displaying objects is always the same: the public good. Who defines the "good," and who embodies "the public"? The answer may vary from institution to institution; it certainly has evolved over time. In the nineteenth century and much of the twentieth, an unchallenged cultural paternalism perceived museums as temples of knowledge, constructed to house the treasures of a community, whether the community is an entire nation, a small town, or a social elite. Since the last half of the twentieth century, particularly since the 1980s, museums have evolved into more democratic institutions. They have become places of learning, encouraging public discourse on subjects of both academic and popular culture.

But the essential nature of museums remains: museums are cultural institutions that collect, preserve, and display objects. All of these activities presume a physical structure, a collection, and an audience. These three elements—building, objects, and public—will shape much of the intellectual and interpretive work done by staff and scholars, including oral historians. Every museum program takes place inside a defined public space: a small exhibit could be one thousand square feet; a large exhibit might be ten thousand square feet. That space will, in many cases, reflect the architectural vocabulary of the museum building: a historic house, for example, will impose different restrictions than a neo-classical building filled with large square rooms. Inside this public space, the museum's staff will place collected or borrowed objects, selected to create a narrative experience. The traveling exhibition "The Quilts of Gee's Bend," for example, assembled a selection of twentieth-century quilts produced by the women of Gee's Bend, Alabama.[1] While the exhibit visited such urban centers as San Francisco, New York, and Washington, its vibrant quilts recalled an African American experience set distinctly in the rural South. These objects, even in the context of such institutional settings as the Corcoran Gallery of Art in Washington, D.C., introduced visitors to the people and traditions of Gee's Bend.

If objects create a narrative experience, it is up to the visitor to interpret that experience, albeit with some help from the museum. Every institution knows the demographics of its visitors, their average age, income, racial and ethnic background, and level of education. A small regional museum, for example, might welcome the same local visitors several times a year. A large national museum knows that at least half of its visitors are there for the first time. These factors help define the museum's role as an educational institution: all learning occurs in a public space animated by selected objects in which visitors come and go at their own pace and at their own direction. This background is essential to understanding the use of oral history in museums, particularly in museum exhibits.

Oral History and Museums

My work with museums began in 1985, when I was invited to produce video programs for "A More Perfect Union: Japanese Americans and the United States Constitution," a new exhibition planned for the Smithsonian Institution's National Museum of American History, in Washington, D.C. Working with the curatorial team, I conducted a number of oral history interviews for use as both background research and within the exhibit itself. All of the interviews were videotaped, since we intended to display them in the exhibit on laserdisc. Over the next twenty years, I continued to work with U.S. museums, primarily in large national and regional institutions, conducting oral history interviews on many different topics and editing them into exhibit programs. I learned much about American social history in the process, and I learned much about museums—and about the use of oral history in museums—working with curators to integrate interviews into exhibits.

Museums were able to incorporate oral history in the late 1980s because of

a critical new tool, the computer-driven laserdisc. (A laserdisc records both visual and oral data and can play it back in "real time" or by advancing frame by
frame, accommodating both moving pictures, as a video source, or single-
frame databases.) This tool gave museums the capacity to introduce the voices
and faces of "real" people into exhibits. A simple, reliable mechanism, it was
also frame-accurate, which meant that visitors could reach out and touch the
screen, select an informant's name, and listen to that person's oral history. This
touch-screen control made the laserdisc a dynamic tool for exhibits. Granted,
interviews were "curated," much as the rest of an exhibition was curated; they
were collected and edited to supplement exhibition themes. But the laserdisc
gave the oral history a directness and an immediacy that made it especially effective for exhibitions. It also was a compact tool that gave museums the
means to install these programs in a small physical space. The practical aspects
of this technology cannot be exaggerated: it was essential to the introduction
of videotaped oral histories into museum exhibitions.

At the same time, placing oral history into a museum exhibit imposed some
restrictions on the curator. While other exhibit elements (text label, even artifact) allowed the visitor to determine the length of time he or she might allocate
to a specific element, the laserdisc—because it introduced a moving picture—
imposed its own timing on both visitor and exhibition, again for very practical
reasons. A laserdisc playing in real time gave the visitor access to thirty minutes
of program time, but no curator expected (or wanted) the visitor to spend that
length of time on a single exhibit element. At the Smithsonian, we edited the oral
histories into short pieces—thirty-second, sixty-second, even ninety-second segments that could stand alone. While the visitor might stand in front of an interactive program for as long as ten minutes, touching the screen to hear a series of
such segments, that was a choice built into the program. No one was obligated to
spend the full thirty minutes of available program time listening to the interviews. It is not a practical option for an exhibit program.

Space, like time, imposes a different set of expectations on the oral histories, and the oral historian. Museum exhibitions are site-specific: they present
a topic within the confined space of a gallery. Design not only controls visitor
access to subject, object, and text; it also defines the visitor's relationship to the
subject. The more space that is dedicated to a specific topic, for example, the
more significance that topic is assigned. In the case of oral history, a videotaped interview presented in a secluded alcove brings the visitor into more intimate contact with the narrator, whereas an interview presented in a theatrical
setting, seen by multiple visitors simultaneously on a large screen, takes on the
role of a public statement. Understanding the nature of the setting helps the
historian edit and shape the oral history interview to make it an effective exhibit tool.

Finally, the nature of the exhibit space itself—punctuated with historical objects, presented with the authority of a major cultural institution—imposes a different set of needs on the videotaped oral history. If an exhibition's narrative is organized and articulated by a physical setting, its authority is established by the authenticity of the material presented. Artifacts—nineteenth-century lathes, eighteenth-century silver sets, and, more recently, slave shackles—speak to museum visitors with an authenticity that is unchallenged. Paper documents, like an original draft of the U.S. Constitution, enjoy unparalleled respect as authentic historical material. Oral histories, placed into the same setting, next to historical artifacts and documents, must display the same integrity. While admittedly an electronic representation of a real person, a videotaped interview must address the visitor with a credibility that is incontestable. Again, this need will determine how the historian edits and presents the material.

In the following discussion, I examine several exhibits that made effective, even acclaimed, use of oral history, addressing the way in which the historian working within the context of a museum exhibit shapes an oral history into an exhibit component.

A More Perfect Union

"A More Perfect Union: Japanese Americans and the United States Constitution" opened at the National Museum of American History on 1 October 1987. The exhibit examined the experience of Japanese Americans during World War II, including their internment in ten isolated camps across the United States and their military service in the specially created (and segregated) 442nd Regimental Combat Team. Executive Order 9066, signed by President Franklin D. Roosevelt on 19 February 1942, allowed the United States military to designate areas from which "any or all persons may be excluded" in the interests of national security. Although the order did not specify Japanese Americans, it was used to move persons of Japanese ancestry away from their homes in the western states of Washington, Oregon, and California and into internment camps. The executive order identified both aliens and "non-aliens" (i.e., citizens) as eligible for internment, and more than 120,000 Americans of Japanese ancestry were removed into the camps, where they lived in military barracks surrounded by barbed wire fences and looming guard towers. Almost a year after the executive order was issued, on 1 February 1943, the federal government established the 442nd Regimental Combat Team, which consisted of Japanese American volunteers. These troops, recruited from the internment camps and sent to fight the war in Italy, distinguished themselves through their actions and became one of the most highly decorated units in U.S. military history.

Decades later, when Roger Kennedy, then director of the National Museum of American History, was searching for a way to celebrate the two hundredth anniversary of the Constitution in 1987, he selected this singular Japanese American experience—of internment, the 442nd, and EO 9066—as a means of exploring the rights and privileges that the Constitution promises to Americans. The significance of Kennedy's decision for museum practice, for historiography, and for American culture was considerable. He brought the authority of a major national museum to the consideration of a historical experience that—while not exactly secret—had rarely been discussed in a public forum.[2]

"A More Perfect Union" explored the abstract notion of civil liberties, but it took as its central premise that the true meaning of the constitutional promise—and the consequences of the constitutional crisis precipitated by EO 9066—is most effectively, maybe even most accurately, examined at the level of real human experience. The exhibit used a rich material culture to recall the pre–World War II lives of Japanese Americans in both rural and urban settings, including strawberry baskets from the agricultural fields of northern California where Japanese Americans labored and a concrete sidewalk and storefront from Little Tokyo in Los Angeles. It included paper documents such as period newspapers and a copy of the executive order, as well as a reconstructed barracks room—like those that were home to thousands of internees for as many as four years—to make the years of internment come alive for the visitor.

But none of these documents, neither text nor object, spoke with the voice of those Americans who were removed from their lives and their livelihoods simply because of their ancestry. Without these voices, the exhibit and the story of EO 9066 were incomplete. In lieu of populating the gallery with real people, the exhibit team decided to conduct oral history interviews and to incorporate them on interactive laserdisc as integral elements in both the narrative and the design of the exhibit. I conducted all of the interviews and edited them into four exhibit programs. "A More Perfect Union" thus introduced visitors to twelve individuals whose oral histories helped interpret the events of the executive order, internment, and military service of volunteer internees during World War II. The exhibit featured four different programs, each of which relied on oral history to supplement the written record and to bring the emotional reality of personal experience to an otherwise abstract history lesson about constitutional rights.[3]

The first program the visitor encountered was the reconstructed barracks room, minimally furnished with bed, table, and clothing. The room was enhanced by a video projection of two life-sized figures, a father and his young daughter, standing in a doorway opposite the visitor. They stood (it seemed to the visitor) against the pink desert landscape of Manzanar, an internment camp in the Owens Valley of California, with the snow-capped Sierra Nevada mountains behind them. The two walked on and off screen a total of five times; each time they appeared they talked to each other for approximately sixty seconds. Just beyond the barracks room, in a quiet alcove, visitors encountered the exhibit's first interactive video program, informally called "Conversations" by the exhibit team. This introduced five internees—Nancy Araki, Sue Kunitomi Embrey, Gordon Hirabayashi, Mary Tsukamoto, and Morgan Yamanaka—who, answering questions posed by the visitor by means of the interactive program, spoke movingly of their lives before, during, and after internment. As the exhibit continued, a second interactive video, located in a section focusing on the military experience of the 442nd combat unit, presented several decorated veterans talking about their wartime experience and used the tools of war—a helmet, an M-1, a jeep, all situated around the video—to help visitors understand actual combat. The final video in the exhibit, located near the exit, allowed those individuals whom the museum visitor had already seen in the show to answer the question: "How do you explain this experience to your grandchildren?"

Working as an integral part of the exhibit team, I nevertheless had a clear role: to identify the best informants, interview them on videotape, and shape those interviews into effective exhibit programs. Throughout, the curatorial process informed my own work as historian/filmmaker. Like the exhibit curators and historians who were conducting a thorough search for possible artifacts, I collected more stories, first in informal conversation, later on videotape, than I knew I could use. Also like the curators, I consulted the familiar historical record—major scholarly works, government documents, local histories, photograph collections, and other archival material. These provided a basic chronology and a social and political context for the interviews and helped frame the questions we would ask narrators. For example, the photographs—which would become an essential part of the exhibition—depict a world of everyday events and familiar scenes: children playing baseball, celebrating Christmas, and sitting in a class, and adults working as teachers, doctors, and farmers, all taking place behind barbed wire fences. Nothing in the archival documents explained that adult internees worked, but photos of doctors caring for elderly patients made us wonder where they got their supplies and what their contact with the outside world was like. Likewise, images of schoolchildren celebrating Halloween, Christmas, and the Fourth of July reminded us that internment was not a brief experience. Partly because of the specificity of the photographs, and partly because we wanted to create an incontestable document, we asked people to address the specifics of their own lives. We asked: "Where were you living in 1941? When did you first hear about the executive order? How did you get to camp? Where did they take you? With whom did you live and what did you do? When did you leave and how do you explain this experience to your grandchildren?"

These interviews were conducted for use in a national museum, and in order to address the widest possible audience, I, like the curators, wanted to include a broad range of experiences and remind visitors that the history of the executive order was a national history. So I worked hard to include as many different individual situations and places as I could, in both the initial selection of narrators and in the final, edited programs. In the "Conversations" video, Gordon Hirabayashi tells us, "I was living in Seattle, a student at the University of Washington." Mary Tsukamoto describes her life as a young wife and mother in the Santa Clara Valley of California. Nancy Araki explains that she was interned at the age of four and moved away from the family farm in Mendocino County, California, to the high desert of Colorado. In "Tools of War," veterans from Kansas and New York address the visitor and tell the story of their experiences while serving in the 442nd. And in the final video, individuals from Hawaii, including U.S. Senator Daniel K. Inouye, answer the question: "How do you explain this to your grandchildren?"

While all of the video programs are edited to stand alone, the parameters of the exhibit provide enough context to allow us to use the interviews as we intended, to provide the authentic, first-person voice of experience. By the time visitors walked up to the video screen in "Conversations," for example, they already knew from photographs and text labels and from the material evidence of newspapers and suitcases that people had been moved from their homes to camps. They knew that copies of EO 9066 had been distributed throughout the west coast states, warning Japanese Americans that they were being removed from their homes. Thus, all of my questions could directly relate to the narrators' personal chronology and experience, giving the exhibit programs an intimate and moving human presence unavailable elsewhere. All four programs bring to the exhibit the immediacy and intensity of a primary source that is instantly recognizable to museum audiences. And they introduce that incontestable authenticity that lies at the heart of a museum exhibit's power.

While the power of these exhibit installations flowed incontrovertibly from the first-person narratives, they required considerable editing to accommodate the parameters of the exhibit and to keep pace with audience expectations. The exhibit included two kinds of oral history programs, each with its own particular challenges. Visitors first encountered the barracks room oral history. The room itself, though historically accurate, was incomplete as a visual record. Visitors can see the cramped quarters of this room, but they don't see the densely populated camp outside it. They don't see the lack of privacy or the barbed wire fences that confined internees. The exhibit needed to create a more active connection to this context; placing real people in the room via oral history seemed the most accessible and effective way to do this. But we had to respect the sense of scale and the theatrical quality that had been created in this installation. And we had to respect the integrity of the artifact itself—the real barracks room.

We had a relatively easy technical solution to the design problems: we projected a "life-size" video image of two people, father and daughter, just outside a screen door on one wall in the room. Visitors walking up to the barracks room could "eavesdrop" on their conversation on the other side of the screen. But this was the easy part. Much more challenging was deciding what kind of narrative to construct for that projection. Should we place a "real" person on the other side of the door, perhaps one of the people whom visitors would meet in the "Conversations" video? Should we acknowledge the theatrical setting of the room and create a scripted experience? Or was it more honest, and appropriate to the exhibit, to project an unedited interview? We decided on a scripted narrative based, in part, on the experience of a real person, that is, the actor playing the father, Sab Shimoto. We felt that to keep the pace of the video program moving and to respect the artifice of the exhibit setting, we needed a crafted story. At the same time, we wanted the authenticity of a story that was based in a real experience. Yet we also felt that we needed a surrogate interviewer to pose questions to the father, so we created the character of the young daughter. Peering into the room, she asks: "Did you really live in a room like this?" He answers: "Yes, with my mother, my father, my brother and my dog, Columbus." She asks: "What did you do all day?" and he replies: "We went to school. We went to Boy Scouts. We played baseball." When, finally, she asks: "Didn't it make you angry, living in a room like this?" he reminds her that he was a child, that there was a war going on, that people wanted to be patriotic.

In the barracks room, the visitor plays no role in constructing, or altering, the narrative. Visitors are free to stop and eavesdrop as the two actors talk, or they can walk past the room to another part of the exhibit, but that is the extent of their choice. The exhibit's second kind of installation is exemplified by the interactive program "Conversations," which allows visitors to choose the stories they wish to hear by touching the video screen and "asking" a series of predetermined questions of the five real persons presented. That format, though new at the time, has become a standard means of introducing oral histories into exhibits. Yet here too we had to adapt the videotaped interviews, not only to the temporal and spatial constraints of the exhibition, but also to the interactive format. Unlike the script in the barracks room, the words of "Conversations" belong entirely to the interviewee. Though they were stripped from the full interview context, I pulled only complete statements from the interviews. I didn't edit the excerpts themselves. Instead of masking an edit by cutting away from the person speaking and inserting a series of photographs or archival film (a common video trick), the camera stays on the interviewee while he/she makes a complete statement. This approach challenged the usual means of editing film, but it helped us create a program that seemed more candid, less constructed than the standard documentary interview.

Since this was a computer-controlled program, we could have given visitors the means of interrupting an informant; instead, having determined that this was a "conversation," we decided against this on the grounds that, in real life, it is rude to interrupt. Visitors touch the screen, ask a question, and then must listen to the complete answer before going on to another question or another person. They listen as interviewees answer, speaking directly to the camera. Nancy Araki reveals: "I was five years old. I started kindergarten at Amache" (an internment camp in Colorado). Mary Tsukamoto says, weeping at the memory: "I never will forget. . . . Human beings were standing there, behind that [barbed wire] fence and they were going to put us in there with them." She describes her efforts, as a young married woman, to create a domestic refuge for both her elderly father-in-law and her young daughter, trying to keep the dust of the Arizona desert away from their home in a hastily constructed Army barracks. Morgan Yamanaka says: "I was an honor student [in high school] and an athlete" living in San Francisco with parents and a brother, preparing to go to college. Instead, he tells us, he was sent to Topaz, Utah, or, as he describes it, "to the middle of nowhere." Listening to him, one can easily imagine the shock of being moved from a vibrant urban environment to an isolated desert. The layers of narrative, ranging from the overall exhibition to the oral histories to the interactive video screen, also include the visitor's own narrative, the background, questions, and expectations he/she brings to the installation and that lead him/her to select this informant and that question. The visitor thus becomes invested in the personal history recounted in this exhibit program. Indeed, visitors to "Conversations" often remain for many minutes, listening carefully to the individual stories, and frequently staying to hear multiple stories.

Museum Exhibits and Oral History

Since "A More Perfect Union," many museums have used oral-history-based media installations in an effort to introduce museum audiences to social history, including their own local histories, though individual experiences. In 1990, for example, I worked with the Children's Discovery Museum in San Jose, California, to develop "A Step into the Past," an exhibit that helped residents of the Silicon Valley recognize the agricultural past of the region, a past almost obliterated by miles of highways and concrete boxes that currently house the nation's high-tech industry. Set in the front porch of a reconstructed farm house, where people typically have sat around telling stories, the exhibit introduced six local farmers who, in telling the story of their lives in and around San Jose, reminded visitors that the Silicon Valley once had been the Valley of Heart's Delight, a region of prime agricultural land, growing apples, peaches, plums, and cherries.

These farmers recalled a life, a community, and a landscape that were inconceivable to the museum's young visitors, describing one-room schoolhouses, family farm stands, and windmill-powered wells. While the technique of conducting and editing the interviews was similar to that employed in "A More Perfect Union," the visitors were different. Not only were they children, they were also locals, residents of the Silicon Valley. Because of that, I crafted the interviews and the video program to address familiar geographic spots, on the assumption that the most direct means of addressing the fact that the world described by the elderly farmers had disappeared was by evoking these recognizable places. In every edit we included place names. Interviewees told us (and visitors): "I was born on Seventh Street." "I went to school on Peach Blossom Drive." "We never came in to downtown San Jose." The street names were familiar, but the children watching the program had to grapple with the remarkable change that these simple statements masked: Peach Blossom Drive was, in 1990, a high-tech cul-de-sac, home of IBM and other Silicon Valley entrepreneurs, not the place where a local school was located.

Several years later, in December 1997, I interviewed two young Thai women, Malinan Radomphon and Praphaphron Pongpid, for a temporary exhibition at the National Museum of American History: "Between a Rock and a Hard Place: A History of American Sweatshops, 1820–Present." These women had left their homes in a remote part of Thailand, lured by unscrupulous businessmen, to work for a clothing manufacturer in a notorious sweatshop in southern California. They were rescued, literally, when the federal government and the state of California arrested the owners of the shop. They were permitted to remain in the United States as material witnesses against the businessmen who had enslaved them, and others like them.[4]

I interviewed them after their rescue. We spoke through a translator, but when the young women described their plight, their pain and shame were unmistakable. Told by their recruiters that they were coming to Hollywood, they were shown photos of Disneyland and Universal Studios and promised that the good life awaited them in Los Angeles. Instead, when they arrived at Los Angeles International Airport, they were immediately taken to a modest house in El Monte, California, and literally imprisoned. The house, surrounded by barbed wire fences, had bars on the windows, and the women had to stand on chairs just to see daylight. They slept in shifts in an upstairs bedroom and worked the sewing machines downstairs during twelve-, fourteen-, or sixteen-hour days. They never had an opportunity to leave the house where they were imprisoned, and, to discourage them from running away, their captors told them stories of girls who had escaped only to meet a worse fate on the violent streets of Los Angeles.

Both women wept as they told their stories. But both also insisted that "people should know" about the injustice that persists in the shadow of Disneyland—and, they said, what better public forum than a Smithsonian exhibition? The museum exhibition gave their experience a platform and an authority that were irrefutable. By recalling the deep human cost and dislocation that the textile industry has historically extracted from its workers, their testimony also gave credibility to the exhibition. Since the early nineteenth century, as the exhibit made clear, textile workers have typically been young women, most often women from rural communities who see the promise of economic independence in a "modern" industrial job. The two contemporary oral histories helped museum visitors recognize this dynamic in the historical photographs of earlier textile workers.

Malinan's and Praphaphron's interviews were presented starkly in the exhibit, on a single video monitor. Facing the camera, in extreme close-up, they addressed the visitor in their native tongue while a young Thai American woman translated off-screen. They spoke simply of their experience: "I first heard about El Monte [their shorthand for the sweatshop] from another worker." They described their flight from Thailand to Los Angeles and their confusion when they were hidden in darkened vans for their ride to El Monte. They expressed the despair they felt when, day after day, they were made to work long hours, forbidden to step outside, and threatened by their captors. While most visitors were unable to understand the women's own language, the emotion in their voices and on their faces was unmistakable, and it made real the very human cost of the industrial sweatshop, in any culture and in any era. Incorporating these oral histories into the exhibit also forced visitors to acknowledge that sweatshops are not a thing of the past. In the context of the exhibit, which presented visitors with a "clothing food chain," the oral histories helped visitors evaluate the often unacknowledged cost of "cheap" clothing. Visitors were reminded that the cost of their own clothing—especially inexpensive clothing—was based on the availability of sweatshop labor.

On a personal note, as I worked on this exhibit I found myself thinking about the role of the museum in revealing a nation's history. Sitting in Los Angeles with two women who spoke only a Thai dialect, I was surprised by how easily I could understand them, even before the translator spoke. They listened carefully to my questions (they were able, clearly, to understand my English), and they struggled to be precise and accurate in their replies. They spoke slowly and without hesitation. They tried to monitor their emotions and, for the most part, succeeded, but the pain was still visible on their faces. What surprised me, though, was their faith in the museum. These two young women had come from a rural province in Thailand to visit Disneyland, and they had somehow acquired a faith in the authority of the Smithsonian. They knew that if they spoke to the museum, people would listen and people would know about their experiences. Moreover, they recognized that by placing their story in a museum, they were preserving it and enhancing its significance. Finally, although the federal government had shut down El Monte, both Malinon and Praphaphron wanted to ensure that no one else would endure the same experience, and they determined that this exhibit would help prevent that possibility.

This recognition made me think again of "A More Perfect Union," which had opened ten years before the sweatshop exhibit. Both exhibits had made effective use of oral history to help museum visitors—indeed, the American public—come to terms with difficult historical experiences. Both exhibits depended on the willingness of interviewees to allow their private memories to become public history. In speaking to me, on behalf of the museum, both the Japanese American internees and the young Thai women shared their stories with a national audience. At the same time, in both instances, the stature and authority of the Smithsonian's National Museum of American History helped transform their memories into a history worth preserving.

Final Thoughts

Much oral history collected by museums will eventually become public history: even the most painful recollections potentially will be shared with thousands, even millions of strangers. For that reason the process requires strong trust between interviewer and interviewee. The interviewer trusts that the interviewee will be honest and open. The interviewee trusts that the interviewer will be respectful. For me, interviewing is invasive, especially since I conduct my interviews on videotape: we are surrounded by lights, cameras, microphones, and a camera crew of at least two other people. But the most invasive aspect of these interviews is the museum exhibit. Here, what began as a relatively personal exchange is transformed into a public program.

The responsibilities of this process are multiple, and sometimes conflicting. First, I have a responsibility to the public record. I am obligated to conduct a direct, open, and professional interview. If this interview inflicts some degree of emotional pain on the interviewee, that comes as no surprise to either me or the narrator. But I also feel a responsibility to the interviewee—precisely because I am engaged in placing that person's oral history into a large public forum. If I represent the public, do I have the right to press when I sense an emotional reticence? Instead, isn't our exchange similar to that between two casual, if compatible, acquaintances? While I may feel a friendship with the interviewee (and, in some cases, have developed such friendships), I can't presume it, nor can I extend it on behalf of the museum.

This dilemma was brought home to me while working on a recent exhibit. I was interviewing a well-known retired racecar driver and NASCAR owner, a man then in his seventies. He recounted the story of his childhood in rural South Carolina, a story familiar to friends and colleagues but not to the museum-going public. His mother had died when he was young, and his father was difficult, by his own account. By the age of seven, this future driver was stealing off to racetracks, since, as he told me: "I knew if I could get there, they [the drivers and team owners] would take care of me." They fed him, gave him a job cleaning engine parts, and also gave him a place to sleep. At the age of eleven, he found a job with Noah Smith, who ran a junkyard. Smith paid him for his first day of work, saying: "Here's your money, you can go home now." But when the young boy admitted that he was no longer welcome at home, Smith found a car—a large car, a Hudson—and outfitted it for him. That Hudson became his home for the next five years, though he took meals with Smith and his wife, Louise.[5]

This elderly man freely told me the story of his childhood, but I found that story so difficult that I had to struggle to maintain my composure. At the same time, listening to his tale, I realized that it was incomplete. He never told me why his father had disowned him at age eleven. He hadn't described the details of life inside a Hudson—the heat and cold, the lonely evenings—nor did he acknowledge his lack of schooling. These details were truly private, and since he was speaking both to a virtual stranger and to a camera, he kept them private. With some reluctance, I tried to press. But though he remained affable and relaxed during the interview, the retired racer made it clear—by evading my questions—that he was editing his memories to tell only part of a story. I was interviewing him on behalf of a racing museum. Did he, or the museum, or the public, need to relive the most personal experiences of his youth? Did the museum or the public need to know those experiences? Did I, on behalf of the public record, have the right to press him? The tension between the public right to know and the individual's right to privacy is ever-present in oral history, but I feel that tension most keenly when the interview is intended to be part of a museum exhibit. If Malinan Radomphon and Praphaphron Pongpid welcomed the museum's scrutiny, and exposure, this elderly man did not, and I had to respect his decision. I stopped pressing and allowed him to tell the story he wanted to tell. Not all informants share all their memories. The questions of a stranger, the presence of a camera, and the promise of a museum exhibit—these elements remind informants that they are transferring their memories to a public forum, and it is the curator/filmmaker's challenge, and responsibility, to protect the integrity of the interview while still recognizing its real limits.

Museums add texture to the spoken word, and they place it within a site-specific context. They combine oral history with music, images, and objects, and place that dynamic combination within a carefully constructed narrative that is both intellectually and architecturally defined. While the historian/film-maker must collect and present good history, the historian working inside a museum must also produce effective programs within these parameters. Good history is a necessary ingredient for effective programming, but it is not sufficient. Inside the museum, oral history—any history—is the first step in a process whose goal is public discourse. That goal, along with the very practical parameters of an exhibit, imposes itself on all exhibit elements, including oral history. In the end, oral history must take its place in the context defined by a museum's geography, collections, and audience and play both an integral and a supporting role in the narrative constructed by that context.

NOTES

1. "The Quilts of Gee's Bend," a traveling exhibition that debuted in 2002, was organized by the Museum of Fine Arts, Houston, Texas, and the Tinwood Alliance, Atlanta, Georgia. It features sixty quilts made by forty-two women from the African American community in Gee's Bend. These vibrant textiles are also reproduced in *The Quilts of Gee's Bend* (Atlanta: Tinwood Books, 2002), with essays by Peter Marzio, John Beardsley, William Arnett, Pauljane Arnett, Jane Livingston, and Alvia Wardlaw.

2. An online version of "A More Perfect Union," available at http://americanhistory.si .edu/perfectunion/experience, provides a full list of credits and an essay on the making of the exhibit.

3. Historian Michael Wallace, reviewing "A More Perfect Union" in *History News* 44:4 (July/August 1989): 5–8, 30–33, described the "revolutionary use of media, [which] allows museums to deploy memory itself as an artifact." Wallace's review cites two exhibit components, the barracks room and "the moving and powerful testimonies of Mary Sukamoto's [*sic*] and her peers," suggesting that these programs "brilliantly complement the show's assemblage of the era's more 'material' artifacts." Historian Ronald Walters, writing in *Public Historian* 13:2 (Spring 1991): 101–6, noted of the exhibit: "Its videotaped testimony of men and women who lived through internment has a power and authenticity that no lay viewer is likely to challenge. . . . It gives voice and life to the reconstructions and objects that comprise the rest of the exhibit."

4. See the website for the exhibit: http://americanhistory.si.edu/sweatshops/.

5. Louise Smith, "the First Lady of Racing," born in Georgia in 1916, was herself a famous driver, competing from 1946 until 1956.

PART II

RECREATING IDENTITY AND COMMUNITY

Part II

RECREATING IDENTITY AND COMMUNITY

~

Oral history is frequently used to promote or celebrate a common identity—that is to say, a sense of community—within a particular social group. This occurs particularly when a group, or a community, has been silenced, threatened, or destroyed. Interviews, often invoking loss, thus become acts of cultural survival; programs and projects based on them, important means of maintaining or re-establishing connections with the past and nourishing hope for a more humane future. In one way or another, the five chapters in this section all draw upon oral history in creative ways to speak to issues of identity and community.

We begin with Sean Field, who, drawing upon oral history interviews conducted in two Cape Town, South Africa, communities over many years, opens up broad questions about the social and psychological functions of memories irrevocably shaped by the apartheid state. As he tells it, oral history interviews can be understood as part of a broader process of negotiating a relationship with a difficult, sometimes brutal past; made public, they are a way of gaining recognition for suffering endured. A sophisticated understanding of the ways in which memories are rooted in specific places undergirds Field's discussion of local museums, including the well-known District Six Museum, created both to commemorate a once-diverse community destroyed by apartheid's forced removals and to regenerate a new community in the face of post-apartheid development. Such museums, Field avers, can be places where memory is enacted and reconstituted, using oral history as a medium by which people actively participate in connecting with the past and with each other.

Finally, Field acknowledges the presence of idealized memories of the past among those who have endured the losses of apartheid. He suggests that this idealization creates a zone of psychological safety even as it misrepresents the historical past, and he challenges those engaged in cultural work among traumatized communities to both respect the ways people make sense of suffering and loss and encourage a more "forward-thinking" and complex understanding of the past.

Gail Dubrow's chapter on changing interpretations of the heritage of Japanese in the United States takes another long view of both oral history and, in this case, Japanese American history. She places contemporary interviewing projects with Japanese Americans within the context of a century-long tradition of relying on personal testimony and insider accounts to shape public understanding of their experiences. For Dubrow as for many scholars, the World War II internment of Japanese Americans was the pivotal event in their history: driven by racism fueled by outsider accounts of "dangerous foreigners," the internment was followed by three decades of collective silence within the Japanese American community. Eventually, however, sparked by the civil rights and ethnic power movements of the 1960s and 1970s, Japanese Americans and their allies spoke out and secured redress for wartime confinement and losses, events that in turn led to an efflorescence of oral history and related efforts to develop a new, more sympathetic public understanding of Japanese Americans. Like other authors in this volume, Dubrow understands that oral history and other narratives of personal experience are deeply political, both expressive and constitutive of existing relations of power. This view leads her finally to consider the significance of the current reassessment of the internment for concerns about tolerance, justice, and civil rights.

Senka Božić-Vrbančić's discussion of the representation of Dalmatian and Maori workers in New Zealand's gumfields similarly understands how representations of the past are shaped by relations of power in the present. Playing off the official story as presented at the Matakohe Kauri Museum, which absorbs these workers into the national myth of sturdy pioneers while ignoring the discrimination they suffered at the hands of Anglo settlers, she counterposes it to stories told at two family museums, one Dalmatian, one Maori, run by descendants of these gum workers. Yet Božić-Vrbančić does not suggest that these vernacular museums simply posit an alternative Dalmatian or Maori identity; rather, as she explains it, they unselfconsciously present a more complex biculturalism: the Jurlina brothers' museum, evoking powerful— indeed loving—memories of the old country, also seeks to legitimize Dalmatian workers as New Zealand pioneers; Tony Yelash's museum, deliberately seeking to claim a positive Maori identity in the present, nonetheless recognizes the common subordination of Maori and Dalmatian gum workers within an Anglo-dominated society. Božić-Vrbančić's use of oral history is unique among all the chapters in this volume: she does not—cannot—explicate its role in presenting an alternative past because the museums under discussion do not draw upon interviews in any way. Rather, it is the interviews that she herself conducted with these guardians of the past, the Jurlina brothers and Tony Yelash, that communicate both the sense of loss and the urgent needs of the present that often frame discussions of identity and community.

Horacio Roque Ramírez's chapter also focuses on cultural work undertaken within a context of loss as he describes his use of oral history to document the history of queer Latinas and Latinos in the San Francisco Bay area at a time when HIV/AIDS was claiming hundreds of lives within the community. Detailing two public events in which he represented the community's history back to itself, Ramírez suggests how oral history can matter to a community. Even as mourning framed his interviews, narrators and the people who heard their words found the solace of memory and hope for the future in these stories about discrimination, erotic pleasure, community building, and political mobilization.

Oral history, Ramírez avers, *is* public history, not only because it makes these stories public but because, in his experience, narrators invariably intertwine personal history with public events and lives lived in community. Ramírez's chapter also articulates his own sense of public responsibility: although his research was conducted for his dissertation, he also held himself to a high standard of community accountability. Because he was able to gain the trust of community members, he was given access to unique collections of photographs and other materials generally absent from the archival record, which represents queer history as white and represents Latina and Latino history as heteronormative. Blurring the line between scholarship and advocacy, Ramírez refers to his work as "historiographic activism," a term that might apply equally to several other chapters in this volume.

Robert Jefferson's chapter, focusing on the stories black GIs have told about their World War II experiences in the Jim Crow Army, also suggests several interesting connections between oral history and public history. The chapter itself implies an expansive notion of oral history, for it is grounded in stories told not in the intimacy of a one-on-one interview, but in the ritualized public setting of veterans' reunions. Furthermore, these stories, as much about fighting racial segregation and oppression in the Army as about fighting foreign enemies, have been told within the context of a public memory that has, until quite recently, ignored, minimized, or denigrated the service of black GIs. These narratives are, therefore, deliberate attempts to counter the dominant narrative, as well as efforts to sustain identity and pride. Like several other contributors to this volume, Jefferson has a keen sense of the power of place:

black GIs' stories are powerfully linked to specific sites of battle and resistance and are evoked by reunions held at Fort Huachuca, Arizona, where black units received their military training. Most importantly, though, the stories Jefferson has listened to and recorded are not exercises in nostalgia, but moral tales told to inspire action in the present against a still-pervasive racism, deliberate efforts to connect personal memories with pressing public issues facing the African American community. Thus this chapter, like all of the contributions to Part II, demonstrates how oral history, though documenting an often private, always personal past, is nonetheless also very much about a community's present conditions, needs, and desires.

6

IMAGINING COMMUNITIES: MEMORY, LOSS, AND RESILIENCE IN POST-APARTHEID CAPE TOWN

Sean Field

≈

The South African city of Cape Town was forged through conflicts that reverberate in the memories and representations of its past in the present. The city center is squeezed geographically between Table Mountain on the south and the shoreline of Table Bay on the north. As a port it has been a place of arrival, interaction, and departure for travelers from across Africa and the Atlantic and Indian oceans. Dutch colonial settlement began in 1652, displacing local Khoi and San inhabitants.[1] English colonial occupation replaced the Dutch in 1806 and continued until 1910. During the twentieth century, Cape Town evolved from a small colonial outpost to South Africa's second-largest city, with more than three million inhabitants. While colonial influences are widespread—evident in architecture, language, and culture—the contemporary landscape of Cape Town is profoundly scarred by the apartheid government policies of 1948 to 1994, which systemically legalized white domination through the racial registration, separation, and control of all South Africans. These scars are visible in the sites of forced removals and racist re-engineering of the entire city. Drawing upon oral history interviews, this chapter focuses on how residents of two Cape Town communities remember apartheid and how their memories are shaped by both loss and resilience.

The first study is of the black African community of Langa; the second, contrasting study is of the multicultural, predominantly coloured community of District Six.[2] These communities include several sites that evoke memories saturated with pain, sadness, and anger. Both Langa and District

Six residents have shaped their memories to contain these emotional legacies, and as they do, patterns of historical memory are revealed. In the wake of land restitution policies in the post-apartheid period, local museums in both Langa and District Six have become significant venues for community regeneration.[3] Oral histories are central to these museums and are presented through the medium of audio-visual exhibitions. But this is neither another article about the extensively researched District Six community nor an effort to address the lack of research on black African experiences in Cape Town. Rather, by comparing how different Capetonians are remembering *and* imagining communities of the past, this chapter seeks to stimulate open-ended thinking about the representation of memories in the present and to move conceptual practice beyond the closed concepts and spaces inherited from apartheid.[4]

Remembering Langa

Langa's vibrant history reveals a interweaving of different living and working arrangements, political resistance, and histories of churches, schools, and legendary sporting and musical icons.[5] The Langa story begins with the forced relocation of residents from the black settlement of Ndabeni to the "new township" of Langa.[6] From 1927 to 1959, Langa was the only official housing area for black Africans in Cape Town, which pre-apartheid and apartheid governments identified as the "natural home" of "Cape Coloureds." Langa rapidly became overcrowded, especially after 1937, when it became illegal for black Africans to own land outside the rural "homelands," thereby forcing black property owners from other city areas.[7] Overcrowding in Langa was further exacerbated during World War II by the influx of rural Africans into Cape Town, as the state temporarily relaxed the pass laws to relieve labor shortages in manufacturing industries. After the onset of the apartheid state in 1948, pass laws were reinforced in 1952 and expanded to include women in 1956. From then on, all adult Africans were compelled to carry an identity book at all times. Popularly referred to as "the *dompass,*" this book was a central means through which the pass law system imposed control over their movements between rural and urban areas and access to jobs and accommodation.

> So if you don't have your pass on you when you see the police, you go for your pocket. If you change clothes that morning and unfortunately your pass is not with you—you have got to run to save your life. Otherwise you're arrested and you got to pay a fine or go to jail. So everybody was sick of that. WE were sick. We were so fed up and sick and tired of living with this pass.[8]

Integral to the pass law system were migrant labor structures, such as Langa's migrant hostels and barracks, which housed thousands of so-called bachelor male workers, in contrast to most families, who lived in subeconomic houses (i.e., houses of a low standard).[9] The built remains of the pass law system in Langa to this day evoke painful memories. For "bachelors" and families, the pass office epitomized this despised system:

> I remember the old office—it used to be packed with migrant workers [and other residents] who were trying to fix their passes up. There was sign saying DO NOT SPIT in Xhosa and there was a fine, you would be fined five pounds [if you spit]. That was a human hellhole because on a daily basis you saw human misery there.[10]

In the same building complex, the administration of passes functioned alongside the magistrate's court for prosecuting pass offenders:

> Whooo, it was terrible. It was not nice, it was not nice to go to the pass office. Because now, even the boys who were issuing the passes, they will harass the people and tell people, you know who could not speak nice and all that—whooo, it was never nice. See some of them will get arrested. . . . "No, no, no, your pass is expired, take him to get locked. He's going to the magistrate's to talk, there you're guilty or not guilty." That was the way. Guilty. That's the way.[11]

The harsh injustices of the pass law system resulted in countless episodes of resistance. One famous incident occurred on 21 March 1960, when Langa residents attempted to march in protest to the Langa police station (Fig. 6.1). At 6:00 P.M. the police asked the crowd to

> disperse in two or three minutes. That was impossible because there were more than twenty thousand people, how were we supposed to disperse. . . . I strongly believe that we should have never listened to that white police captain. . . . The mistake was made to believe that we must go back and our leader, Philip Kgosana, would come at 6 o'clock and then we would talk to your guys and they would give a report of decisions taken. We should never have believed that. . . . They were smart, they tricked us, and we fell for that. But when we realized that our leaders were locked up . . . that's when the trouble started, that's when people got shot and killed.[12]

The crowd was positioned opposite a square—today known as Sobukwe Square—when the shooting began.

Fig 6.1   Old Langa flats, opposite Sobukwe Square; site of the 21 March 1960 police ambush of marchers protesting against apartheid pass laws. *(Photograph by the Centre for Popular Memory, University of Cape Town; photograph by Connie Knopp.)*

> We were standing here—it was five of us—I saw the cop, policeman taking aim and hit this guy here, the guy fell, you know. It was so painful, man, between his eyes. I mean his head was not splattered or splashed, you could just see the hole here and then blood coming down . . . then all hell broke loose, they started shooting.[13]

These are visceral memories. Langa residents remember anywhere from three to more than fifty being killed during the 21 March protests. Written sources are no more reliable, ranging from a report of three killed, from a commission of the apartheid government, to a claim of twenty killed, from a post-apartheid member of Parliament.[14] Historical facts are important, but what is significant here is how these memories of resistance are traces of the "unimaginable taking place."[15] These collective acts of resistance seemed unimaginable to many individual witnesses because they constituted a significant challenge to the omnipotent apartheid state. But the "unimaginable" also refers to the linguistic and psychological limits of narrating memories of a traumatic episode. Thousands from across Cape Town then protested the events of 21 March by marching into Cape Town's city center on 30 March in what was to become famous as "the Langa March," but I have frequently encountered residents who compressed their memories of these two protests into one epic-like event.

For the next generation, 1976 represented the pivotal moment of resistance. Langa High School students mobilized in alliance with students from the neighboring coloured community of Bontehuewel. Significantly, many of the African and coloured activists of 1976 were the descendants of people removed from Ndabeni to Langa in the 1920s and, as will be discussed below, from District Six to Bonteheuwel. The 1976 clashes with police on Vanguard Drive, a boundary between Langa and Bonteheuwel, crossed the racialized spatial boundaries around these communities.

Popular memories of several generations clustered around spaces within and across the boundaries of Langa to create a sense of place for Langa residents. The memories of earlier Langa generations refer to various experiences of subjugation and resistance, which they have imaginatively reconstructed around sites of memory such as public spaces (e.g., the pass office), physical objects (e.g., the identity book), and collective actions (e.g., the Langa marches).[16] For later generations, the focus of memory is the racialized boundary.

Novelist Richard Rive has written, "To have a sense of place is to have an empathy and identification with that place, a mental attitude towards it, an appreciation of it."[17] "Sense of place," then, is an imaginative act that combines ongoing sensory inputs from the surrounding social and physical landscape with a person's internal world of selected and constructed memories. And for these memories to be sustained, "We situate what we recollect within the mental spaces provided by the group. . . . No collective memory can exist without reference to a socially specific spatial framework."[18] The closed space called "Langa" and the sites of memory contained within are the spatial framing. Memories of Langa were shaped by its function as a spatially bounded community created by "racial zoning" as well as by the surrounding coloured communities and highways, rail lines, and industrial zones. The apartheid government's determination that black Africans did not belong in urban Cape Town—residential pockets like Langa were tolerated to meet labor market needs—constituted the broader ideological frame. The systemic discriminations of the pass law system created common localized experiences for Africans, which were identified with and politically organized around, and which gave coherence to shared memories *and* excluded unshared memories. Moreover, Langa did not face widespread forced removals but rather absorbed Africans who were displaced through removals from other urban and rural areas. In contrast, District Six was physically, culturally, and emotionally shattered by apartheid forced removals.

Remembering District Six

In the period before 1948, South African governments implemented racial separation to varying degrees through job reservation and regulating accommodations. But in Cape Town residential life remained culturally heterogeneous until the 1950s. From the city center all along the Southern Suburbs railway line, District Six, Woodstock, Observatory, Mowbray, Rondebosch, and other communities included white, coloured, and African residents. With the exception of isolated areas of cultural diversity, other South African cities were less culturally mixed, and apartheid laws tended to reinforce pre-existing racial divisions. In Cape Town, however, they ripped apart families, friends, and neighborhoods and dispersed people to racially separate townships. District Six is the best-known example of these displacements.

District Six lies within walking distance of the city center and since the 1830s provided low-cost housing to emancipated slaves, textile and other workers, sailors, and passing travelers from around the globe.[19] Although its population was predominantly coloured, District Six was home to many white and African families and soldiers returning from the South African War and both World Wars.[20] It supported a diverse cultural life including various music genres, dance bands, New Year's carnivals, shopping areas, bioscopes, youth gangs, and groups of political intellectuals (Figs. 6.2–3). By the late 1940s District Six was deemed a "slum." At the same time, its proximity to the city center excited urban planners with its economic potential, and its cultural diversity was anathema to apartheid ideology.

Under the Group Areas Act of 1950, the Group Areas Board had powers to "racially zone" all spaces in South Africa according to the "group" classifications: "white," "coloured," "African," and "Asian." District Six was zoned a "white area" in 1966, and from 1968 to 1982 more than sixty thousand people were forcibly removed from their homes, the vast majority of which were then bulldozed down.[21] People classified as "African" relocated to the apartheid township of Guguletu, and people classified as "coloured" went to the townships of Bonteheuwel, Hanover Park, and Mitchells Plein.[22] Today, with the exception of a few churches and a mosque, the familiar features of District Six are gone, and rubble and weeds are all that remain. As one former District Six resident said:

> Oh! Don't talk to me about that, please don't talk to me. I will cry. I will cry all over again. There's when the trouble started. When they chucked us out like that. When they chucked us out of Cape Town, my whole life became changed! There was change. Not just in me, but in all people. What they took away they can never give back to us again (weeps). Oh I want to cry so much all over again.[23]

Fig 6.2 and 6.3. Prior to its destruction by apartheid's forced relocations, District Six around 1970 was a lively and dense urban community. *(Courtesy of the Centre for Popular Memory, University of Cape Town; photographs by Jurg Ruedi)*

The interviewee fears feeling her loss "all over again." But without prompting she describes apartheid removals as "changing people," and so her tears begin to flow. In the midst of this emotional expression, she reflects that "what they took away they can never give back to us again." Today the restitution process offers the promise of return to District Six. But displacement was not solely about the removal of people from physical houses and spaces. It was also about the loss of emotionally and symbolically meaningful places, particularly "home" and "community." The impact of these losses is enormous: these were the places where people played, worked, and lived and that were central to their development from children to adults. Within the familiar landscape of home, neighborhood, and the city, people felt connected.

> En as ons op onse stoepe staan en dan het ons die hele Table Mountain gesien. En as ons in die backyard stand en dan sien ons die hele docks. Soe lekker het ons gewoon. En ons wil nie uit nie, ons wil nie gemove het nie. Maar dis was really lekker gewees om in die Kaap te bly, homely en lekker bymekaar gebly.

> *(And if we stood on our verandas, then we could see the whole of Table Mountain. And if we stood in the backyard, we could see the whole of the docks. And it was really nice to live there. We did not want to move out. But it was really nice to stay in the Cape, homely and nice staying together.)*[24]

But the memories of places recalled in interviews are often expressed in idealized terms. For example:

> There will never come, another place like District Six. There were very good people and there were fair people. . . . District Six was a nice place, it was a lovely place. . . . Ja so was District Six! But it was a beautiful place. Here [Bonteheuwel] everybody's for themselves. They don't worry with nobody. It was a happy family that stayed in District Six.[25]

The loss of home and community is palpable, and that loss is frequently expressed in the trope of the "happy family."[26] The collective sense of belonging in District Six is contrasted to the post-removal, racially closed townships where "everybody's for themselves." Narrators' mental images of the past yield clues about their conscious and unconscious struggles with forms of loss. Nostalgia is an imaginative process of finding words to make sense of memories laden with uncomfortable images and feelings evoked in the present but linked to what has been lost from the past. Oral historians have learned to listen to how interviewees remember and narrate the past, whether or not it is factually accurate, to consider how memories and myths have influenced people's actions and sense of agency.[27]

For residents who experienced forced removals, memories of losses are forged in relation to what was once had, experienced, and felt, to what existed prior to the loss. Most interviewees compressed pre-removal memories into an undifferentiated "that time" as opposed to the present. These memory strategies contribute to an exaggerated sense of community before forced removals. The public myth goes as follows: everything was fine before apartheid, during "the good peaceful times," but the evil of apartheid destroyed everything, and then "the bad violent times" commenced. To be sure, while these collective memories of District Six are myth-laden, they are also accurate assessments of change. For example, statistics show a rise in crime in the townships where people were relocated beginning in the late 1970s, with the most dramatic increases after 1990.[28] But how can we understand the psychological motives shaping these partly mythologized memories?

Linguistically, "loss" suggests absence. But this loss of home and community has an ongoing emotional presence. Interviewees' repeated enunciation of the words "home" and "community" is evidence of their working through feelings of loss. The actual loss of home and community is felt as a loss of personal security, stability, and autonomy. Most of all, when the social world people grew up in is destroyed, it is experienced *as if* the inner self is being fragmented or *as if* "all is lost."[29] In response, many protect themselves by psychologically splitting off parts of the self to create imaginary places framed by nostalgic memories. For these trauma survivors, nostalgia protects the self from the pain, sadness, hatred, and losses inflicted by the apartheid system. This psychological manifestation is encountered in interviews as myth-laden memories of "home" and "community," which "hold together" an imagined "whole" self.[30]

Yet the idealized past is not the only construct oral historians confront in interviews with former District Six residents. There is little sense of myth when some interviewees confront the social fragmentation inflicted by removals:

> In those days I didn't know why they chuck us out. What did we do, that they chuck us out like this? We wasn't murderers, we wasn't robbers, like today. . . . It was wrong what the white people did. These people did wrong. They had everything that a person's heart yearns for. And we had nothing but we were satisfied. They broke us up. They broke up the community. They took our happiness from us. The day they threw us out of Cape Town that was my whole life tumbling down. I don't know how my life continued. I couldn't see my life in this

raw township far away from family. All the neighbours were strangers. That was the hardest part of my life.[31]

These effects of dislocation are exacerbated by racist discourses that justified apartheid's forced removals. Far removed from District Six, most former residents lived in poverty-stricken racialized ghettos, circumstances that produced bleak worldviews. In this context, people weave together nostalgia and historical facts to create memories of solace, helping them bear both their emotional losses from the past and the socioeconomic problems of the present. These reconstructed memories are evidence of people's resilience, their will to survive. They also reveal a resolve to imagine a better future, which results in popular memories that look backward *and* forward with ambiguity.

Imagining Communities in Post-Apartheid Cape Town

The remembered and imagined local communities are not separate from people's different senses of the city. While city spaces were racially segregated under apartheid, over time cross-cultural, cross-generational, and other border-crossing relationships blurred these boundaries. Similarly, people's sense of the city cannot be stereotyped as "black" versus "white" or "from above" versus "from below." Rather, there is a kaleidoscope of *popular and unpopular imaginings* from different cultural, spatial, and temporal vantage points. Since 1994, apartheid laws have been removed, but post-apartheid Cape Town is "not simply a rainbow city of cultural diversity and exotic spice. It is also a space of social polarization, ghettoization, and fortified shopping malls and suburban homes."[32]

Both Langa and District Six are historically significant, but how they are remembered, imagined, and represented is contested within the nonracial transformation—or lack thereof—of the post-apartheid city. Langa is imagined as the "proud elderly African" township of Cape Town. But as it has become a congested mixture of houses, flats, hostels, barracks, and shanties in informal settlements, it has also come to be viewed as a poverty-stricken ghetto with different generations and migrant groups competing for scarce resources. In contrast, District Six's multicultural past has led a range of people across the racialized working- and middle-class areas of Cape Town to make valid claims to its past. For many—especially for coloured former residents—it has an iconic status.

The post-apartheid government created two legal processes to redress past abuses. The first was steered by the Truth and Reconciliation Commission (TRC), which began its work in 1996 and wound up operations in 2000. Its scope was limited to identifying "horrendous abuses of human rights" committed between 1961 and 1994, with the reconciliatory aim of granting amnesty to perpetrators and redress to victims of human rights abuses.[33] The second process, still in operation in 2007, is the Commission for Land Rights and Restitution, which enables survivors of forced removals either to return to their original land or to receive alternative land or a symbolic financial compensation. The land restitution cases are handled administratively and legally, and in contrast to the TRC, which held public hearings, there is no public space where land claimants can tell their stories. Many have suggested that just such a public process is necessary.[34] Financial compensation for those who cannot return to their land or communities will provide material restitution, but will it alleviate people's emotional losses? Furthermore, those who can return to their land and houses might be reconnected to the "original spaces," but is this sufficient?

Recognizing that "remembering well a shared injury is something which people cannot do by themselves, but must be shared by a group of diverse voices," oral and public historians have pragmatic contributions to make to regenerative forms of memory work.[35] First, recording people's narratives—in oral, visual, and written forms—in a sensitive and empathic manner can help people to feel that they are heard and seen. Second, the dissemination of people's stories through books, radio programs, films, and audio-visual productions can help them gain public recognition and support. Third, memorialization in collaboration with local museums creates opportunities for people to share memories and make meaningful connections with each other.

Furthermore, instead of ignoring idealized images of a past community, oral historians need to empathize with these imaginative recreations and to facilitate and guide that process in a forward-thinking fashion. The process of *imagining communities* provides coherence to communities that were fragmented and/or violated in the past. These imagined communities provide perceptual framing for individual and collective struggles, but they also exclude stories that do not fit anti-apartheid frames of reference.[36] For example, having "the community" speak with a singular and united voice was a crucial antiapartheid political strategy, but post-apartheid oral historians need not replicate this.[37] Given that democracy allows a diversity of voices to seek expression, oral historians need to record shared *and* unshared memories and interpret how these have shaped moments of unity *and* disunity. We need to think through how both shared *and* unshared memories influence the framing of dominant community stories.

How have post-apartheid community museums responded to these challenges? In Langa the process of setting up a museum is at an embryonic stage. A group of residents, local councilors, and municipal officials launched the Langa Heritage Foundation in 2003. The pass law office and court were renovated in the same year and in 2004 opened as the Langa Museum. The main museum space contains one exhibit, comprising storyboards and the actual benches where the court proceedings occurred. The storyboards include photographs and excerpts from oral history interviews that discussed pass laws, as well as other community stories. Because the court and holding cells were a site of apartheid repression, the museum has an austere atmosphere. Its central appeal is to the older generation of Langa residents, who together with tourists are its main visitors. In consultation with teachers, the museum is planning programs to attract school students both from Langa and across Cape Town. Memorializing the witnesses of pass law abuses is central to the museum, but it is the younger generations and newer residents from the informal settlements who are future target groups.[38] The Langa Museum also commissioned a film documentary based on videotaped oral history interviews with Langa residents, which is displayed in the museum.[39] Various sites of memory across Langa, including the museum and pass office site, are also publicly signified with concrete pillars covered with colorful mosaics telling brief stories about each site. These pillars mark a heritage trail through the community. The Langa Museum has political support from city government but lacks sufficient financing.

In contrast, the District Six Museum is the leading community museum in South Africa. The "Hands Off District Six" campaign, a coalition of anti-apartheid groups that stopped economic development on the District Six site during apartheid, was a significant forerunner to the formation of the museum. Former residents also played a central role in creating this museum and in materially and emotionally rebuilding the community. In 1995 a temporary exhibition about District Six was launched and planned to run for only two weeks. But it was such a popular success that it developed into a permanent museum, located within a Methodist church that had previously served District Six residents.

Oral history recordings, photographs, and objects are creatively displayed in permanent and temporary exhibitions.[40] The museum has different styles of presenting oral histories. For example, "Nomvuyo's Room" presents a typical District Six bedroom and kitchen of the 1950s. Oral history recordings of a black African woman, Nomvuyo Ngcelwane, and other residents relating memories of District Six are played through a radio. The exhibition also contains family photographs and other familiar objects presented in dim lighting. This integrated presentation of sounds, images, and objects has a realistic atmosphere, giving the visitor a close approximation of what it felt like to live in a District Six home of the 1950s and 1960s. Because Nomvuyo's Room presents an African women's story, it breaks the stereotypical framing of District Six's history as only a "coloured story."[41] "Rod's Room" presents a stylistic contrast. Developed in collaboration with former resident and visual artist Roderick Saul, this room is brightly lit. The family objects from Rod's past are not presented in a natural setting but are artistically molded into the walls and appear as fragments piercing the room. The floor is relatively bare, and some photographs are displayed on the walls. On the recording playing in the room, Rod not only recounts his memories of living in District Six but also reflects on the meanings of this exhibition. Through the participation of both Nomvuyo Ngcelwana and Roderick Saul in these exhibits, the museum created "an opportunity for conventional scholar-informant relations to be overturned," allowing oral history interviewees to become co-authors of the public presentation of their stories.[42]

This community museum places considerable emphasis on engaging and stimulating visitor experiences. Visitors are given opportunities to inscribe their names and stories onto memory cloths and diaries, and when opportunities arise during visits, former residents are interviewed on site. As suggested earlier, people's sense of place frames an imaginative "holding together" of both their own and their community's identity. This is represented by former residents writing their names onto a street map of District Six on the location of their former homes. The map is covered by transparent plastic sheeting and is located near the museum's main entrance, below the floor of the central exhibition space. As one commentator noted: "The map works as a mnemonic device, which both allows the recall of place but also puts the rememberer back into it, as they literally have put their names back into District Six by writing them on the map. It produces a re-identification . . . for each District Six starts from the epicenter of *their* home, *their* street, *their* place."[43]

From 1966 to 1995, former residents sustained a community-in-memory by imagining their community of the past, even when they had no contact, or only sporadic contact, with each other. But since 1995, through the work of the museum, epitomized by this mnemonic map, each individual's name and place in District Six is reinscribed in the community's history. This is an evocative space: as a museum education officer said, "Every day at least one person cries here."[44] These tears are links to the past but are evoked within the safe museum space of the present, where former residents disconnected through removals and dispersed across the city have the opportunity to re-experience an emotional connection to District Six and to each other. Put differently, it rekindles a pre-removals connectedness, which over time was sustained through memory *and* imagination. Moments of connection often happen through spontaneous meetings of former residents at museum exhibitions and organized book launches, musical and memorial events, and public education programs. But the regeneration of a community is also fraught with contestation. Museum staff acknowledge a community

> both diverse and fractured but that simultaneously lays claim to a version of the concept that has more to do with the 'imagined' coherence . . . than with the diverse and sometimes antagonistic polity that it actually represents. This is the uncompromising tightrope that the museum has chosen to walk in the interests of 'community'.[45]

The museum's central commitment is to the community, but dialogues among residents and with academics and heritage professionals have triggered heated debates. For example, how should competing voices with differing versions or interpretations of the past be represented? What is the role of professionals in a community museum? Should the District Six Museum assume the role of city museum? The museum also attracts vast numbers of foreign visitors and is a member of an international network of Sites and Museums of Conscience.[46] These audiences and dialogues have helped the museum to produce vibrant results, which might not match everyone's remembered or imagined community, but nonetheless provide space for the memories of loss and resilience to be expressed, recorded, archived, and represented. Most significantly, the museum provides an overarching *framework* to hold many viewpoints, memories, emotions, and imaginings of District Six.

For individuals reliant on the collective identity of "District Sixer" or "Langa People," the imagined coherence of community or wholeness of self bolstered their resilience under apartheid. These imaginings have been affirmed through the work of these post-apartheid museums. But these are delicate, associative links, between self and community and between past and present, and they will endure future disappointments. The communities people return to will neither be the same as they experienced them in the past nor what they imagined over time. Certainly the idealized community cannot be realized. It is too early to tell how imagining communities assists or hinders returnees' possible acceptance of their altered communities in the present. Nevertheless, the resilience shown during apartheid is evidence of people's capacity to adapt. The District Six Museum's current oral history project is recording the stories of returnees and will, in the long run, have much to say about these questions. The museum also plans to have the original District Six area declared a national heritage site; as its former director, Valmont Layne, stated: "It must be something that isn't static and limited. It must combine many elements—visual, oral, and memory. People don't want a monument or statue."[47] To date, nine residents have returned to District Six, and more than three thousand houses are to be built there.[48] Former Ndabeni residents in Langa are also waiting for houses to be built, but they will not be returning to the original Ndabeni area, as it was turned into an industrial zone. They will be moving to alternative land provided at the defunct Wingfield aerodrome, approximately five kilometers from Langa. The Langa community as a whole is not connected through forced removal experiences in the way that the District Six community is. But the Langa Museum is committed to appealing to multiple groups, and representing *unshared* memories and interests of the "Capeborners" and rural newcomers will be challenging.[49] There is much to be learned from how the District Six Museum used the iconic status of this diverse community to appeal across cultural, generational, political, religious, and sexual distinctions. Nevertheless, Langa's status as the oldest African community in Cape Town provides that museum with vital political capital in attracting more visitors and more funding. The Langa and District Six museums are beginning to forge links, which bodes well for building relationships across the different communities they represent.

A persistent challenge for both museums is to transmit the lived memories of apartheid to the second, third, and coming generations. Recording the oral histories of living witnesses, before they become frail or die, is therefore urgent. While I have emphasized the cohesive function of imagining communities for apartheid witnesses, the next generations will also need to imagine these communities in empathic ways—to understand the past they did not experience and to ensure that communities are regenerated. In Cape Town today there are very few nonracialized sites such as the District Six Museum. The city government is developing programs to foster "a home for all" the culturally diverse people of the city. Oral historians can play a constructive role in overcoming the social divisions of apartheid by recording and disseminating a range of people's stories through books, radio, film, exhibitions, memorials, and the internet, across communities and generations. These media open possibilities for shared and unshared memories to be recognized publicly and contribute to imagining the city and its communities as a place for *all*. But imagining a nonracial future must be tempered by acknowledging that "no one knows what the past will be made of next."[50] This caveat creates opportunities for oral historians to be self-reflective and engage in disquieting dialogues with historians and history.

NOTES

Sincere thanks to Linda Shopes, Paula Hamilton, Renate Meyer, and Jane van der Riet for their constructive comments on drafts of this chapter.

1. Vivian Bickford-Smith, Elizabeth van Heyningen, and Nigel Worden, *Cape Town: The Making of a City* (David Philip: Cape Town, 1998), 12–83.
2. Under the Population Registration Act of 1950, all persons in South Africa were

classified according to the following "races": "white" (European ancestry), "Bantu" (African ethnic "tribes"), "Asian" (Indian ancestry), and "coloured" (mixed cultural ancestry, significantly including Khoi, San, and slave ancestors). These terms have been historically contested but retain popular and legal currency in post-apartheid South Africa.

3. The restitution process promises redress to those removed from their homes and land by the racist actions of regimes in power from 1913 to 1990.

4. Sarah Nuttal and Cheryl-Ann Michael, eds., *Senses of Culture: South African Cultural Studies* (Oxford: Oxford University Press, 2000), 2–21.

5. Rachidi Mahlope, "Sports, Festivals and Popular Politics: Aspects of the Social and Popular Culture in Langa Township, 1945–70" (M.A. thesis, University of Cape Town, 1994); Nazeema Mohammed, "The Struggle for Existence: The First Twenty Years in the History of Langa High School" (honors diss., University of Cape Town, 1989).

6. Ndabeni was set up in 1901 in response to racist fears of Africans bringing diseases into the city. During this "scare" some Africans were removed from District Six to Ndabeni. Thus, some Langa residents were twice removed, first from District Six and again from Ndabeni. Christopher Saunders, "From Ndabeni to Langa," *Studies in the History of Cape Town* 1 (1979): 167–204.

7. This was reinforced during the apartheid era, when black South Africans effectively became "foreigners" inside South Africa. For example, Xhosa-speaking Africans of Cape Town were deemed to be citizens of either the Ciskei or Transkei. Barry Kinkead-Weeks, "Africans in Cape Town: State Policy and Popular Resistance, 1936–1973" (Ph.D. diss., University of Cape Town, 1992).

8. Interview with Ignatius Zuma, Langa, 7 April 2002. All Langa quotations are drawn from twenty interviews I conducted with residents for the Cape Town City Council and the Langa Heritage Foundation. The interviews were undertaken as part of the research to identify heritage sites in Langa and to contribute to launching the Langa Museum in 2004. All these interviews are lodged at the Centre for Popular Memory archive: www.popularmemory.org.

9. Mamphele Ramphele, *A Bed Called Home: Life in the Migrant Hostels of Cape Town* (Athens: Ohio University Press, 1993).

10. Interview with Fatima Dike, Langa, 24 April 2002.

11. Interview with Stoto Zibi, Langa, 18 March 2002.

12. Interview with Colenso Mama, Langa, 10 April 2002.

13. Interview with Gilbert Fezi, Langa, 17 April 2002.

14. Justice Van Dieman, *Commission of Enquiry into the Events in Langa Location, District of Wynberg, on 21st March 1960.* The parliamentary source is: www.info.gov.za/speeches/2005/05032208451005.htmh.

15. Similarly, Auschwitz witnesses remember several gas chamber chimneys exploding during an act of resistance and not the one chimney that actually exploded. Shoshana Felman and Dori Laub, *Testimony: Crises of Witnessing in Literature, Psychoanalysis and History* (London: Routledge, 1992), quotation from p. 62.

16. Compare Pierre Nora, "Between Memory and History: Les Lieux de Memoire," *Representations* 26 (1989): 7–25.

17. Richard Rive quoted in Ciraj Rassool and Sandi Prosalendis, eds., *Recalling Community in Cape Town: Creating and Curating the District Six Museum* (Cape Town: District Six Museum Foundation, 2001), 31.

18. Paul Connerton, *How Societies Remember* (Cambridge: Cambridge University Press, 1989), 37.

19. Shamil Jeppie and Crain Soudien, eds., *The Struggle for District Six, Past and Present* (Cape Town: Buchu Books, 1991).

20. My father, a World War II veteran of Irish descent, left his family in England and came to Cape Town in 1949. After he and my Afrikaner mother married, they lived in District Six from 1956 to 1962, and I was born there in 1961. Too young to remember District Six, I grew up listening to my parents tell stories about family life on Lemmington Terrace. But fearing stigmatization, my parents (who are white) deliberately located these stories in the neighboring white suburb of Vredehoek. I was in my mid-twenties when I heard from my older siblings that our Lemmington Terrace home was on Upper Constitution Street in District Six.

21. Felicity Swanson, " 'Ja! So Was District Six! But It Was a Beautiful Place': Oral Histories, Memory and Identity," in Sean Field, ed., *Lost Communities, Living Memories: Remembering Forced Removals in Cape Town* (Cape Town: David Philip, 2001).

22. From 1962 Guguletu was the "new" township, where most African residents in Cape Town were relocated because Langa was massively overcrowded.

23. Mrs. G. J., interviewed in Cape Town between 1986 and 1989 (documentation is incomplete). All quotations in this chapter from District Six interviews are drawn from ninety-four interviews conducted by Bill Nasson, Shamil Jeppie, and others between 1986 and 1989 for the Western Cape Oral History Project (WCOHP). These interviews are located in the District Six Collection, Centre for Popular Memory (www.popularmemory.org).

24. Mrs. A. P., interviewed by Bill Nasson, London, 16 September 1987, WCOHP.

25. Mr. B. C., interviewed by Ciraj Mohammed, Cape Town, 1989, WCOHP.

26. Kay Mcormick, *Language in Cape Town's District Six* (Oxford University Press: Oxford, 2002), 47.

27. Alessandro Portelli, *The Battle of Valle Giulia: Oral History and the Art of Dialogue* (Madison: University of Wisconsin Press, 1997).

28. Vivian Bickford-Smith, Nigel Worden, and Elizabeth van Heyingen, *Cape Town in the Twentieth Century* (Cape Town: David Philip, 1999), 138.

29. For definitions of "the self," see Richard Stolorow, "An Inter-subjective View of Self Psychology," *Psychoanalytic Dialogues* 5 (1995): 393–99.

30. Raphael Samuel and Paul Thompson, eds., *The Myths We Live By* (London: Routledge, 1990).

31. Interview with Mrs. G. J.

32. Steve Robins, "City Spaces," in Nuttal and Michael, *Senses of Culture*, 423.

33. Debbie Posel and Graeme Simpson, eds., *Commissioning the Past: Understanding South Africa's Truth and Reconciliation Commission* (Johannesburg: Witwatersrand University Press, 2002).

34. Uma Mesthrie, "Land Restitution in Cape Town: Public Displays and Private Meanings," *Kronos: Journal of Cape History* 25 (1998–99): 239–58.

35. Richard Sennett, "Disturbing Memories," in Patricia Fara and Karalyn Patterson, eds., *Memory* (Cambridge: Cambridge University Press, 1998), 12.

36. Benedict Anderson, *Imagined Communities: Reflections on the Origins and Spread of Nationalism* (Verso: London, 1983).

37. Gary Minkley and Ciraj Rassool, "Orality, Memory, and Social History in South Africa," in Sarah Nuttal and Carli Coetzee, eds., *Negotiating the Past: The Making of Memory in South Africa* (Cape Town: Oxford University Press, 1998).

38. Personal communication from museum staff, 19 April 2005. Since 1990, informal settlements, previously referred to as "shantytowns," have proliferated around the outer edges of Langa.

39. The documentary, entitled *We Are All History: Stories from Langa*, was researched and produced by the Centre for Popular Memory (2005).

40. Peggy Delport, "Signposts for Retrieval: A Visual Framework for Enabling Memory of Place and Time," in Rassool and Prosalendis, *Recalling Community*, 31–46.

41. *Nomvuyo Ngcelwane, Sala Kahle District Six, An African Women's Perspective* (Cape Town: Kwela Books, 1998).

42. Ciraj Rassool and Valmont Layne, "Memory Rooms: Oral History in the District Six Museum," in Rassool and Prosalendis, *Recalling Community*, 149.

43. Charmaine McEachern, "Mapping the Memories: Politics, Place and Identity in the District Six Museum," in Abebe Zegeye, ed., *Social Identities in the New South Africa* (Cape Town: Kwela Books, 2001), 232–33.

44. Personal communication, 7 March 2003.

45. Annie E. Coombes, *History after Apartheid: Visual Culture and Public Memory in a Democratic South Africa* (Johannesburg: Witwatersrand University Press: 2003), 142.

46. The museum hosted a 2005 conference entitled "Hands on District Six: Landscapes of Post-colonial Memorialization," at which international and local participants debated how the site should be memorialized.

47. Quoted in "March to Site of First and Last Removals Rounds Off District Six Conference," *Cape Times*, 30 May 2005, 3.

48. A website of the District 6 Beneficiary Trust is under development: www .d6bentrust.org.za.

49. Marianne Merthen, "A Winter of Discontent," *Mail and Guardian*, 27 May 2005, 5.

50. Nora, "Between Memory and History," 17.

7

CONTESTED PLACES IN PUBLIC MEMORY: REFLECTIONS ON PERSONAL TESTIMONY AND ORAL HISTORY IN JAPANESE AMERICAN HERITAGE

Gail Lee Dubrow

In this chapter I examine the public memory of the Japanese American experience. First I explain how it was formed and circulated in the first half of the twentieth century; then, turning to the second half of that century, I consider the ways in which personal testimony before official commissions and in community oral history projects has reshaped public memory of the World War II internment of people of Japanese ancestry. This long view demonstrates that insider accounts have not merely added more facts about Japanese Americans to the historical record; instead, they have reshaped public understandings of American history. The view has shifted from one that repeatedly rationalized discrimination, based on the putative motivations and characteristics of Japanese immigrants, to one that indicts the long history of racial intolerance in America. Making these voices public though community history projects, educational outreach efforts in schools, official recognition of Japanese American heritage sites, and other means has opened up a more critical view of the nation's past and has framed new opportunities for public engagement with unresolved issues of social justice in America.

Japanese first immigrated to the United States mainland in significant numbers during the last two decades of the nineteenth century. Initially welcomed as replacements for Chinese laborers, who were barred from the country with the passage in 1882 of the Chinese Exclusion Act, Japanese immigrants themselves soon became the target of an exclusion movement. During the early decades of the twentieth century, newspapers circulated images of Japanese immigrants as inassimilable aliens who posed a threat to American labor. The Japanese government capitulated to the exclusionists by implementing the Gentlemen's Agreements of 1907–8, enacting its own restrictions on the emigration of laborers to the continental United States. Beginning in 1913 and fueled by antiforeign sentiment after World War I, first California and then other western states enacted anti-Japanese legislation in the form of prohibitions against alien land ownership as well as discriminatory local ordinances. The U.S. Immigration Act of 1924 effectively ended Japanese immigration.

The long history of anti-Japanese sentiment culminated in Executive Order 9066, which mandated the removal of nearly 120,000 people of Japanese descent from designated areas in the western United States during World War II and their forced incarceration in internment camps for the duration of the war. Two-thirds of the internees were American citizens, and more than half were children. The justification for this wholesale suspension of civil liberties, based solely on race and ancestry, has occupied contested terrain from the first roundups of Issei community leaders immediately following the Japanese bombing of Pearl Harbor on 7 December 1941; through the mass removal and forced incarceration that followed the signing of EO 9066 on 19 February 1942; through the period of postwar resettlement; into the fight for redress and reparations during the late 1970s and 1980s; and up to the present day, when, in the wake of the terrorist attacks on the United States on 11 September 2001, new questions are being raised about the appropriate balance between protecting civil liberties and waging a war on terrorism.

Although World War II internment is widely regarded as the nadir of Japanese American history, negative representations of Japanese immigrants and their American-born children had been circulating in American popular culture and official government documents throughout the first half of the century. Core features of these representations included the notions that Japanese immigrants were loyal citizens of a military power that constituted a threat to the United States and the American people; that they were inassimilable aliens, who neither sought nor were biologically capable of integration into the social and cultural norms of western civilization; and that their hard work, low standard of living, and high fertility would lead them to overrun white economic competitors. The attribution of negative character traits to Japanese immigrants reinforced these beliefs.

Newspapers played a critical role in fabricating and circulating these harmful images by transforming innocent activity into sensational coverage.[1] Rural farmers seen shooting birds were suspected of practicing for war between Japan and the United States. Immigrants observed drawing maps or taking photographs were accused of being spies seeking optimum locations for enemy cannons, though they were likely scouting for rural farmsteads. Annual assemblies of Japanese immigrants in public parks for celebratory spring picnics aroused undue fear and suspicion when sack races and calisthenics displays, during which participants waved the Japanese flag, were misinterpreted as military maneuvers. While the suspicions and fears of any vocal American citizen were privileged as newsworthy, a combination of language barriers, limited access to major media, and internal hierarchies led Japanese immigrants to rely on official spokesmen, particularly representatives of the Japanese Association of America, to respond to these sorts of rumors and try to quell fears by explaining the cultural context for public gatherings in the Japanese American community.

Federal hearings on Japanese immigration, held on the west coast by the House Committee on Immigration and Naturalization during the summer of 1920, reflected the rising power of the exclusion movement after World War I. These congressional hearings, which studied the so-called Japanese problem as a prelude to imposing new immigration restrictions, provide a clear view of how Japanese immigrants appeared in the public record, both as the objects of public scrutiny and as expert witnesses to their own condition. Fewer than one-fifth of those who testified before the committee were people of Japanese descent, despite ample opportunity to find them at the California hearing sites in San Francisco, Sacramento, Stockton, Angel Island, Fresno, Turlock, Auburn, and Los Angeles, and in Seattle and Tacoma, Washington, each of which was home to a substantial Japanese population.

Caucasians effectively dominated the contest for claiming expertise about the "Japanese problem" in the hearings. Senator James D. Phelan of California and Valentine S. McClatchy, publisher of the *Sacramento Bee*, championed the exclusionist cause. Those favoring exclusion grounded their expertise in studies of looming dangers posed by immigrants, drawing upon public office, official documents, and governmental processes to reinforce the legitimacy of their claims. Defenders of the Japanese, on the other hand, largely drew upon personal knowledge arising from missionary work or close contact with Japanese immigrants in the labor market. Caucasians generally were given ample time to lay out their arguments. Archexclusionist Phelan effectively extended his lengthy testimony by entering into evidence a virulently anti-Japanese official report, "California and the Oriental," produced by the California State Board of Control, which Phelan presented as "doubtless in every respect true."[2]

Japanese testimony at the hearings, on the other hand, typically was quite brief.[3] The only Japanese to speak at any length were representatives of three Nikkei (overseas Japanese) organizations: the Japanese Association of America, the Japanese Agricultural Association, and Furuya, a major import/export company.[4] Each witness's testimony, moreover, was repeatedly interrupted by hostile interrogation. Even the most able defender of Japanese immigrants, the publicist Kiyoshi Karl Kawakami, was prevented from mounting an articulate rebuttal to the exclusionists' case by the committee's dogged pursuit of an irrelevant topic.[5] Pamphlets entered into evidence by Japanese associations ultimately presented the most coherent arguments against exclusion in the 1920 hearings, since they were mercifully free of interruption. As a result of this rhetorical bullying, by the end of the hearings on 3 August 1920 exclusionists had succeeded in reinforcing the terms and boundaries of the "Japanese problem" as it had been defined for two decades in the public imagination.

Despite a hardening of discriminatory policies and practices, Japanese immigrants generally continued to exercise community discipline in the 1920s by channeling their responses through a select few representatives, particularly spokesmen from the Japanese Association of America. In 1919 members of Hiroshima-Kenjinkai, the Hiroshima prefectural association located in western Washington, photographically documented the real property members had developed in an attempt to persuade the Japanese government to intervene before laws restricting alien land ownership spread from California to Washington.[6] Although Hiroshima-ken and others failed to stop state legislators' passage of the land laws, these protests indicate a preference for highly orchestrated diplomatic initiatives on behalf of the larger community, as opposed to individual voices of dissent, mass protest, or direct action.

The fact that Issei (the immigrant generation) were denied the right to become American citizens no doubt informed their turn to Japan for diplomatic intervention. But cultural norms of behavior within a hierarchically organized community surely played a part in muting and channeling their response to prejudice. The supreme ethical norm guiding Japanese conduct, including that of Japanese tenuously settled overseas, was to prevent harm to the group by moderating individual behavior.[7] Alternatively, communities sometimes attempted to transcend language and cultural barriers by communicating through symbolic action. Thus in 1919 Issei leaders of the Americanization movement in Seattle, which was organized under the auspices of the Japanese Association, implemented a strategy of minimizing signs of difference— literally by darkening and removing commercial signboards in the Japanese language—in an effort to undermine exclusionist claims that the Japanese were inassimilable aliens who did not merit the rights of citizenship.[8]

World War II internment of people of Japanese descent was not without contemporary critics, such as Walt Woodward, editor and publisher of the *Bainbridge Review*, who recognized wholesale removal and incarceration as an infringement of civil liberties. Many more outside the Japanese community, however, supported removal, believing—without evidence—that people of Japanese ancestry, both resident aliens and American citizens, represented a threat to national defense. Still others claimed that the incarceration was necessary for the Japanese American community's protection. While the Japanese bombing of Pearl Harbor and American entry into the war were the immediate precipitants of racial hostility, the longer history of anti-Japanese sentiment fed into these new calls for exclusion.

Contemporary studies of the internment shed light on how Japanese American voices were received during the war years. Ethnographic field studies conducted in the internment camps by a sociologist from the University of California at Berkeley, Dorothy Swaine Thomas, with the assistance of Japanese American fieldworkers, produced an extraordinarily rich but problematic set of personal narratives.[9] Methodologically, Thomas and her assistants combined covert research in the form of systematic observation recorded in field notes and reports with direct interviewing, which was then stripped of information that could be used to identify individuals. In both cases, Japanese Americans' experience of forced confinement was mediated by the perceptions and conceptual frameworks applied by the ethnographic researchers. As Lane Ryo Hirabayashi has aptly pointed out in *The Politics of Fieldwork: Research in an American Concentration Camp,* Thomas's bland and euphemistic definition of the internment as an "enforced mass migration" signaled the inadequacy of existing conceptual frameworks to grasp the meaning of the event, particularly from a Japanese American perspective.[10] In fact, within the context of community oral histories that emerged in the postwar period, no single issue would come to matter more than the terminology used to name the event, as the words "evacuation," "internment camp," and "concentration camp" each signified a slightly different political perspective. The core concepts that guided Thomas's research—culture conflict, social and personal disorganization, and reorganization—drawn from classic models of race relations, did little to inject internees' perspectives into the interpretation of the data collected, though the use of Japanese American fieldworkers represented a methodological advance. A fuller voice, however, would await the emergence of community oral history projects initiated in the redress era.

Collective silence about the incarceration characterized the period between postwar resettlement and the rise of the redress movement in the 1980s, both within the Japanese American community and in the wider realm of public memory. Tetsuden Kashima has called attention to the reasons for this state of social amnesia:

Expressing opposition toward the government was much more difficult from the 1940s to the mid-1960s than it was to become later. Soon after World War II and the post-war adjustment phase, America entered into the Korean War. Senator Joseph McCarthy's anti-Communism/infiltration crusade and the start of the Cold War reflected—or resulted in—a national attitude that discouraged criticism of the government.[11]

During this period, the recollections and views of a few Nisei (American-born Japanese) writers had to stand in for the collective experience of the Nikkei in America, most prominently Toshio Mori's short story collection *Yokahama, California*, Monica Sone's largely autobiographical *Nisei Daughter*, and John Okada's *No-No Boy*.[12] These few works, however, were overburdened by the larger silence about the internment experience and the resulting suppression of the full range of personal experiences and political perspectives within the Japanese American community.

Public re-examination of the meaning of the internment awaited the enormous social changes wrought by the civil rights and liberation movements of the 1960s and 1970s. While the story of the U.S. civil rights movement usually focuses on the African American experience, an important dimension—particularly in west coast cities—was mobilization for social justice in Asian American communities. Within Japanese American communities, demands for justice focused on winning a public apology and federal redress payments for those incarcerated during World War II.

Prior to the redress movement, however, recognition in the 1960s of the imminent passing of the Issei generation led a number of communities to try to capture their memories. Japanese journalist Kazuo Ito played a pioneering role in gathering the memories of elderly Issei in the Pacific Northwest, with support from Seattle's Japanese Community Services organization. Instead of recording oral accounts, Ito gathered compelling first-person narratives through letters and other written testimony as sources for a history of Japanese immigrants to that region. His 1969 book, *Hokubei Hyakunenzakura*, was first published in Japanese, reflecting its focus on the immigrant generation. Several years later, Ito worked with Seattle's Japanese Community Services to translate the book into English in response to a growing hunger on the part of the Nisei to learn about their parents' generation.[13]

Reviewing the literature on Japanese immigration in preparation for writing *Issei*, Ito was disappointed by the absence of information on the actual lives of immigrants.

I noticed that one big thing was missing in those publications from 1908 right on up to today. Specifically, I couldn't find the life of immigrants, which was the most important thing, though there were some good books which serve as dictionaries of the history of immigration. Wherever people are involved, there must be real lives, feelings, and human dramas. There must be failures behind successes, for victories and defeats have always gone hand in hand. But I couldn't find in those books the living people, or even the shadow of life.[14]

Ito also believed in the power of personal narratives to reduce international conflict and racial discrimination by kindling human empathy. He firmly believed that a lack of understanding between Japan and the United States had fueled a century of poor relations. Moreover, he was convinced that the failure of American leaders to understand the hardships and feelings experienced by Japanese immigrants undergirded the history of racial discrimination in America. Thus Ito's work was intended to do more than fill gaps in the historical record. He also aimed to disrupt the exclusionists' monopoly over defining the "Japanese question" by identifying the exclusion of minorities as an overarching and problematic theme in American history. In his view, "each minority group was excluded in one period or another and had to endure unreasonable insult"; but "the exclusion of Japanese was probably the most severe of any discrimination against foreigners in American history."[15] A full decade before the redress movement successfully claimed space in public venues for Japanese Americans to receive a fair hearing about their experience of discrimination, Issei voices "testified" to its persistence in the pages of Ito's work.

Unfortunately, collecting Issei narratives prior to redress meant that few people were prepared to speak openly about the darkest chapter in their personal and collective history. One consequence of this silence is that while the personal narratives Ito collected recalled—with great poignancy—memories of immigration, settlement, and early work in sawmills, on farms, and in other industries that dated to the opening decades of the twentieth century, they avoided discussion of the internment altogether.

The rise of Asian American social and political activism from the1960s on spawned community-based history projects, such as the Japanese American Research Project (JARP). Planned and initiated by the Japanese American Citizens League (JACL), the nation's oldest and largest Asian American civil rights organization, this documentation project amassed an enormous collection of correspondence, diaries, photographs, and other materials in Japanese and English that have found a home in the Special Collections at the University of California, Los Angeles.[16] JARP's survey, undertaken from 1962 to 1972, was an important forerunner of the myriad Japanese American community oral history projects that would emerge during the next quarter-century. More than four hundred tape recordings and oral histories eventually were added to JARP's collection of print materials.

The years that followed the publication of Ito's book and the JARP survey witnessed the rise of the redress movement. In 1980 efforts to win redress led to a congressional act establishing the Commission on Wartime Relocation and Internment of Civilians (CWRIC). From July to December of 1981, CWRIC held twenty days of hearings in ten cities that ultimately incorporated the testimony of more than 750 witnesses. First-person testimony would take center stage in the movement's efforts to document the losses, suffering, betrayal, and injustice of forced removal and incarceration,[17] but hard work was required to break more than three decades of collective silence on a painful subject. Robert Shimabukuro has noted the importance of the JACL's efforts to gather first-person testimony to build the case for redress.[18] When Seattle was chosen by CWRIC as a site for redress hearings, the JACL's Community Committee on Redress/Reparations "worked feverishly" in the winter of 1981 to identify and then prepare volunteers willing to testify. As a result, the testimonies presented at the hearings, while authentically moving, were also well orchestrated or, in Shimabukuro's words, "prepared in advance."[19] While the Japanese immigrant community had once relied on official spokesmen to counter discrimination, the redress movement made space for testimony from a wider range of individual voices, while maintaining community control over public memories of this difficult period in American history.

As Tetsuden Kashima points out in his foreword to a recent reissue of the commission's report, *Personal Justice Denied*, "most of [those who testified] were formerly incarcerated Japanese Americans and Aleuts or Pribilof Islanders," though the list of witnesses also included "former internees brought up from Peru, noted scholars, and a few apologists of the incarceration or internment experience."[20] The predominance of Nikkei voices in the hearings reversed the racial balance of expertise on the Japanese American experience that had persisted for most of the twentieth century. Similarly, the commission report's integration of first-person testimony by people of Japanese descent is conspicuous. For the first time, the Japanese American community presented its claims for justice in multiple voices, and those voices would be accepted in the official record as authorities on their own experience. As a result, the report is striking in its condemnation of the internment as unjustified, its refutation of the argument of "military necessity," its articulation of the forces that led to the denial of civil liberties, and its documentation of the resultant losses at both the individual and the community levels.[21] Moreover, the report had enormous influence in altering the U.S. government's official position on the internment, as its recommendations, according to Kashima, led directly to a presidential apology and financial restitution from Congress.[22] Survivors received their long-overdue public apology and payments of $20,000 each beginning in 1990. Moving out of silence, Japanese Americans' willingness to speak publicly about their experience of discrimination has reshaped public memory of the internment. It has also helped to extend the relevance of the civil rights movement beyond its roots in the African American experience.

A small but vocal conservative group, however, has remained steadfast in its opposition to redress and reparations from the 1940s to the present day. This group regards the public apology and payments as "a blackening of America's honor" based on "falsification of World War II history."[23] Until her death in 1996, prolific writer and amateur historian Lillian Baker stood at the center of this political backlash, arguing that the suspension of civil liberties was justified by military necessity, while claiming that most Japanese Americans chose to go to the camps and that the experience of internment did not constitute suffering. More recently, journalist Michelle Malkin has taken up where Baker left off in a provocatively titled book, *In Defense of Internment: The Case for Racial Profiling in World War II and the War on Terror.*[24]

Both Baker and Malkin rely heavily on decoded Japanese diplomatic communications, known as the "Magic cables," to support their claims of military necessity. These cables demonstrate that the Japanese government sought to establish espionage and spying networks on the U.S. mainland, although scanty evidence of that government's success undermines the cables' value in justifying the internment. Baker and her followers also selectively use World War II photographs and personal testimony by Japanese Americans to buttress their claims that internees did not suffer in the camps and thus do not merit redress and reparations.[25] For example, Baker attempted to counter *Star Trek* actor George Takei's commission testimony, in which he recalled "being afraid" of the barbed wire fence, armed soldiers, and guard towers, with quotations from an interview a decade later, with a reporter for a theater magazine, in which Takei spoke more nostalgically about his time in the Arkansas internment camp:

> My own memories of camp, ironically enough, are fun memories: a kid growing up, playing in the swamps in the summer, playing in the snow in wintertime. I do remember the barbed wire and the guard towers but they were just things that were there—no more intimidating than the chain link fence at a schoolyard would have been for me or a telephone pole, a high, ominous, looming thing. But they were just things that were there. It wasn't until I was much older that I understood.[26]

Clearly the emotional tone of memories can shift from moment to moment and over the years. Moreover, the process of preparing and giving testimony in the context of a movement for redress allowed survivors of the internment to reflect critically on the meaning of their experience. This level of critical reflection was unlikely to be welcome in a theater magazine. Not surprising to anyone who has come to new insights as an adult about naïve perceptions formed in childhood, those, like Takei, whose memories of the internment dated to childhood came to different and more troubled views of forced confinement after mature reflection on their experience. In Takei's words, "It wasn't until I was much older that I understood." Apologists for the internment represent the instability of memory as "rewriting World War II history" in response to political pressure from the redress movement.

The higher social value conventionally assigned to certain branches of history and a particular kind of historical evidence has also played a role in this debate. Baker and Malkin appeal to the tradition of privileging military and diplomatic over social and ethnic history; they rely on the convention of valuing official documents over personal narratives as authoritative forms of evidence. Their approach harks back to the turn-of-the-century exclusion movement, in which the authority of official documents and political leaders drowned out the voices of those who were the subject of the inquiry.

In the quarter-century since the commission's hearings, oral history projects focused on the internment have built upon the momentum generated by the redress hearings, allowing Japanese Americans to continue to articulate a new version of events and, ultimately, a new interpretation of American history. One of the earliest of these projects was established on Bainbridge Island, Washington, whose Japanese American community was the first to be forcibly removed during World War II, and to which an exceptionally high percentage of internees returned after the war. Bainbridge Islanders' efforts to gather oral histories have led to the development of a Japanese American community archive, a speakers' program for local schools, public exhibitions, and several films. Their archive, in turn, has been the source of documentary evidence for popular representations sympathetic to the Japanese American historical experience, such as David Guterson's novel *Snow Falling on Cedars*, and the Hollywood film based on it.[27]

Most community oral history projects have relied on volunteers to conduct and, wherever possible, transcribe the interviews. In recent years, some of these independent projects have found permanent and somewhat more accessible homes in university-based archives and special collections. The Department of Special Collections and University Archives at California State University, Sacramento, for example, has built its Japanese American Archival Collection on a 1994 gift of more than sixty oral histories conducted by the Florin, California, JACL's Oral History Project, as well as the collection of Mary Tsukamoto, a retired schoolteacher who had gathered materials on Japanese Americans in California for more than forty years. This material was augmented by the 2001 donation of 162 oral history interviews, conducted between 1969 and 2000 by the Issei Oral History Project.[28] A rare example of an operation that adopted professional standards at an early stage is the Japanese American Oral History Project established by Arthur Hansen at California State University, Fullerton, which has been active for more than thirty years.[29] For the most part, however, from the 1970s through the early 1980s, volunteers ran local oral history projects in a decidedly haphazard manner, with limited resources to index, transcribe, and preserve their collections, and few channels for distributing findings in the public realm.

The conditions for doing this work changed dramatically with the passage of the Civil Liberties Act of 1988, which supported the publication and distribution of findings of the Commission on Wartime Relocation and Internment of Civilians and established the Civil Liberties Public Education Fund (CLPEF), which in turn underwrote a massive amount of oral history research and related educational activities. Among the most significant CLPEF-funded oral history projects are those conducted by the Japanese American National Museum, which in conjunction with local partners conducted forty videotaped oral history interviews in Los Angeles, Chicago, San Diego, and San Jose;[30] the Department of Special Collections and University Archives at California State University, Sacramento, which catalogued its Florin JACL and Tsukamoto collections; and JACL chapters in northern California, which conducted oral history interviews with selected individuals and made the bound transcripts available within the organization. An infusion of funding from one source to so many oral history projects simultaneously allowed project directors to gather, compare notes, engage in mutual education about professional practices, and consider ways to connect their work with public audiences. The new emphasis on dissemination has brought oral histories out of basements and archives and into such public venues and media as classrooms, films, historic sites, and scholarly publications, where they are positioned to influence public awareness and understanding of the internment from the perspective of those who experienced it.

The influx of funds also brought attention to diversity within Japanese Americans' experience of internment, as new oral history projects gave voice to the distinct experiences of Japanese Americans in the military, in the draft resistance movement, and in the campaign for redress, as well as those of Japanese Alaskans and Japanese Latin Americans. The Military Intelligence Services (MIS) Association of Northern California conducted thirty-eight interviews with Japanese Americans who had served in the MIS, and these interviews were later summarized in a video.[31] Sylvia Kobayashi conducted oral history interviews with Eskimo-Japanese Alaskans, while Grace Shimizu led the effort to interview Japanese Peruvians incarcerated during World War II. Many of these oral history projects included a public education component, and a new wave of scholarly publications, such as Robert Shimabukuro's study of the origins of the redress movement in Seattle, not only found a critical source of funding from CLPEF but also benefited from the oral history interviews conducted under CLPEF auspices.

In addition to supporting oral history research, CLPEF also funded research projects that adopted a more critical perspective on the question of historical memory. Alice Yang Murray's project " 'Silence, No More': Japanese American Internment, Redress and Historical Memory" focused on the evolution of memories and representations of internment and redress between 1942 and 1998.[32] Unlike most CLPEF-funded projects, which regarded first-person narratives as unproblematic forms of historical evidence, Murray's work recognizes that portrayals of the interment were shaped over time by the evolving political objectives of the redress movement in the 1970s and 1980s.

CLPEF closed its operations in August 1998, but its mission was extended by similar statewide projects in Washington[33] and California.[34] From 1999 to 2003, the California Civil Liberties Public Education Program (CCLPEP) awarded competitive grants to individuals, organizations, and units of government developing projects related to the incarceration of Japanese Americans. Among those employing oral history were Frank Abe's film *Conscience and the Constitution,* which highlighted the previously suppressed story of young Japanese Americans incarcerated at Heart Mountain in northwest Wyoming who refused to be drafted from an internment camp; Eric Fournier's documentary on the life of Fred Korematsu, who challenged internment orders; James Omura's memoir based on interviews conducted by Arthur Hansen; the JACL's interviews in the community of Florin; and Rita Takahashi's interviews with thirty-five Japanese Americans who were not incarcerated.[35] The raw materials of oral history also found expression in a wide array of creative endeavors funded by the CCLPEP: a musical composition built around digital samples of audiotaped interviews from the Japanese American Research Project (JARP) housed at the University of California, Los Angeles, a quilt, multimedia educational presentations, films, dance performances, and plays.[36] Buttressed by the compelling emotional quality of well-chosen oral history excerpts, the message of the redress movement reached new audiences in a wide array of creative forms.

Perhaps the most ambitious attempt to connect oral histories of the internment with public audiences is the Seattle-based Densho Project. Started in 1996, when the hope of financial support from CLPEF nurtured ambitious ideas for community history projects, Densho adopted digital technology as the basis for recording, indexing, and disseminating videotaped oral history interviews with Japanese Americans incarcerated during World War II. Over time Densho evolved from its initial goal of documentation into "a mission to educate, preserve, collaborate and inspire action for equity."[37] Inspired by the uses of technology in Steven Spielberg's "Survivors of the Shoah" project, Densho set out to record the memories of internment survivors on high-quality digital videos to ensure that the archive would be usable in film and television broadcasts. Beyond that objective, Densho's founders were determined to overcome problems of dissemination that have chronically plagued oral history projects by using the internet to guarantee widespread public access to its archive. By 2004 Densho had completed more than two hundred hours of interviews and had amassed over one thousand historical images with some financial support from CLPEF.[38] Much of this collection is publicly accessible from the Densho website.

The oral histories in Densho's and other collections did more than just fill gaps in the historical record. As Japanese American perspectives on the internment entered public awareness through the educational system, literature, the visual and performing arts, and mass media, they contributed to a transformation of public awareness, understanding, and interpretation of the meaning of this history. These personal testimonies countered official justifications for the internment and proffered moral judgments about the curtailment of civil liberties in times of national peril that differed profoundly from the ethos that had prevailed in America from World War II through the Cold War. Densho's website, for example, does not merely present the oral histories but also interprets their meaning from the standpoint of Japanese Americans, identifying four main factors that led to the internment of people of Japanese descent: the long history of racism in America, a failure of national leadership, wartime hysteria, and economic motives among those who stood to profit from the dislocation and dispossession of Japanese Americans. The website also provides teachers with readings and lessons that explore this historical event as well as the underlying principles of democracy that it engages. In this way, first-person testimonies have been positioned as resources in support of social change, intended both to transform public memory of the World War II incarceration of people of Japanese ancestry and to understand its meaning for current and future struggles for tolerance, equal justice, and civil liberties.

Not surprisingly, critical reflection on the interment has motivated leaders of the redress movement and directors of related oral history projects, such as Densho, to become vocal advocates for protecting the civil liberties of people of Middle Eastern descent in the wake of September 11. Linking racial hysteria after Pearl Harbor to racial profiling in the post-9/11 period, the founders of

Seattle's Densho Project, Scott Oki and Tom Ikeda, for example, used the platform of op-ed columns to suggest the need for Americans to learn from the past.[39] In particular, they have argued that it is a mistake to leap from suspecting particular terrorists to discriminating against an entire population based on a shared ethnic and religious heritage.

For Ikeda, Oki, and others engaged in documenting the losses, suffering, and injustice of the internment, this knowledge carries a moral obligation to promote tolerance, encourage respect for other cultures, and nurture democratic practices. Their public stand against discrimination has renewed relevance in light of Malkin's reactionary defense of internment.[40] In her view, the civil liberties of people from the same ethnic and religious backgrounds as terrorists must be modified, or possibly suspended, in times of great threat to national security, and revisionist historians who have condemned the internment are undermining current efforts to fight terrorism. Current controversy over the World War II internment of people of Japanese descent thus offers insight into what is at stake, both socially and politically, in the contested terrain of public memory. Just beyond the charged intellectual controversy over historical interpretation lies a higher-stakes debate over which values will govern public policies and practices in the civic realm.

Though the process of conducting oral histories has no doubt contributed to shaping memory within the Japanese American communities by moving many people from personal shame to a shared understanding and a more critical perspective on civil liberties, the oral history projects undertaken within these communities during the past three decades might have gathered dust on a shelf had they not been the cultural initiatives of a broader redress movement. For that reason, this particular story resonates with a theme also addressed by other chapters in this volume—the active role that oral history can play not only in reshaping public memories but also in advancing social change. In this case, oral histories of the internment have become inextricably linked to the project of protecting the rights of ethnic minorities.

The extraordinarily rich collections of personal testimony and oral histories have also provided documentary evidence for historians to utilize in a virtual outpouring of work on Japanese American history in recent years. While historians have re-examined early documents, particularly those produced by the exclusion movement, often reading them against the grain, they have also included more Japanese American sources in their work—oral history accounts, organizational records, and community newspapers—to balance the record.[41] Historical scholarship thus joins other vehicles for transforming public memory and represents one of the clearest acts of revisionism—directly challenging the long legacy of anti-Japanese sentiment cultivated in American popular culture, official documents, and public memory.

By giving voice to those who experienced history, personal narratives and oral histories have played a critical role in changing community and public memory of Japanese Americans in the twentieth century, and particularly of their World War II internment. What role might narratives and oral histories play in the future? Success in changing public perceptions both of Japanese Americans and of their experience of internment has allowed differences to emerge from within the community that previously were hidden from public view. A prime example is the longstanding conflict between the Japanese American Citizens League and those who resisted military service. More nuanced understandings of the varieties of experience and range of views that co-exist within ethnic communities ultimately may be the key to undermining the homogenizing force of racism, and of resistance, which relies on internal community discipline to present a united front against discrimination. The combination of individual and group experiences that emerges from oral history interviews with various segments of a community allows these commonalities and differences to come into view.

Oral histories allowed the Nisei to better understand both the hardships and accomplishments of their parents' pioneering generation, and to break the national silence on the interment experience. Having done this both within families and in the larger community, and having achieved substantial success in securing social equality, future generations may not feel the same need to interview their elders and scrutinize their history. If anything, the privilege of exploring personal identity may come into focus for the next generation. Hence, the popular periodical *Giant Robot* features narratives by youths irreverently focused on "Skateboarding at Manzanar," mocking the solemnity of Nisei treatments of the internment experience.[42] Impatience with the internment story and its cultural rituals—its pilgrimages, reunions, books, and exhibits—may indeed become a defining generational experience for the children (Sansei) and particularly the grandchildren (Yonsei) of the Nisei. For some people of Japanese ancestry, questions specific to other aspects of their identity will spawn public conversations: for example, out gay, lesbian, bisexual, and transgendered people of Japanese descent;[43] or Hapa, Asian Pacific Islanders of mixed heritage.[44] In each of these cases, individual identity is informed by several factors, making it difficult to construct future narratives of Japanese American heritage that are either as univocal as the official protests of the opening decades of the twentieth century or as choral in their coordination as the narratives of the redress era. The more complicated politics of identity in our own era, combined with high levels of personal access to recording technology and digital dissemination, suggest that polyvocality is likely to characterize Japanese American oral history—perhaps all oral history—and its many variants in the future.

NOTES

1. Gail Dubrow, "Deru Kugi Wa Utareru or The Nail That Sticks Up Gets Hit: The Architecture of Japanese American Identity, 1885–1942—The Rural Environment," *Journal of Architectural and Planning Research* 19 (2002): 319–33, esp. 329, citing "Japs Caught Drawing Maps," *Seattle Times,* 1 February 1908; "Picnic Shows There Are Many Japanese: South Park Residents Wonder Where All of the 2,000 Brown Men Who Met There Came From," ibid., 17 March 1908; "Mysterious Japanese about Vashon Island: Take Note of Topography and Prepare Map for Locating Batteries to Command Waterways," ibid., 24 February 1908; and "Jap Farmers Creating Alarm: Are Holding Mysterious Meetings at Night on the White River Farms and Whites are Perplexed: Lights Burned from Tops of Their Houses: Former State Land Commissioner Robert Bridges Says They Are Overrunning the Valley and Getting Control," ibid., 20 January 1908.

2. U.S. House of Representatives, 66th Congress, 2d Session, Committee on Immigration and Naturalization, *Hearings on Japanese Immigration Part 1, Hearings at San Francisco and Sacramento, California, 12, 13, and 14 July 1920* (Washington, DC: USGPO, 1921), 3.

3. The modal length of Japanese testimony, when transcribed, was between one and four pages. In contrast, Phelan's oral testimony filled nearly thirty pages. The additional Board of Control report brought his total contribution to 153 pages, or one-tenth of the whole proceedings.

4. The longest Japanese testimonies, at between thirty-three and 103 pages, including supplementary reports by the organizations they represented, were by K. K. Kawakami, a well-recognized publicist for Japanese interests in America; D. Matsumi, general manager of the [F]uruya Company; and K. Kanzaki, general secretary of the Japanese Association of America.

5. Kawakami had published at least five books prior to the 1920 hearings of the Immigration and Naturalization Committee, including *The Political Ideas of Modern Japan* (Iowa City: University Press, 1903); *American-Japanese Relations: An Inside View of Japan's Policies and Purposes* (New York: Fleming H. Revell, 1912); *Asia at the Door* (New York: Fleming H. Revell, 1914); *Japan in World Politics* (New York: Macmillan, 1917); and *Japan and World Peace* (New York: Macmillan, 1919). Immediately after the hearings he published the aptly titled *The Real Japanese Question* (New York: Macmillan, 1921).

6. Beikoku Seihokubu Hiroshima-Kenjinkai, *Ken No Hitobito: Soritsu Nijunen Kinen* (Tokyo: Beikoku Seihokubu Hiroshima-Kenjinkai, 1919).

7. On the ethical norm of group solidarity and survival, see Stephen S. Fugita and David J. O'Brien, *Japanese American Ethnicity: The Persistence of Community* (Seattle: University of Washington Press, 1991), 37–41.

8. Gail Dubrow, "The Nail That Sticks Up Gets Hit: The Architecture of Japanese American Identity in the Urban Environment, 1884–1942," in Louis Fiset and Gail Nomura, eds., *Nikkei in the Pacific Northwest: Japanese Americans and Japanese Canadians in the Twentieth Century* (Seattle: University of Washington Press, 2005), citing Kazuo Ito, *Issei: A History of Japanese Immigrants in North America,* trans. Shinichiro Nakamura and Jean S. Gerard (Seattle: Japanese Community Service, 1973), 148.

9. These narratives were collected under the rubric of the Japanese American Evacuation and Resettlement Study (JERS). The assistants included Richard S. Nishimoto, Charles Kikuchi, James Sakoda, and Tamie Tsuchiyama.

10. Lane Ryo Hirabayashi, *Politics of Fieldwork: Research in an American Concentration Camp* (Tucson: University of Arizona Press, 1999), 64.

11. U.S. Commission on the Wartime Relocation and Internment of Civilians, *Personal*

Justice Denied: Report of the Commission on the Wartime Relocation and Internment of Civilians, 2 vols. (Washington, DC: USGPO, 1982–1983); reprint ed., with a new foreword by Tetsuden Kashima (Seattle: University of Washington Press, 2000), xix.

12. Toshio Mori, *Yokahama, California* (Caldwell, ID: Caxton, 1949); Monica Itoi Sone, *Nisei Daughter* (Boston: Little, Brown, 1953); John Okada, *No-No Boy* (Rutland, VT: C. E. Tuttle, 1957).

13. Kazuo Ito, *Hokubei Hyakunenzakura* (Tokyo: Hokubei Hyakunenzakura, 1969); English ed.: *Issei: A History of Japanese Immigrants in North America* (see n. 8 above).

14. Ito, *Issei*, 980.

15. Ibid., 93.

16. Yasuo Sakata, *Fading Footsteps of the Issei: An Annotated Check List of the Manuscript Holdings of the Japanese American Research Project Collection* (Los Angeles: Asian American Studies Center, Center for Japanese Studies, University of California, Los Angeles/Japanese American National Museum, 1992).

17. Robert Sadamu Shimabukuro, *Born in Seattle: The Campaign for Japanese American Redress* (Seattle: University of Washington Press, 2001).

18. Ibid., 66–67.

19. Ibid., 70.

20. Kashima, "Foreword," xvii.

21. Ibid.

22. Ibid., xx.

23. Lillian Baker, *The Japanning of America: Redress and Reparations Demands by Japanese-Americans* (Medford, OR: Webb Research Group, 1991), 11. An insightful review of Baker's arguments can be found in Robert Ito, "Concentration Camp or Summer Camp?" *Mother Jones News*, 15 September 1998, http://www.motherjones.com/news/feature/1998/09/ito.html.

24. Michelle Malkin, *In Defense of Internment: The Case for Racial Profiling in World War II and the War on Terror* (Washington, DC: Regnery Publishing, 2004).

25. For a characteristic example of the selective use of photographs to buttress Baker's arguments, see *Japanning of America*, 176–86.

26. Ibid., 94, citing Takei interview in *Drama-Logue*, 24–30 January 1991.

27. David Guterson, *Snow Falling on Cedars* (New York: Vintage Books, 1995); and the 1999 motion picture *Snow Falling on Cedars* (videodisk: Universal Studios, 2000). The community's archives have been used to produce documentaries as well. See, for example, *Visible Target* (Chris Andersen, producer, 1985), a twenty-eight-minute video documenting the incarceration of Bainbridge Island's community.

28. For a description of the collection, see http://library.csus.edu/collections/jaac/overview.html.

29. Arthur A. Hansen and Betty E. Mitson, eds., *Voices Long Silent: An Oral Inquiry into the Japanese American Evacuation* (Fullerton: Japanese American Project, California State University, Fullerton, Oral History Program, 1974); Arthur A. Hansen, ed., *Japanese American World War II Evacuation Oral History Project* (Westport, CT: Meckler, 1991). For a description of the Fullerton collection, see http://coph.fullerton.edu/JAOHPAbout.asp.

30. *Regenerations Oral History Project: Rebuilding Japanese American Families, Communities, and Civil Rights in the Resettlement Era* (Los Angeles: Japanese American National Museum, 2000): vol. 1: Chicago; vol. 2: Los Angeles; vol. 3: San Diego; vol. 4: San Jose.

31. A ninety-minute video, *The Color of Honor* (Loni Ding, producer, 1989), documents

the experiences of Japanese Americans during World War II who served in the U.S. armed forces as translators and interpreters in military intelligence.

32. Alice Yang Murray, " 'Silence, No More': The Japanese American Redress Movement, 1942–1992" (Ph.D. dissertation, Stanford University, 1995).

33. In Washington, the Civil Liberties Public Education Project was established by the state legislature in 2000. This project made funds available through the State Office of the Superintendent of Public Instruction to: (1) educate the public about the history and lessons of the World War II exclusion, removal, and detention of Americans of Japanese ancestry through the development, coordination, and distribution of educational materials and the development of curriculum materials to augment resources currently available on the subject matter; and (2) develop videos, plays, presentations, speakers' bureaus, and exhibitions for presentation to elementary and secondary schools, community colleges, and other interested parties.

34. The purpose of the California Civil Liberties Public Education Program is to "provide competitive grants for public educational activities and the development of educational materials to ensure that the events surrounding the exclusion, forced removal and incarceration of civilians and permanent resident aliens of Japanese ancestry will be remembered and so that causes and circumstances of this and similar events may be illuminated and understood." See http://www.library.ca.gov/grants/cclpep.

35. Frank Abe *Conscience and the Constitution* (Hohokus, NJ: Transit Media, 2000).

36. For a description of the CCLPEP and lists of grant recipients, see http://www.library.ca.gov/grants/cclpep.

37. Website: http://www.densho.org/about/About.asp.

38. See http://www.densho.org.

39. Scott Oki and Tom Ikeda, "Japanese American Internment Not Justified," *Seattle Post-Intelligencer*, 12 August 2004.

40. Malkin, *In Defense of Internment*.

41. Scholarly works that have undermined official claims of military necessity for the internment and given voice to various aspects of the Japanese American experience during World War II include: Roger Daniels, *Concentration Camps North America; Japanese in the United States and Canada During World War II* (1971; reprint Malabar, FL: Krieger Publishing, 1993); Stephen S. Fugita and Marilyn Fernandez, *Altered Lives, Enduring Community: Japanese Americans Remember Their World War II Incarceration* (Seattle: University of Washington Press, 2004); Peter Irons, *Justice At War: The Story of the Japanese American Internment Cases* (Berkeley: University of California Press, 1983); Tetsuden Kashima, *Judgment without Trial: Japanese American Imprisonment during World War II* (Seattle: University of Washington Press, 2003); Greg Robinson, *By Order of the President: FDR and the Internment of Japanese Americans* (Cambridge: Harvard University Press, 2001); John Tateishi, ed., *And Justice for All: An Oral History of the Japanese American Detention Camps* (1984; reprint ed., Seattle: University of Washington Press, 1999); Jacobus tenBroek, Edward N. Barnhart, and Floyd W. Matson, *Prejudice, War and the Constitution: Causes and Consequences of the Evacuation of the Japanese Americans in World War II* (Berkeley: University of California Press, 1968); and Michi Weglyn, *Years of Infamy: The Untold Story of America's Concentration Camps* (1976; reprint ed., Seattle: University of Washington Press, 1996).

42. "Skate Manzanar," *Giant Robot* 7. The irreverent magazine, focused on Asian popular culture, was launched in 1994 by Eric Nakamura and Martin Wong.

43. The San Francisco International Asian American Film Festival, for example, which held its twentieth anniversary in 2002, featured numerous films by and about gay and lesbian Asian Americans.

44. Information and resources relevant to hapas are indexed at http://www.hapas .com/. The website includes a link to the Hapa Issues Forum, which is dedicated to enriching the lives of Asian Pacific Islanders of mixed heritage and developing communities that value diversity, also available at http://www.mixedasians.com.

8

"SCARS IN THE GROUND": KAURI

GUM STORIES

~

Senka Božić-Vrbančić

The gumfield is a memory place for me. Everything is completely different now but I can read scars in the ground. There were a lot of homes here . . . everybody shared the land. We all dug gum. People used to say that a shantytown was here. I don't call it a shantytown. I call it home.
MAORI WOMAN WHO AS A CHILD WORKED IN AHIPARA GUMFIELD,
NEW ZEALAND

Kauri gum is the fossilized resin of the massive kauri trees that once formed vast forests over the northern half of the North Island of New Zealand. From 1860 to the 1950s, kauri gum was used for oil varnishes, and gumdigging played an important role in the New Zealand economy. During the 1950s, when the gumdigging industry stopped because synthetic substitutes were created, most gumdiggers left the gumfields and moved to cities or nearby villages in search of new work. They left behind empty shanties and small huts, machinery used for digging and washing gum, schools they had built for their children, dancehalls, post offices. In short, places once populated by hundreds or even thousands became ghost towns.

New Zealand is full of ghost towns, places that were formed quickly as a result of industries such as gold mining and gumdigging and deserted in an instant when the industry stopped. Very often these dead economies of the past have found a place in local heritage museums, where they usually come to represent the pioneering era of British immigrants in New Zealand. In this chapter I examine a triptych of kauri gum stories as they are told in three different museums: Matakohe Kauri Museum, which tells the official story of the kauri gum industry in New Zealand, focusing mostly on the British gumdiggers; the Jurlina Museum, a family museum concentrating on the story of Dalmatian gumdiggers who initially settled in New Zealand at the end of the nineteenth century;[1] and the Yelash Gumfield Museum, which presents the story of the Maori, the indigenous people of New Zealand, and their relationships with Dalmatians on the gumfields.

Maori and Dalmatians were the two largest non-British groups on the gumfields of the Far North. Both groups experienced stigmatization, which simultaneously excluded them from the dominant culture and constituted the condition for their relationship to one another, including a significant number of intermarriages. The stories about Maori and Dalmatian encounters on the gumfields have not been recorded in official New Zealand history but have stayed within the local community, transmitted orally from one generation to the next. As the industry ceased to exist, only to become memorialized in museum exhibits, Maori and Croatian memories of this era became part of their identity, often full of descriptions of the weird objects used for digging gum, and the people and shanties that once filled the gumfields. These memories very often take highly emotional forms: images of grandparents, souvenir pieces of kauri gum, stories told by people who once lived in the gumfields, very often laced with a nostalgic longing for lost moments of happiness. Here I compare the kauri gum stories as they are told in two private Maori-Dalmatian museums—institutions that are not on the official list of New Zealand museums—to the story on display in the Matakohe Kauri Museum. I visited these museums several times and conducted nine in-depth interviews with their owners and employees. Their stories differ widely, but a parallel reading reveals many similarities. All of them chart not only the power relations that existed in colonial New Zealand, but also the antagonisms and forms of struggle that exist in the country today.[2]

Matakohe Kauri Museum

WELCOME TO THE KAURI MUSEUM! Our displays tell the story of the magnificent kauri tree, its timber and its gum. This was a very important part of pioneering in northern New Zealand. . . . [The museum] provides a stimulating insight into New Zealand history.[3]

Matakohe Kauri Museum opened in 1962 as a memorial to the district's pioneers and gumdiggers. Visitors are encouraged to see the Sterling Family Wing (Mervyn David Sterling was a founder of the museum), the Smith Family Wing (named after one of the first British settlers in Matakohe), the Tudor Collins Wing, and the Bob Ross Family Wing. Using tableaus and dioramas, the museum tells us "little stories" about the day-to-day experiences of the early pioneers and their indoor and outdoor life. A large space in the basement

Fig 8.1   Mannequin of the "happy gumdigger" at the Kauri Museum, Matakohe, North-land, New Zealand, 2002. *(Photograph by Senka Božić-Vrbančić.)*

houses the kauri gum collection, a gumdigger's shelter,[4] a saw mill, and old machinery once used in kauri milling. Next to the glass cases where kauri gum pieces are displayed is a "typical gumfields scene" with two life-size man-nequins, modeled after real people (Fig. 8.1).[5] On the wall behind the figures is a framed poem:

> *The happy gumdigger who lived in shack*
> *Ti tree for a bed and a mattress of sack*

He worked at times just when he wished . . .
An era has gone of the gumdigger's boom . . .
For the happy gumdigger of yesterday.

Visitors are constantly reminded that everything they see is displayed with the intention of showing what "real life" was like in early New Zealand history. But this "early New Zealand history" is represented only through the "real life" of four British families. Thus the stories these four British families tell about the past are now understood as part of the regional collective memory. Roger Mulvay, director of the Kauri Museum, explains that those four families donated the materials and set up the displays and therefore can be seen as the "museum makers." But it would be naïve to believe that the "museum makers" are the only ones responsible for the content of the museum and the politics of its exhibitions. Artifacts, photos, panels, and captions are organized in the Kauri Museum in accordance with a larger ideological project of creating a New Zealand identity. Let me explain this point. The Kauri Museum was built in 1962, before the policy of biculturalism or multiculturalism was publicly discussed.[6] At that time the most common story of national identity, expressed by various politicians, was that of the unity of peoples in one nation.[7] This story of integration was based on the European ideal of a homogeneous national culture, but, as in all settler societies, in New Zealand this notion was also connected to the transplanted culture of the mother country, Britain. At the beginning of the kauri gum industry, the majority of gumdiggers were Maori. Maori in the Far North who traditionally depended upon cultivation of the land worked as gumdiggers when the crops failed; and Maori from other parts of New Zealand sometimes traveled north to earn and save some money. During the 1880s, the worst years of a long economic depression in New Zealand, many European settlers were also forced to find seasonal work such as gumdigging. At the same time, because the kauri gum market was well established in the American and British markets, the gumfields attracted individuals from around the world. However, the goal of colonial New Zealand was to establish a proper settler society. The development of land was understood as the only possible means of progress, and a high value was placed on a stable domestic life, strictly gendered work roles, abstinence from alcohol, and other markers of middle-class life. In that context the gumfield industry was seen as one that could not produce long-term prosperity. The nature of gumdigging, moreover, required diggers to move from field to field in search of gum, and most were men. Given the nomadic character of the job, everyone who worked as a gumdigger, including English, Scottish, Irish, Maori, Italian, Croatian, or Chinese workers, was suspected of being "wild" and "problematic." Any person who moved to the gumfields was held in general contempt and considered to have slipped to the bottom of the economic and social ladder. But in the Matakohe Kauri Museum, gumdiggers are clearly incorporated within the pioneering myth: the world of the ideal colonizer, who in emigrating to New Zealand, had "a chance to face life in the raw, to show courage and physical strength."[8] The message is clear: the beginning was full of hardships, but despite this gumdiggers had a good life and succeeded in establishing a community.

The museum's construction of the gumfield way of life includes a large selection of photographs, which provide contexts for the objects and machines on display. Yet there are few photos of Maori and Dalmatian gumdiggers. The labels tell us only that both groups were present on the gumfields and that they developed a "harmonious" relationship working together. We also learn that Dalmatians were very honorable and industrious. But the labels do not tell us that both Dalmatian and Maori gumdiggers were stigmatized and stereotyped. In the nineteenth century more than three thousand Dalmatians worked on the gumfields.[9] They, like Maori, lived and worked in groups, in contrast to the mostly solitary British diggers. Ironically, their industrious habits were seen as a threat to the British gumdiggers. In contemporary newspapers, both Maori and Dalmatians were very often described as "locusts on the gumfields."[10] They were represented as a "horde of barbarians," "the scum of earth," and "inferior races."[11] In 1989 the colonial government responded to these fears by introducing the Kauri Gum Industry Bill, which restrained the movement of Dalmatians to the gumfields. In 1908 and 1910, the government passed additional restrictive laws, and many Maori and Dalmatian gumdiggers were pushed to work in the most isolated areas of the Far North. But the history of British treatment of Maori and Dalmatians, which formed the basis for their relationship, is erased by the main narrative of the Matahoke museum: "locusts on the gumfields" have magically become a model of the "pioneer and indigenous harmony" favored by New Zealand's more recent ideology of biculturalism and multiculturalism.

Following Foucault, we can say that the Kauri Museum narrative demonstrates the relationship between knowledge and power.[12] One of the very few photographs of Maori and Croats working together in the gumfields is labeled "Allan McPherson, Dalmatian gumdiggers and Maori assistants." The caption makes clear what the museum believes is important for visitors to know—the hierarchical order of groups. When I discussed this with one of the museum's attendants, he suggested that I visit Drago Yelavich, a barber from Kaitaia, who could tell me the names of the people in the photo. It seems that the absence of Maori and Dalmatian names is not a concern of the museum.

In short, the Kauri Museum demonstrates that the interest in remembering the past is always an interest in building public memory in the present, and that this memory-building depends on the social relations of power. We could say that the kauri gum story is part of the system of preserving a past that represents New Zealand as a working paradise for British immigrants. The story of Maori and Dalmatians sits on the margins of this idealized story. It lies at the center, however, of the past represented in the Croatian and Maori private museums to which I now turn.

The Jurlina Family's Gumstore-Museum

In the Jurlina family's little shanty in Sweetwater, formerly a gumstore, numerous memorabilia of the gumdigging era and the Dalmatian community have been preserved. The Jurlinas, Milan and Victor, have tried to preserve the past by leaving everything intact. In the little tin shack that used to be dragged by oxen from one gumfield to another and in a large warehouse nearby, everything remains as it was—a museum?

Claustrophobia is soon replaced by an expansive feeling as a whole new world opens up—the world of Dalmatian gumdiggers. On the wall are shelves full of books; above them is an old calendar; in the corner are several different scales for weighing kauri gum, an old phonograph, and a large box of beautiful samples of shiny kauri gum covered with transparent plastic. They have to be kept in the dark to preserve their shine, so Milan Jurlina covers them with a potato bag. There are all sorts of odds and ends, including small bottles. A bottle of wine dated 1929 has the inscription "The Kingdom of Slovenians, Croats and Serbs" and, on the label, a Social Realist drawing of a village girl drinking a glass of wine. Underneath a little window, a table holds boxes filled with Maori carvings; on the wall by the window hangs an old Austro-Hungarian passport; on another wall crowded shelves hold piles of dangling yellowed paper—orders and contracts for Holland, Germany, Sweden, and Denmark, where the Jurlinas sold kauri gum (Fig. 8.2). There are various books: a prayer book in Croatian entitled *Marijin Mjesec* [Mary's Moon], published in Croatia in 1891; *Zivotopis kraljevica Rudolfa*, a biography of Prince Rudolf; and a book by the Croatian poet Petar Preradović, published in America in 1901. And finally there are many invoices, piles of record books, lists of Croatian names, Maori names . . . and photographs.

My informants, Milan and Victor, comment on the objects on display. Maybe the word "display" is inappropriate, since these items are not arranged in any special way. Things have simply accumulated and been stored here for almost one hundred years. Victor shows me some objects and then carefully returns them to the shelf. Any displacement would produce an irrevocable chaos, the collapse of this little microcosm. But each of these objects is associated with particular memories, and soon, while Victor's and Milan's hands carefully

Fig 8.2. Milan Jurlina in his family's Gumstore-Museum, Sweetwater, New Zealand, 2002. *(Photograph by Senka Božić-Vrbančić)*

examine every nook and cranny, I am flooded with stories and anecdotes about the people who were once involved in this almost forgotten industry:

> Victor: When you come here you can almost dream what it was like in the past. . . . My father used to sit on this chair late into the night filling in the ledger books. . . . This place is full of memories, of things forgotten and people who were once here and they have all gone.[13]

Names can be followed through the old ledger books from the moment gumdiggers were signed in: how many dollars they borrowed, how many kilos of kauri gum they sold, how many kilos of flour and sugar they bought. Looking through the old papers, Victor starts to read some names: "Petričević Ilija, Stanić Šime, Nizić Mate, Tomasović, Jerković, Jelaš Ivan . . . Jurkušić Ivan. . . ."

Victor pauses after each name, adding a ceremonial dimension to his recitation, and after a few minutes Milan starts to comment:

> Jurkušić Ivan, you know . . . he died here, never got married, didn't even want to get married. The Brajkovićs . . . later went into the wine business. The Urlićs, a large family . . . yeah . . . Simon Urlić married a Maori woman. Nicholas Čović married a Maori woman too. . . . There are photos here, plenty of photos. There was an Englishman here, Northwood, and he was a photographer, took thousands of photos.

The Jurlinas keep photographs in a wooden box under the table. Some of them are copies of those exhibited in the Kauri Museum, but here, in the little gumstore, these photos evoke quite different meanings. First of all, they do not serve to provide a context for objects that are on display, since the objects here are not divorced from their original context as they are in the Kauri Museum; they are already in their authentic place. Second, the photos have no written labels to guide visitors, just stories told by Milan and Victor that were passed down from their father and other gumdiggers and that bring life to each photo. Milan starts with a photo of his father, Kleme:

> Father came out from Dalmatia in 1903, aged fourteen. He had two pounds spending money for the journey, yet after four years he'd set up as a trader. He came to his uncle. The choice was between one uncle in America and one in New Zealand. The situation at home was bad—a peasant country with others taking over—not good futures. They were called Austrians, but they came to get away from the Austrians. They were called square-heads too. . . . After a few years of being here Dad helped bring others out from Dalmatia. The intention was to come and make money and go back, but Dad never went back . . . like all those others . . . Srhoj, Ujdur, Grebić, Belić. . . . They had a good life here. . . . There was social card playing and dances like the *kolo* done in a circle. . . . Between North Cape and Kaitaia there were fifty big shops. There were five billiard saloons in a range of five hundred meters around here. The circus would come around . . . , and one-man entertainments like silent movies, violinists, and magicians.

When I asked Victor and Milan about Dalmatian relations with Maori, they continued with a new series of stories:

> Milan: Dalmatians got on well with Maori . . . both gregarious and both a bit outcast. It was always easy to communicate, and there was a

lot of intermarriage. . . . Dalmatians got on well with the Maori from the start, but not with British . . . the British diggers didn't like our people.

Victor: There were many Maori girls around and just a few British girls. I think that the ratio was ten diggers to one girl . . . and that's why Sweetwater was called "girls' paradise." There were many dancing halls around but British girls avoided Dalmatians . . . so many married Maori or brought their fiancées or families from Dalmatia and all of them became respectable settlers. . . . See these wedding photos here.

Each photo is accompanied by a story, and each story cross-references other things "exhibited" in the museum. However, Milan and Victor do not like to use the word "museum" for their father's gumstore. For them, it is a special place, a place of memory:

Victor: This is a memory place for us . . . and we haven't actually encouraged visitors . . . but anyhow people who come here have an interest. . . . Usually they have some relations with something recorded somewhere here . . . there are so many names recorded here . . . and when someone comes in and mentions the name and says my grandfather was so and so . . . and we go through the books and find that name . . . it is like a dream . . . it is like catching a big fish. . . . It gives them a great satisfaction to see a little of the history of their family.

Unlike the Kauri Museum, where the story of gumdigging could be seen as a political construct of the time, the Jurlinas' little gumstore appears as an outstanding example of what Pierre Nora refers to as a "private" site of memory—a "place of refuge," where one finds "the living heart of pure memory."[14] In that little gumstore, it looks as if no time has passed; things are kept without regard for what is typical or representative. But it would be naïve to think that Victor and Milan's stories are unaffected by the colonial discourse that linked gumdigging with the pioneering myth and the making of New Zealand. Traces of the mythologizing found in the Matakohe Kauri Museum surface in the Jurlinas' narrative as well:

Victor: Dalmatian gumdiggers were treated badly by the British . . . but gradually, because of their industrious habits and because they were mostly honest men, they were accepted into the society, and many of them moved to the cities and became successful wine-makers, and some of them were successful politicians . . . for example Jim Belić was the mayor of Wellington . . . and Cleme Simić . . . very respectable people. . . . There is a historian Trlin and he published a book, *Once De-spised Now Respected.* Yeah . . . our people have done a great job in this country. . . . They started with nothing, but now they are respected.

The story of hardship on the gumfields has become an icon of Croatian cultural identity in New Zealand, an identity rooted in hard work and also in the strength and growth of the community. The Jurlinas' story becomes one of success and acceptance. In this context Victor and Milan's stories do not escape the pioneering discourse that legitimizes the effort to establish their group identity in New Zealand. And as in many other diaspora museums, the story of living in a new country told at the Jurlina museum simultaneously opens questions about displacement and memories of the homeland.

At the end of our interview, Victor showed me a photograph of a group of "old-timers," gumdiggers who decided to stay and die on the gumfields. In the early 1950s only a few Croatian diggers were left on the Sweetwater gumfield. They were receiving state pensions, their shacks were on state land, and they had the right to use them for the rest of their lives. Victor particularly likes the story about old Jure, who lived all his life in a little shanty. At the age of eighty he had no food, he had no friends, he had no family. There was some gossip that Jure had had a child with a Maori woman. He dreamt about his homeland every day; he wanted to die in Dalmatia. Victor's father, Kleme, who used to visit Jure once a month, decided to buy him a plane ticket. Kleme was busy the week he bought the ticket, and when he went to see Jure, he found his dead body in front of the shanty. Jure had very few belongings: some old yellowed letters written in Croatian, a cigarette case, a few family photos, barely enough money to cover the cost of the funeral. His letters and photos are in the Jurlinas' museum. One of the photos is a portrait of a young Jure, dressed in his Sunday best. That picture was probably taken to be sent to his family in Dalmatia. In another picture, taken on the gumfields, Jure's clothes do not fit well: his shirt is dirty and too small, and his hat is clearly too large. When Victor finished his story and silently looked at this photograph of Jure, I saw tears in his eyes.

On one level, Victor tells the life story of one gumdigger; on another level, through his imagination, fantasies, and memories, he makes meaning of his own identity. Like most Croatian immigrants in the late nineteenth and early twentieth centuries, Jure sought a better life for himself and his family. By immigrating to New Zealand, "the workers' paradise," Jure became the other, the foreigner, the displaced person. He worked hard all his life, but he had no money. Wanting his family in Dalmatia to see a different picture of his life, he sent them the portrait of the well-dressed Jure, not the gumdigging photo. If a photograph freezes one moment in time, then these images of Jure give us two moments connected by his desire. The questions to ask here are: For whom is

Jure enacting these roles? Whose gaze is imagined through these photographs? Whose gaze is imagined when Victor Jurlina tells the story of Jure's life?

As an old man, Jure still felt like a newcomer, an immigrant. Stressing the importance of the old man's wish to die in Dalmatia, Victor emphasized the doubleness of Jure's life, and of his own. When he talks about his own life, it becomes clear that his story is dominated by the stories of the previous generations, by memories that are not his own:

> Where you came from is what you are . . . and finally we came from Croatia and that influence is still here. You look at photographs and you see *baba* [grandmother] and *dida* [grandfather] up there and you know how it all started. And you can't forget about Croatia, even though I my-self have never been there, but it makes you realise that you are part of a different land in some way . . . and when you hear the *tamburica* play, for example, or old songs like "Daleko mi je biser Jadran" ["The pearl of the Adriatic is far away"], it is not just a song. . . . It is a song that goes through the heart. . . . You feel it. . . . It is more than a pleasant song, it is a song of feeling.

Memories of the first generation of Croats in New Zealand have become the memories of their children, creating the multi-placedness of home. But this multi-placedness in the imagination of Croatian descendants does not mean that they do not feel anchored in the place of settlement. Of course they do, but their anchoring is like a daydream in which past, present, and future are strung together on the thread of the wish that runs through them. Their attachment to New Zealand establishes itself as a continuous search for full identity.

Yelash Gumfield Museum

The Yelash Gumfield Museum is located on the top of Ahipara Hill, beyond huge, golden sand dunes. Among local people in the town of Ahipara, the hill is known as Opoka, one of the last gumfields in New Zealand. The Yelash Gum-field Museum is not in tourist books or on maps. In the course of my research, I found a few articles in old newspapers about Toni Yelash, the last gumdigger in New Zealand, who decided to stay and live by himself on the Ahipara gumfields and make a museum dedicated to Maori and Croatian gumdiggers where he could house his various gum machines, tools, samples, and other memorabilia. But he died in 1982 in his small tin shanty, and the museum project remained unfinished. In 1998, when I was in Ahipara interviewing some Maori-Croatian descendants, I decided to look for remnants of Yelash's shanty museum.

The road from Ahipara to the Opoka gumfield meanders over barren and broken country. The soil is a grayish-white sandy clay, and all that seems to grow is thin, scrubby *manuka*.[15] The hill rises into a gloomy, barren plateau. It is a bleak and desolate place. I was overwhelmed with a feeling of emptiness when suddenly I saw an old corrugated iron shack with a signpost in front of it: "Yelash Gumfield Museum." The door was open, but nobody was there—an abandoned museum on the abandoned gumfields. It started to rain, and I decided to stay for a while in the museum. Inside I felt almost as if I was in the Jurlinas' museum: bottles stacked on dusty shelves, a gramophone from the 1920s, a wooden mask, pieces of kauri gum sorted in boxes, a gum scale, newspaper clippings, and on the wall a photo of an old Toni Yelash. On a small table in the corner were many old letters written in Croatian, some from the 1930s but mostly from the 1940s. Next to the table was a boxful of photographs, mostly of Maori and Croatian gumdiggers along with some Maori family portraits. I felt like an intruder in the abandoned museum, surrounded by photos and letters that seemed unread, as is the history of Maori and Croats who are tied to this area.

The next day in Ahipara I was told that Yelash's grandsons live in a shack close to the museum. I went back, eager to find its owners. This time a young Maori man opened the door of the museum and introduced himself: "I am Tony Yelash, a grandson of the old gumdigger Toni. Welcome to our gumfield museum" (Fig. 8.3).

Tony explained that his grandfather spent almost all of his life in that shanty. He came to New Zealand from Dalmatia in 1926, when these vast hills were just beginning to be recognized as the rich gumfield of the Far North. In the late 1940s, as the price of kauri gum started falling and the golden days of the Ahipara Hills began to fade, endless rumors spread that the gumfields would be depleted or that the demand for gum would cease overnight. Naturally, gumdiggers began to abandon Opoka. It did not happen quickly; the industry died slowly. Many gumdiggers switched to farming, but Toni Yelash kept digging. Finally, his shack was the only thing left on Ahipara Hill. Toward the end of his life Toni started to dream about a museum and took some initial steps to establish it. But he died before his project was finished:

> When my grandfather died, my father wanted to continue with the museum project. We got some money from the government, we made plans, paid professionals to make plans, wanted to employ a lot of people, our local people, Maori. . . . We proposed a big project, and an important part of the project was accommodation for visitors who wish to stay and take in the unique atmosphere of the gumfields. We wanted to build small cosy shanties for visitors, styled from the original type that the gumdiggers used, and we wanted to build a large *marae*-style[16] accommodation unit for groups to stay. We wanted to provide a venue

Fig 8.3. Tony Yelash, right, with his brother Leroy and their children in front of the Yelash Gumfield Museum, Opoka, Ahipara, New Zealand, 2000. *(Photograph by Senka Božić-Vrbančić)*

for those who wish to study this unique environment by way of accommodation, walkways, information, and identification of trees, plants . . . for individuals and groups. We had many meetings in our local marae in Ahipara and at the end, nothing . . . the government decided to stop everything. . . . Why . . . I cannot tell you. . . . I think it's the land issue. . . . Some of this land is Maori land, but some is still the crown's land. . . . Of course, we Maori want our land back . . . and the government stopped the museum project. My father left because there are no jobs available for us here in Ahipara, but I decided to stay, I renovated the shack, I mean I just turned the shop into a museum . . . and I think that I am doing history here, I am telling stories about our way of life, Maori way of life . . . and gumdigging was our way of life. I read a lot of books, and I tell you, I am well prepared to be a guide.

The Yelash Museum project, in line with the new museology, aimed to attract visitors to consume the gumdigging way of life, to stay in replicas of gumdiggers' shanties for several days and relax by digging gum. At the same time gumdigging was to be represented mainly as a Maori way of life, inherited from the Maori past. A dead economy was supposed to be reborn as a tourist destination. But the project did not attract outside support, and the Ahipara gumfields are not even on the New Zealand map. And Tony, as his grandfather once did, hosts lost tourists who somehow manage to find his museum. Tony acts as professional guide and expert on the kauri gum industry and, most importantly, on Maori culture. He starts his story with Maori mythology, the creation of the mythical homeland Hawaiki, and Tane, the god of the forest. He showed me a photo of a huge kauri tree (*Tane mahuta*), and he explained how kauri forest once covered much of Aotearoa (i.e., New Zealand) but then disappeared: "Nobody knows what really happened, but when Pakeha [the Maori name for the mainly British settler population in colonial New Zealand] arrived they destroyed the last pockets of the forest." Maori knew that kauri gum was valuable and used it for several purposes—as a treatment for vomiting and diarrhea, as a firelighter, on torches used for attracting fish, and so on. But, again according to Tony, Pakeha destroyed everything. They discovered that gum could be used for varnish and linoleum and started to exploit it. Many Maori worked as gumdiggers in order to survive:

> After signing of the treaty in 1840, Pakeha did everything to destroy Maori. Maori didn't have money, they lost their land, so they did gumdigging. Gum supplied cash and many Maori families survived because of that. My people, Te Rarawa, dug gum from the beginning of the industry, but Ahipara gumfield become known during 1920s, during the depression time in New Zealand. I say that for Maori the depression time started already in the 1840s, after signing of the treaty, but in books on New Zealand history you can read that the Depression was in the late 1920s.... Anyway ... during the 1920s this gumfield attracted *Tarara* [Dalmatian] people.... I mean Opoka is a Maori gumfield, but during 1920s many Tarara joined Maori to work here.... Tarara were oppressed by Pakeha, but Maori welcomed them. For example, my grandpa is from Dalmatia, he came in 1926.... Within a few years, Opoka had become a boom town with a population greater than Kaitaia and there were one thousand diggers here.... I think that there were more than four hundred Tarara gumdiggers here. Yeah, as I said, those were depression days in New Zealand, but in Ahipara my grandpa and many others prospered.[17]

Tony explains how by 1940 there was a gumtown with a few shops, billiard rooms, dancehalls, a school, a hotel, postmaster, fire brigade, and many gumbuyers' offices:

My grandpa became a storekeeper and gumbuyer. He also was one of the men who helped to organise and supervise the road-building. You know, at that time the road between Opoka and Ahipara didn't exist. Every time gumdiggers had a dance my grandpa collected money for the road. It was his grand idea, the great road that would finally connect gumdiggers with the harbour at the foot of Ahipara Hill.

At the end of the interview, Tony took me on a tour around the gumfields. He showed me where the vanished town once sprawled, where the houses, saloons, and school were. He pointed with his finger as if the old shanties and houses were still there: "Try to imagine . . . try to picture . . . use your imagination and you will learn much about Maori and Tarara gumdiggers." But all I could see was tall grass and scrub. It looked as if nobody had lived there for a thousand years. But for Tony, every square meter was unique. There were a thousand landmarks for him, and each one told a story:

Here, where the soil seems to be raised in a line, was once a dam. See that fig tree . . . there was Yelavich's house. Many Tarara planted fig, olive, and lime trees, they had small vineyards behind their shanties. My grandpa said to us that Tarara smelled of garlic, which was constantly eaten, thanks to the old belief that it can cure heavy colds and many other diseases. . . . See there . . . that was a billiard room . . . and here Maori used to have *hangi* [an earth oven]. . . . They were good pig hunters and they did fishing. Maori were always good fishermen . . . they also did shark fishing. . . . Fish was eaten smoked or dried. . . . And there . . . there Maori had vegetable gardens . . . people cultivated kumara, potatoes, and corn.

Tony read the land. He picked up gum along the way, explaining its origin and quality. He talked about Maori being guardians of the land, the only people in New Zealand who are actually linked to the land and can read its different layers. He explained the special meaning of Ninety Mile Beach as the location of the pathway along which, according to Maori mythology, the spirits of all Maori dead must travel to reach their first and final home, Hawaiki. The journey of spirits starts in Ahipara. He talked about *tapu* (sacred) places around the gumfields, and he finished with a story about how the New Zealand government does not care about the Maori past and presents Maori culture in its own way, which is not the Maori way:

What I want to show here is that the Maori way of life survived. . . . Many Maori who live in the cities are not real Maori. They know nothing about

Maori culture. They transformed into Pakeha. I cannot speak Maori as well, but I want to learn. One day I will be able to talk on the marae. . . . Our elders here say that we, young Maori, cannot speak on the marae because we cannot speak the language . . . but that's not right. . . . We cannot speak because we have never been taught our own language. . . . It's not our mistake . . . but I'm going to school now and I'm learning . . . to be able to fight against the system. You have to know your own culture . . . and my culture is in my blood. . . . I have strong Maori blood as well as Tarara blood.

Heritage, according to David Lowenthal, is commonly understood as passed on in the blood, determining the character and fate of individuals and groups.[18] Heritage seen in that way is used widely by both dominant and dominated groups, the majority as well as minorities. Tony sees his heritage as rooted in dual allegiances: to the Te Rarawa tribe, which justifies his position as a guardian of the land, and to his Croatian grandfather, which has made him a lonely curator. But this emphasis on the strength of Maori and Tarara blood plays a much bigger role in Tony's worldview than just essentializing and legitimizing what he sees as oppressed cultures. It functions as a tool in the wider struggle of his community on issues such as unemployment, land rights, and Maori education. For Tony, the Pakeha oppression continues, and he links Maoriness with suffering and resistance and distinguishes between true and false Maoriness. True Maoriness is not entirely based on tradition (he cannot speak Maori) but on resistance to oppression, and if some Maori do not resist, for Tony they are transformed into Pakeha, misled in their true identity. In this way the social order is represented as the division between oppressed and oppressors, and the connection of Maori and Tarara on the gumfield is understood as a brotherhood, a relationship of oppressed peoples who resisted Pakeha domination.

When I asked Tony about his grandfather's relationship with his grandmother he said:

How did my Grandpa meet Grandma? I am not quite sure. People say that he had a wife in Croatia . . . and children. . . . They are my relatives . . . I suppose, but I don't know anything about them. . . . Here he lived with my grandma, and when she gave birth to my father, he said, "Lipi je," which means, "He is beautiful" in Croatian language, and that's how my father got his name—Leapyear—which is pronounced in the same way as Croatian "lipi je." . . . There are plenty of Granddad's letters in the museum, but I cannot read them . . . they are written in Croatian language. . . . You know, there were many Tarara here

and they lived together with Maori, no problems at all. . . . Nice people . . . everyone says that . . . Pakeha didn't like Tarara, so, many
Tarara experienced oppression and they connected with Maori . . .
that's really how they started to live together . . . that was the only way
to survive.

Tony represents the Maori and Croatian way of life on the gumfields as resistance to the Pakeha system, and as he struggles to retain the memory of his
forebears, he highly romanticizes their relationship. The next day Tony invited
more than sixty of his relatives and friends to meet me. All of them were connected with Maori or Tarara gumdiggers who once worked on the Opoka
gumfield. A hangi was prepared, and while some of the older women spoke
nostalgically about their childhoods on the gumfields, Tony asked me to read a
few of his grandfather's letters. Most of the letters were from Croatia, from
Yelash's family, but some were written by Dalmatian gumdiggers who were
working on other gumfields. In one of them, one of Yelash's friends who was
working on the Mangawhare gumfield wrote:

Dear Toni . . . I hear that you have many Maori friends there, but I also
hear that you live with one Maori woman. People talk about that. That's
not good, Toni. You know that everyone in this country who lives with
natives cannot make money. In general, natives are known to be lazy
and they are not able to save any money. Remember, the natives were
cannibals . . . and the house with the black woman's hand in it is not a
good house. . . . It is a disgrace and I hope that you will soon change
your mind. I am writing this for your own good. Some of our people
married Maori, but I know that many of them made a big mistake. . . .
They are going to stay poor forever . . . and we are here to make a better
future for us. . . . We suffered a lot in our own country and there is no
need for us to suffer again. . . . My advice—stay away from Maori.

I felt uncomfortable reading this letter to Tony, but he smiled and said:

See, that Tarara was writing under the influence of Pakeha. . . . See
how Pakeha were working against us. . . . They wanted to destroy our
brotherhood but they haven't succeeded. . . . They were only partially
successful and this letter is proof of that . . . and it's still going on. . . .
Pakeha think that they are superior, I'm sick and tired of being told by
Pakeha who I am and what is my culture. . . . I know where I come
from. . . . I know my past . . . and this museum project is not just
about our past, it's about our present as well, it is about our future. The

government blames us because we are unemployed, they say that we
are radical and have marijuana farms . . . but at the same time they
don't want to support this project, they don't want to give us the possibility to work and live here, on our land. . . . They lock our culture into
their own museums . . . we are removed from their maps . . . so
tourists cannot find us . . . but a few months ago we had more than
twenty Germans here . . . and they will be back. . . . They liked what
they saw . . . and they'll send others. . . . We'll survive.

Though *on* the frontier, the Yelash Museum is not a museum *of* the frontier; though enmeshed in immigrant histories, it is not a diaspora museum;
though on Maori land to which a contemporary tribal community is attached,
it is not only a tribal museum. James Clifford writes about museums as contact
zones, spaces where a relationship between peoples who came into contact historically becomes, usually through the museums' collections, "an ongoing historical, political, moral relationship—a power-charged set of exchanges, of
push and pull."[19] Even though we can analyze both the Kauri Museum and the
Jurlinas' Museum as contact zones, for in both the exhibited objects provoke
ongoing stories of struggle, in my view it is the Yelash Museum that most represents this notion of a museum as a contact zone. It is an ongoing site of
struggle for control of the past, as well as the present and future. It evokes
Maori history before European contact; it provokes memories of colonization,
land alienation, and displacement, of an industry that has disappeared, and of
Dalmatian gumdiggers and their contact with Maori; but most importantly it
is a site of ongoing conflict and negotiation of identity.

In this chapter I have analyzed the story of the kauri gum industry as it is
told in three museums. Even though these three narratives look completely different from each other, they actually have much in common. All are preoccupied
with establishing a particular group's position in the social order. The Matakohe
Kauri Museum is the official site of memory, where the story is framed by notions of colonial history and the pioneering era of New Zealand, and where the
representation of the kauri gum industry is part of a larger ideological project of
creating New Zealand identity. The Jurlina Museum and the Yelash Museum are
voices from the margins, voices ignored by the official history, voices that reveal
the gumdigging past in a new way. They have not been imposed on communities
from above by the government or some official organization; they are not tourist
destinations; they are not on the map of New Zealand; but still, as I show in this
chapter, they cannot be seen as sites "where the living heart of memory beats,"
since both describe the antagonisms that have beset Maori and Dalmation
gumdiggers while trying to establish the kauri gum story. Pure memory exists
neither in official nor in marginalized sites of memory. Clearly, through pro-

cesses of remembering, the gumfields have gained new meanings for both those who are included in official representations of the past and those who are on the margins; they have become a kind of invisible living memorial through which the past is constantly negotiated. These three museums are hybrid places, where different groups of people establish ongoing relations. Of course, as Clifford has emphasized, these are not relations of equality, but what I want to stress here is that all three museums use the kauri gum story in their own way as a constitutive element in the formation of collective identities. In short, the kauri gum story becomes a site of social struggle.

NOTES

1. Today, Dalmatia is a province of the Republic of Croatia. In the nineteenth century, when the first groups of Dalmatians were arriving in New Zealand, Croatia was part of the Austro-Hungarian empire, and even though Croats were never treated by Vienna as Austrians, in many parts of the British empire immigrants from Austria-Hungary were simply labeled as such.

2. Ethnographic field research for this chapter was conducted as a part of a more comprehensive research project on the relationships between Croats and Maori in New Zealand. In the course of my research, I interviewed many Maori-Croatian gumdiggers and their descendants. All of the interviews addressed similar themes: New Zealand history, life on the gumfields of the Far North, positions of Maori and Croats on the gumfields, personal biography, family life, and so on. Different elements of my own identity as a Croatian woman recently arrived in New Zealand became significant during the research. As it turned out, my ethnicity and gender were very important for many of my Croatian informants, who felt that I was "one of them," sharing the same cultural background and a similar "foreign" status in New Zealand. In a similar way my Maori informants positioned me as a non-British (non-Pakeha) person, which had implications for our interactions.

3. M. D. Sterling and J. C. M. Cresswell, "Otamatea Kauri and Pioneer Museum" (Matakohe: Matakohe Kauri Museum, 1985).

4. As gumdiggers moved around the various gumfields, they typically lived in small, often temporary camps. Some camps, however, were large enough to become permanent settlements. Gumdiggers worked from dawn till dusk. They went out with a spear (used to probe the ground and locate the gum), spade, and *pikau* bag to dig by day and scrape by night.

5. The two gumdiggers, Steve and Bob, are set in a corner against a mural backdrop of the gumfields, artfully drawn to portray the vast, barren fields, "a typical swampy, scrubby area where the gum was found." The museum director told me: "The models are extremely good, life-like replicas of local pioneers and provide a sometimes eerie insight into past lives."

6. Today New Zealand represents itself as bicultural, a product of the historical interaction of two peoples: Maori, the indigenous people, and Pakeha, the mainly British colonial population and their descendants. Diversity is celebrated over sameness, multiplicity over monoculturalism. These new bicultural and multicultural policies have nurtured a re-examination and rewriting of New Zealand history and a re-emergence of suppressed memories.

7. Andrew Sharp, *Justice and the Maori: The Philosophy and Practice of Maori Claims in New Zealand since the 1970s* (Auckland: Oxford University Press, 1997).

8. Jock Phillips, *A Man's Country? The Image of the Pakeha Male* (Auckland: Penguin, 1987), 5.

9. More than half a million Croats were part of the European migration to America at the beginning of the twentieth century, the biggest exodus in Croatian history. Suppressed by Austrians and Hungarians, even in the 1900s many Croats lived under a remnant of the old feudal system, and Dalmatia, more than other Croatian lands, experienced hard times. As emigrants flooded into New World countries, a small trickle ended up in New Zealand, usually on the Far North gumfields.

10. "According to the majority of the diggers, the greatest pests of all are the Austrians [Dalmatians] who are now flocking to the different fields" (*Supplement, New Zealand Herald*, 25 March 1893, p. 1). "Since the Austrians have passed over like locusts, it is impossible to earn a living" (*New Zealand Herald*, 29 April 1898, p. 3). "This field, as well as others between this and Auckland, is flooded with Maoris, who come from as far as the Waikato and the King Country, also from the North, in crowds—men, women, and children—who are covering the hillsides like swarms of locusts, sweeping all the gum before them, so that shortly there will be none left for the legitimate European digger, who at the present time of retrenchment has nothing else to look to for a livelihood" (*Weekly News*, 19 May 1888, 14).

11. Senka Božić-Vrbančić, "Celebrating Forgetting: The Formation of Identities and Memories by Tarara in New Zealand" (Ph.D. diss., University of Auckland, 2004), 204.

12. Michel Foucault, "Truth and Power," in Colin Gordon, ed., *Power/Knowledge: Selected Interviews and Other Writings 1972–1977* (New York: Pantheon, 1980), 109–34.

13. All quotations from Victor and Milan Jurlina, as well as those from Tony Yelash in the next section, are taken from interviews conducted by the author between July 1999 and 2002; the tapes and transcripts of the interviews are in the author's possession. The interviews with the Jurlinas took place in the village of Sweetwater in the Far North of New Zealand; the Yelash interviews took place in the village of Ahipara.

14. Pierre Nora, *Realms of Memory: The Construction of the French Past*, 3 vols. (New York: Columbia University Press, 1996), 1:19.

15. The Manuka tree (*Leptospermum scoparium*) is unique to New Zealand. The trees are often found in harsh terrain exposed to strong winds and salt air.

16. *Marae* is a meeting house with open space in front of it.

17. The Maori name for Dalmatians is "Tarara." Maori listeners were attracted by the sharp "r" in the Croatian language; they also termed the land from which Dalmatians emigrated Tarara (thus Williams's dictionary of the Maori language refers to the land between Italy and Greece as Tarara). See Hans Peter Stoffel, "Slaviches in Polynesian zum Serbokroatisch-Maorisch-Englischen Sprachkontakt in Neuseeland," *Selecta Slavica* 12 (1988): 344–58.

18. David Lowenthal, *The Heritage Crusade and the Spoils of History* (Cambridge: Cambridge University Press, 1998).

19. James Clifford, *Routes, Travel and Translation in the Late Twentieth Century* (Cambridge: Harvard University Press, 1997), 192.

9

MEMORY AND MOURNING:
LIVING ORAL HISTORY WITH QUEER
LATINOS AND LATINAS IN SAN FRANCISCO

Horacio N. Roque Ramírez

> *The politics of mourning might be described as that creative process mediating a hopeful or hopeless relationship between loss and history.*
>
> DAVID L. ENG AND DAVID KAZANJIAN[1]
>
> *The violence we encounter is relentless, the violence of silence and omission almost as impossible to endure as the violence of unleashed hatred and outright murder. Because this violence also desecrates the memories of our dead, we rise in anger to vindicate them. For many of us, mourning becomes militancy.*
>
> DOUGLAS CRIMP[2]

More than one decade ago, on a hot and sunny August afternoon in 1994, I crossed the Oakland–San Francisco Bay Bridge into that grand and gayest City by the Bay. I was moving from Los Angeles, having come out as a gay man only three years earlier, and yearning for personal adventure and excitement, perhaps a new life. While I was moving formally to begin graduate studies at the University of California, Berkeley, across the bay, I was really going next door to San Francisco, a twenty-four-year-old gay Latino wanting to taste the history of the city's gay past and queer present, however mythic or exaggerated.[3] But I was also somewhat afraid of San Francisco, for I knew that it was one of the epicenters of the AIDS epidemic, even more so than Los Angeles. To be gay in the early 1990s, in the age of AIDS, meant to think of erotic pleasure alongside risk and of the real possibility of early death, just as it had occurred for hundreds of thousands in the 1980s. To be gay in the age of

AIDS also meant mediating between the celebration of gay sexual consciousness and these fears and anxieties over desire, our bodies, and life.

To land in San Francisco as a gay *Latino* in the mid-1990s was to arrive in the midst of queer community loss and destruction. But at this time there was also a specifically queer Latino and Latina renaissance in the making, with a new generation of artists, health workers, educators, and activists forging a varied culture and politics of visibility and identity. There remained also the artifacts, memories, and ghosts of the dead among the living. An earlier generation of community members, activists, and cultural workers had passed on through the ravages of AIDS, while a younger queer Latino body sought to reflect on those losses and what it needed to do to remain alive. As a community, we were forced to ask questions. How do we narrate simultaneously these politics of mourning, the passions of our queer lives in the present alongside the recognition of the loss of bodies just like our own? How do we become part of a productive process of mourning that activates our sense of hope for survival? Finally, how do we make public our memories of the missing, claiming their loss as part of our histories of the present?

In this chapter I reflect on this process of memory and mourning based on an extensive oral history project I conducted with queer Latinas and Latinos in the San Francisco Bay Area starting in the mid-1990s.[4] Specifically, I discuss the dilemmas I encountered as a community researcher and academic oral historian wanting to document and record memories of the living amid trauma, suffering, and ongoing uncertainty over the community's future. I then consider how oral history facilitates the activation of public memories, literally the collective, communal practice of facing loss while transforming it into processes of healing. Finally, I discuss the layers of memory and truth that oral history unearths, and how public memorial events serve as further moments where oral culture builds community history.

Background

The mid-1990s marked a distinct historical juncture for many of us younger queer activists, artists, and scholars: we came into sexual consciousness in part thanks to at least two decades of gay liberation, lesbian feminism, and Third World and nationalist radicalisms, but, at the same time, we had to consider the decimation of parts of those queer generations, mostly gay and bisexual men and male-to-female (MTF) transgender women.[5] Among the dead were many of the men who helped to build San Francisco's Gay Latino Alliance and the Third World Gay Caucus; those who were from the Bay Area or who landed there in the 1970s and made their way to the historic 1979 Gay March on Washington, D.C., as part of the large Third World Gay March contingent;

and the men and transgender artists in the famed gay Latino strip of San Francisco's Latino barrio, the Mission District.[6] This gay Latino bar strip, 16th Street, more commonly referred to in Spanish as *la dieciséis*, had been a popular destination since 1979, when the first openly gay Latino bar opened its doors. However, while those of us interested in these earlier histories, spaces, and leaders knew of their existence, the larger public simply did not recognize them. The intersection of narrative exclusions was all too clear: queer historiography of the Bay Area remained white, while the Latino historiography of the region—what there was of it—erased the queer specificity of our lives.

Such narrative exclusions were in part a product of the success of the identity-based liberation politics of earlier decades. While the social and protest movements of the 1960s and 1970s professed racial and gender inclusion and all-round liberation from all forms of oppression and exclusion, essentialist practices were the norm: the Black Power and Chicano movements were essentially male-controlled, patriarchal, and homophobic; and the feminist and gay and lesbian movements were overwhelmingly white and middle-class.[7] The conceptualizations of gay as white and Latino as heterosexual that emerged pitted "gay community" against "Latino community." Such diametrically exclusionary conceptualizations, of course, were simply inaccurate and outright offensive for those women and men inhabiting these social markers at one and the same time: Chicana lesbians, Puerto Rican gay men, Cuban male-to-female transgender performers, and so on. In historical practice, these intersecting narrative exclusions worked their way into publications, libraries, and archives: even now (though this is slowly changing), what publications there are about gay and lesbian/queer Bay Area history and the gay and lesbian archival repositories remain generally white, and Chicano/Latino and ethnic studies historiography, libraries, and archives similarly privilege heteronormative experience and struggle.[8]

When I began to record oral histories in the spring of 1995, it was by no means the first time anyone had taken an active role in documenting life and loss among queer Latinos in San Francisco. Local, community-based, artistic and cultural productions had, since the mid- to late 1980s, recorded the lives and labors of a dying generation. Overwhelmingly, these grassroots initiatives sprang out of the desperation and desire to address HIV and AIDS, those directly and indirectly affected by the disease, and the fears and active forms of denial of much of the queer and straight Latino community—including many community leaders in the nonprofit sector. It is critical to note that up to the early 1990s, there were no significant medical treatments available.[9] My project therefore was rooted in an effort to document life at the moment of its loss.

Many narrators recall their exhaustion, physical and emotional, from attending funeral after funeral. In this period of death and despair, queer visibility and identity took on greater dimensions for the mourners. Thus, annual celebrations such as the PRISMA Awards (1987–1991), the brainchild of the late gay Chicano activist Rodrigo Reyes (1945–1992), served as fundraisers for the street-based HIV education outreach project he founded, CURAS (Comunidad Unida en Respuesta al AIDS/SIDA—Community United in Response to AIDS/SIDA). These performing events showcased the artistic talents, political gains, and survival of queer Latinos and their allies in the local community. Yet another gay Chicano activist and cultural worker, the late Henry "Hank" Tavera (1944–2000), similarly coordinated cross dressing/drag shows on *la dieciséis* to raise funds but mostly to keep knowledge about HIV risk and sexual safety alive in this queer Latino bar community. His "We Will Survive" annual safe sex shows (1989–2001), sponsored by his organization California LLEGÓ (Latino/a Lesbian, Gay, Bisexual and Transgender Organization), were reminders of the ongoing epidemic. Similarly, the gay Mexican immigrant activist Gustavo Martín Cravioto, with the support of the Mission health agency Instituto Familiar de la Raza, used *la dieciséis* to create awareness around HIV through the queer beauty and talent contests, "Mr. and Mrs. Gay Safe Latino" (1996–present). On still-larger scales, Tavera coordinated his annual Performing Arts Show of Latino/a Gay, Lesbian, Bisexual and Transgender Artists (1990–2000), while QUELACO (Queer Latina/o Artists Coalition) established a tradition through its annual Queer Latina/o Arts Festival (1990–present), both held at the Mission Cultural Center for Latino Arts (MCCLA). While attendance at these community gatherings has varied from standing-room-only to sporadic (sometimes as a result of adversarial stances taken by some of the organizers against one another), they symbolized an active process of celebrating queer Latina and Latino lives while the community was still in the midst of mourning.[10]

One generation later, my own oral history project represented activist cultural work in the service of memory. Like the PRISMA Awards, it recognized and documented queer Latino community life. But whereas my oral history project sprang from the historical experience of AIDS, unlike PRISMA it was not always bound to HIV, AIDS, and loss. My own queer Latino political birth took place in this context of risk, desire, and community loss, but the oral history project brought forth narratives that included the larger experiences of migration, forms of cultural and political activism, and a sense of the future. Still, AIDS, and the geography it marked locally through suffering and loss, created an affective experience for which cultural work remained one of the most important means of responding.

Several factors combined to make my oral history project possible. First, although I had begun graduate work in Comparative Ethnic Studies and History at UC Berkeley, researching gay Chicano/Latino history, I was finding no primary sources. There were clues and bits and pieces in the literary works of John Rechy, Arturo Islas, Cherríe L. Moraga, and Gloria E. Anzaldúa, but no fuller accounts of queer Latino community life in historical perspective. En-rolling in a graduate research seminar on oral histories and immigrant com-munities in spring 1995 grounded for me the methodology I would use to document and analyze community life. At this point I also became aware of the foundational working-class lesbian oral history, *Boots of Leather, Slippers of Gold* by Elizabeth Lapovsky Kennedy and Madeline D. Davis.[11] This exemplary community study helped me imagine what was possible through oral history, and convinced me that it was not too late to begin to look at my own commu-nity's history. Last but most crucially, just as I enrolled at UC Berkeley in 1994, through my activism I had entered and slowly become part of San Francisco's dazzling queer Latina and Latino community.[12] In sum, I was able to tap into the academic resources of an educational institution as well as the social and cultural capital of a broad-based LGBT/queer community of Latinas and Lati-nos willing to support this oral history effort. Thus, while the project was to be part of my doctoral work and dissertation, it would also be received in other forms by the community at large.

Recording Life and Loss on *La Dieciséis*

To commit to recording loss and destruction requires courage and the recog-nition of one's own fears: to face histories of sexual desire in our communities while knowing the forms of silence, denial, and erasure that still challenge the reality of our lives.[13] One graphic example of this was the literal loss of com-munity members from the public bar life of the community. The significant loss of this vibrant community sector through the death of many female-impersonating artists and MTF transgender performers and many patrons, turned *la dieciséis* into a local repository of ghosts and memories. To record and rescue even part of this queer Latina and Latino history of San Francisco and its Latino barrio, two young gay Chicano artists, Valentín Aguirre and Augie Robles, took the initiative to video and make an audio record of a wealth of community oral histories. Through their twenty-three-minute video docu-mentary, *¡Viva 16!*—a multilingual collage of voices, images, and life narratives on this gay Latino strip—Aguirre and Robles created a collective portrait that highlighted the dazzling contours of gender, desire, race, and nationality within this queer urban landscape.[14] While men—queer and some straight—predominated on *la dieciséis*, lesbian and bisexual Latinas, butch and femme, and (mostly) MTF transgenders also turned to this strip with regularity. Speaking about their video documentary, Aguirre notes:

> *¡Viva 16!* was a way to give back, to my friend Francisco [Zamora] who had died. And after Rodrigo [Reyes] had died, it was a way for me to

reconnect to 16th Street when it was most painful to walk down the street because my friend Francisco lived on 16th. So all of it. There's just steps where there's so much death. Cindy Lu was a drag queen that lived like half a block from here [on 16th Street] . . . who killed herself on Valentine's Day. So just walking down the street became extremely painful. *¡Viva 16!* was personally my way I was giving myself back to my past.[15]

In Aguirre's narrative, what is central is the proactive process of turning loss and mourning into documentary action, a conscious project of historical self-giving. This return to a public self provided a way to remember community life through the traces of death (and life) in narrators' recollections rather than remain stuck in the loss itself. What he chose to undertake was a community-based enterprise necessarily dependent on the memories of those who, like him, were mourning one another, with the result that he was also allowing them to enter into this queer dialectic of historical self-giving in the age of AIDS.

As Aguirre recalls further, once *¡Viva 16!* was completed, the video became a reflection of multiple queer community dynamics, just as the production itself had been dependent to some degree on other community members' contributions to the documentation of local life. The archival artifacts—including family photographs, organizational flyers, and newspaper clippings that narrators had kept since the 1950s—evidenced the cross-generational roots of the community. However celebratory the sense of community has been since the 1960s, the relationships among all these members have not always been smooth. Yet, as Aguirre explains, the desolation that came with AIDS signified a common experience of loss to which all were responding:

[The community] wanted to see [*¡Viva 16!*] out there. And it did get out there on a limited basis—film festivals, universities, organizations, events and on 16th Street for sure. So that was great. I got to interview Ronnie [Salazar] right before Ronnie got sick. I have lots of footage from Ana Berta Campa who's extremely helpful in giving me access to all of her footage; she had like 10 years of footage—greatly indebted to her. . . . We had great political fights. She and I have had separations just like past separations with Rosa Maria Zayas and Rodrigo [Reyes], and then re-connections. . . . It was a time of such devastation where the street was being devastated and people were just desperate. I remember an air of desperation around too, "Oh, we're losing history, we're losing history as we speak. And if you will have the time and the stupidity to go ahead, to think you can document some of it, put it together, then please do. I will help you." And that's what happened.[16]

Fig 9.1. Chicano activist Rodrigo Reyes, c. 1990. *(Courtesy of Luis Alberto Campos de la Garza and the Archivo Rodrigo Reyes; photograph by Del Toro.)*

The unfolding devastation was directly in relation to the actual deaths from AIDS. In these two brief recollections alone, Aguirre invokes the lives and deaths of four queer Latinos and Latinas with whom he had shared part of his life in the Mission District—Francisco Zamora, Rodrigo Reyes, Cindy Lu, and Ronnie Salazar (Fig. 9.1). But community destruction was also in the form of memory loss—"we're losing history as we speak." *¡Viva 16!* thus became a means through which collective speech acts mitigated against the devastation of silencing.

Oral history for public memory functions at least on two levels. On one level the oral histories themselves narrate life and loss; on the other, these oral histories produce public events that allow audience members to build on them through further dialogue within themselves and with one another. Avery Gordon explains that in social analysis, conjuring has a central place in our mediation of life material and its faint traces and memories. "Conjuring," she argues:

> is a particular way of calling up and calling out the forces that make things what they are in order to fix and transform a troubling situation.

As a mode of apprehension and reformation, conjuring merges the analytical, the procedural, the imaginative, and the effervescent.[17]

In the troubling personal and collective historical moment of community destruction that was queer Latino San Francisco in the 1980s and 1990s, to conjure through oral history was to invoke the dead and the still living, "to fix and transform" the troubling bridges between all of us. Recording for the very first time his life history, and how it feels to be a survivor living with AIDS while hundreds of other gay Latinos had died in the previous fifteen years, for example, allows a narrator to make public the presumably private struggles of being queer and of color. For a Chicana lesbian narrator moving to the Bay Area in the 1980s, conjuring the memory of her late gay brother entails positioning herself as the teller of his stories, those he never told while living.

Aguirre narrates his own process for making ¡*Viva 16!* Just walking down 16th Street had become painful, he recalls, feeling and recalling the ghosts in the queer Latino streets of San Francisco. Although I, a Los Angeles transplant in the mid-1990s, had been spared this direct experience of queer community loss, I became a conduit for re-enacting the meaning of that loss through the public oral history project. Like Aguirre, other narrators recalled how walking down a familiar Mission street, or having a drink at a local bar in the heavy absence of close community friends, took them back to that challenging relationship between loss and history. These powerful memories of their lives that narrators constantly described in the interviews are the "ghostly matters" that Gordon believes are critical parts of social life. "If we want to study social life well," she argues:

> and if in addition we want to contribute, on however small a measure, to changing it, we must learn how to identify hauntings and reckon with ghosts, must learn how to make contact with what is without a doubt often painful, difficult, and unsettling.[18]

It was in the spirit of studying my own community well, and contributing in what may be only a small measure, that I undertook this project in the mid-1990s. In the more than one decade since its beginnings, I feel the most productive work has occurred at the public gatherings where we have reflected on memories and community records and dealt with the difficult and painful process of remembrance. Two public events stand out: the first annual PCPV's [Proyecto ContraSIDA, Pro Vida, or Proyecto Por Vida ("For Life")] Awards on 16 September 2001, days after the attacks on New York and Washington, and the QUELACO Visual Art Exhibit, held in June 2002.[19]

Activating and Returning Memories 1:
The Por Vida Awards at Proyecto

In the spring of 1995, when I formally began the first phase of my project by recording oral histories in relation to AIDS, I faced great trepidation among potential narrators and within myself about what it would mean for all of us to tap into memories that centered on suffering, pain, and death. Despite the fact that health agencies and grassroots community efforts continued to challenge silence and denial with HIV educational campaigns and street outreach projects, the simple truth was that many of us were still afraid to talk honestly and openly, in nonstigmatizing ways, about our sexual longings and needs and how they related to AIDS.

At the same time, the project was also about analyzing through these oral narratives the intersections between race, sexuality, culture, and immigration. The recorded memories constantly shifted between the personal experiences of the narrators and the public lives they lived with others in the community. Thus, a narrator was as likely to share the details of her erotic encounters at a bar as another was to show his collection of flyers from a gay Latino political organization. In the mediation between the personal and the public that emerged in the narratives, it became yet more clear to me how effective oral histories could be for building public memory.

Thoughts and feelings about risk, AIDS, and desire were easier to approach in the company of others less afraid to embark on a frank historical discussion of their erotic lives. Meeting the late MTF transgender artist and live singer Alberta Nevaerez (1940–2002), better known to the community as Teresita la Campesina, was a turning point in my project and in my life (Fig. 9.2).[20] As a long-term queer survivor already living with AIDS by 1994, Teresita symbolized a living queer Latino history spanning six decades. Born in 1940 in Los Angeles to a large working-poor Mexican family, Teresita—in those days, the young Alberto—confused his family with his already powerful singing voice. It was this talent, together with her legendary sexual escapades and all-round loud mouth, that took Teresita to numerous performing venues across California and beyond: restaurants, bars and clubs, health agencies, private homes, organizational meetings, and the street. It was the fact that Teresita had a big mouth about her own life and often—to their detriment—about others that created a living narrative of her queer life, especially in surviving AIDS. Public about her HIV-positive status, about living with AIDS, and always and repeatedly invoking the dozens of friends she had already lost to the disease, Teresita helped keep alive the reality of AIDS and our community's mourning for its losses. As one of the most vocal narrators in my oral history project and in the community at large, Teresita certainly did not have

Fig 9.2   Transgender artist and singer Alberta Nevaerez/Teresita la Campesina. *(C. 1985, (Courtesy of Luis Alberto Campos de la Garza and the Archivo Rodrigo Reyes; photograph by Rodrigo Reyes.)*

to wait for the tape recorder to be on to share the memories and meanings of her life.

I met Teresita at Proyecto ContraSIDA Por Vida (PCPV, or simply "Proyecto"), the same place where I met several other, usually much younger narrators. This queer HIV Latina and Latino agency in the Mission District supported a corps of artists and activists to devise creative strategies for addressing HIV and AIDS.[21] Steadfastly multigender, sex-positive (non-sexually stigmatizing), and neighborhood-based, Proyecto became a critical bridge between different generations of queers. Just as Teresita, already in her late fifties, made her way to Proyecto to use the telephone, get some water to take her medications, talk to staff, and not dwell in further queer isolation, many queer Latino teens and those of us in our twenties came into the agency as volunteers, clients, or supporters of this new vision. While sitting on a couch, we listened to Teresita's (in)famous tales about her struggles and triumphs as a transgender Latina live *ranchera* singer.[22] For an oral historian, there simply could not have been a better community ally than Teresita. She was vocal about the historical links between the living and the dead, the queer and the straight, and the multiple geographies she herself had lived and shaped as a queer pioneer long before AIDS. Just as she celebrated and entertained, Teresita was also living in mourning.

Teresita enabled me to meet and eventually interview others (such as Manuel Castillo, better known as the cross-dressing Mission performing legend "Ookie la Tigresa") who had shaped gay Latino space since the 1950s. I began to uncover as well a forgotten visual record in photographs, news clippings, diaries, flyers, scrapbooks, and other materials that they still kept. In every single one of my interviews with these "elders," AIDS and the mourning it signaled were central anchors in their memories: when they first heard of the new "gay disease" spreading in the Castro District; who was the first beloved bartender on *la dieciséis* to die; the persistent and convenient denial that a "gay white men's disease" could affect the Latino community; or the often charged debates about who did and did not actually die from AIDS. These interviews were archaeological explorations, digging for facts, names, dates, and places, as much as they were confrontations with others' memories of the epidemic.

As I proceeded with the project, concerns grew over what to do with the oral narratives, and also the visual, material record that I had been gathering, as narrators, like Teresita herself, grew sicker. While the dissertation was going to be one of the outcomes, I knew that more accessible public creations were in order. Oral history projects like mine, which interact with the academic world and with community life and death, mandate that we think critically and in explicitly political ways about what we do with our intellectual labor. Dozens of narrators had made a significant investment to bring the oral history project to life in the first place; as a community member myself, it was simply a question of personal and professional responsibility to engage the community with the results of our collaboration.[23] Thus, as I began to complete the phase of gathering oral histories, I took advantage of queer, Latino, and queer-Latino community gatherings to showcase the "memory footage" that would allow collective reflections on queer Latino life and death.

In 2001, to raise funds and to bring Proyecto's work and vision back to where they had been years earlier, the agency coordinated the first annual Por Vida ("For Life") Awards. As a way to celebrate the life of the agency itself, its work in the community, and the local leaders, activists, and artists who continued to support the queer Latino community, the event gathered hundreds of queer Latinas and Latinos and straight allies on 16 September in the Mission, a Sunday evening less than a week after 9/11. Given that this was to be a multigenerational and multigendered gathering of Proyecto founders, current staff, allies, and extended local and regional communities, it was the ideal space in which to "return" to historical and contemporary roots: *before* AIDS, and *in* AIDS. Mourning and celebration would go hand in hand, with the living, with those living with HIV or AIDS, and those struggling in every way possible against the disease's stigma and its destruction—that is, all who were collectively experiencing hope and loss.

Putting together an oral history–based audio and video presentation that could do justice to the years-long project was impossible during this time of transition between doctoral and postdoctoral work. The half-hour Power Point presentation I eventually organized was actually part of a multidimensional performance about community life.[24] I worked for months gathering hundreds of images, editing them to highlight key individuals, historical events, and places, and preparing the digital computer presentation. But I also knew that someone like Teresita la Campesina, with her powerful voice, backed by live *mariachis*, would—literally—bring to life for the audience the meaning of life, loss, and survival represented in the images. Thus, as image after image, alongside descriptive text, filled the large screen at Theatre Artaud, Teresita and the Mariachi Jaliciense delivered from the stage in front of the screen a powerful medley of *rancheras* songs. Because these songs in Spanish evoked strong popular sentiments of loss, love, and longing, and were performed most passionately by one of our queer community elders and a masterful storyteller, they worked well with the visual record of life and loss. As women and men in the audience heard and saw queer Latina and Latino history performed and displayed, including images of queer community members lost to AIDS, they processed the multiple meanings of these narratives and affective encounters.

"Returning" history to those who allowed its reconstruction in the first place is not easy. For communities long held in narrative, cultural, and politi-

cal exclusion, to get history "wrong" yet again through a public event is potentially dangerous. Crossing but also bringing together time and space, the public memory that places oral history alongside visual culture allows for creative
reflection about historical meanings. An audience member who had been one
of the best-known MTF transgender performers on *la dieciséis* since the late
1980s shared her emotional excitement and pain when witnessing and listening to the performance. Others who had never seen a public, collective presentation of these images but were aware of the oral history project also
communicated their support for more public gatherings to acknowledge these
historical precedents. Although I generally arranged slides in chronological order, the clustering of several subjects—such as gay Latino political mobilization, HIV prevention efforts, and gay Latino bar life—allowed audience
members who were reflected in the slides to reinterpret their place in this
retelling. This reassessment of one's place in history is part of a larger political
process for social change whereby different queer genders and generations
(and their allies) consider both the work completed and that yet to be done. At
the same time, and specifically in the conjuring and mourning of the dead
among the living, there is a therapeutic process for audience members living
with and surviving AIDS as they reflect on their lives. As audience members
gathered informally for hours after the performance of this history, their conversations activated community memories. Over coffee and dessert, or juice,
wine, and beer, attendees told one another where or when they had first met a
cross-dressing performer from *la dieciséis*, now deceased; the name of a "survivor" from the pre-AIDS generation who remained alive; or how important it
was to continue producing similar events. This dimension of the Por Vida
Awards was a coming together of living oral history, public memory, and community reflections about itself.

For queer communities of color generally not part of the national historical imaginary, these public gatherings are key moments for celebrating accomplishments. Similarly, because the national imaginary reduces "significant
memory" to the lives of heteronormative white leaders, events that produce
queer public memories of color are that much more crucial. Events like the Por
Vida Awards also call for community members to come together and put differences aside, if only momentarily. Personal animosities based on previous
disagreements over different organizational visions or strategies are suspended; and agencies that periodically compete for resources can appreciate
together the need for at least an occasional form of celebration. Finally, because queer Latino life and death are after all about the survival of bodies and
their distinct historical desires, these gatherings offer yet more opportunities
for erotic belonging among queer women, among queer men, and among
queer women and men, thus rebuilding community presence.

Activating and Returning Memories 2:
The QUELACO Visual Art Exhibit

A second event the following year again brought to life Teresita's memories of self and community and allowed the entire community to engage with them. "Dándole la Cara a la Historia: La Cara y la Boca de Teresita la Campesina" (Face-ing History: Teresita's Face and Mouth), a photo-text installation, was part of the annual QUELACO production of a LGBT Latina and Latino visual art exhibit. "Face-Ing History" was a multigenerational collaboration based on memories and archives. Once again, it was the exclusionary practices of regional archival and library collections that prompted me to look to the narrators themselves to provide documents and other materials related to their lives and the lives of those around them. Because queer collections failed to recognize the wealth of queer lives of color, and racial or ethnic collections had yet to pay attention to material culture from queers of color, the oral history project came to include archiving as well: identifying, organizing, and using a myriad of materials from narrators' collections. It was through this dynamic process of combining oral historiography with archival work that I found in a local collection the portraits that made "Face-Ing History" possible. More than anything else, it was also the need to remind the community that the elder Teresita was growing sicker that pushed me to act quickly on behalf of this specific facet of our queer Latino public memory.

In the early 1990s, one of the few known collections of gay Latino materials in the Bay Area belonged to Luis Alberto Campos de la Garza, a student at the University of California, Berkeley, and a staff member at the Chicano Studies Research Center Library. Since his arrival in San Francisco in 1987, Campos de la Garza had taken the lead in gathering materials related to queer Latino life regionally and nationally, including some from his home state of Texas. When his close friend Rodrigo Reyes died from AIDS in 1991, Campos de la Garza inherited Reyes's personal collection of unpublished manuscripts, correspondence, art, photographs and slides, posters, and ephemera. Once he had organized this collection as the "Archivo Rodrigo Reyes," Campos de la Garza began to consider where he could deposit it, negotiating the delicate balance between public access and preservation.[25] After meeting Campos de la Garza in the fall of 1994, I began to use the Archivo Rodrigo Reyes to supplement the oral history narratives I was gathering.[26] There I found by chance a set of undeveloped film negatives from the 1980s that, upon processing, revealed a healthier Teresita with a penetrating, elegantly mocking stare.

In the spring of 2002, as Teresita's condition worsened, there was no time to lose. Applying for funding support of any kind was not an option time-wise; personal resources had to be mobilized to develop the slides into the graceful framed portraits they became. Alongside Teresita's transcribed memories of escapades and struggles, the portraits would create a visual narrative of queer Latina survival across six decades of the twentieth century. Even though professional and personal demands had forced me to relocate to Los Angeles by this time, I chose the Bay Area for presenting a public display of the life and history of Teresita and, through her, the life and history of queer Latina and Latino life in the United States. The postdoctoral fellowship I held at this time, with no teaching requirements, allowed me the time to dedicate to this project for queer Latino public memory.

Public memory events and projects require planning, resources, and, most of all, a space. The timing of my serendipitous discovery of Reyes's black and white photo negatives coincided perfectly with QUELACO's 2002 production of the LGBT Latina and Latino visual art exhibit for that year's gay pride festivities. I formally proposed "Face-Ing History" for the exhibit, knowing that it would take place in the heart of the Mission District, at the easily accessible Mission Cultural Center for Latino Arts (MCCLA) building.[27] This is the building at which LGBT Latina and Latino artists and activists have been "queering" since the 1980s, usually in connection with the gay and lesbian pride events held in June. Several bus lines, the nearby metro station, and a constant flow of foot traffic day and night make the MCCLA a highly visible community site for displaying and experiencing art, culture, and politics. As such, it is a pivotal place for enacting queer Latino public memories on several levels: as queers in the historically Latino barrio; as Latinas and Latinos dealing with notions of queer history, survival, and community presence in the city; and as participants in queer *and* Latino life in the present.

Through "Dándole la Cara a la Historia," part of that year's QUELACO's Queer Latina/o Arts Exhibit, Mission District residents had the opportunity to reflect on the images and memories of a local legend, one whom many of them had placed at the center of their oral histories of gay Latino life in the city. Eight framed transcribed excerpts and the eight black and white portraits of Teresita made up the installation at the MCCLA. Based on the oral history Teresita had recorded with me in previous years, the excerpts outlined several facets of her life, which, in turn, spoke to others' experiences as queer Latinas and Latinos. In her recollections, reflected in the eight excerpts on display, Teresita spoke about being institutionalized in her youth "to cure" her; why other "sexiles" like her had made their way to San Francisco since the 1950s; what it took to be a MTF transgender in the streets; and what HIV and AIDS had been doing to her generation of queers, among many other queer moments in her life.[28]

In the excerpt that I entitled "La Familia: 1956," Teresita bridged the queer histories and geographies of Los Angeles and San Francisco. Here she recalls the particular context of her queer beginnings:

And then I left home when I was 16. I wasn't in drag yet. I was wearing boy's clothes, Khakis . . . you know how they used to wear the little crosses. I come from the *pachuco* days [in Los Angeles]. But I was very—*con la mano caída* [with a limp wrist]. I was never butch. I was, *but I wasn't!* So I ran into a coffee shop they called Cooper's Dough-nuts, and it was only a nickel for a doughnut. And there was this heavy-set person there, nice looking, *very* good looking when he was young. . . . His name was Joe Dejola; she was my gay mother. They called [her] "Lola." She passed away not too long ago at the [San Francisco] General Hospital; her kidneys went out on her.[29]

Referring to the "*pachuco* days" of Los Angeles, from the 1930s to the 1950s, Teresita invokes the racial/ethnic history of young Mexican American adolescent men (and other young men of color in urban cities) who wore distinctly countercultural and gendered zoot suits—baggy trousers worn high on the waist and cuffed snugly at the ankles, a sport coat wide at the shoulders and hanging halfway down the thighs, and pointed Florsheim shoes. Already aware of her own countercultural gender identity, Teresita survived in this period thanks to the chance meeting with her gay mother, "Lola," whose death is also highlighted in this brief recollection. To conjure up Lola gives us insight into the creation of queer kinships in the street, a survival move for queers like Teresita who were pushed out of their blood family units because of their sexuality or gender identity, and who needed this queer solidarity to feel less isolated.

While hundreds experienced the multiple layers of truth and memory in Teresita's oral history at the MCCLA, she was herself experiencing her own public oral history. There on opening night, already visibly ill because of her failing liver, she recognized herself in the photographs the late Reyes had taken in an earlier period of their lives. But Teresita, illiterate, could not read the excerpted transcriptions of her own oral history, and relied on Campos de la Garza, also in attendance, to tell her what the text said about her life.[30] Though visually and textually framed at the center of that queer Latino public memory, Teresita, who had made the oral histories possible in the first place, needed the community itself to help her understand the commemoration and mourning it was already engaged in just weeks before her passing.

Public memory events such as the 2001 Por Vida Awards and the 2002 "Dándole la Cara a la Historia" installation confirmed what oral histories can achieve as critical ingredients for community memory.[31] In 1996, when I was still in the beginning stages of my oral history project, Teresita and other elder Latina and Latino queers were already coming forth as narrators with their understandings of the relationship between survival and death in the age of AIDS. For Diane Felix, long-term butch Chicana activist and then coordinator for women's programming at Proyecto, the life of someone like Teresita needed to become public community knowledge as soon as possible to permit an appreciation of the generational links between those living with the disease and those fighting it through prevention campaigns. In Felix's recollection of Teresita's shared life, she recounted how vital it is to reveal and record community memories in order to recognize the value of queer struggle:

> You know, we have survived *un chingo de* [a lot of fucking] stuff. Teresita, for instance, her survival, her stories always amaze me. From your *familia*, from [being] a baby, giving you shock therapy and sending you to all these whackos to change you, torturing her, cutting her hair, putting her in institutions. And then she finally runs away to *aquí en el Valle de San Joaquín* [here in the San Joaquín Valley], in a *mexicano* town and goes underground as a *cantinera* [woman bartender]; nobody knows she's a man. When they find out she's a man, what they do to her; they take her to jail, what they do to her in jail. And she survived, and she survived, and she survived, and she survived! And she's still standing here, *loca* [crazy] as ever, singing. *She survived!* And then it's this fucking disease that's killing her. And it's amazing, our stories are just amazing, all that we've survived.[32]

Survival was at the center of Felix's narrative: not just Teresita's survival in particular, but Teresita's survival as an individual record of collective queer survival: despite the homophobia from blood family, incarcerations by the state, and general community distrust of queer genders and sexualities. Teresita survived only six more years after I conducted the oral history interview with Felix in 1996, but the memories and mournings of both—through public events and installations with images and narratives, through their respective oral histories, and through this writing—remain.

On 21 November 2002, four months after her death from AIDS-related complications, the board of directors of the MCCLA selected Teresita la Campesina as a posthumous recipient of one of its Twenty-fifth Anniversary Awards. Alongside famed singer Carlos Santana and Chicana lesbian playwright Cherríe L. Moraga and other artists who forged connections with San Francisco in their Latina/o and/or queer visions, Teresita continued to mark queer survival that day. The oral narratives she had created for herself and her queer life over the decades, which others like Diane Felix and Valentín Aguirre echoed and interpreted in yet more oral histories, had also become a means to mark the public passing and mourning of the queer Latino community.

Oral history *is* public memory. In the meandering oral narratives I have recorded and the documentary projects such as Aguirre and Robles's *¡Viva 16!*

it is people's public lives and the collective forms of making public space and identity that stand out. Queer oral histories that find audio, textual, and visual spaces for public and communal experience in the ongoing age of AIDS are necessarily a living archive that must constantly refer back to its losses. This oral history documentation is part of a historiographic activism that privileges historical documentation and the reconstruction of community narratives before its makers pass on into silence. This commitment to history mourns just as much as it celebrates the lives it records. To experience all the losses of community, friends, families, and lovers, and even of self is to inhabit a place of mourning on multiple levels, a mourning which, David Eng and David Kazanjian argue, finds meaning in "the individual and the collective, the spiritual and the material, the psychic and the social, the aesthetic and the political."[33] Indeed, in oral history and in the public memory events we make possible through that history whenever and wherever we turn the individual voice into the recorder of public lives, mourning is nothing less than the social and political responsibility to remember.

NOTES

I acknowledge the support from the narrators quoted herein—Valentín Aguirre, Diane Felix, and the late Alberta Nevaerez (Teresita la Campesina)—and appreciate their trust in sharing their lives with me. I also thank Luis Alberto Campos de la Garza for feedback and technical support, and for permission to use his photographic image and that belonging to the late Rodrigo Reyes. Thanks also to Paula Hamilton and Linda Shopes for their comments. Financial support from a University of California MEXUS Dissertation Completion grant and a University of California President's Postdoctoral Fellowship at UCLA made the research possible.

1. David L. Eng and David Kazanjian, "Introduction: Mourning Remains," in David L. Eng and David Kazanjian, eds., *Loss: the Politics of Mourning* (Berkeley: University of California Press, 2003), 2.

2. Douglas Crimp, "Mourning and Militancy," in *Melancholia and Moralism: Essays on AIDS and Queer Politics* (Cambridge: MIT Press, 2002), 137, emphasis in original.

3. Although the abbreviation "LGBT" ("lesbian, gay, bisexual, and transgender") has become popular globally, particularly through what can be referred to as the "NGOization" of lesbian and gay rights and related HIV and AIDS education, I privilege the more politically charged "queer" in this writing. This term reflects the spirit of several cultural and political currents in San Francisco and other western urban cities from the late 1980s to the mid-1990s: less accommodationist stances usually associated with the in-your-face tactics of the political action group Queer Nation, and also less well known regional organizations and service agencies, including San Francisco's queer-identified Latina/o Proyecto ContraSIDA Por Vida ("Project against AIDS for Life," PCPV). I use "queer" as I remain conscious of its problematic conflation of distinct sexual and gender experiences: butch, femme, bisexual, lesbian, and MTF (male-to-female) and FTM (female-to-male) transgenders, for example, especially outside Anglocentric histories and cultures. For an insightful

discussion of the "queering" of Latino cultures in the context of the Mexican American experience in the United States—that is, Chicana and Chicano liberation—see Cherríe Moraga, "Queer Aztlán: The Reformation of Chicano Tribe," in *The Last Generation: Prose and Poetry* (Boston: South End Press, 1993), 145–74. For an analysis of the "queering" of the "heteronormative" organization of society, see Michael Warner, "Introduction," in Michael Warner, ed., *Fear of a Queer Planet: Queer Politics and Social Theory* (Minneapolis: University of Minnesota Press, 1993), vii–xxxi.

4. A larger book project is meant to document and analyze community building and community destruction, and to help create public and archival records of community life. See Horacio N. Roque Ramírez, "Communities of Desire: Queer Latina/Latino History and Memory, San Francisco Bay Area, 1960s–1990s" (Ph.D. diss., University of California, Berkeley, 2001).

5. I explore my personal investment in this cross-generational juncture through oral historiography in "My Community, My History, My Practice," *Oral History Review* 29:2 (Summer/Fall 2002): 87–91. While HIV infection rates and AIDS cases have historically shifted to include more sexually, racially, nationally, and linguistically diverse populations in the United States, compared with the more homogeneous gay, white urban male population first afflicted, in the San Francisco Bay Area, the epidemiological profile remains overwhelmingly queer and male, but with an overrepresentation of people of color, especially queer youth, as well as MTF transgender women. A useful overview of HIV as it impacts queer men of color in the United States is provided in George Ayala, Claire E. Husted, and Andrew Spieldenner, *Holding Open Space: Re-Tooling and Re-Imagining HIV Prevention for Gay and Bisexual Men of Color* (Los Angeles and New York: Institute for Gay Men's Health, 2004).

6. The Gay Latino Alliance played a pivotal role socially and politically in bringing recognition to gay Latinos and, to a lesser degree, lesbian Latinas in the Bay Area and nationally. See Horacio N. Roque Ramírez, " 'That's My Place': Negotiating Racial, Sexual, and Gender Politics in San Francisco's Gay Latino Alliance, 1975–1983," *Journal of the History of Sexuality* 12 (2003): 224–58.

7. Useful discussions on the exclusionary dimensions of identity politics, and the challenges to consider regarding the intersectional qualities of identity and experience in history, are Cherríe Moraga and Gloria Anzaldúa, eds., *This Bridge Called My Back: Writings by Radical Women of Color* (1981; reprint ed., Berkeley: Third Woman Press, 2002); and Kimberlé Crenshaw, "Mapping the Margins: Intersectionality, Identity Politics, and Violence against Women of Color," in Kimberlé Crenshaw, Neil Gotanda, Gary Peller, and Kendall Thomas, eds., *Critical Race Theory: The Key Writings That Formed the Movement* (New York: New Press, 1995), 357–83.

8. Two useful overviews of queer cultures in the Bay Area (again, not significantly about communities of color) are Susan Stryker and Jim Van Buskirk, *Gay by the Bay: A History of Queer Culture in the San Francisco Bay Area* (San Francisco: Chronicle Books, 1996), and Nan Alamilla Boyd, *Wide Open Town: A History of Queer San Francisco to 1965* (Berkeley: University of California Press, 2003). On Latinas and Latinos, see Juan Felipe Herrera, "Riffs on Mission District Raza Writers," in James Brook, Chris Carlsson, and Nancy J. Peters, eds., *Reclaiming San Francisco: History, Politics, Culture* (San Francisco: City Lights Books, 1998), 217–30, and Alejandro Murguía, "Tropi(lo)calidad: Macondo in La Mission," in *The Medicine of Memory: A Mexican Clan in California* (Austin: University of Texas Press, 2002), 118–46.

9. However exaggerated, or at least misleading, pharmaceutical promises have been in recent years, these new medications have kept tens of thousands of people living with AIDS

from dying. By keeping those with access to these medications alive, protease inhibitors (more popularly known as antiretroviral "cocktail therapies") have changed the cultural and political landscape for mourning. Today, in wealthy nations like the United States, queer losses from AIDS are simply no longer what they were in the 1980s. I do not mean to suggest that all racial/ethnic groups, economic classes, and queer gendered and sexual identities have equal access to HIV medications, or that all people living with AIDS respond well to protease inhibitors; neither is true. For a useful background on the history of AIDS in San Francisco, see Benjamin Heim Shepard, *White Nights and Ascending Shadows: An Oral History of the San Francisco AIDS Epidemic* (London: Cassell, 1997). The University of California, San Francisco, has an extensive oral history of AIDS project available online at www .library.ucsf.edu/collres/archives/ahp/ohp.html.

10. These decades-long efforts to create visibility, forge identities, and claim space and rights regionally speak to the idea of cultural citizenship, for social, cultural, and political belonging not reduced to state-sanctioned legal claims. See Horacio N. Roque Ramírez, "Claiming Queer Cultural Citizenship: Gay Latino (Im)Migrant Cultures in San Francisco," in Eithne Luibhéid and Lionel Cantú, Jr., eds., *Queer Migrations: Sexuality, U.S.A. Citizenship and Border Crossings* (Minneapolis: University of Minnesota Press, 2005), 161–88, and William V. Flores and Rina Benmayor, eds., *Latino Cultural Citizenship: Claiming Identity, Space, and Rights* (Boston: Beacon Press, 1997).

11. Elizabeth Lapovsky Kennedy and Madeline D. Davis, *Boots of Leather, Slippers of Gold: The History of a Lesbian Community* (New York: Routledge, 1993).

12. Those most supportive of my work during these early forays into community dynamics and history were all gay, lesbian, or MTF transgenders and were usually affiliated with HIV and AIDS education agencies, including Marcos Bañales, then at STOP AIDS San Francisco; Gustavo Martín Cravioto, then at Instituto Familiar de la Raza ("the People's Family Institute"); Ricardo A. Bracho and Diane Felix, both then at PCPV; the late Alberta Nevaerez (better known as Teresita la Campesina, live singer and client of several of these agencies; and Luis Alberto Campos de la Garza, then with the Chicano Studies Research Center Library at UC Berkeley.

13. The encounter between two generations of gay Latino men through an oral history project can be an emotionally loaded research experience, given their different relationships to the earliest stages of the HIV/AIDS epidemic, prevention knowledge and sexual practices, and antiretroviral medications. I explore such research dilemmas in "To Face History," *Words and Silences* 2:2 (June 2004): 8–9.

14. "¡Viva 16!" 23 minutes long, was produced, written, and directed by Valentín Aguirre and Augie Robles (21st Century Aztlan Productions, 1994).

15. Valentín Aguirre, interviewed by the author, audiotape recording, San Francisco, California, 12 January 2001. Rodrigo Reyes was one of the co-founders of the Gay Latino Alliance in 1975.

16. Ibid. Rosa Maria Zayas was at the center of a public controversy over the (mis)management of CURAS close to the time of Reyes's death.

17. Avery F. Gordon, *Ghostly Matters: Haunting and the Sociological Imagination* (Minneapolis: University of Minnesota Press, 1997), 22.

18. Ibid., 23.

19. Two previous events around queer Latino public memory also relied to different degrees on my oral history research and the archival materials found through that work. The June 1999 "Making a Case for Community History" was sponsored by the Gay and Lesbian Historical Society and the Center for the History of Sexual Diversity. The exhibit consisted of

eight large glass cases with archival materials, which traveled to several city locations. One case was entitled "¡Gente de Ambiente Presente!" (Gay People Present!). The June 2000 "Pedazos de Tu Historia (Pieces of Your History): A Historical Retrospective," was a queer Latino archival exhibit at the MCCLA, coordinated with Karla E. Rosales and Héctor Meléndez.

20. I explore the role the late Teresita played in my oral history project and in my life in "A Living Archive of Desire: Teresita la Campesina and the Embodiment of Queer Latino Community Histories," in Antoinette Burton, ed., *Archive Stories: Facts, Fictions, and the Writing of History* (Durham: Duke University Press, 2005), and in "Teresita's Blood/La Sangre de Teresita," *CORPUS: An HIV Prevention Publication* 2:2 (Los Angeles and New York: Institute for Gay Men's Health, 2004), 2–9.

21. I discuss the critical role this queer Latina and Latino HIV agency played in this period of community rebirth, celebration of life, and mourning in "Praxes of Desire: Remaking Queer Latino Geographies and Communities through San Francisco's Proyecto ContraSIDA Por Vida," in Matt García, Marie Leger, and Angharad Valdivia, eds., *Geographies of Latinidad: Latina/o Studies into the Twenty-First Century* (Durham: Duke University Press, forthcoming). See also the discussion of the various forms of queer and racial activism carried out through the agency in Juana María Rodríguez, *Queer Latinidad: Identity Practices, Discursive Spaces* (New York: New York University Press, 2003).

22. *Ranchera* is a distinctly Mexican style of music that emerged in the postrevolutionary period, especially in the state of Jalisco, based on rural, traditional forms that include *mariachi* musical groups. The late Lola Beltrán (1934–1996), the "queen of rancheras," had an unmistakably strong voice and was Teresita's artistic idol.

23. For an excellent discussion of the benefits and challenges of being both an insider and an outsider in community research, see Maxine Baca Zinn, "Field Research in Minority Communities: Ethical, Methodological, and Political Observations by an Insider," *Social Problems* 27 (1979): 209–19.

24. I originally had planned to produce this presentation with Luis Alberto Campos de la Garza, but he was unable to support the final stages of this production because he was stuck in Washington, D.C., after 9/11.

25. The Archivo Rodrigo Reyes will become part of the permanent collection of the Ethnic Studies Library at the University of California, Berkeley, upon donation by Campos de la Garza. Campos de la Garza and I spent more than a year in 2000–2001 organizing more than 150 boxes of materials remaining after the death of Henry "Hank" Tavera. The Hank Tavera Collection is already part of the Ethnic Studies Library.

26. For a preliminary discussion of the late Rodrigo Reyes's archival collection, see Luis Alberto Campos de la Garza and Horacio N. Roque Ramírez, "Community History and the Evidence of Desire: The Archivo Rodrigo Reyes, a Gay and Lesbian Latino Archive," in Lillian Castillo-Speed and the REFORMA National Conference Publications Committee, eds., *The Power of Language/El Poder de la Palabra: Selected Papers from the 2nd Annual REFORMA National Conference* (Englewood, CO: Libraries Unlimited, 2000), 181–98.

27. Although there was no formal opposition to the photo and text display I proposed— and it was accepted—I later found out that the coordinator responsible for the exhibit found it to be "gray," or, as she described it in Spanish, "*gris.*" She was likely referring in part to the color tones of the display itself—black and white photographs enclosed in silver gray frames next to text in a large black font on white paper enclosed in similar frames—but also to the subdued mood evoked through the display. Part of my intent through this color scheme was to avoid overshadowing the subtle texture of the photographs or the timelessness suggested by black

and white photography, but I also wanted to contrast this calm visual mood with Teresita's own words in the accompanying framed texts, narratives that were forceful, comical, ironic, richly reflective, and multilayered—anything but "gray."

28. The notion of "sexile," of leaving one's nation of origin on account of sexuality, is from Manuel Guzmán, " 'Pa' la escuelita con mucho cuida'o y por la orillita': A Journey through the Contested Terrains of the Nation and Sexual Orientation," in Frances Negrón-Muntaner and Ramón Grosfoguel, eds., *Puerto Rican Jam: Rethinking Colonialism and Nationalism* (Minneapolis: University of Minnesota Press, 1997), 209–28. See also the bilingual graphic novel by Jaime Cortez, based on an oral history project with MTF Cuban transgender Adela Vásquez, *Sexile/Sexilio* (Los Angeles and New York: Institute for Gay Men's Health, 2004).

29. Alberta Nevaerez (Teresita la Campesina), interviewed by the author, audiotape recording, San Francisco, 22 August 1999.

30. I thank Luis Alberto Campos de la Garza C. for providing me with the details of this encounter with Teresita at the MCCLA on the opening night of the exhibit.

31. For an earlier discussion of the importance of a nonacademic, community focus in oral history research, see Laurie R. Serikaku, "Oral History in Ethnic Communities: Widening the Focus," *Oral History Review* 17:1 (1989): 71–87.

32 Diane Felix, interviewed by the author, audiotape recording, San Francisco, 27 April 1996. Felix is one of the featured butch narrators in the award-winning video *Mind if I Call You Sir?: Masculinity and Gender Expression in Chicana/Latina Butches and Latino Female-to-Male (FTM) Transgender Men,* conceived and produced by Karla E. Rosales, directed by Mary Guzmán, 30 minutes (Stickygirl Productions, 2004).

33. Eng and Kazanjian, "Introduction," 3.

10

INTERFACED MEMORY: BLACK WORLD WAR II EX-GIS' AND VETERANS' REUNIONS OF THE LATE TWENTIETH CENTURY

Robert F. Jefferson

Is that thing on? Make sure that you get this down. Since the early 1970s, I have periodically called the roll of a selected group of surviving veterans. Many of those who responded to my calls have discussed their military experiences as well as the problems in their communities when we've met. Let me tell you . . . those reunions were much more than a "drums and bugles" history of World War II.

LTC (RET.) MAJOR CLARK

Over the years a number of soldiers' reunions have been held at the oldest military installations in the United States to commemorate the contribution of African Americans to World War II. The first of these was a 1975 gathering at Fort Huachuca, Arizona, sponsored by the Department of the Army and various black veterans' organizations. In June of that year, members of the World War II Regular Army and their guests assembled at Fort Huachuca to commemorate the two-hundredth anniversary of the American Army and renew friendships with those with whom they had served during the wartime period. During the three-day event, veterans of wars past and present participated in an assortment of festivities that ranged from nostalgic tours around the historic post, battlefield re-enactments, awards banquets, tree dedication ceremonies, golf tournaments, and evening entertainment. Among the conferees were civic leaders, military spokespeople, business people, and members of the press. During their visit, ex-GIs and their family members and friends walked past their old barracks and gazed at the Huachuca Mountains, recounting their collective hardships and personal triumphs in the segregated army of the 1940s.

For many of the soldiers, Fort Huachuca held special relevance. Since 1877 the installation had served as the only military base where black units received training. Considered the home of the renowned 24th and 25th Infantry Regiments, or "Buffalo Soldiers," and the segregated units that followed, the base later housed the U.S. 92nd and 93rd Infantry Divisions and their supporting units, as well as the black Women's Army Corps and Nurse Corps units during World War II.[1] As the veterans moved around the post, the past and present merged with a special intensity. Many of them could be heard asking: "What outfit were you with?" "Do you remember so-and-so?" "Hey, I recognized your name but you've changed."

Among the crowd of former servicemen who made the trip to Arizona was Frank Little, retired First Sergeant of the famous 25th Infantry Regiment. A native of South Philadelphia, Little had enlisted in the Army in 1935 at the age of sixteen to escape the poverty of the Great Depression. Like so many Fort Huachuca veterans who gathered that day, he had fought in the Second World War as a member of the all-black 93rd Infantry Division. After a brief introduction by the post commander, Little launched into an awe-inspiring address, ticking off the achievements of his illustrious unit before reminding his fellow GIs that the reunion was intended to pay honest tribute to fighting men whose record in peace and war was equal to any who wore the nation's uniform. But the highlight of the reunion occurred when Virginia resident and World War II veteran Jesse Johnson took the stage that Friday evening. A recently retired officer who also served in the desegregated army of the 1950s and 1960s, Johnson began his presentation with a graphic description of the service records, dates, humiliations, oppression, and achievements of his predecessors who had served in the segregated army and called on fellow veterans to prepare their communities for the battles for equality that lay ahead. Speaking to the audience as if he were not only a family member, but the appointed recorder of the family history, he concluded his address by issuing an injunction that stayed with most of the observers at the gathering: "Much of what I say here is known in varying degrees by most of us. Lest we forget, we must recount and teach this history to our children and neighbors." This struck a responsive chord among those who sat in the audience that day. For example, Carl Jones of Altadena, California, listened intently and interrupted Johnson before he had concluded his remarks by pointing at the speaker and declaring loudly to his fellow veterans: "He is telling it like it is. We have plenty of work to do yet."[2]

For the ex-GIs who gathered for the occasion, Johnson's gripping statement and Jones's concurrence represent much more than exercises in nostalgia. They reflect forces that held and continue to hold special value and meaning. To be sure, Johnson's references to World War II as a defining experience summoned

forth for many in the audience their own memories of the social and political
currents that shaped their identities as young adults in the early decades of the
twentieth century—namely, military service and war. It became apparent that
black GIs of World II used the sharing of memories within these ritualized settings to promote positive images of their wartime contributions. Their descriptions of military service reminded them of the various twists and turns that
most of them had taken in their subsequent lives. But the ceremonial events and
situated storytelling also provided them with a stage from which they could im-
part their unique value systems to members of their families and respective
communities.

By observing the interaction of black World War II–era ex-GIs and their
families, this chapter explores some of the ways in which group storytelling
performances during veterans' reunions in late twentieth-century America facilitated a collapsing of public memory and private history. First, I examine the
"memory-telling" experiences among black ex-GIs and the sites in which they
took place during the last two decades of the twentieth century. Following the
lead of Francis Yates but extending his analysis outward, I suggest that
memory-telling in a performative sense has a figurative purpose, as well as being a primary means of expression among black ex-GIs when in a familiar ceremonial or ritualized setting such as a veterans' home, a reunion hall, or an
armory.[3] Second, I present examples of occasions on which the dramaturgical
aspects of memory-telling among these veterans provided direction to their
respective communities to be more politically active. The ex-GIs' memories
and identities reflected the conversations they held with each other regarding
their wartime contributions, and their concerns about the general condition of
their respective communities. In addition, through the vernacular storytelling
sequences enacted during veterans' reunions and anniversaries, one can
glimpse the manner in which black collective memory is linked to place.

First Roll Call: The Historical Context

When Johnson and other African American ex-GIs shared memories and attempted to forge collective memory into political instruction at these veterans'
gatherings, their actions were deeply rooted in the public debate over the combat record of black troops in the immediate aftermath of World War II. During
the early months of 1945, Washington officials, led by Assistant Secretary of
War John J. McCloy and a civilian aide to the secretary of war, Truman Gibson,
held a series of conferences and meetings with members of the Advisory Committee on Special Troop Policies to discuss the employment of African Americans in the postwar military establishment. Among the topics that animated
their discussion was the effectiveness of black officers and enlisted personnel in

front-line combat. After exploring possible changes in army racial policies for several months, members of the committee resolved to dispatch questionnaires to senior army commanders in Europe and the Pacific, soliciting their views on the performance of the all-black 92nd and 93rd Infantry Divisions, which were serving in their respective theaters of operations during the spring of that year.[4]

The negative responses presented by senior officers were hardly surprising. Many of them were rooted in racist notions of white supremacy and couched in stereotypical language stressing black cowardice and incompetence under fire. The 92nd Infantry Division Commander, Major General Edward M. Almond, tried to link the division's perceived shortcomings to "the lack of dependability in Negro officers and enlisted men; especially is this the case in infantry combat." General Almond concluded: "My experience of three and one-half years in an attempt to create a combat infantry division comprising of [sic] only Negro units convinces me that it is a failure."[5] Almond's statement was echoed among the unit's staff and junior officers. For example, Major Thomas Saint John Arnold, the division's operations section chief, expressed his contempt for the fighting abilities of black troops, stating: "I don't trust Negroes. White officers who work with them have to work harder than with white troops." Perhaps even more revealing were the views expressed by the intelligence section commander, employing a baseball analogy: "The Ninety-third Division was one out. The Second Cavalry Division was the second out; and now the Ninety-second Division is at bat with one strike already over on us."[6]

Similar views circulated widely among senior army commanders and junior officers in the Southwest Pacific Theater of Operations when they were queried about the combat record of the first major all-black unit created during the war, the U.S. 93rd Infantry Division. In response to an inquiry from Army Chief of Staff George Marshall regarding the 93rd Division's contribution to the war effort, Southwest Pacific Theater Commander in Chief General Douglas MacArthur claimed: "In its only combat experience which occurred in the South Pacific, the Ninety-third's infantry was reported to me as extraordinarily poor. All those to whom I have spoken regarded it as unreliable . . . lacking in initiative, and entirely incapable of matching the Japanese forces in combat."[7] MacArthur based his opinion on a report filed a year earlier by 14th Corps Commander General Oscar Griswold. Shortly after the division had arrived in the South Pacific during the spring of 1944, Marshall ordered Griswold to assign elements of the division to patrolling missions after an inadequate training period. After hastily converting several units into regimental combat teams and witnessing the division stage a series of patrolling exercises against the enemy on unfamiliar terrain, the corps commander wrote to his superiors:

"Experience has shown me that to date they are unreliable and it is impossible to determine how they will react in any given situation."[8]

As the worldwide conflict ground to a halt, popular, professional, and service newspapers, journals, and magazines were filled with stories that offered a negative assessment of the wartime performance of the 93rd Division and other all-black units. Throughout the spring of 1946 and well into the winter of the following year, publications such as *Survey Graphic, American Journal of Psychiatry, Annals of the American Academy of Political and Social Science*, and the *American Journal of Sociology* featured articles describing the shortcomings of black troops in the Pacific Theater of Operations.[9] In April 1946, for instance, *Harper's Magazine* carried a story by Warman Welliver, a company commander who had served with the 92nd Infantry Division during the war, and who now argued that the "policy for colored troops has been an almost absolute failure." In addition to casting doubt on the fighting capabilities of his own unit during the Fifth Army Offensive of 1945, Welliver blamed the black press for playing up the activities of the 93rd Infantry Division in the Pacific when the unit was "actually doing little more than mopping up in the wake of other divisions' conquest."[10] Later that year, the *Infantry Journal* reported a story by a staff officer who served with the division in the Southwest Pacific. Using the same headline as Welliver's, "Report on the Negro Soldier," the author downplayed racial discrimination and prejudice as underlying reasons for the problems experienced by black members of the 93rd Infantry Division in the Jim Crow army—stating that discrimination had, after all, been an everyday reality for most of them prior to their entrance into the military.[11] Like Welliver, he laid much of the blame for the controversy surrounding black units' combat record at the feet of the black press. At the same time, he expressed contempt for black soldiers themselves: "Full success and maximum efficiency cannot be ensured by the War Department alone. A grave responsibility rests with the colored soldier himself. By exemplary demeanor and a determined effort to do his level best, he can go a long way toward breaking down the prejudices that now exist."[12]

Quick to recognize the threat posed by these negative images, black political leaders, reporters, and white sympathizers spoke out vigorously against attempts to scapegoat black soldiers who served in the field. As the summer months faded into the fall of 1945, black newspapers, most notably the Pittsburgh *Courier*, the Baltimore *Afro-American*, the Chicago *Defender*, and the New York *Amsterdam News*, sided with the soldiers in uniform and were filled with feature articles, reports, and editorials complaining about the negative assessments of the fighting capabilities of black soldiers in Europe and Asia. In a letter to the editor of the *American Journal of Sociology* that was published in the spring of 1947, Lawrence D. Reddick, historian and curator of the Schomburg Collection of the New York Public Library, addressed what was at stake in the public debate:

It is worthwhile to watch the fabrication of the social myth of the Negro's role in World War II. Not only are the news stories that came back from the war fronts, outbursts of oratory of certain members of Congress, and the 'official' releases of the War and Navy departments worthy of analysis, but the studies of 'scholars' deserve to be examined with some attention to orientation and attitude content. Their conclusions do not vary too much from the basic thesis of more crudely stated observations that (1) the Negro was not much good as a fighting man and (2) little could be done about racial discrimination and segregation because American society is as it is.

Reddick went on to stress the need to get all sides of the story: "It is as important to get impressions and opinions about Negro servicemen as held by white officers and administrators of the military as it is to get comparable sets of impressions of and opinions about white officers and others held by Negro servicemen."[13]

After The War: Weaving Military Recollections into Postwar Realities

Reddick's suggestion reflected the way in which the memory-telling performances staged by black ex-servicemen during the postwar period also became impromptu sense-making exercises.[14] And he was not alone in this realization. After returning home from military service in 1945, Luther M. Fuller, an ordained minister and former 93rd Division chaplain, went on to complete a doctorate in American history at Columbia University while working with New York City's Department of Public Welfare. By the time Fuller earned his degree in 1955, he was highly regarded for both his wartime struggles against racism in the Jim Crow Army and his academic promise. In fact, his doctoral dissertation on the War Department's racial policies during the war captured the attention of the faculty in the history department at West Virginia State College, who promptly offered him a position. Fuller's quest to set straight the wartime record of African American GIs met an abrupt ending, however. Two years later, while toiling to revise his dissertation into a publishable manuscript, he succumbed to asphyxiation; he was found dead in his apartment, located near the university.[15]

Walter R. Greene, the son of a well-known Detroit city constable and a seamstress, also continued to reflect on his wartime experience. Like Frank Little and Jesse Johnson, Greene used the memory of his participation in the worldwide conflict and the lessons he learned while in uniform to frame his response to life in the postwar years. After attending Officers Candidate School at Fort Benning, he joined the 93rd Infantry Division's 25th Infantry Regiment while the unit was undergoing maneuvers training in the Mojave Desert in California in 1943. Greene later traveled with the unit to the Pacific Theater of Operations, where he and the rest of his comrades participated in patrolling missions on Bougainville Island, New Guinea, and Morotai Island. In the Pacific, Greene and other members of his regiment fought the hostile enemy, the treacherous terrain, and endless bouts of racism from within their own army. For example, he and other soldiers were ordered to unload ships while less seasoned white combat units advanced toward the Japanese. To make matters worse, Greene and nine other black officers were ordered to attend a special officer-training school that had been established on a nearby island by division headquarters for underperforming soldiers. After discussing the rank discrimination that they faced and the looming prospects of courts-martial, Greene and the others formed a group they called the Treasury Island Nine. Shortly afterward, they began to contest federally sanctioned indignities at every turn, staging sit-down strikes and refusing to answer to roll call on a number of occasions.

Mustered out of the service in late 1945, Greene returned home to Detroit. Although the racial climate in the city had not changed significantly, he noticed, he had changed a great deal. Greene allied himself with the sites, sounds, and people he had encountered while in uniform. Beginning in 1951 and continuing through to the 1980s, Greene and other members of the self-styled Treasury Island Nine would gather to renew their bonds of community. On many occasions their meetings produced long, sleepless nights during which they revisited sweat-filled days in the South Pacific while catching up on recent issues affecting their communities. Greene and other veterans made numerous treks to the Californian desert site where they had trained during the early 1940s. For the long-time Detroit resident, discussing his wartime experiences with his fellow servicemen evoked a flood of emotions. It became evident that their wartime contributions served as a vivid reminder of his present commitment to the people in his community. When he was tapped by Detroit's Mayor Roman S. Gribbs to join his staff as chief deputy in 1969, a time of rising racial tensions in the Motor City, Greene reflected in the comfort of friends and family. Gesturing toward his former comrades-in-arms, he said: "We went through so much over there . . . like most of the fellows here, I want our military service to count towards something positive, not to be a witness to a city tearing itself apart." Greene was not the only participant who walked away from reunions relating the wartime past to the present situation. Of their gatherings, fellow Michigan resident Francis Ellis recalled: "Our meetings really kept me going. During our reunions, I recounted how I met Walter Greene, Harold Biddiex, and the guys all those years ago and it helped me to realize that we were using what we learned back then to better the situations of our communities. This was the message that stayed with me even when I came back to Ann Arbor to start my own business."[16]

For Walter's wife, Freida, the settings for these ritualized gatherings and the memories they elicited also retained special relevance, but for different reasons. Years later she recalled how ex-GIs from the 93rd would banter while discussing their wartime experiences:

> The house meetings that Walter and his war buddies had throughout that period were full of stories but they also had a tremendous impact on his spirits. One time, in particular, they had a meeting at George and Helen Higgins's home in Pasadena in February of 1969 and as they were talking about their army experiences, the fellas would turn to each other and refer to Dr. King's death, the rioting and burning taking place in Detroit, Washington, D.C., and New York, and this affected Walter because he was in city government at the time. Sometimes he would get some ideas about the situation by just listening to the others talk. But their storytelling also educated the children because along with our children, Gregory and Trey, Linzy and Eleanor Jones, John and Vera Serazen, and Ezra and Theresa Henderson were all there and many of them were in junior high and high school at the time. So they were getting history lessons of a different kind as well.[17]

Freida Greene's account clearly demonstrates the efforts of her husband and the other ex-GIs to weave personal recollections of military service into their postwar realities. As black veterans made the transition to civilian life, they combined their shared memories of a not-so-distant World War II–related past with their transformed identities as *veterans* to produce powerful counternarratives challenging the biased depictions of their battlefield performance and to effect real change in their respective neighborhoods and communities across the country. The lessons that Greene and Ellis learned while in uniform during the 1940s served them in good stead more than twenty-five years later. Not only that, but, as their reunions demonstrate, their sense-making sessions implicitly provided cardinal points of instruction for successive generations. Although Greene and Ellis emerged from different class, work, generational, and ideological backgrounds and may have possessed political perspectives as diverse as their ranks, they clearly understood that the need to present their own versions of their military contributions and the desire to shape the direction of their communities were two sides of the same coin of empowerment. Thus, for folks like Greene and Ellis, the training sites and battlefronts of Fort Huachuca in Arizona and the South Pacific became emotive avenues through which memory and social learning were filtered and transmitted.

Interfaced Memories: Reunions and Memory-Telling in the Late Twentieth Century

In September 1992, the Department of the Army held a conference at the U.S. Army War College at Carlisle Barracks, Pennsylvania, commemorating the fiftieth anniversary of the Second World War. Among the wide array of veterans' organizations in attendance were members of the all-black Tuskegee Airmen Association, the 366th Infantry Veterans' Association, the Women's Army Corps Association, the Buffalo Rangers' Association, and the 92nd Infantry Division Association. During the gathering of ex-GIs, military officials, and their family members, Jehu Hunter, Dennette Harrod, and Dovey Roundtree gave presentations on their wartime experiences.

All three began with the problems that they encountered in the Jim Crow Army and concluded with the deployment of African American units overseas. Both Hunter and Harrod's recollections revolved around the training of the 92nd and 93rd Infantry Divisions in the early 1940s. Hunter, a former 92nd Infantry Division officer and an active member of the unit's veterans' association, evoked a sense of camaraderie tinged with resentment as he told of how he and the nearly four thousand black enlisted personnel and officers arrived at the arid Arizona base:

> The training of the Division at Fort Huachuca brought its own set of problems. The post was isolated, around 60 miles from Tucson, the nearest town of any size with a significant black population. The post had few recreational opportunities and very limited social opportunities except for prostitution. It was right then that I realized that the Army General Staff had it in for us because it preferred to assign white officers to black units because it assumed that most southern white men knew how to deal with black men better than most northern white men. Much of the reason for the less than optimal performance of the 92nd Infantry Division must be laid at the feet of the army because it promoted the idea that African Americans could not be developed into good combat soldiers.

At one point in his address, Hunter stated, "Let me tell you . . . most of the kids in the Washington, D.C., public school system know this history because my association has gone to discuss this at various schools around the area.[18]

Later on during the gathering, Philadelphia native Dennett Harrod, a veteran of the U.S. 366th Infantry Regiment, told the audience that the experience related by Hunter was all too familiar to him. Moving back and forth between 1940 and 1945, Harrod began with his own entry into the army and offered his recollection of the 92nd Infantry Division commander, General Edward Almond, before providing the audience with a harrowing description of his unit's combat experiences in Italy:

> After we arrived in Pisa, Italy, the Commanding General of the 92nd Infantry Division addressed us, or should I say, 'Up jumped the devil!' He told us that he didn't ask for us nor did he want us. We were there because the black press and our black leaders wanted us to be there. Since we were there he was going to make us fight. We fought two wars . . . one on the battlefield and another with the Commanding General of the 92nd Division.

Harrod concluded his remarks with the bitter fighting that had taken place near the village of Sommocolonia, Tuscany, in 1944, and the exploits of his company commander, Lieutenant John R. Fox. A young officer with the 366th, Fox distinguished himself on the field of battle in 1944 when he called artillery fire on his own position during an attack by a German formation, resulting in his own death while safely securing the Allied location. Harrod recalled: "Fox was my boyhood friend and one of the best damned officers in the 366th. If nothing else comes from this meeting, let's agree to try to get the president to issue a congressional medal for him because it should have happened long before now. Our community could use such a lift right now."[19]

The judgments rendered by the two men regarding their wartime experiences and Harrod's appeal for national honor to be bestowed on a fallen comrade might seem sentimental. But special attention should be paid to the ways in which the two men used the formal setting and their reunion stories to share experiences as well as call attention to present-day concerns. For example, Harrod's plea for national recognition for the heroism of his company commander was translated into reality in 1996 when President Bill Clinton awarded John Fox, along with six other African American veterans of World War II, the Congressional Medal of Honor.

Harrod's remarks were echoed, more or less, by other veterans who shared the stage with him that day. Later that afternoon, Dovey J. Roundtree, a District of Columbia attorney and former officer with the Women's Army Corps during the war, enthralled the audience with descriptions of her wartime experiences and her admiration for African American educator Dr. Mary McLeod Bethune:

> When Dr. Mary McLeod Bethune invited me to come to Washington, D.C., in the summer of 1941, and explained to me that there was a bill before Congress, and it would be passed she assured me, and since she had met me and my family, she wanted to recommend me to be in the

first class of officers of women for the Women's Army Auxiliary Corps . . . I had somewhat of an ambivalent reaction to it all. But she was so enthusiastic. She told me that black women had to carry their fair share in the fight for freedom. If we were good enough and smart enough we could be selected. Well, that got my dander up and I told her that I would go back home and discuss it with Mama and Grandma and then let her know.

Roundtree described her struggles to enter the Women's Army Corps and the sense of camaraderie she witnessed among black women training at Fort Des Moines, Iowa, while fighting racism and sexism both in and out of uniform. But in contrast to black servicemen, whose narrative performances revolved around their dual battle to perform well in the field and demand dignity for their role in the Jim Crow Army, Roundtree used her reunion story to convey her sense of anger, resentment, and bitterness at what she and other women experienced while challenging the interlocking systems of racial, gender, and sexual oppression in the armed forces and the wider society throughout the period: "There was such misinformation that was spread that we were going to be the mistresses for the black soldiers and all such sex-oriented tales, none of which were true. In the first place, there were just a handful of us and how in the world could we service all the black men. That was just too ridiculous to make any sense."

But, like Hunter and Harrod, Roundtree also developed her reunion narrative of the distant past into a discussion of the current problems that black neighborhoods, towns, and communities were experiencing as a result of structural changes in the nation's economy:

I always remember the challenge of Dr. Mary McLeod Bethune. Maybe you are not good enough, maybe you are not smart enough, maybe you are not physically well enough. It is a challenge. Of course, you are not well enough if you are filled with drugs when you are a teenager. Drugs are just crazy in our communities. In the best homes, in the lowest homes. You cannot get well enough if you do not go through and study and complete high school and get some additional training. That, my friends, is a task that I believe that you and I must take into consideration and wherever we go miss not one chance to inspire young folks, regardless of the color of their skin, to be their best selves. Marching forward but looking backward. Wearing a uniform, serving in our country is not enough. We must continue to serve in our local communities and do it with the same smartness and diligence as we served in the military.[20]

Roundtree's reconstruction of her experiences in the Women's Army Corps, her reunion story, and her pleas for mobilization among her fellow ex-GIs made a great impression upon those in attendance. Martha Putney, a fellow Women's Army Corps veteran noted: "Dovey Roundtree brought back some memories to me, some pleasant and some not so pleasant in the corps. We had much to overcome, and if those who served with us but are no longer here could speak today, they would say we still have so much to do in our neighborhoods."[21] But more importantly, Roundtree transformed her points of reflection into keen insights into the severe problems of poverty and joblessness facing postindustrial cities across the country. In that instance, private history interfaced with public memory to take on a broader, more powerful, meaning.

The wider implications of the memory-making performances by black ex-GIs and the ritual spaces in which their recollections and past identities were revived do not stop there. As veterans gathered at Bliss Hall that evening, very few of them were unaware of the inextricable connection between their struggles to promote a positive image of their previous wartime contributions and the current struggles of their respective communities. In the 1990s, the similarities between the two issues were too great to ignore. Throughout much of the country, racial profiling was rife in black neighborhoods, black men were killed by police officers in Detroit, Michigan, and Pittsburgh, Pennsylvania, and the videotaped beating of a young African American motorist at the hands of several police officers in Los Angeles triggered an urban rebellion. Meanwhile, black communities suffered increased economic distress and unremitting poverty, resulting from factory closings, the movement of heavy industry to less populated areas and overseas, intense housing discrimination, and the cutting back of city expenditures for public housing, parks, recreation centers, public schools, health care delivery systems, and youth programs. In addition, enormous tax cuts for the wealthy, huge federal deficits, heavy defense spending, and corporate downsizing spelled huge disparities in income between vast segments of society and diminished entitlement funding for veterans. In Texas, California, and Florida, federal courts dismantled state affirmative action programs, largely eliminating race-based admissions criteria to achieve diversity.[22] By the end of 2007, while the number of crimes committed by African Americans continued to decline, the percentage of African Americans imprisoned tripled as a veritable boom in privatized prisons-for-profit grew out of the racist stereotypes of the Reagan-Bush-Clinton-Bush eras.[23] At the same time, the actions of black World War II GIs had become the subject of reinvention in popular newspapers, magazines, and books. By the summer of 2000, these servicemen had become, in the hands of Hollywood filmmakers, pundits, and historians, either invisible soldiers or victims of circumstances beyond their control. While *Saving Private Ryan* and *The Thin Red Line* provided graphic depictions of the fighting that soldiers faced in Europe and the South Pacific, the absence of the men who served in the 320th Anti-aircraft Barrage Balloon Battalion or the 24th Infantry Regiment—who also saw front-line action at the time—was particularly glaring. On the other hand, John R. Fox and Reuben Rivers, veterans, respectively, of the 366th Infantry and the 761st Tank Battalion, along with six other servicemen, were awarded the Congressional Medal of Honor in 1996. And by late 1997, monuments were erected to commemorate the exploits of the men of the 9th and 10th Cavalry, at Fort Riley, Kansas, and those of the Women's Army Corps, at the World War II Memorial in Washington, D.C.

Certainly, in the minds of many ex-GIs, these bronze and granite statutes brought public attention to the political struggles they had waged during the war. But the monuments also stood in the midst of the social inequalities that they hoped would be redressed during their lifetimes. For many of the veterans I interviewed, the ideological and material discrepancies between their personal historical images and the deteriorating conditions of their respective communities produced frustration and despair regarding the future direction of the country. At a reunion for ex-GIs who had served with the 93rd Infantry Division, held in San Francisco in 1994, Southside Chicago resident Nelson Peery, a former infantryman, chose to recount his wartime experiences in the following manner:

> The monuments symbolize a damned lie, and they are only erected to have people forget about the larger struggle out there: the struggle to organize. Let me tell you why I think that this is so. My first assignment was Guadalcanal and it was unforgettable. We went from the desert directly into Guadalcanal and everybody almost died. It was at that moment I learned that we, as a people, were on the bottom and that organizing was the key to getting anything that you want. We staged sit-down strikes on the docks from time to time to let the crackers know that we were not having any of that. By then, I realized that I had already become revolutionary, in the true sense of the word. That was the best thing that I learned while being stationed in Guadalcanal. I can tell you . . . no damn statute or monument anywhere in the world is going to teach you that.[24]

After Peery spoke, Arnett Hartsfield, a longtime Los Angeles resident and a former officer in the same division, collapsed his military experiences into a somewhat different social reality: an environment marked by racial progress. Hartsfield graduated from the University of California, Los Angeles, the first African American to graduate from the university's Reserve Officer Training Corps before entering the military in 1942. He recalled his army career and his friendships with classmates and future sports stars Jackie Robinson, Kenny Robinson, and Mayor Tom Bradley with great pride:

> Little did I dream that my best friend at UCLA would become mayor of Los Angeles. Just like little did I dream, after I went into the segregated military that I would live long enough to see the Chairman of the Joint Chiefs of Staff not only a brother but a fellow ROTC graduate. Today, as I look out at all of the former captains and battalion commanders who have served in the military, they are younger than my children. We have grown old and our sacrifice was worthwhile.[25]

Reuben Frasier, a Minnesota resident and former officer with the 93rd Infantry Division, echoed some of these sentiments but added a slight twist of irony. When Frasier was interviewed along with fellow World War II–era ex-GIs John O. Howard and Conway Jones in his home in Apple Valley, he stood and launched into a lecture about his military activities that lasted approximately forty-five minutes. Like Arnett Hartsfield, he fashioned elements of his tale around a central theme of military service but arrived at a different interpretation of its meaning. Looking at his twenty-six-year-old granddaughter, an Air Force Academy graduate who was present in the room, Frasier stated:

> Monuments are fine. But they are saying that everything is great now when it isn't. Everything wasn't so great back then, either. When I got out to Fort Huachuca, Arizona, in 1942, the army had no plans for those of us in uniform then, and American society doesn't have any plans for young people now. In fact, there are still some places in my native state of Minnesota where I can't even go to get a cup of coffee. Young people in my hometown of Saint Louis are dissatisfied, standing on the corners. They are not standing there because they're loafing, but because there're not enough jobs. Monuments are for the dead; not the living.

Like Walter Greene, Frasier blended his memories of his wartime past with present-day reality. Throughout the 1980s and 1990s, he and a small party consisting of his wife, daughter, and granddaughter continued to travel down to southern Arizona as a way of making sense of his military career as well as reflecting on conditions affecting their community.[26]

Perhaps the clearest instance of the memory-making process being folded into community instruction occurred in May 1997, when Frasier joined approximately 140 World War II veterans to commemorate the two-hundredth anniversary of Fort Huachuca. Among those in attendance were members of the Southwest Association of Buffalo Soldiers, the 92nd Infantry Division Association, and the Women's Army Corps Association. Also among the spectators were Ohio natives Henry Williams, Thomas White, Fred Ezelle, and Clarence Gaines—all members of the Cleveland-based Huachucans Veterans' Association. While enjoying the local cuisine, ex-World War II service personnel and their families listened to speeches delivered by Sierra Vista city officials, business people, and the post commander. However, they were brought to their feet by Southwest Association of Buffalo Soldiers chairman Harlan L. Bradford: "Comrades, we gather here today to honor our past activities here at Fort Huachuca. But we represent more than social/party organization. Let us remember that Fort Huachuca symbolizes our continuing commitment to informing the public and especially young people of our contribution to the making of this country and our continuing commitment to our communities." His words touched many in the audience that day because, for them, Fort Huachuca was the place where the past intersected with their immediate condition.[27]

Here we find the ultimate irony. While Peery delivered his impromptu address, the 1,400 base dwellings that provided many of these veterans with the political lessons that informed their postwar lives were scheduled for demolition.[28] Moreover, while journalists and scholars celebrated and eulogized the historical roles of black World War II GIs like Frasier, they failed to confront the wider significance of these memory-making sessions or the instruction that Frasier and others were imparting to successive generations or the reunion sites in which these dynamic processes were taking place. Little did the veterans realize it, but at that moment their precious sites of memory were being wiped away in a public epidemic of forgetting. And yet for many of the family members, spectators, and public officials who gathered at the military base, the memory-telling performances of the black ex-GIs and the context in which their stories were revived, resuscitated, and relived reflected an interactive process through which the veterans themselves became walking monuments of social and political struggle.

By carefully examining the dynamic interplay of sites of memory and memory-making performance, we move closer to understanding the relationship between public memory and private history in the African American experience during World War II. Although the stories are as diverse as the units in which they served and the ranks they held, in the minds of the ex-GIs the reunion hall, the armory, and the parade grounds became sites where the telling of their own life experiences provided the keys to future direct action for their respective communities. Of course, the memory process is both semantic and episodic, prone to moments of inaccuracy and distortion, and subjectively constructed. But by attempting to understand the social, cultural, and political settings that shape the construction of memory, we move toward a reconceptualization of the significance of race, power, and identity formation in the African American experience of twentieth-century wars.

NOTES

I would like to acknowledge Leslie Schwalm and Stephen Vlastos for their helpful suggestions on earlier drafts of this manuscript.

1. The term "Buffalo Soldiers" refers to the all-black 24th and 25th Infantry and the 9th and 10th Cavalry regiments that served in the trans-Mississippi West in the late nineteenth century. Authorized by Congress after the Civil War, the units engaged in patrolling assignments throughout the West, protecting settlers who traveled from Missouri to the west coast and the Southwest from attacks by outlaws or American Indians. Renowned for their activities in the region, members of the cavalry units were named "Buffalo Soldiers" by American Indians, a reference to the animal that roamed the plains during the period. For more on these units, see William Leckie, *The Buffalo Soldiers* (Norman: University of Oklahoma Press, 1967); William Loren Katz, *Black West: A Documentary and Pictorial History of the African American Role in the Westward Expansion of the United States* (New York: Doubleday, 1971).

2. Press release, "Reunion at Fort Huachuca" (Washington, DC: U.S. Department of the Army, 1995), 2–9.

3. My idea of memory theater is drawn from Frances A. Yates, *The Art of Memory* (Chicago: University of Chicago Press, 1966), 129–59; Susan G. Davis, *Parades and Power: Street Theatre in Nineteenth Century Philadelphia* (Philadelphia: Temple University Press, 1986); Jill Taft-Kaufman, "How to Tell a True War Story: The Dramaturgy and Staging of Narrative Theatre," *Theatre Topics* 10:1 (2000): 17–38; Jens Brockmeier, "Autobiography, Narrative, and the Freudian Concept of Life History," *Philosophy, Psychiatry, and Psychology* 4:3 (1997): 175–99; Elizabeth A. L. Stine, "Commentary: Is Memory Something We Have or Something We Do?" in Graham M. Davies and Robert H. Logie, eds., *Advances in Psychology 100: Memory in Everyday Life* (The Netherlands: Elsevier, 1993), 447–60; Sheldon L. Messinger, Harold Sampson, and Robert D. Towne, "Life as Theater: Some Notes on the Dramaturgic Approach to Social Reality," *Sociometry* 25 (September 1962): 98–110; Earl Lewis, "Connecting Memory, Self, and the Power of Place in African American Urban History," in Kenneth W. Goings and Raymond Mohl, eds., *The New African American Urban History* (London: Sage Publications, 1996), 116–41; Howard Schuman and Jacqueline Scott, "Generations and Collective Memory," *American Sociological Review* 54 (1989): 359–81. I thank Angelita Reyes for bringing this source to my attention.

4. "War Department to Study Tan Yanks' Utilization," *Baltimore Afro-American,* 6 October 1945, 12; Morris J. MacGregor, *Integration of the Armed Forces, 1940–1965* (Washington, DC: Center for Military History, 1981), 130–32. For more on the Army's postwar studies of the participation of African Americans in the U.S. armed forces, see Sherie Mershon and Steven Schlossman, *Foxholes and Color Lines: Desegregating the U.S. Armed Forces* (Baltimore: Johns Hopkins University Press, 1998); Gerald Astor, *The Right to Fight: A History of African Americans in the Military* (Novato, CA: Presidio Press, 1998); Bernard C. Nalty, *Strength for the Fight: A History of Black Americans in the Military* (New York: Free Press, 1986); Richard O. Hope, *Racial Strife in the U.S. Military: Toward the Elimination of Discrimination* (New York: Praeger, 1979); Neil A. Wynn, *The Afro-American and the Second World War* (New York: Holmes and Meier, 1975); Jack D. Foner, *Blacks and the Military in American History* (New York: Praeger, 1974); Richard M. Dalfiume, *Desegregation of the U.S. Armed Forces: Fighting on Two Fronts, 1939–1953* (Columbia: University of Missouri Press, 1969); Richard Stillman, *Integration of the U.S. Armed Forces* (New York: Praeger, 1968); and the landmark study by Ulysses G. Lee, *United States Army in World War II, Special Studies: The Employment of Negro Troops* (Washington, DC: Office of the Chief of Military History, 1966).

5. Approving Action of Commanding General, 92nd Infantry Division of Proceedings of Board of Review Appointed by Letter Orders dated 23 June 1945 to Consider the Combat Effectiveness of Negro Officers and Enlisted Men, 2 July 1945, RG 407, Records of the Adjutant General's Department, Entry 291.2, File: "Top Secret: 92nd Infantry Division Combat Efficiency Analysis and Supplementary Report," National Archives and Records Administration, Military Field Branch, Suitland, MD.

6. Memorandum, 92nd Commanding General, Major General Edward M. Almond, to John J. McCloy, undated, Subject: Expressions showing Attitudes towards the Fighting Abilities of Negro Troops, RG 107, Records of the Civilian Aide to the Secretary of War, Box 359, Entry 236, Folder: 93rd Division, National Archives and Records Administration, Military Field Branch. For a fuller elaboration of the viewpoints that circulated among the 92nd Division High Command during the period, see Paul Goodman, *A Fragment of Victory: In Italy during World War II, 1942–1945* (Carlisle Barracks, PA: U.S. Army War College, 1952); Lee, *Employment of Negro Troops*; Ernest F. Fisher, Jr., *Cassino to the Alps: United States Army in World War II* (Washington, DC: Center of Military History, 1977); Robert W. Kesting, "Conspiracy to Discredit the Black Buffaloes: The 92nd Infantry in World War II," *Journal of Negro History* 72:1–2 (1987): 1–17; Hondon B. Hargrove, *Buffalo Soldiers in Italy: Black Americans in World War II* (Jefferson, NC: McFarland, 1985); and Dale Wilson, "Recipe for Failure: Major General Edward M. Almond and Preparation of the U.S. 92nd Infantry Division for Combat in World War II," *Journal of Military History* 56 (1992): 473–88.

7. Radio Message, Douglas MacArthur to George C. Marshall, Chief of Staff, 4 March 1945, RG 4, Box 17, Folder 3, C-N-C, USAFPAC, War Department, Correspondence, 901-1000, 31 December 1944–29 April 1945, Douglas MacArthur Memorial Archives, Norfolk, VA.

8. Secret Radiogram, George Marshall, Chief of Staff, to Major General Millard Harmon, 18 March 1944; and Secret Letter, General Oscar Griswold to Major General A. J. Barnett, 6 May 1944; both available at RG 407, Records of the Adjutant General's Office, Entry 427, Box 13712, Folder: Negro Troops-Bougainville, First Battalion of the 25th Infantry Regimental Combat Team, NARA II, College Park, MD.

9. For example, see Arnold M. Rose, "Army Policies toward Negro Soldiers," *Annals of the American Academy of Political and Social Science* 244 (March 1946): 90–94; Rutherford B. Stevens, "Racial Aspects of Emotional Problems of Negro Soldiers," *American Journal of Psychiatry* 103 (January 1947): 493–98; Stewart Wolf, "Mental Illness among Negro Troops Overseas," *American Journal of Psychiatry* 103 (January 1947): 499–512; Charles Dollard and Donald Young, "The Negro in the Armed Forces," *Survey Graphic* 36 (January 1947): 66–69, 111–16; Edward T. Hall, Jr., "Race Prejudice and Negro-White Relations in the Army," *American Journal of Sociology* 52 (March 1947): 401–9.

10. Warman Welliver, "Report on the Negro Soldier," *Harper's Magazine* (April 1946): 333–338ff; quoted material, p. 335.

11. Between the Civil War and World War II, the African American presence in the U.S. military was limited to service in racially segregated battalions and regiments. The term "Jim Crow" refers to the systematic segregation in the treatment, assignment, and employment of these units.

12. Robert F. Cocklin, "Report on the Negro Soldier," *Infantry Journal* 54 (December 1946): 17.

13. Lawrence D. Reddick, "Race Relations in the Army," *American Journal of Sociology* 53 (July 1947): 41. Reddick was referring to a speech delivered by James Eastland, the junior senator from Mississippi, on the Senate floor in June 1945, in which he disparaged the conduct of African American GIs under fire. For more on this issue, see *Congressional Record*,

79th Cong., 1st Sess. (29 June 1945), vol. 91, pt. 5: 7420–22; and *Congressional Record,* 79th Cong., 2nd Sess. (1 February 1946), vol. 92, pt. 1: 392-489. "Representative Gahagan Lauds Colored Servicemen," *Michigan Chronicle,* 2 February 1946, 13; "GI Mother Rallies 2,500 Against Senator Eastland," Baltimore *Afro-American,* 21 July 1945, in Tuskegee Institute Newspaper Clippings Files (hereafter TCF) (Ann Arbor: University Microfilms International, 1976), Reel 92, Frame 356; "What Afro Readers Say; Animal Cracker-ology," Baltimore *Afro-American,* 29 September 1945, 4; "Army Jim Crow Continues in Face of Record of Tan Yanks," Oklahoma *City Black Dispatch,* 17 August 1946, TCF, Reel 96, Frame 484;

14. The idea of sense-making in rituals like reunions is borrowed from Keiko Ikeda's remarkable study *A Room Full of Mirrors: High School Reunions in Middle America* (Stanford: Stanford University Press, 1998). I would like to thank Paula Hamilton for bringing this work to my attention.

15. "Professor Found Dead in Gas-Filled Room," Norfolk *Journal and Guide,* 30 November 1957, 1. For more on the wartime travails of Luther Fuller while serving in the 93rd Division, see Robert Jefferson, "Tempered Hope," manuscript.

16. Interview with Francis Ellis, Ann Arbor, MI, 1 March and 3 March 1995; interview with Freida Bailey Greene, Phoenix, AZ., 26 March 1998.

17. "Bowen and Greene to Vet Administration," *Michigan Chronicle,* 19 March 1946, 5; Walter R. Greene clipping file, in the author's possession; interview with Francis Ellis, 3 March 1995; interview with Freida Bailey Greene, Phoenix, AZ, 19 March 1998; Jefferson, "Tempered Hope," epilogue.

18. Jehu Hunter, conversation with author, Carlisle Barracks, PA, 9 September 1992; also Major Clark and Jehu Hunter, "Triumph and Tribulation: Reflections on the Combat Experience of the Ninety-second Infantry Division in North Italy," in *Proceedings of the First Conference on Black Americans in World War II,* 9 September 1992 (Carlisle Barracks, 1992), 5.

19. Dennette Harrod, conversation with author, Carlisle Barracks, PA, 9 September 1992; also Harrod, "The 366th Infantry and Lieutenant John R. Fox," in *Proceedings,* 2–3.

20. Dovey J. Roundtree, "Looking Back and Marching Forward," paper presented at the Conference on Black Americans in World War II, Carlisle Barracks, PA, 9 September 1992.

21. Interview with Dr. Martha Putney, Carlisle Barracks, PA, 9 September 1992.

22. Stephen Steinberg, *Turning Back: The Retreat from Racial Justice in American Thought and Policy* (Boston: Beacon, 1995), 175.

23. Robin D. G. Kelley, *Yo Mama's Disfunktional!: Fighting the Cultural Wars in Urban America* (Boston: Beacon Press, 1997), 98–99; Michael Tonry, *Malign Neglect: Race, Crime and Punishment in America* (New York: Oxford University Press, 1996).

24. Interview with Nelson Peery, Chicago, 8 December 1994.

25. Interview with Arnett Hartsfield, Jr., Los Angeles, 1 December 1994.

26. Interview with Reuben Frasier, Apple Valley, MN, 1 August 1998.

27. Harlan L. Bradford, Sr., "Remembering Our Forgotten Heroes," Fifth Annual Salute to Buffalo Soldiers Days, Fort Huachuca, AZ, 2 May 1997 (photocopy), 14.

28. Fifth Annual Salute to Buffalo Soldier Days, souvenir program, Fort Huachuca and Sierra Vista, AZ, 1–4 May 1997; Bill Hess, "Historian Lauds Black Soldiers' Service," *Sierra Vista Herald,* 30 April 1997, 1, 5; "Passing of an Era: Demolition of World War II Wood Buildings Continues," *Huachuca Scout,* 8 January 1998, 3–4.

PART III

MAKING CHANGE

Part III

Making Change

⁓

While an interest in creating a democratic, inclusive public history underlies much work in oral history, including work described in the previous parts of this volume, the chapters in this final part focus on oral history driven by an explicitly activist agenda. The work is quite eclectic, drawing on a variety of theories, methods, and media, and blurring the boundaries between past troubles and present needs, between scholar and citizen, between research and action. Some of it is broadly cultural, aimed at changing minds and influencing ideas; some is more directed at empowering individuals and creating social change.

Riki Van Boeschoten's chapter describes an activity that will be familiar to many readers: using a classroom oral history project to challenge students' "common sense" notions and open them up to other points of view. An anthropologist teaching in Greece, Van Boeschoten sought to create for her students an experience akin to the "culture shock" felt by anthropologists in the field as they confront an unfamiliar way of life. Thus she had them interview Albanian migrants to Greece, a group often presented in stereotypical, indeed xenophobic, ways in Greek popular culture. Subsequently, she had another group of students interview Greeks who had migrated to Germany after World War II in search of economic opportunity, a phenomenon that is not unlike the experience of contemporary Albanians but about which there is an uncomfortable silence in Greece. The interviews had the desired effect: students had the sort of "aha!" reaction Van Boeschoten hoped for, seeing the person underneath the stereotype in the case of the Albanian interviews, understanding something about the desperate circumstances of postwar Greece in the case of the Greek interviews. Van Boeschoten describes the entire process of her classroom project, from preparing students to do the interviews to developing a radio program that compared Albanian and Greek migrant experiences. Yet the chapter is more than a comprehensive "how to," since Van Boeschoten places her students' work within the broader contexts of Greek history, an analysis of mass-mediated culture, and anthropological theory.

Daniel Kerr's chapter suggests oral history's broad educative value outside a formal classroom setting as he reflects upon his years of work with the very public Cleveland Homeless Oral History Project. Beginning with a series of videotaped interviews with homeless men and women in Cleveland, Ohio's, Public Square, the project aimed to counter the triumphalist rhetoric about the city's presumed "renaissance" by giving voice to those for whom urban renewal has meant further marginalization. Quoted extensively in the essay, the interviewees articulated an incisive critique and a sophisticated analysis of the relationship between gentrification and poor living and working conditions among the unhoused. For some, the interviews provided an opportunity to express an already well defined understanding of their situation; for others, they promoted consciousness raising, offering a means of thinking about their circumstances in new ways. A key element of these oral histories was Kerr's interviewing strategy. Rather than focusing on narrators' personal histories, inevitably narratives of declension and an all-too-frequent humiliating ritual for homeless people, he asked about causes of homelessness. In their answers, details of personal life became embedded in a broader context. The project did not end with the interviews; rather, they became a starting point for both community education and activism: video interviews were shown and discussed at homeless shelters; they served as the basis for a locally produced radio program and a platform for those pressing—successfully, in some cases—for changes in the management of homelessness and the employment of the unhoused in Cleveland. Kerr reflects thoughtfully on his own efforts to link scholarship with activism, a concern of many involved in local oral history projects. Above all, the chapter suggests that work like the Cleveland Homeless Oral History Project requires commitment, patience, and the recognition that ordinary people can think critically and make change—an ethic deeply embedded in the practice of oral history.

Silvia Salvatici's discussion of her work documenting the experiences of Albanian women in Kosovo during the Balkan wars of the 1990s further suggests how oral history may contribute to a broad program of social change. Undertaken under the auspices of the Archives of Memory project of the International Organization for Migration, Salvatici's interviews sought to inform the organization's efforts to attend to the psychosocial needs of a population traumatized by war and displacement. The narratives revealed an interesting tension: while women often framed their stories within the conventions of nationalist discourse, especially the trope of the "suffering victim," they also undercut these conventions with stories of unconventional behavior, individual courage, and resistance within what had been a deeply patriarchal society. As Salvatici richly illustrates, the exigencies of war created opportunities, if we may call them that, for an expanded sphere of action and a redefinition of identity for Albanian Kosovar women, a promising hint at a more equitable future for them. More importantly for Salvatici, the accounts narrators gave of their lives suggest cracks in a monolithic nationalist identity among Albanians, which, if made public, can create cultural space for divergent voices in a post-war world.

Social trauma forms the context of Pilar Riaño-Alcalá's work also as she discusses the memory workshops she and colleagues conducted among those forcibly displaced by a generation of violence in Colombia, South America. These workshops, like Kerr's Cleveland Homeless Oral History Project, combine the narrative aspects of oral history with action-oriented research and popular education. They engage participants in a complex act of group storytelling with both personal and collective ramifications. As individuals tell of terror and loss, they also create a new identity as survivors; as they reconstruct their pasts, they develop a sense of a plotted—or purposeful—life. As individuals share their stories with others, they gain a sense of community; and as these temporary workshop communities reflect on participants' stories, they begin to develop a critical social consciousness. These communities of memory also become a shield against the state-sanctioned forgetting encouraged by the rhetoric of reconciliation in present-day Colombia. Here oral history is a means both of proceeding through the mourning that accompanies profound loss and of recreating community anew. In its awareness of this dual function, Riaño-Alcalá's chapter harks back to those of Sean Field and Horacio Roque Ramírez in Part II, suggesting the interconnected themes that run through many of the chapters and much work in oral history.

11

PUBLIC MEMORY AS ARENA OF CONTESTED MEANINGS: A STUDENT PROJECT ON MIGRATION

~

Riki Van Boeschoten

Mass Migration into Southern Europe and Public Memory

This chapter explores the use of oral history in education by focusing on a project designed to explore migration issues with Greek undergraduate students. For scholars interested in the relationship between subjectively told oral narratives and the shaping of public memory, the subject of contemporary migration into the Mediterranean has much to offer. Greece, Italy, Spain, and Portugal have over the last two decades witnessed an impressive turnaround—from emigration to immigration—scarcely paralleled in the history of migration.[1] For most of the twentieth century, these countries sent millions of mainly illiterate migrants of peasant origin abroad in search of economic opportunity. After the mid-1980s, as the European "Rio Grande" dividing prosperous nations from their underdeveloped southern neighbors moved north, they have become (reluctant) hosts to a mass influx of new migrants from Africa, Asia, Latin America, and Eastern Europe. This phenomenon has not only restructured local societies in multiple ways; it has also changed the ways in which their citizens remember their past, represent their present, and imagine their future. The social impact of these developments in any of these countries can hardly be overestimated.

For Greece, adjusting to its sudden transformation into a multicultural society is a major challenge. Greece has an exceptionally large immigrant population, estimated at about 10 percent of the total, whereas Italy, Spain, and Portugal have figures between 2.3 percent and 2.6 percent, well below the European average.[2] Because Greece lacks an efficient legal framework for integrating newcomers into society, most of these immigrants are undocumented. Moreover, in contrast to the other three countries, where the ethnic origin of migrants is quite diversified, about 80 percent of all migrants in Greece are from neighboring Albania. The predominance of one particular ethnic group has favored its "demonization" in public discourse and the development of xenophobic attitudes. Opinion polls taken in 1989 still showed Greece as one of the European Union (EU) countries most tolerant toward foreigners; only three years later, it had become one of the most xenophobic. Foreign migrants are blamed for unemployment and the rise of criminality. Although some of the latest opinion polls show that a majority of Greeks now accept that migrants are likely to stay and favor their naturalization, there is also convincing contrasting evidence that Greece continues to be the most xenophobic and intolerant country of the EU.[3]

This negative stereotyping of Albanian migrants has also influenced the way in which Greeks have come to see themselves and their past.[4] The fact that Greeks massively participated in the post–World War II migration to Western Europe to escape similar, if not worse, living conditions than the ones Albanians endure has been erased from public memory. Recent prosperity, brought about, among other factors, by EU membership, can help explain why Greek xenophobia is strongest against the group with which it shares a common past (both countries were part of the Ottoman empire) and to which it is culturally most similar.[5] By employing Albanians for jobs or household chores they used to do themselves, Greeks confirm their improved status and self-image.

In addition, contemporary Greeks are not used to the presence of ethnic "others" apart from tourists.[6] The ethnic, religious, and linguistic variety that had characterized the country's Ottoman past,[7] as well as the continued presence of many of these old linguistic minorities within the Greek nation-state, had been erased from public memory in the nation-building process of the nineteenth and twentieth centuries as Greek national ideology was constructed around two core ideas: homogeneity of the nation and continuity with the classical past.[8] Until the 1990s young Greeks grew up with the idea that they belonged to a monolingual nation.

Today, the high visibility of the new immigrants undermines these two traditional pillars of the Greek nation. Strolling through the streets of Athens, one encounters Chinese restaurants and tiny shops selling cheap and shiny clothes, Indian and Pakistani street vendors, building sites employing Albanian construction workers, Africans selling CDs, and Filipinas resting in a nearby park. Baffled by this new urban landscape and lacking the conceptual tools to make sense of it, modern Greeks resort to two contradictory stereotypical images inherited from the past. On the one hand they refer to the nineteenth-century ideal of ethnic homogeneity, a discourse that has already led to strong social pressures for assimilation or to open hostility toward the newcomers. On the other, they stress the notion of hospitality (*philoxenia*), a virtue supposedly inherited from the ancient Greeks. Balancing these two opposite values is an arduous—and ultimately impossible—task.

Bringing Migration into the Classroom

When I started to teach anthropology at the University of Thessaly, I faced a major challenge. Most of our students had no idea what anthropology was, and I had no clear idea of my students' "common sense knowledge" of culture. One of the most efficient ways to develop anthropological insights is to produce a culture shock—to "otherize," by listening to the "native" point of view, what had seemed familiar, and to come to recognize as familiar what had seemed strange, different, or threatening. Migration seemed an ideal field to produce such a culture shock at home.

Because Greece had been a nation of migrants through most of the twentieth century, some of my students, as I expected, had relatives who had taken part in the post–World War II migration to Western Europe; some students had even grown up as second-generation migrant children in Germany, where most Greeks had migrated. Yet students are not immune to the xenophobia pervading Greek society. Among students at the University of Thrace in 1996, 97 percent thought foreigners (mainly Albanians) were to be blamed for the rise in crime. Albanians were thought to be dirty, dangerous, and poor.[9] I assumed that most students would be familiar with or might even share such stereotypes, and that they would be unfamiliar with the historical background leading to the mass migration from Albania or with the lived experiences of Albanian migrants. Discovering the migrants' subjectivity through the intimacy of an oral history interview in a migrant's home might, I thought, be an appropriate way to discover the "other" at home, or even to "otherize" the evening newscaster whose banal racism had previously gone unnoticed.

The oral history courses I developed in 2001 and 2002 thus were designed to confront students both with contemporary xenophobic stereotypes about the new migrants from Albania and with public amnesia about the Greeks' own history as migrants. Students were asked to work as a research team to interview Albanian immigrants to Greece and Greek former migrants to Germany and then to compare the experiences of both groups. Because I wanted to show how oral history interviews can play a more active role in society and help shape a different public memory from the one molded by the mass media, I asked the students to reflect on how interviews generated by the class could be used to develop course material for primary or secondary schools in Greece. In addition, during the second year of the project, a different set of students combined material from interviews with Albanian and Greek narrators to produce a radio program, which was broadcast on a local station.

Public Memory and Migration: Celebrating the Nation—but Whose Nation?

A controversy involving a schoolboy made headlines in the Greek press in 2001 and 2003 and awoke the public to the fact that Greece had become a multicultural society. The conflict—concerning the right of foreign-born students to hold the Greek flag at national holiday celebrations—brings us to the core of public memory as an arena of contested meanings. It also shows the central role education plays in shaping national identities and its potential for integrating migrants into the host society. The social actors involved in this event were Odysseas Tsenai,[10] a high school student of Albanian origin, the community of Nea Michaniona[11] in Northern Greece, and high-ranking Greek politicians. The conflict itself arose on the occasion of the annual parade on 28 October, celebrating the refusal in 1940 of Greece's dictator, General Ioannis Metaxas, to comply with the Italian Fascists' demand to occupy the country, an event that marked the beginning of Greece's involvement in World War II. This national holiday is known as *Ochi* ("No") Day.

Ceremonies commemorating historical events play an important role in shaping public memory.[12] They consolidate and legitimate the authority of those in power; they show the public which versions of the past people should remember and which they should forget. Especially in times of rapid sociocultural change, when nations may feel threatened from without or from within, they also show who should be included or excluded from the national body. In this case the perceived threat was the "pollution"[13] of a national symbol in the hands of a migrant boy. Yet even as commemorative events serve to consolidate power from above, they also incorporate "popular attitudes and desires."[14] Thus, the passions aroused nationwide by the 28 October celebration in Nea Michaniona can only be fully understood by taking into account the "popular attitudes and desires" incorporated in the ritual.

Paul Connerton has argued that to understand the nature of social memory, we should shift our attention from the content to the form of such rituals, and especially to the bodily practices involved.[15] The latter play, in fact, an important role in the traditional school parades commemorating *Ochi* Day. After long and exacting rehearsals, primary and secondary students neatly dressed in the national colors of white and blue proudly parade along the main street of towns throughout Greece. Drilled by their teachers and marching docilely to the tunes of the local brass band, their young bodies are transformed into symbols of the nation and thus remind the community of its identity.[16]

The mainstream attitudes incorporated in the ritual reveal themselves also in a very material—indeed bodily—way when the parading students are enthusiastically applauded by the public and especially by their parents in a powerful fusing of national and familial pride. But often public attitudes have less to do with the nation than with social prestige. The privilege of holding the Greek flag is reserved for the best pupil in each school. In Nea Michaniona, in 2001 and again in 2003, the best pupil was Odysseas Tsenai, an Albanian immigrant. By his very excellence at school, young Tsenai involuntarily contested the implicit meanings of the 28 October parade, which were made quite explicit in the ensuing debate in the national press.

The crucial question raised by the event and hotly debated in the newspapers was "Who belongs to the nation?" A second question arose from the first: are identities determined by nature or by culture? Greeks were divided into two camps, each headed by a high-ranking politician. Both camps agreed that only Greeks belong to the nation, but each espoused a different version of "Greekness." The first opted for nature, as in the remarkable words of Panayotis Psomiadis, the right-wing prefect of the northern town of Salonica: "You can only be born a Greek, not become one." The second version opted for culture. "Greeks are those who take part in Greek education" was a famous quotation attributed to the ancient orator Isocrates and invoked by President of the Republic Constantine Stefanopoulos in his attempt to settle the dispute in favor of young Tsenai.[17] The issues remained unresolved when Tsenai, faced with this public pressure, renounced his right to lead the parade. Three years later, although he had passed the entrance examination for the university in Salonica, he left Greece to study in the United States.

The events in Nea Michaniona clearly show that public memory is an arena of contested meanings and that migration is one of the major issues at stake in contemporary Greece. If commemorative practices sanction and interiorize a notion of a common heritage and identity, they also exclude alternative versions of that past.[18] And yet, especially in periods of swift social change, alternative versions of the past as well as a different vision of the future are bound to emerge to challenge dominant versions of public memory. In many other places school parades take place on Greek national holidays without any major conflict. This was what happened, for example, in a depopulated mountain village in southern Greece, where agriculture's survival depends on the Albanian migrant workers who have settled there. The local school had only ten pupils, all of them Albanians. On *Ochi* Day all ten proudly marched through the village holding the Greek flag, acclaimed by the elderly peasants who employed their fathers.[19] So if public memory is about contested symbols, how can oral history contribute to alternative versions of a common past, present, and future? The students' project I developed tried to find some answers to that question.

Developing Culture Shock

The two one-semester oral history courses I developed were designed to offer students the opportunity to think critically about their own and others' stereotypes through the life stories of migrants they interviewed. This experience indeed produced the expected "culture shock": students' direct confrontation with the "native point of view" worked as a catalyst and proved to be a very efficient way to introduce them to the concepts of "anthropology at home" and reflexivity.

I began the first course (2001) by asking the students about their own "spontaneous" perceptions of Albanian migrants. Contrary to what I expected, their responses did not precisely mirror the dominant negative stereotypes. Some mentioned that the Albanian workers settled in their home villages were well received by the locals; others had already developed personal friendships with Albanian young people in our university town. On the other hand, those who grew up in rural villages employing Albanians as a seasonal work force voiced existing stereotypes about the Albanian "mafia" and links with criminality. The fact that responses varied according to students' degree of familiarity with the Albanian "other" seemed to confirm a tendency revealed by recent ethnographic studies. But I wondered if the students expressed more moderate views in the classroom in order to conform to the teacher's expectations (as they imagined them) or to avoid exposing their stereotypical views to the other students. Indeed, even among the more open-minded students, the deep structure of dominant stereotyping emerged at some points in their interviews and their final essays.

Of particular interest in our early discussions was the fact that nearly all students recounted a version of the "tale of the Albanian migrant worker." Though they presented this story as something that had happened to a close relative or neighbor, it is, in fact, a stock tale recounted all over Greece. According to the story, an Albanian who had worked for years for a Greek employer decided to leave one day and went to thank his boss, who had offered him food and shelter for so many years and had stood by him like a father. Before leaving, however, he advised his boss never to employ an Albanian again, because Albanians are ungrateful and he himself had many times considered killing his employer.

This story seems to belong to what Alessandro Portelli has defined as a narrative genre,[20] conforming to the trope of "standing up to the big man" (to the extent that the narrator had thought of killing his boss) but with a twist at the end, as the protagonist adopts a negative view of this own ethnic group. This and other stories introduced the students to the heart of oral history: the selectivity of memory, the relationship between myth and history, and the role of subjectivity. It also generated long discussions on the alleged criminal nature of Albanian workers. I asked the students to read and present in class published sources on this subject, which revealed the extent to which Albanian criminality is constructed by the media, the silence surrounding Greek criminality toward Albanian migrants, and the fact that the behavior of their Greek employers—for example, the refusal to pay wages—may trigger Albanian acts of violence. This discussion opened a pathway for the students to discover the migrants' own subjectivity.

We then proceeded to study the historical and political background of out-migration from Albania, paying particular attention to the effects of the breakdown of the Communist regime on the Albanian economy and social structures. We also examined the global context of new migration movements and legal frameworks in the host countries. Finally, we analyzed the role played by the media in constructing stereotypes of Albanians, focusing on ways in which the discourse varied by medium and by political orientation. We found that electronic media displayed xenophobic attitudes most aggressively, especially in the evening television news programs and talk shows on commercial television stations. Shortly after the arrival of the first Albanian migrants in 1991, the nighttime news changed its format, increasing in length from thirty to ninety minutes and focusing on sensational reporting of crime-related events in which the suspects were invariably Albanian migrants. In the print media, two variants of ethnic stereotyping appeared. The conservative press conveyed a pervasive sense of moral panic: the Greek nation was being threatened by an "invasion" of illegal male Albanian migrants, who were criminals, socially inferior, undesirable, and visually recognizable (poorly dressed, strong and muscular, subdued demeanor). Greeks, on the contrary, were presented as loyal citizens, good family men, honorable but defenseless, terrorized by the increase of criminality. The progressive press distinguished between "good" and "bad" Albanians and reversed the terms of the dichotomy (portraying good Albanians and bad Greeks) while leaving intact the mechanisms by which Albanians are stigmatized. In this discourse, the "bad" and criminal Albanian is presented as an exception, while "good" Albanian workers are represented as poor and hungry victims of exploitation and racist attacks, honorable, hard-working, and frightened underdogs. Greeks are portrayed as unscrupulous and pitiless employers and as born racists.[21]

Against this background, my students and I set out to discover those aspects of Albanian migration that were so obviously lacking in the media discourse: the historical background and motivations of the recent wave of migrants, the variety of individual experiences, an understanding of Albanian migrants as gender-specific and socially constructed individuals, and, above all, the voice of the migrants themselves.

Our interviewees were not selected to be representative of the whole Albanian population in Greece, but to show a diversity of social backgrounds and thus deconstruct the stereotype of "the Albanian" as exclusively male, uneducated, and poor. We identified nine interviewees, four men and five women, mostly in their twenties or thirties. Their social backgrounds and reasons for migrating varied, but their present occupations in the main conformed to prevailing patterns of employment: the women were domestic workers, and the men worked in the construction sector. The sample also included a male university student and a ten-year-old schoolgirl.

The students worked in teams to prepare the interview guide. For most this was their first experience with interviewing. Each team prepared questions on a particular aspect of a life story (childhood, reason for emigrating, the journey, reception in the host country, work experience, relations with Greeks, future plans). The content, phrasing, and order of these questions were discussed and adjusted in the classroom, and then all were combined into an interview guide. We concluded our preparation with a role-playing session. The students worked in groups of three, each assuming in turn the role of Albanian migrant, interviewer, and observer. The practice interviews were recorded, and the students discussed the results. This exercise proved very difficult, as the dominant stereotypes had started to crumble but nothing was yet available to replace them. While students had no difficulty playing the role of the Greek interviewer, they had a hard time imagining the Albanian perspective. As a result, most students trying to assume the role of the Albanian migrant portrayed their relations to Greek society as either extremely positive or extremely negative. Only during their "real life" interviews did they began to develop a sense of the nuances.

Most students found the interview itself an interesting experience and were able to establish rapport with their interviewees in spite of initial tensions. They produced summaries of their completed interviews and a diary of the interviewing process in which they commented on changes in the interviewee-interviewer relationship during the interview and the effects of gender, age, and ethnicity; they also reflected on their own perceptions. The summaries were shared within the class so that each student could obtain a more comprehensive view of the material collected. At this stage the students wrote their first paper, which had to include three excerpts from their interview that they considered particularly revealing, along with an explanation of why they selected these texts. Finally, all the selected excerpts were divided into thematic categories, including gender relations, perceived racism, religion, work, and changed perceptions of the country of origin, and subjected to a horizontal analysis. This exercise was designed to enable students to assess those aspects of the migration experience that differed according to gender, age, and social background and those aspects that were shared among all migrants. The course concluded with a final essay in which each student had to consider stereotypical representations of Albanian migrants in the Greek media in light of the evidence from the interviews.

In the second course (2002), we focused on Greek migrants' experience and on comparing that with the experience of the Albanians. We reviewed the social context of Greek migration to Western Europe and considered the cultural silence that surrounds the Greek emigrant past, contrasting it with the abundant cultural commentary about Albanian migration to Greece. The social profile of Greek migrants to Germany is much more homogeneous than that of post-1990 migrants from Albania to Greece. Most came from rural villages in northern Greece and were employed in German factories. Therefore, it was neither necessary nor possible to ensure the same diversity of social backgrounds in our sample of Greek interviewees that we had sought in our Albanian group. Yet our small sample revealed some variation: some went to Germany on tourist visas instead of with organized labor schemes; others had moved to small urban centers in Greece before their departure for Germany. The sample included four women and three men. All but one had been employed as factory workers and had returned to Greece in the 1970s. As their final essay assignment, students had to discuss the contribution of oral history to the study of migration, supporting their arguments with evidence from their own interview.

In the second phase of the 2002 course, we developed ideas for combining the Greek and Albanian interview material to produce a radio program. I thought that a comparative approach, focusing on aspects of the migration process common to both Albanians and Greeks, would most likely engage the widest audience. After transcribing the interviews, the students worked as a group to produce a draft script. We first defined thematic units that had emerged from the interviews and seemed relevant to both Albanian and Greek migrations: reasons for migrating, relations with the host society, work, gender, and kinship. Then each student selected excerpts from both her own interview with a Greek former migrant and an interview with an Albanian migrant that matched these thematic units. We next juxtaposed the experiences of Greek and Albanian migrants to produce the first draft of the script. We then made final selections and reordered the fragments, taking pains to put the voices of Greeks and Albanians into dialogue with each other.

But the most difficult task still lay ahead: connecting the fragments with brief but substantial commentaries. At this point the students needed a lot of help, as this task required three very different skills: a thorough knowledge of the migration experience of the two groups, a level of abstract thinking, and the ability to express essential ideas in language accessible to a broad audience.

Students drafted their own connecting links, and we worked on them in class until they seemed satisfactory. Our final task was exciting but extremely time-consuming: to record and put together the actual radio tape, including interview excerpts, commentary, and selected musical fragments.

The final product was a radio program, approximately forty minutes long, called "Journey into Infinity." It was broadcast on a daily morning show called "Good Morning, Neighbor," which deals mainly with social and political issues of local and national interest. The program began with a well-known Greek popular song, "At Munich Station," in which a singer plaintively describes the ordeal of Greek migrants to Germany. This was followed by an Albanian folk song about migration, which is sung also on the Greek side of the border. Then Matilda, one of our Albanian interviewees, took the floor, observing that Albanian migrants had come to Greece just as Greek migrants had once gone to Germany; she was immediately followed by Haris, a Greek interviewee, who asserted that the difference between Greek and Albanian experiences was like "night and day." That opening sequence brought the selectivity of public memory immediately to the fore. In the narrative that followed, the students explained that in order to find out which of the two was right, they had interviewed both Greek and Albanian migrants. For the remainder of the program we juxtaposed Albanian and Greek voices talking about different aspects of the migrant experience. The program ended with Ilias, an Albanian migrant worker, thanking us in broken Greek for the opportunity to "talk about the Greeks and the Albanians. In both countries there are goodies and baddies, and finally we are the same everywhere. Thank you so much."

Migrants' Voices: What We Learned from the Interviews

The interviews produced a wealth of information and ample food for thought, thus creating the opportunity for students to reconsider mainstream attitudes toward present and past migration. The surprisingly high quality of the interviews, considering the students' lack of prior experience with oral history, was due partly to the migrants' eagerness to have their voices heard and partly to pre-existing rapport, since many of the students interviewed individuals whom they already knew.

At a subjective level, the most thrilling experience for the students was to discover the human being behind the label "migrant." As one student wrote: "The 'other' is transformed from a product of our imagination into a real person with visible needs, possibilities, and feelings."[22] Indeed, migrants consented to be interviewed for precisely this reason. In a society that they felt treated them as less than human, they sought public recognition of their collective history and an opportunity to reclaim their dignity: "The most important thing is that we are human beings."[23] Narrators also spoke of transformations, identities shaped and reshaped. As their stories unfolded from childhood to repatriation or to plans for the future, they brought home to the listener how deeply transformative the migrant experience is. One of the Greek migrants called it "a popular university."[24] A clear example can be found in the way migration restructures gender identities. Both Greek and Albanian women came from societies with strong patriarchal ideologies and changed their perspective on gender relations through contact with the host society and participation in the labor market. From this perspective the Greek/Albanian dichotomy introduced by the media became meaningless.

The individual life stories of the Greek migrants paradoxically became a means of reclaiming a collective history. They restored the visibility of a common past that had been condemned to oblivion and undermined the common sense view of migration as a pathway to prosperity. Greek migrants had left for Germany out of sheer poverty. All our interviewees came from poor mountain villages and were poorly educated. "Home? What home? We just had one room and a kitchen and there wasn't even a lock on the door. We didn't have any olive oil for our food. We used to go and borrow half a cup in the neighborhood."[25] The Albanian migrant stories, on the other hand, undermined the stereotypical view of a racially defined, ahistorical, and reified subject (male, poor, uncivilized, and criminal). All the migrants had completed eight years of compulsory education, and some had university degrees. While some came from rural villages, others belonged to the urban elite. If they had decided to migrate for economic reasons, these were linked to the social chaos brought about by the breakdown of Communist rule, but their childhood memories evoked idyllic images of harmony, peace, and security. Their stories also reveal many other motives for migrating: love, adventure, study, escape from parental authority or restrictions on women's freedom of movement. Most of all they wanted to discover a new world lying beyond a border that had hitherto closed them off from the rest of the world and about which Communist leader Enver Hoxha had lied: "Enver Hoxha told us that we in Albania are better off than anywhere else in the world, he told us that Greece is a poor country!" "We were restless like animals locked up in a cage for years and then set free. Hoxha had locked us up for forty-five years!"[26]

Work experiences are another important part of the life stories. Greek migrants left on organized work schemes within the framework of bilateral agreements between Greece and Germany. Upon arrival they were granted a factory job, rudimentary living quarters, and health insurance. Therefore they remember Germany as a country with "good systems," much better than those in their home country. But there was a high price to pay: long hours of work in unhealthy conditions and long separations from their children: "Until 1986 I worked very hard with my wife. Then I got ill from asthma because I worked at the painting shop of this car factory. I said to my wife 'Efthimia, let's get out of here, or else I will leave my bones here.' "[27]

Although the prospects for upward social mobility for Greek *gastarbeiter* (guest workers) were almost nonexistent, the change from peasant to factory worker was a modest social improvement. Most Albanian migrants, on the contrary, found themselves in social positions inferior to those they had occupied at home. Anna, a student, and Natasha, a former accountant, are now cleaning house for middle-class Greek women. Albanian migrant workers usually do not have health insurance and are more dependent on their employer than were Greek laborers in German factories. But they can more easily change jobs: "I worked as a housekeeper in a big villa in Lechonia. That lady had seventeen dogs and it nearly drove me mad. I woke up at 6:30 A.M. and went to bed at 12:30 after midnight. I cleaned the whole house and the garden, fed the dogs and at night I wept all by myself. Well, I didn't even stay for a fortnight; I couldn't stand those dogs any longer."[28] In spite of these marked differences, the Greek and Albanian stories about work experiences are similar in two aspects: both groups take pride in their work skills, and both claim a personal dignity denied to them by the host society.

There are other points on which Greek and Albanian migrant experiences mirror each other. For example, both groups, as a result of living in another country as less-than-welcome guests, have developed more critical attitudes toward the home country. And both groups have suffered from social exclusion and xenophobic attitudes in the host country. Although Greek migrants are less explicit about such humiliating experiences, these memories emerged during our interviews. One of the Greek men, for example, remembered that Greek migrants were called *"Zigeuner"* (Gypsies) and "dirty *gastarbeiter*" and that he himself was once falsely accused of theft just because he was a foreigner.[29] Greek xenophobia was a more common theme in the Albanian interviews. For example, Dora, a young schoolgirl, said that when the Greek lady who employed her mother had proposed having her baptized, the girl agreed, even though her parents were Muslims. Pressed by her interviewer to explain why, she admitted that she did not want to be labeled "Albanian" by her schoolmates. "That annoys me, because they don't only say I am Albanian, they also say I should get back to Albania."[30]

These few examples clearly show the multiple ways in which the migrants' lived experiences undermined existing stereotypes. The Greek stories brought to the surface aspects of the recent past that modern Greeks now wish to forget: the poverty and insecurity of the 1950s and 1960s, the experience of being treated as underdogs in Germany, the failure of migration to materially improve their circumstances. More generally, they suggested social and cultural similarities between Greeks and Albanians that often go unrecognized. As one student aptly remarked, the recent revival of "balkanisms" has led many Greeks to dissociate themselves from their Balkan past and to stress instead their European identity.[31] The Albanian stories, on the other hand, restored gender to the migration story, reconstructed the image of the Albanian migrant as a well-educated and skilled subject, undermined the link between ethnic identity and criminality, and introduced an assertive migrant counter-discourse.

Reconstructing Public Memory: Students' and Migrants' Responses

The interview is a search for self through the other. That's how I experienced giving the floor to an Albanian Gypsy and I asked myself what alterity actually is. For me what is familiar is also what we know less, and the unknown is most frightening because it can at any moment reveal itself as desperately familiar.

During this semester I deconstructed the stereotypes I had transposed from the television screen to my own consciousness. With their memories the migrants helped us understand much about their life back home. We were able not only to reverse many stereotypes, but also to face Greek reality.

When I set out for this interview, somewhere at the back of my mind I had a certain idea about Albanian migrants, which to some extent was influenced by mainstream representations in Greek society. Initially I felt very surprised when I saw before me a nicely dressed, intelligent, and well-educated woman and stepped into her large and elegant living-room, which formed a stark contrast with images of Albanian dwellings I had seen on television. When we started talking, I understood I was dealing with a proud and dignified person. What I gained from this interview was to see migration from a human point of view, to obtain a different view of the mentality and culture of Albanian migrants, and to look at migration through the eyes of a woman.

I grew up in a rural area employing many Albanian migrant workers. Many of my co-villagers consider these people as an "infamous race" and call them "the Albanian mafia." Imperceptibly I had been influenced by these attitudes. I learned to widen my horizon and to see things in a more critical way. The migrants' voices we heard in this course helped to reverse preconceived ideas associated with racist attitudes and to see things more objectively.[32]

As these excerpts from the students' essays show, their direct confrontation with the migrants' lived experience provoked a profound culture shock that made them see in a different light not only the "other," but also the self. For the students it was shocking to discover that not all Albanians were uneducated and poor; in fact, they were more educated than Greek migrants of the 1960s and had been forced to accept work well below their skill level in Greece. Having grown up in a culture that attaches the utmost importance to national identity and its link with religion, the students were even more shocked by the social pressure put on Albanian migrants to change their names and their religion. Although some had known their informants before the interview, they had known them only by their Greek names and had not realized all the implications of the name change. As they were now able to incorporate this issue within the larger framework of ethnic stereotyping, they considered it a brutal and unjust form of forced self-denial and an unnecessary break with an individual's personal past. It was equally shocking for them to discover that not all Greek migrants could boast of a success story and that the strict constraints of capitalist work processes in German factories had placed severe strains on migrant families.

As for the migrants, they felt proud that a university was interested in their stories and hoped that their interviews could contribute to a better public understanding of the migrants' "real life." This expectation confirmed the value of oral history in migration studies as a way to empower individuals and advocate for a greater respect for the migrants' own perspectives.[33] The most explicit examples of oral history's capacity for empowerment can be found in the Albanian interviews, where narrators developed a counter-discourse to the national narrative on immigration and criticized aspects of their host society. Vasiliki, a former factory worker now cleaning for a Greek teacher, expressed opposition to the expectations for assimilation and the social pressure on Albanian migrants to change their names by claiming back her own identity and demanding equal treatment: "They try to make us forget who we are. My boss says that with our new name we will become equal to the Greeks, but they still treat us differently." Yannis, an Albanian student whose family belonged to the former elite, openly confronted his interviewer with the pervasive amnesia about the Greek migrant past: "It happened to me to get on a bus and to hear somebody say that Albanians are the worst people in the world. Why are we the worst people? We may be poor, but the Greeks have had similar experiences. Ask the Greeks who went to Germany: the Germans said the same about them. You see, at least the Greeks should not say something like that, because they have lived through the same experience. They shouldn't forget." And Matilda, daughter of a former police officer, defiantly criticized Greek employers who refuse to pay their Albanian workers. She explained how her uncle had forced his reluctant boss to pay him by denouncing him on the local television channel: "My uncle had his papers in order and had a lively character. What about other Albanians who can't speak and don't know where to go? Should they work for peanuts?"[34]

Beyond the Classroom: Multiplying the Effects

The ultimate aim of the course was to explore oral history's potential for reconstructing public memory. We targeted two essential arenas where public memory is produced: education and the media. Although the interview material seemed suitable for course work in primary or secondary education, lack of time and experience prevented us from developing curricular materials. By good chance, however, one of my students was a primary school teacher, and he subsequently applied his new knowledge in the classroom. Although he presented only a short exercise, at the end of it most pupils had begun to question notions they had taken for granted (the "honest" Greek, the "criminal" Albanian). A few months later the teacher presented his work at a large conference on intercultural education for primary school teachers. As most teachers face similar problems with intercultural relations in the classroom but never think of bringing in migrants' voices, his presentation had considerable impact. Thus, through the mediating role of one of our students who functioned as a "multiplier," we were able to reach a public audience well beyond the walls of our university.

The second way in which we tried to reach a broader audience was by developing the radio program "Journey into Infinity." In addition to being aired on a local commercial station, the show was transmitted once again by the local branch of the National Radio Broadcasting Corporation, on a weekly program mainly targeting an Albanian audience. Although we received no feedback from either audience, an unexpected development further multiplied its effects. When Matilda went home to Albania with enthusiastic reports about being interviewed and a tape of our radio program, young Albanians who worked in Greece and, like Matilda, were home on holidays initiated a similar project. They gathered a group of twenty Albanian migrants from Greece and produced a television documentary presenting the migrants' perspective on their experiences. This was broadcast on a local channel in the southern Albanian town of Korytsa and aroused much local interest and debate.

Oral history, by offering an alternative to a dominant narrative of migration, can serve as a form of shock therapy for students, deconstructing their ethnic stereotypes and reshaping their perceptions of both history and contemporary social life. Our work shows how a classroom oral history project can snowball and reach a broader audience than originally intended. The Greek response to mass in-migration is to some extent specific to that country, combining a laissez-faire policy at the institutional level with strong social pressures for assimilation. But transnational migration is rocking the foundations of societies all over the globe, provoking reactions similar to those described here. Both within "Fortress Europe" and in traditionally multicultural societies such as Canada and Australia, the moral panic provoked by the mass influx of migrants has produced xenophobic attitudes and restricted the democratic rights of both new and old citizens. In an age of mass mediation, public memory is often short-lived: as I am writing these lines, four years after the completion of the project, the extreme demonization of Albanian migrants has been somewhat muted, although ethnic stereotyping continues to be a persistent feature of media discourse. In other countries such as the Netherlands, the recent rise of xenophobia threatens to condemn to oblivion a long national tradition of tolerance. In this context, projects such as the one I have described not only have advantages for the students involved; they can also create a memory bank for the future—one that holds both the remembered experiences of migrants and the dominant views of society at a particular moment in time. These accounts may become an important resource for future generations and a strong antidote to the ephemeral character of public memory. They can be an important tool not only for historians seeking to reconstruct forgotten aspects of a society's history, but also for ordinary citizens working to make their societies more democratic, and for second-generation migrants wanting to remember where they came from.

NOTES

1. This spectacular turnaround is linked, among other factors, to the breakdown of Communist rule in Eastern Europe, and in the host countries to geography ("open borders"), the modernization of the economy, the development of the tertiary sector, the flexibility of the labor market, and low birth rates. See Russell King, "Southern Europe in the Changing Global Map of Migration," in Russell, King, Gabriella, Lazaridis, and Charalambis Tsardanidis, eds., *Eldorado or Fortress? Migration in Southern Europe* (London: Macmillan, 2000), 3.

2. Martin Baldwin-Edwards, "Southern European Labour Markets and Immigration: A Structural and Functional Analysis, Mediterranean Migration Observatory," working paper no. 5 (Athens: University Research Institute of Urban Environment and Human Resources, Panteion University, November 2002), 13–14.

3. An opinion poll carried out in November 2003 by the Greek Centre of European Studies and Research showed that 64.54 percent of Greek citizens think that migrants should obtain full constitutional rights and be naturalized after one year (11.49 percent), five years (33.4 percent), ten years (15.62 percent), or twenty years (4.03 percent) of residence: *Eleftherotypia*, 4 January 2004. The immigration law of 2001 allows naturalization only after ten years of residence. But other opinion polls carried out during the same period showed that more than 80 percent of Greeks thought that there were too many migrants: *Eleftherotypia*, 12 December 2003; see European Social Survey, at www.ekke.gr/ess.

4. Anna Triandafyllidou, " 'Racists? Us? Are You Joking?' The Discourse of Social Exclusion of Immigrants in Greece and Italy," in King et al., *Eldorado or Fortress?* 186–206.

5. Laurie Hart, "Culture, Civilization and Demarcation at the Northwestern Borders of Greece," *American Ethnologist* 26:1 (1999): 196–220.

6. Public discourse makes a clear distinction between migrants and tourists. The term *allodapos* (literally "coming from another territory") is commonly reserved for economic migrants from outside the European Union (cf. the use of *extracommunitari* in Italy) and has consequently acquired a negative connotation. Other foreigners are commonly labeled by the more neutral term *xenos*, meaning "foreigner, outsider," or, according to the context, "tourist."

7. Until the end of the nineteenth century, Muslims lived alongside Orthodox Christians and Jews, while a variety of languages other than Greek were spoken, including Turkish, Ladino, Vlach, Albanian, and South Slav dialects. Today these languages have either disappeared or are spoken by small groups of mainly elderly peasants. The only recognized minority are the (mainly Turcophone) Muslims in Thrace.

8. Michael Herzfeld, *Ours Once More: Folklore, Ideology and the Making of Modern Greece* (Austin: University of Texas Press, 1982); Michael Herzfeld, *Anthropology through the Looking Glass: Critical Ethnography in the Margins of Europe* (Cambridge: Cambridge University Press, 1987).

9. Vasilis Karydis, *I egklimatikotita ton metanaston stin Ellada* [Criminality of Migrants in Greece] (Athens: Papazisis, 1996), 150.

10. The very name of this brilliant student is extremely revealing in this context and demonstrates the conflicted position of migrants. His surname (Tsenai) is Albanian, but he acquired a "safe" Greek first name (Odysseas), referring to the classical past, when he decided, as have so many of his co-nationals, to be baptized and embrace the Orthodox religion.

11. Significantly, the inhabitants of this community had come from Turkey as refugees in the wake of the population exchange between Greece and Turkey in the 1920s. At their arrival in their new country, they faced the same contempt from the local population (who labeled them as "Turkish-born") that they now display toward the Albanian newcomers. As we know from Erving Goffman, *Stigma: Notes on the Management of Spoiled Identity* (Englewood Cliffs, NJ: Prentice-Hall, 1963), memories of past stigma may lead to overcompensation.

12. A vast and growing literature on the subject of commemoration and public memory includes Paul Connerton, *How Societies Remember* (Cambridge: Cambridge University Press, 1989); David Middleton and Derek Edwards, eds., *Collective Remembering* (London:

Sage, 1990); John Gillis, ed., *Commemorations: The Politics of National Identity* (Princeton: Princeton University Press, 1994).

13. For a more general perception of Albanian migrants as a polluting danger, see Nadia Seremetaki, "In Search of the Barbarians: Borders in Pain," *American Anthropologist* 98 (1996): 489–91; Mary Douglas, *Purity and Danger* (London: Routledge, 1966).

14. Anastasia Karakasidou, "Protocol and Pageantry: Celebrating the Nation in Northern Greece," in Mark Mazower, ed., *After the War Was Over: Reconstructing the Family, Nation and State in Greece, 1943–1960* (Princeton: Princeton University Press, 2000), 223.

15. Connerton, *How Societies Remember*, 1–5, 52–53, and passim.

16. On the disciplining of bodies, see Michel Foucault, *Discipline and Punish: The Birth of the Prison*, trans. Alan Sheridan (New York: Pantheon, 1978).

17. Both quotations were extensively reported in the Athenian press. See, for example, *Eleftherotypia*, 27 October 2003.

18. Middleton and Edwards, *Collective Remembering*, 8.

19. *Eleftherotypia*, 29 October 2003.

20. Alessandro Portelli, "Oral History as Genre," in *The Battle of Valle Giulia: Oral History and the Art of Dialogue* (Madison: University of Wisconsin Press, 1997), 7. On the mythical transposition of Albanian workers' conflicts with their Greek bosses from the workers' own perspective, see Penelope Papailia, " 'Money of *Kurbet* Is Money of Blood': The Making of a 'Hero' of Migration at the Greek-Albanian Border," *Journal of Ethnic and Migration Studies* 29 (2003): 1059–78.

21. See Christina Konstantinidou, "Koinonikes anaparastaseis tou egklimatos: I egklimatikotita ton Alvanon metanaston ston athinaiko typo" [Social Representations of Crime: The Criminality of Albanian Migrants in the Athenian Press], in Afroditi Koukoutsaki, ed., *Eikones egklimatos* [Images of Crime] (Athens: Plethron, 1999), 103–41. This article is based on a content analysis of the Athenian press from 1991 to 1999, with a special focus on the period from February to May 1998.

22. Styliou Lambrini, final essay, 2001.

23. Spyros Tzanos, interviewed by Gesthimani Mertzemekidou, April 2001, tape MET-12. All recorded interviews and their transcripts have been preserved in the oral history archives of the Department of Social Anthropology of the University of Thessaly. Interviewees who objected to the use of their full name are indicated by their first name only.

24. Charis M., interviewed by Jenny Roussos, 5 April 2002, tape MET-19.

25. Kallinikos N., interviewed by Efi Navrouzoglou, 3 April 2002, tape MET-20.

26. Enver Hoxha was the General Secretary of the Albanian Communist Party, which held absolute power over Albanian society until the breakdown of Communist rule. Quotations from Matilda, interviewed by Dimitra Kofti, May 2001, tape MET-9; and Apostolis, interviewed by Alexandra Siotou and Christos Kiouroglou, April 2001, tape MET-4.

27. Interview with Kallinikos N.

28. Interview with Matilda.

29. Christodoulos Dimou, interviewed by Mary Margaroni, 12 April 2002, tape MET-17.

30. Dora, interviewed by Gerasimos Tsimbloulis, her teacher, 30 May 2001, tape MET-5. Albanian migrants face strong social pressures, especially from their employers, to be baptized in the Orthodox Church and adopt Greek names. This pressure is even stronger for migrants who belong to Muslim families. In Albania three major religions—Islam, Greek Orthodoxy, and Catholicism—were practiced until 1967, when the Communist regime under Enver Hoxha banned religion and closed down all churches and mosques.

31. Maria Todorova, *Imagining the Balkans* (Oxford: Oxford University Press, 1997).

32. Quotations taken from final essays by Alexandra Siotou, Maria Karasteryiou, Lambrini Styliou, and Elizabeth Pitsiona, spring semester, 2001.

33. Alistair Thomson, "Moving Stories: Oral History and Migration Studies," *Oral History* 27:1 (1999): 30.

34. Vasiliki, interviewed by Maria Vlachaki, 21 April 2001, tape MET-13; Yannis Yanglare, interviewed by Maria Karasteryiou, April 2001, tape MET-7; Matilda interview.

12

COUNTERING CORPORATE NARRATIVES FROM THE STREETS: THE CLEVELAND HOMELESS ORAL HISTORY PROJECT

~

Daniel Kerr

In 1978 Thomas Vail, editor and publisher of the Cleveland, Ohio, *Plain Dealer,* founded the New Cleveland Campaign (NCC), a civic marketing organization charged with advertising and promoting the city in order to attract corporate investment, conventions, and downtown tourism. At the time of the organization's founding, deindustrialization was wreaking havoc on the region. By the close of World War II the city had become one of the largest industrial regions in the world, specializing in the manufacture of steel, machine tools, industrial equipment, automobiles, and electrical appliances. By the 1950s, however, companies had already begun to relocate out of the central city and into the outer suburbs. By the 1970s companies were closing their Cleveland-based plants and moving out of the area altogether. Between 1974 and 1983 the metropolitan area as a whole lost 100,000 of its manufacturing jobs (one-third of the total); half of those losses occurred between 1980 and 1983. As local industrialists shut down their plants, the housing market in Cleveland's eastside working-class African American neighborhoods collapsed. Unable to sell their properties, landlords stopped paying taxes and abandoned and set fire to thousands of homes and apartment buildings. The city used nearly its entire allotment of federal redevelopment money for demolition costs. During the 1970s the largely African American Hough, Glenville, Fairfax, and St. Clair neighborhoods alone lost 17,309 housing units. Vail assigned NCC the task of marketing this tragedy as an opportunity for profit.[1]

During its first two decades NCC developed substantial corporate support. By 1997 the city's top fifty corporations were funding NCC's $750,000 annual budget. During the 1980s and 1990s, the organization aggressively promoted Cleveland's "urban renaissance," touting each new downtown attraction, capital investment, professional sports arena, stadium, luxury hotel, shopping mall, and office complex as evidence of the city's re-emergence. It also publicized the "revitalization" of the city's neighborhoods as luxury town homes, condominiums, and single-family mansions sprang up in areas where disinvestment had occurred. Millions of dollars were spent on advertising campaigns in the national media. The group produced glossy brochures and videos and even designed "The Cleveland Curriculum" to present the corporate interpretation of the city to third and fourth graders. In 1996 NCC's executive director, Sandra P. Dunn, reveled in her organization's accomplishments:

> Cleveland—once all but given up for dead by many of its own people, not to mention outsiders—has, indeed, come back to life. Through the work of "urban pioneers," Cleveland has been transformed from a national laughingstock to the New American City. . . . Where once Clevelanders could see only the traces of a brilliant past and the harsh realities of a difficult present, we now find ourselves looking forward to a bright and prosperous future.[2]

Unquestionably NCC crafted an alluring narrative that captivated many people in northeast Ohio. The problem with NCC's marketing campaign, however, was that it did not address the reality of most working-class and unemployed Clevelanders. While NCC promoted the "revitalization" of Cleveland, the city's homeless shelter population ballooned to the largest number since the Great Depression. By 2003 Cleveland residents faced the highest poverty rate of all major cities in the United States.[3] Clearly something was wrong with the corporate narrative.

In contrast, from 1996 to 2002 the Cleveland Homeless Oral History Project (CHOHP) developed a low-budget, high-intensity campaign to interpret the city's condition from the bottom up. The need for CHOHP became apparent to me after I co-founded the Cleveland chapter of Food Not Bombs in January 1996.[4] Every Sunday from 1996 through 2003, I worked with other volunteers to prepare a free picnic on Cleveland's Public Square, a downtown park located at the center of the city. The contradiction between the rhetoric of renaissance and the reality of dispossession was readily apparent as hundreds of unhoused men and women came to the meal each weekend.

Although I was new to the phenomenon of homelessness in Cleveland, after graduating from college I had independently organized around issues of housing, squatted in abandoned buildings, and participated in anti-eviction struggles in the Lower East Side of New York City from 1993 through 1995, ac-

tions that had developed out of my undergraduate study of the history of social movements and housing struggles. Although initially I had sought to move
as far away from academia as I could, several important role models prompted
me to consider the possibility that community work could be integrated with
academic research. In particular I became intrigued with the possibility that
oral history could provide a tool for the unhoused to collectively analyze their
condition. So I moved to Cleveland in November 1995 with the intention of
attending the graduate history program at Case Western Reserve University
the following fall.

By the time I entered CWRU in 1996, I had already established Food Not
Bombs Cleveland and considered developing an oral history project in conjunction with the meal program. I recognized that such a project could provide
a backbone for future graduate research. Linking my community work with my
academic labor would also reduce the fragmentation of my everyday life and offer me more time to spend in the community. However, I was hesitant: I did not
want to design an oral history project that would be limited by my needs as a
graduate student. An even bigger concern was betrayal—the risk of subjugating
the needs of people in the community to the demands of academia.

Ultimately the work of oral historians Alessandro Portelli and Michael
Frisch convinced me that I could minimize these risks by designing the research
project in such a way that the interviewees could use the project for their own
ends. Drawing on the work of Gianni Bosio, Portelli contends that researchers
should view themselves as organizers and be prepared to teach and learn, study
and be studied. If we address rather than avoid our internal contradictions as
intellectuals, Portelli argues, the embodied practice of the interview can provide
a unique avenue for consciousness raising—for both interviewee and interviewer: "Fieldwork is meaningful as the encounter of two subjects who recognize each other as subjects, and therefore separate, and seek to build their
equality upon their difference in order to work together." Reflecting on his own
work in oral history, Frisch argues for the adoption of democratically organized
research projects that offer "a more profound sharing of knowledges, an implicit and sometimes explicit dialogue from very different vantages about the
shape, meaning, and implications of history." He contends that this dialogue
will "promote a more democratized and widely shared historical consciousness,
consequently encouraging broader participation in debates about history, debates that will be informed by a more deeply representative range of experiences, perspectives, and values."[5] Beyond participating in historical debates, I
concluded that a properly organized oral history project could also lead to efforts by unhoused participants to intervene in the world around them.

Emboldened by Frisch and Portelli's work, I formally launched the Cleveland Homeless Oral History Project in the fall of 1996. To fulfill a graduate

research seminar requirement, I purchased a thirty-dollar microcassette recorder and began conducting formal interviews on Public Square. The project started slowly. From 1996 through 1998 I conducted one-hour life history interviews with one Latino and three African American unhoused individuals. I spent a great deal more time hanging out in parks and on street corners developing relationships with unhoused people in the city. This period of informal ethnographic research allowed me to learn who people were by name and gain a greater understanding of the reality of their lives, and enabled others to learn who I was. By establishing relationships independent of social service agencies, I sought to ensure that people would not see me as either a direct avenue or a barrier to the assistance programs they needed. I also worked to cultivate a space where unhoused interviewees could develop an unveiled and uncensored analysis of their predicament. Increasingly I hung out in the common spaces of shelters, soup kitchens, and drop-in centers as well—out of earshot of agency staff and security guards. As my relationships grew and trust developed, I discovered that a critical analysis could also emerge within the bowels of the shelter system itself.[6]

My initial interviews provided a dramatically different perspective on the city than the one marketed by NCC. While Sandra Dunn touted the city's "bright and prosperous future," my first interviewee, J. D., stated baldly: "I don't see anything getting better. This is not the worst. I hear people saying, 'Well things can't get worse.' That's the biggest piece of doodoo I've ever heard." There were, however, significant problems with the methodology I adopted in the early interviews. Many of them stemmed from my own attachment to the notion that an oral history interview is solely an examination of a person's life story. This misunderstanding restricted the ability of the narrators to discuss and analyze structural changes in the city that had occurred during their lifetime. As we sat in a quiet area of Public Square and I asked the interviewees how they became homeless, the discussions at times became therapy sessions, confessions, or at the very least individualized declension narratives. This pattern mirrored the structure of interviews in which social workers and case managers ask homeless people about their life histories in order to peg them into a category of deviance. Most unhoused people participate in these interviews solely to gain access to vital resources. After telling me about his personal addiction to crack cocaine, Deuce abruptly ended the interview: "Basically end this conversation right now. There's little in it for me." By explicitly delving into my interviewees' life histories, I unintentionally invaded what little privacy they were able to maintain in their all-too-public lives. After the initial interviews were finished, all four of the people I had talked with asked that I either change their names or not use their interviews at all.[7]

Yet oral history's potential to allow homeless men and women to draw out and refine an analysis of their circumstances continued to intrigue me. I approached the research with renewed vigor in the fall of 1999 after I completed my comprehensive exams and officially decided to base my dissertation research on the CHOHP interviews. I promptly ditched my microcassette recorder and replaced it with a video camera. During the interviews I had conducted with the mini-tape recorder, many narrators seemed to forget that they were talking to anyone other than me. The physical presence of the video camera, however, emphasized the public and performative aspects of the interview, thereby minimizing the confessional mode. Instead of seeking out a quiet corner of Public Square, I conducted interviews in the midst of the busy Foods Not Bombs picnic. Furthermore, I played the interviews back on the following Sunday on a television and videocassette recorder I set up in the park, making it clear to the interviewees that the recordings would be readily accessible to the largely unhoused audience that attended the picnics. Finally, I consciously avoided asking questions related to personal life histories. Instead, I asked about the causes of homelessness and the transformation of the city of Cleveland within their lifetime. Avoiding the pressure and manipulation of direct personal questions was not designed to prevent people from talking about their own experiences. Rather, interviewees shared their life histories as they came up within the course of their discussion of more public issues. The video interviews became very popular among those who attended the weekly picnics, and I showed tapes of the interviews in homeless shelters and meal sites throughout the winter of 1999–2000. By ensuring that the unhoused were also a primary audience of the interviews, I intended to establish a forum where individuals in these circumstances could share their ideas and learn from one another.

In developing the concept of reciprocal ethnography, anthropologist Elaine Lawless stresses the importance of a research structure that includes spaces for the collective discussion and analysis of research data with subjects.[8] Drawing from her research model, in January and February 2000 I conducted three workshops at a drop-in center for the homeless where seventeen project participants analyzed the videotapes, outlined future directions for the project, and identified strategies for moving in those directions. The participants in these sessions identified six themes in the video interviews that were crucial to their everyday lives: the upscale transformation of residential neighborhoods over the last thirty years, the impact of downtown development on affordable housing, the expansion of the criminal justice system, the rise of temporary labor agencies, the collapse of federal and state welfare programs, and the institutionalization of homeless shelters designed to remove and contain unhoused people outside the central business district. Exploitation and abuse at the hands of the temporary labor agencies, which hired many of the unhoused on a day-by-day basis, attracted the most vigorous discussion. Participants complained of low wages, a myriad of agency fees that further reduced pay, dangerous working conditions, and racial and sexual harassment. In order to investigate how systematic these conditions were, the group proposed conducting a large number of standardized interviews with day laborers. Lastly, although the videotapes offered an important avenue for unhoused people to critique their circumstances, they recommended exploring the use of other media to broaden the reach of these discussions.

This last recommendation led to the development of a weekly show, called Frost Radio, on Case Western Reserve University's 15,000-watt student-run radio station. One workshop participant suggested the title of the show and its slogan: "The crystallization of ideas on the airwaves." From May 2000 through August 2002, I along with project collaborator Chris Dole conducted fifty-seven separate on-air interviews with thirty-six unhoused individuals.[9] In addition to these live interviews, I conducted twenty-one off-site interviews with seventeen unhoused individuals that were subsequently broadcast. The demands of carrying out the weekly broadcasts led me to scrap the video project. Participants on the show, however, ensured that the unhoused would continue to be an active audience for the interviews by tuning into the program at homeless drop-in centers and sharing copies of their own broadcasts with friends at local shelters.

We next addressed problems with the day labor industry. During the early winter of 2001, I collaborated with a small group of unhoused day laborers at the office of the Northeast Ohio Coalition for the Homeless (NEOCH) to design an extensive questionnaire to document the abuses of the industry. NEOCH functions as an advocacy organization that primarily focuses on issues related to shelter conditions. The day laborers analyzed their own experiences as well as data from the video and Frost Radio interviews to craft standardized questions. After participating in a workshop I organized on conducting interviews, throughout the spring and summer my collaborators and I conducted seventy-seven interviews with unhoused day laborers across the city. Although the interviews were conducted in confidence, out of fear that day labor agencies might blacklist participants, several interviewees also publicly discussed their grievances on Frost Radio. The project prompted two exposés of the day labor industry in the local press and led a member of Cleveland City Council to promise that he would conduct a public hearing on the industry.

Throughout the summer of 2001 I conducted practice sessions for the hearing, arranged for transportation to City Hall, and helped organize a rally in support of the day laborers on the day of the hearing. At the hearing on 4 September 2001, eighteen day laborers testified on the abuse and exploitation they faced at local day labor agencies and released the final report of the summer study of the industry. Nearly all of those who testified had actively participated in the research project. CHOHP—encompassing the initial audio interviews, the workshops, the video project, the radio show, and the grassroots day labor research study—had provided several powerful low-budget tools to form and promulgate a critical analysis of the city from the bottom up.[10]

Interpreting the City from the Streets

CHOHP participants provided a radically different interpretation of the city than the narrative of "revitalization" promoted by NCC. Like NCC, CHOHP participants examined developments going on in city neighborhoods, the transformation of the downtown area, and changes in the organization of work across northeast Ohio. But while NCC fixated on the prospect of "a bright and prosperous future," CHOHP participants highlighted the growing levels of dispossession and exploitation facing the city's working-class residents.

Unlike many east and west coast cities, Cleveland does not attract unhoused people from other parts of the country. Nearly all the unhoused people I have formally and informally interviewed grew up in the city, and most were raised in the African American neighborhoods on the eastside, the area hit hardest by abandonment, arson, and demolition during the 1970s. The historical transformation of the Hough neighborhood in particular plays a prominent role in the analysis of homelessness among those I have interviewed. It also features heavily in the rhetoric of revival promoted by NCC. In the summer of 1966, the predominantly African American residents of Hough rose up in rebellion in response to landlord disinvestments that had resulted in deteriorating housing conditions, cutbacks in city services, high prices for goods of questionable quality, lack of job opportunities, and ongoing police brutality and harassment. So-called rioters focused their wrath on the police, urban renewal offices, and specific merchants and landlords before being suppressed by the National Guard. The landlord disinvestment and abandonment that preceded and helped spur on this unrest continued unabated in the 1970s as Hough alone lost 8,412 housing units—nearly 40 percent of its total stock—to arson and demolition.[11]

Two decades later, in December 1994, the Cleveland *Plain Dealer* reported that in Hough "a weedy, deteriorated community already is transforming itself. Shabby wooden houses and vacant lots, scars lingering from the infamous Hough riots of July 1966, are slowly being joined by the type of large brick homes more often found in the rolling hills of [the outer suburbs]." The massive single family mansions were a part of a development called "Renaissance Village," built on an eight-acre site in the heart of what had been the most densely populated neighborhood in the city in the 1960s. City planners and officials heavily subsidized the new construction with tax abatements and land grants in hopes of luring prosperous families back into the city. Lauding the development, Community Development Director Terri Hamilton emphasized that the new homes were not "causing the displacement of people." She argued, "Most of the housing is being built on land that was vacant pieces of property."[12]

CHOHP narrators who grew up in Hough contested the erasure of their displacement from public memory and clearly identified the economic interests behind it. On the very first day I brought a video camera to Public Square, John Appling, an older black man experienced at politicking, discussed the changes in Hough:

> If you go down into the Hough area now, it is a planned thing. This is not just something that came about overnight. This has been a planned thing, because I heard something said to me by [former Mayor] Carl Stokes back in 1967. . . . He said, "You know John, in about thirty, no more than thirty-five years, there's not going to be any set areas where blacks are concentrated. They are going to spread them all out over the city." Back in the sixties when the Hough riots were going down, people couldn't get to work. They were scared to come down Chester; they were scared to come down Euclid; they were scared to come down Superior [major thoroughfares through Hough]. Because you see, in order to get downtown to the business district, you had to come down through those streets. And they said, never again will it be like this.
>
> And if you look around here today, it is not like that anymore. If you go down to the Hough area, you have 300,000-dollar homes down there now. You have got apartments that cost 700, 750, 800, 900 dollars a month now, which we cannot afford. The whole area, in which I was raised up in until I was a grown man, now is taken over by Cleveland Clinic, Mount Sinai, and University [Hospitals]. . . . The black people that live in that area now are doctors and lawyers: professional people—white-collar people. And all the so-called low-income blue-collar working people are spread out all over the city.

Michael Taylor, a former resident of Hough who lived in the city emergency shelter and volunteered as a cook at a local free meal program at the time of the interview, highlighted the basic economics of displacement:

> And the people that are coming around and building [are] not the people in the community. It's the big boys downtown that are building on

our community land . . . , but if you look at the average person in the community, they are barely making 10,000 dollars a year. If they are making 12,000 dollars, you're still making it impossible to pay for [one of the new homes] under the wage scale that they are living under. . . . I remember back in the day when houses were 10,000 dollars—a nice house. People were able to afford to buy a house. You can't really afford to buy—the people that I'm speaking of. Now your people that have good jobs can afford to pay [for] house notes like that. But the people that cannot, these are the heart and soul of the community.[13]

While NCC lauded the development of luxury $300,000 homes in Hough, by the year 2000 more than 30 percent of Cleveland's households earned less than $15,000 a year. Many of those who lost their homes in Hough and the surrounding neighborhoods were pushed toward older inner-ring suburbs. Anthony Gentile argues that the massive expansion of Ohio's prison system during the 1980s and 1990s (the fifth largest in the country) also played a direct role in displacement from these areas:

I see on Jay Avenue and up on Hough Avenue, they are forcing out the poor, the lower middle class, with one-hundred-, two-hundred-, and three hundred-thousand-dollar fucking homes. You know what else they are doing? They are privatizing prisons. . . . Then they put all these poor people in these privatized prisons because they can't afford to live anywhere. Because they are building all of these one, two, three-hundred-thousand-dollar homes in my city. And all my people are going to jail because they don't make fifty thousand fucking dollars a year. They all have work at the temporary services.[14]

Even as Cleveland's corporate and banking leaders sought to rebuild the city's neighborhoods, their top priority was downtown development. Throughout the 1980s and 1990s, billions of dollars were invested in new condominiums, hotels, shopping centers, corporate headquarters, museums, and stadiums in the city core. The inclusion of recreational and cultural facilities in this development was a conscious strategy to attract businesses to the city and retain those that were already there. In literature designed to market the city to corporate executives, the NCC advertised, "Only Cleveland gives you 9,000 acres of work surrounded by 110,000 acres of play."[15]

While the local press and Cleveland's elite hyped the corporate version of the city's downtown transformation, they virtually ignored the destructive side of this flurry of development. CHOHP interviewee Ralph Williams Pack, who had migrated from West Virginia to Cleveland after World War II and lived downtown for most of his life, emphasizes the human costs of the demolition that took place to make way for these downtown projects:

> They have torn down nearly all the low-cost housing in the city. At one time downtown Cleveland was a haven, almost a utopia, for lower-income people. There were a thousand cheap hotels and cheap rooming houses. They have torn them down for the different stadiums. And instead of the three-dollar-a-night hotels, there are the 150-dollar-, 300-dollar-a-night hotels.

Over the past thirty years, Pack continues, they have tried to convert downtown into a "playground for the rich"—a strategy that has had a tremendous impact on the poor:

> They wanted to make downtown look real photogenic and make it look real clean. So they cleared out all the old hotels and all the places that were frequented by the poor guys so that when the well-to-do tourists . . . came in they wouldn't see all this. . . . They wanted to create a complete new image for downtown Cleveland of everyone prosperous, of everyone doing real well, so they really made a sweep on all the poor people there.[16]

The last single-room-occupancy (SRO) hotels and rooming houses downtown were destroyed to make way for the publicly financed Cleveland University's State Convocation Center, Jacobs' Field, and Gund Arena. The Cleveland phone book listed 147 centrally located hotels in 1955—the large majority catering to working-class residents. By 1970, the number of hotels in this same area had been cut in half, to seventy-four. By 1997, eleven hotels remained, and only one catered to the working poor—the Jay Hotel in the Ohio City neighborhood. This hotel closed in 2003 and has been converted to condominiums.[17]

City development strategies have created a fundamental contradiction. While they sought to clean up downtown and city neighborhoods, a growing number of homeless people took refuge on downtown sidewalks during the 1980s and 1990s. In 1980 city shelters maintained 356 beds, and the city papers found it newsworthy when people could be found sleeping outside. By 2002 the city shelters operated at full capacity with over 2,000 beds while unhoused people maintained camps on marginal land throughout the city and occupied nearly every boarded-up building. Robert Jackson, who first moved into a camp across from the Browns' stadium in the late 1980s explains:

People started sleeping around in old buildings and stuff like that and the police and everybody said we're going to have to do something, because there started to be more homeless people, more homeless people. You had to do something. And business, business all around the city wasn't going to let you sleep in their doorway because people had to walk over you.

To contain this population, the city institutionalized an emergency shelter program in 1988 and engaged in periodic campaigns to sweep the homeless off the streets throughout the 1990s. Robert Igoe, who lived on the streets for most of the 1990s, recalls: "There was a definite concerted effort in the early 1990s to move people from the downtown area into the area in front of the Virgil E. Brown Center." The Brown Center, the county welfare office, is located in a warehouse and light-manufacturing district seventeen blocks east of Public Square. Dave "the Homeless President" Campbell, an unhoused activist dedicated to organizing camps outside the administrative structure of the city system, explains:

[Mayor Mike White] had ordered that they sweep the streets of the homeless—in other words, arrest the homeless people if they refused to go to shelters. He criminalized them . . . he was targeting the poor. Instead of looking at the poor as people who need help, he was looking at the poor as being a problem for his mayoral interests.

For many of those sleeping outside the Brown welfare center, the camp served as a protest against the miserable conditions within the shelters and also as a visible demonstration of the failure of the government to address the homeless crisis. Jason Maiden describes the outcome of the city's drive to eliminate the camp:

Now we must find places where they can't see us. Now they want to come around the holiday season and get homeless people off the streets—show things off for the people in the suburbs. That's all they want to do is see things pleasant. They don't want to see us lying on benches.[18]

While the city-led campaigns sought to sweep unhoused people off the streets and into the city shelter system, the residents of the shelters harshly critiqued their living conditions. By the late 1990s the emergency shelter system consisted of a half-dozen converted warehouse spaces near the Brown Center that offered residents the comfort of concrete floors and mats. Draimon Shepard first moved to an emergency shelter with his mother. When he turned fourteen, the shelter staff told him he could no longer live with his mother and sister at the emergency women's and children's shelter. They sent him by himself to one of the emergency men's shelters. Several years later he reflects: "Basically the shelters are horrible. This is my opinion. A lot of people can deal with that, but I wasn't one of them. Because there is too much going on with shelters. It's like prison basically. They tell you when to sleep, when to eat." When Raymond Robinson lost his housing in 2002, the emergency men's shelters had consolidated into one mega-shelter at 2100 Lakeside, also in the warehouse district. Robinson was appalled by the treatment residents received at the hands of the shelter staff: "This particular staff, they are disrespectful, they are uncaring, they are just plain downright full of malice and hatred against the residents that stay at Lakeside." Robinson testified on Frost Radio that the staff frequently refer to residents as "maggots."[19]

Conditions at the emergency women's shelter were no better. Several unhoused women emphasize that the shelters are not designed to meet their needs. In an interview on Public Square, Pamela Wagner discusses the time she spent with her young son in the women's shelter: "The [emergency women's shelter] I think was the most devastating for me, because you sleep on the floor on a mat at night." Wagner explains that there are seventy to eighty women and children every night, sleeping side by side in a church basement with access to only one bathroom: "You can go out one time [between 9 P.M. and 5 A.M.] when [the staff goes] out to have a cigarette. When the doors are shut they don't let anyone in." With the exception of this brief supervised breath of fresh air, they found themselves virtually imprisoned from the early evening until the early morning. Agreeing with Shepard, Brenda Crosby concludes that when she is in the women's shelter, "It's almost like I'm in jail."[20]

Besides countering the notion that shelters are humanitarian institutions, many CHOHP participants confront the misconception that unhoused men and women do not work. In her interview on Frost Radio, Brenda Crosby informed the audience that 75 percent of the women staying at her shelter work, and mostly for day labor agencies. She described her typical day trying to find a job: "You have to get in [the labor agency] at least by 5 A.M. and then if you don't get out, you come back around 12 or 1 to try and go out second shift. Then come back at 10 in the evening to try and go out at third shift." Nearly all the men and women I interviewed have worked through five major day labor agencies in the city. When they are sent out, they clean acid vats at plating factories, operate punch presses, work at injection molding plants, prepare frozen vegetables for packaging, clean the downtown sports arenas, and even dig graves.[21]

Three of the five major day labor agencies in the city were established in the late 1960s. While manufacturing plants in the city closed or relocated to the outer suburbs and beyond, these agencies flourished. For those companies that moved to the suburbs, the day labor agencies provided an indispensable service supplying workers on demand. Furthermore, the day labor agencies helped depress wages in several key industrial sectors. For the NCC this pool of low-wage workers ready to be dispatched at a moment's notice represented a marketable regional asset. A NCC pamphlet designed to attract companies to northeast Ohio highlights this feature:

> Surprisingly, in many kinds of industrial operations, Cleveland wages are lower than the national average, such as in fabricated metal products, household appliances, chemical and allied products and instruments and related products. So employers seeking to move quickly into productive operation with a minimum of costly and time consuming training and start-up problems find Cleveland an excellent location.

In literature designed for the consumption of the region's residents, the NCC emphasizes the presumed relationship between corporate development projects and job creation. In an essay published in the *Plain Dealer*, campaign executive Sandra Dunn writes:

> Our once-dying city in now alive and well, a genuine success story. We are on the way to becoming one of the country's top visitor destinations, a turn of events that will benefit not only Cleveland but the entire northeast Ohio region too. Downtown attractions will continue to generate new jobs, new residences, new tax revenues and new dollars to benefit the region's economy.[22]

Once again, CHOHP interviewees contradict the NCC's rhetoric. Shelter resident and day laborer Alphonso Beverly describes the conditions he is subjected to when working for a day labor agency:

> The bottom line is the homeless are 90 percent of the workers [at the day labor agencies]. . . . Since we're homeless, nobody really cares. . . . A lot of jobs you go to are very dangerous. You are around chemicals with no masks, no safety equipment, no nothing. . . . I've been to Kelly Plating, Atlas Plating, and different plating jobs, and you have no safety equipment, no ventilation, there is no sprinkler system in them. They are not being inspected. The temp agency knows this, they know this, but if we speak out we might never work again.

At a free meal center, Robert Best further analyzes the structural exploitation in the day labor industry:

> Some of these plating companies or painting companies, the type of work you do, you should be making three times as much. Workers need to form their own organization and work for themselves, because these places like AmeriTemps, Minute Men, Area Temps, they are like nationwide. They are making tons of money. All they are doing is just sending [workers to jobs]. They don't produce nothing. They don't train for anything. They just send you to work. All you do is make money for them. They are pimping you really. And what you are getting paid is below poverty level. . . . You are working hard too. You are tearing up all your clothes. You're getting covered with oil. You're breathing in hazardous materials.[23]

Many CHOHP participants emphasize that the day labor agencies are at the core of the city's economic development strategy—a strategy based on reducing corporations' cost of labor. Mark Hennigan discusses the cozy relationship between employers in northeast Ohio and day labor agencies—a relationship that comes at the expense of the worker:

> It is so easy to hire temporary labor. These employers don't have to pay benefits. They are getting cheap labor. They don't have to worry about hiring anybody. They can just get rid of whoever they want to. They can do whatever they want. It makes it so easy for them to exploit people and the law. . . . They are not interested in what tactics these agencies have to use to get the bodies into there as long as they have their workers and they are making their quotas every day.

James Battle places the rise of the day labor industry in the 1980s and 1990s in a larger historical context:

> The struggle between the unions and business has always been a struggle if you look back at American history. And there seems to be a rollback of that using the temporary situation. . . . There has been a meltdown of the worker and his wages. I was talking to a welder, and he said he used to work for twenty or twenty-five dollars an hour back in the sixties and seventies. Now he can hardly get eight, nine, ten bucks an hour for doing the exact same thing. What happened? What happened to the labor movement?[24]

Intervention

Throughout the project CHOHP participants used their interviews and the workshops to strengthen their own efforts at creating social change. They drew from CHOHP material in their persistent interventions to improve the conditions in the homeless shelters, to defend their encampments, to protect their right to stay outside of shelters, and to improve their working lives. One of the more militant CHOHP participants, Vietnam veteran Dave Campbell, referred to Frost Radio as "the air war." In his view the unhoused people living on the streets were the ground troops engaged in fundamental battles to maintain their survival networks in order to establish social change. While CHOHP operated at a comfortable distance from these struggles, he believed it provided essential support. Although I might have chosen a less militaristic metaphor, I shared his view of the structural relationship between CHOHP and the unhoused people's movement in Cleveland, Ohio.

From the earliest video interviews, several unhoused activists used the forum to organize protests. In the very first video interview, Anthony Ball announced, "In the coming weeks you might hear from me again because we plan on protesting down in the welfare building." Ball and a group of other homeless men were seeking to address the terrible conditions within the city emergency shelters bordering the Brown Center. That same afternoon, Clinton Marron declared that the nonprofit organization that operated the city emergency shelter program—Cornerstone Connections—needed to be "kicked to the curb." Several weeks later Ball, Marron, and nearly one hundred other unhoused men led a march from the city's emergency shelters to the offices of Cleveland's only daily newspaper. News coverage of the march and the public outcry that followed prompted the city and the county to drop Cornerstone Connections as operator of the emergency shelter program. Furthermore, the city and county announced that all the emergency men's shelters would be combined under one roof, a "mega-shelter" run by the Salvation Army. The Salvation Army promised that the new site, 2100 Lakeside, would be a "full-service" shelter providing substance-abuse counseling, job services, and links to "transitional housing." Once the massive shelter opened in the spring of 2000, none of the promised services ever materialized.[25]

In 2002 Raymond Robinson used Frost Radio as a platform to discuss his petition drive aimed at getting Cleveland City Council to terminate its contract with the Salvation Army. The petition, signed by 350 shelter residents, prompted City Council to hold hearings on the matter. Initially the city renegotiated its contract with Salvation Army; then the organization fired the director of 2100 Lakeside and reorganized its entire shelter program. Although the new director eliminated most of the worst abuses in the facility, the Salvation

Army still failed to develop support programs. In December 2004 the city and county removed the Salvation Army and turned shelter management over to Lutheran Metropolitan Ministries.[26]

Other CHOHP participants used the interviews to protect their right to stay outside the shelter system. Jason Maiden's video testimony in late November 1999 sparked a flurry of protests. In the interview he revealed Mayor Mike White's holiday campaign to arrest homeless people sleeping on the street in order to force them into the shelters. Maiden argued: "We should get a group together and lay out in front of City Hall or in front of his house on South Boulevard. Hopefully we can get something done." Maiden's testimony led to the publication of several news stories on the arrests and to a public hearing organized by Congressman Dennis Kucinich. Maiden, a coalition of homeless men and women known as Rosewater 2000, an organization led by Dave "the Homeless President" Campbell, and Food Not Bombs Cleveland organized a sleepout on Public Square on 23 December. Amid the Downtown Development Corporation's yearly display of Christmas lights, unhoused men and women and their advocates hung banners saying, "We're Not Dreaming of a White Christmas!" and "I'm Homeless, Arrest Me!" and passed out flyers to holiday revelers. Then they settled in for the evening. At 3 A.M. on Christmas Eve, Mayor White ordered the police to raid the encampment, tear it down, and arrest anyone who refused to leave. The camp came down, and five people were arrested, but the next morning a federal court issued an injunction against the mayor's policy. In February 2000 the city formally agreed not to arrest or threaten to detain any individuals for "performing innocent, harmless, inoffensive acts such as sleeping, eating, lying, or sitting in or on public property."[27]

Others used CHOHP to highlight grassroots networks of support that were essential to their survival outside the shelter system. In November 1988 Chris "Chief" Herman and Tyrone Jordan established a camp built of plywood and milk crates in a deliberate protest over the shelter conditions. By 2000 Herman and Jordan's camp had moved to a massive five-story abandoned bakery and had grown to include more than fifty people. The building stood at the heart of what local planners called the Midtown Corridor—an area designated for corporate offices and high-tech businesses. The camp, dubbed Camelot, joined a network of six other camps under the umbrella of Rosewater 2000. In an interview on Frost Radio, Herman differentiated his camp from the shelters:

> Camelot is for anybody that wants to come over there. Everybody is welcome. I don't turn nobody down. But if you get too loud, that's when you've got to go. Because I don't like no violence over there or nothing

like that. I want that to be a peaceful camp. . . . I got three churches that bring us food three times a week. You don't want for nothing. And me and Dave [the Homeless President], we supply everything—food, clothes, shelter. The only thing I ask you to do over there is be peaceful. Or once in a while come in with something to offer.

I struggled all my life living in the streets. Living in the streets, I can handle that. When somebody new comes along and they say, "Chief, I just got kicked out of my house," I say, "Well, you can come over here and stay. You're welcome." You know everybody looks down on us, but once they see how we treat each other . . . we treat people better than their own family treats them—no hassles and no tussles or nothing like that. We just get along. And whatever I can do I try to do for the people. I built Camelot, and it is my responsibility to take care of the people that come over there.[28]

The encampments were not immune to the city's destructive development policies. In July 2000 the city announced its plans to take over the abandoned building that housed Camelot, demolish it, and turn the cleared lot over to a potential developer at no cost. The residents of the camp first heard of the plan when delegations of outreach workers from nonprofit organizations contracted by the city arrived to inform them where the shelters were located. Dave Campbell read an open letter to Mayor Mike White on Frost Radio: "We wonder why you keep sending people out to ask us to sleep in a shelter when we have our own housing here at Camelot." Campbell invited the mayor and his assistant Linda Hudacek to the building: "We will have food and can provide you with a bunk if you want to sleep over. We would love to sit down and discuss the sad state of the shelters in Cleveland, the lack of affordable housing, or our fine house that we have constructed for ourselves."[29]

While Campbell sought to negotiate with the mayoral administration, his fellow Camelot resident Eduardo Lauriano used the same broadcast to warn the mayor that the building's occupants were ready to defend what they understood to be their home. He announced: "I'm laying my life down, and I will go down with Camelot. Camelot is bigger than you think. They think they know every inch, but they don't know it like we do." The mayor ignored both Campbell and Lauriano. Lauriano's pledge, however, brought flocks of local reporters to the building on the night before and the morning of the planned demolition. Dozens of Camelot supporters set up tents outside the building in an effort to shield those on the inside. Top figures in the mayor's administration, including his development director, chief of police, Safety Department director, and a handful of assistants, stood outside, bewildered by the occupants' militant refusal to leave. Following a nearly twenty-four-hour standoff with the police, the residents agreed to leave the building after a local attorney promised to secure a court injunction against the city's plans. Before the courts opened the following morning, the city hastily began demolishing the structure, only to learn later that their action had released large amounts of asbestos dust into the surrounding neighborhoods. While Camelot's residents failed to block the demolition of the building, they refused to let their displacement go unnoticed and uncontested. Furthermore, Cleveland residents provided significant material aid to those evicted by the city action. As a result, many former Camelot residents were able to move directly into apartments. Others established new camps. No one, however, moved to the emergency shelter as the city had advised. The negative publicity that followed the Public Square arrests and the Camelot eviction figured prominently in Mayor White's decision not to run for re-election in the fall of 2001.[30]

While activism over conditions in the shelters and the maintenance of the encampments flourished, many other CHOHP participants sought to organize to improve their working lives. In the spring of 2000, Robert Best argued in a CHOHP workshop, "Workers need to form their own organization and work for themselves." Later that fall, two dozen residents of 2100 Lakeside formed the Day Laborers' Organizing Committee (DLOC). The DLOC immediately sought to disrupt the close relationship between the day labor agencies and the Salvation Army. More than two hundred residents of the men's shelter signed a petition demanding that any labor agent recruiting on the premises be required to sign a strict code of conduct. Only recruiters offering living-wage jobs, benefits, and safe working conditions would be welcome. Despite the presence of representatives of Minute Men Inc., the largest day labor agency operating in Cleveland, on the advisory board of the Salvation Army, the organization effectively acquiesced to the residents' wishes and banned all labor agents from its facilities.[31]

The DLOC also worked to establish a nonprofit alternative Community Hiring Hall that could lease workers to area companies and pay its workers a living wage. Those who testified at the City Council hearings on the day labor industry on 4 September 2001 indicated that establishing this hall was their top priority. Following the events of 9/11, public officials quickly lost interest in grievances voiced by day laborers, but organized labor backed the hiring hall proposal with a $30,000 grant to hire a development director. After running a pilot project in the summer of 2003, the new agency raised more than $100,000 from foundations and became fully operational in 2005. Furthermore, the DLOC secured enough funding to hire a full-time organizer and commenced a direct-action campaign in the spring of 2004—bringing a busload of day laborers to the home of Larry Dolan, owner of Cleveland's major league baseball team, the Indians. The group demanded that the Indians quit recruiting workers to clean the baseball stadium from the AmeriTemps day labor agency, put an end to the rampant sexual harassment faced by women day laborers at the baseball stadium, and stop the practice of taking fees out of workers' checks that brought their hourly pay below the minimum wage. Although the team refused to break its contract with AmeriTemps, the day labor agency substantially revised its sexual harassment policy.[32]

In September 2002 Frost Radio aired its last broadcast, and CHOHP officially came to a close after conducting 195 interviews with 147 people. The task of continuing the radio show and writing my dissertation proved too overwhelming. Unfortunately, I failed to find someone willing to take on the responsibility of keeping the show on the air each week. As CHOHP came to a close, one unhoused man who had been peripherally involved with the DLOC accused me of organizing CHOHP solely to bolster my resume. The charge raised the specter of betrayal that had plagued me at the onset of the project. There was no denying that I would use information from CHOHP for my dissertation as well as in writings such as this chapter. Although I have benefited from this project, I am satisfied that the design of CHOHP allowed its participants to use the project for their own ends. The video interviews and radio show "amplified" participant voices, deliberately sought out unhoused audiences, and played a role in the emergence of a collective historical and political analysis of the city from the bottom up. Throughout the project CHOHP participants were at the forefront of a movement to address the needs of Cleveland's unhoused men and women. Some of the participants came to CHOHP with established critiques that they sought to broadcast to a larger audience. Others used the project to develop their own voices and understanding of their circumstances. As they grew more confident through their participation, they took on more active roles in protesting city policies and shelter and working conditions. While NCC spent close to a million dollars a year to market the corporate version of the city, a project whose budget was no more than $2,000 over six years ensured that the larger community would have the opportunity to see the city through the eyes of Cleveland's unhoused residents.

NOTES

Ted Steinberg, Rhonda Y. Williams, Jonathan Sadowsky, Wendy Rickard, Alistair Thomson, Alicia Rouverol, and Linda Shopes recognized the value of this research from its early stages. MaryAnn and Douglas Kerr helped shape the project in countless ways. Anthony Ball, Fred Whitlow, Robert Jackson, Robert Molchan, Ralph W. Pack, Clark Cody Campbell, Hakim Rahman Ali, Pam Wagner, and Gerri Chesler all assured me that oral history had relevance in social justice work. Chris Dole was there week in and week out helping to prepare food, organize the radio show, and conduct interviews. Tatiana Belenkaya inspired me to continue this work when I was ready to give up.

1. *Plain Dealer,* 16 September 1998, 1C; Daniel J. Marschall Papers, Folder 15, Container 1, Folder 46, Container 2, Western Reserve Historical Society (WRHS). For more on deindustrialization and the collapse of housing markets in Cleveland, see Daniel Kerr, "Open Penitentiaries: Institutionalizing Homelessness in Cleveland, Ohio" (Ph.D. diss., Case Western Reserve University, 2005). For an outstanding account of race and deindustrialization in neighboring Detroit, see Thomas Sugrue, *The Origins of the Urban Crisis: Race and Inequality in Postwar Detroit* (Princeton: Princeton University Press, 1988).

2. *Plain Dealer,* 21 July 1994, 8F; 19 July 1994, 2C; 27 March 1996, 2C; 21 July 1996, 14A.

3. *Plain Dealer,* 27 August 2004, 1A.

4. Food Not Bombs is a decentralized international network of people who freely distribute vegetarian food at picnics open to the public. For more on the organization, see C. T. Butler and Keith McHenry, *Food Not Bombs* (Tucson: See Sharp Press, 2000).

5. Alessandro Portelli, *The Death of Luigi Trastulli and Other Stories: Form and Meaning in Oral History* (Albany: State University of New York Press, 1991), 43; Michael Frisch, *A Shared Authority: Essays on the Craft and Meaning of Oral and Public History* (Albany: State University of New York Press, 1990), xxi–xxii.

6. James Scott's discussion of the "hidden transcript" and Robin Kelley's elaboration of the concept as it relates to the black working class influenced my attentiveness to the spatial dimension of power as CHOHP progressed. However, it was Maria Lugones who first suggested that I incorporate the "hanging out" approach to this popular education project. In her "Tactical Strategies of the Streetwalker," Lugones argues: "Hangouts are highly fluid, worldly, nonsanctioned, communicative occupations of space, contestatory retreats for the passing on of knowledge, for the tactical-strategic fashioning of multi-vocal sense, of enigmatic vocabularies and gestures, for the development of keen commentaries on structural pressures and gaps, spaces of complex and open-ended recognition." James C. Scott, *Domination and the Arts of Resistance: Hidden Transcripts* (New Haven: Yale University Press, 1990); Robin D. G. Kelley, *Race Rebels: Culture, Politics, and the Black Working Class* (New York: Free Press, 1996); Maria Lugones, *Pilgrimages/Peregrinajes: Theorizing Coalition against Multiple Oppressions* (Lanham, MD: Rowman & Littlefield, 2003), 221.

7. Arrangements have been made to house the Cleveland Homeless Oral History Collection at the Cleveland Public Library. Throughout this chapter I have tried to provide a close rendering of the actual language used by the narrators while making minor editorial changes in the transcriptions when a literal rendition of an interview could cause misunderstanding. Oral historian Donald Ritchie emphasizes that oral sources often look confusing in print no matter how literate the narrator is. See Donald Ritchie, *Doing Oral History: A Practical Guide* (Oxford: Oxford University Press, 2003), 68–69. Interview with J. D., Public Square, Cleveland, 15 September 1996; interview with Deuce, Public Square, Cleveland, 29 September 1996. Unless otherwise attributed, interviews were conducted by the author.

8. Elaine J. Lawless, *Holy Women, Wholly Women: Sharing Ministries of Wholeness through Life Stories and Reciprocal Ethnography* (Philadelphia: University of Pennsylvania Press, 1993).

9. Chris Dole, a Ph.D. candidate in the Anthropology Department at Case Western Reserve University, developed an interest in the project through his own involvement in Food Not Bombs.

10. *Free Times,* 7–13 February 2001, cover story; *Plain Dealer,* 19 August 2000, 1A. A copy of the final report of the summer study—Daniel Kerr and Chris Dole, "Challenging Exploitation and Abuse: A Study of the Day Labor Industry in Cleveland," produced for Cleveland City Council, 4 September 2001—is available at www.neoch.org/challengingtemp.htm.

11. Daniel Kerr, "Open Penitentiaries," 345–70, 430. For a contemporary report on the Glenville uprising in 1968, see Louis Masotti and Jerome Corsi, *Shoot-Out in Cleveland: Black Militants and the Police: July 23, 1968* (Washington, DC: U.S. Government Printing Office, 1969).

12. *Plain Dealer*, 21 December 1994, 18A; 22 March 1993, 1A.

13. Interview with John Appling, Public Square, Cleveland, 5 September 1999; interview with Michael Taylor, 2100 Lakeside Avenue, Cleveland, 6 April 2000.

14. Interview with Anthony Gentile, Public Square, Cleveland, 5 September 1999.

15. George V. Voinovich Mayoral Papers, Accession 89-084, Folder 4, Container 10, Western Reserve Historical Society (WRHS); *Plain Dealer*, 16 September 1998, 1C.

16. Interviews with Ralph Pack, Public Square, Cleveland, 12 September 1999, and Frost Radio, Cleveland, 6 June 2000.

17. Kerr, "Open Penitentiaries," 444.

18. Interview with Robert Jackson, *Frost Radio*, Cleveland, 27 November 2001; interview with Robert Igoe, 8 January 2000, 2902 W. 11th Street, Cleveland; interview with Dave Campbell, Bishop Cosgrove Center, Cleveland, 20 April 2000; interview with Jason Maiden, Public Square, Cleveland, 28 November 1999.

19. Interview with Draimon Shepard, Frost Radio, Cleveland, 26 September 2000; Raymond Robinson, interviewed by Chris Dole, Frost Radio, 18 June 2002.

20. Interview with Pamela Wagner, Public Square, Cleveland, 24 September 2000; interview with Brenda Crosby, Frost Radio, Cleveland, 8 May 2001.

21. Interview with Brenda Crosby.

22. George V. Voinovich Mayoral Papers, Accession 89-084, Folder 4, Container 10, WRHS; *Plain Dealer*, 10 December 1994, 13B.

23. Interview with Alphonso Beverly, Frost Radio, Cleveland, 13 March 2001; interview with Robert Best, Bishop Cosgrove Center, Cleveland, 16 March 2000.

24. Interview with Mark Hennigan, Frost Radio, Cleveland, 15 May 2001; interview with James Battle, Public Square, Cleveland, 23 April 2000.

25. Interview with Anthony Ball, Public Square, Cleveland, 30 May 1999; interview with Clinton Marron, Public Square, Cleveland, 30 May 1999; *Plain Dealer*, 7 July 1999, 1B; ibid., 16 July 1999, 3B; ibid., 1 December 1999, 1B.

26. Interview with Raymond Robinson.

27. Interview with Jason Maiden; "City Chatter," *Free Times*, 29 December 1999–4 January 2000; *Plain Dealer*, 24 December 1999, 1A; *Lynn et al. v. City of Cleveland*, No. 93-cv-3143 (N.D. OH 2000).

28. Interview with Chris Herman, Frost Radio, Cleveland, 2 July 2000.

29. Interview with Dave Campbell, Frost Radio, Cleveland, 17 July 2000.

30. Interview with Eduardo Lauriano, Frost Radio, Cleveland, 18 July 2000; *Plain Dealer*, 1 August 2000, 5B; ibid., 3 August 2000, 1B.

31. Best interview; "Army Wages War Against Minute Men," *The Homeless Grapevine*, March 2001..

32. "First Punch," *Cleveland Scene*, 28 April 2004; "City Chatter," *Cleveland Free Times*, 5 May 2004.

13

PUBLIC MEMORY, GENDER, AND NATIONAL IDENTITY IN POSTWAR KOSOVO: THE ALBANIAN COMMUNITY

~

Silvia Salvatici

Kosovo is a small region in the heart of the Balkans. Until 1989 Kosovo was a region in the Federal Republic of Yugoslavia, enjoying a certain degree of autonomy at the behest of the Albanian population, which represented 90 percent of the region's inhabitants. The remaining population consisted of small Serbian, Romany, and Turkish communities. At the end of the 1980s, the nationalist leanings of the federal government under Slobodan Milosevic resulted in the abolition of the Kosovo region and the emergence of extremely strong tensions between the Albanian segment of the Kosovo population and the Serbian segment, which was supported by the central government of Yugoslavia. These violent tensions would explode dramatically a decade later. The war in Kosovo was the last episode in the violent disintegration of the former Yugoslavia, which began in the early 1990s with the secession of Slovenia, followed by dramatic conflicts in Croatia and Bosnia-Herzegovina. The conflict in Kosovo broke out in March 1999 when NATO attacked Yugoslavia's aerial defenses in support of the Albanian population, whose military organization was the Kosovar Liberation Army (KLA). The war lasted three months, and during the NATO bombing over 800,000 ethnic Albanians left Kosovo, while hundreds of thousands of people were internally displaced. An estimated 7,000 Kosovar Albanians were killed during the hostilities. At the end of the military action, a significant part of the Serbian population (between 25,000 and 100,000 out of the original prewar population of 200,000) hastily left Kosovo, prompted by the imminent threat of violence on the part of the Albanian population. Since that time, the remaining

Serbian population in Kosovo has lived in enclaves protected by an international military force, while Kosovo continues to be a United Nations protectorate. Thus, although the war was confined to a small region of the Balkans, it nevertheless involved the international community to a significant degree. The war needs to be understood in terms of this explosion of violent nationalistic tension within the larger political, economic, and social crises that shook the Balkan region to the core.

In the following pages, I examine the experience and memory of the war among women belonging to the Albanian community, using interviews conducted in Kosovo between December 1999 and July 2000 by the Archives of Memory project. The project was part of the larger program known as Psychosocial and Trauma Response in Kosovo, implemented by the International Organization for Migration (IOM). The aim of this larger program was to create a structured response for the emerging psychosocial needs of a population that had experienced war, exile, and return.[1] In this setting, the Archives of Memory was conceived as a place devoted to both the preservation and the dissemination of the different kinds of documents (interviews, letters, diaries, drawings) remaining from the Kosovo conflict.[2] The production, collection, and circulation of such materials were considered a preliminary step in the sharing of the varied experiences of Kosovar people and a way to affirm the variety of memories documented by the interviews.

Collecting interviews was the main activity of the Archives of Memory in Kosovo. The interviews were conducted in towns and in villages, and the interview subjects were chosen to represent a wide range of ages, social backgrounds, and gender and ethnic identities (Albanian, Serbian, Romany). The goal was to restore a multiplicity of voices, determined not only by ethnic identity but also by a diversity of sociocultural origins, and including generational and gender differences. The specific quality of the female experience quickly became one of the most significant elements in the archives' work, since gender relations provided one of the most revealing perspectives on the experience of the war and also the way in which that experience was recollected. As we will see, the gender perspective turned out to be central both for identifying the fundamental elements of the public memory of the war as forged by nationalistic discourse and for understanding the degree to which individual memories conformed to or diverged from this public memory. In asserting its claims to ethnic and national identity, the Albanian community pursued first the denunciation of Serbian oppression and then the return of Kosovar autonomy, thus providing a privileged point of view on the Kosovo war.

Memories of War: Heroic Martyrs and Suffering Victims

As studies have shown, the Albanian community's collective discourse on the war is marked by a sense of victimization, a trait already identified as a core element of nationalist identities in the Balkans.[3] Among the Albanians of Kosovo, this came to be understood primarily in terms of their status during the course of the twentieth century as the majority population in their region, but a minority population within a nation governed by Serbs. A similar public discourse emerging within the conflict seems to be based on highly gendered imagery of how men and women experienced that conflict. The men's participation in armed conflict has generally given rise to the figure of the "heroic martyr" who is willing to risk or even sacrifice his own life in defense of the community. This masculine hero is the main character of the songs, stories, and images of popular national folklore that embodies the Albanian community's experiences of armed conflict. In contrast, the female experience of war seems to have been reduced to a role both opposite and subordinate to that of the "heroic martyr." The image of women has become that of the "suffering victim," the target of the violence directed toward the civilian population as noncombatants. In addition, women above all represent the bearers of family and community grief as a result of the loss of their men. Widows, mothers who have lost their sons, and daughters who have lost their fathers are the new social subjects of a community stricken by the violence of war,[4] and they are also the figures invoked to express the suffering that has become a constitutive element of national identity. Many monuments erected in public squares or cemeteries after the war showed weeping female figures bending over the bodies of their slain husbands or sons.

Reducing the experience of men and women to the images of "heroic martyr" and "suffering victim," of course, recalls the gender stereotypes that have historically surfaced during periods of armed conflict and are intimately connected with the construction of masculine and feminine social identities.[5] As research has demonstrated, the attribution of such roles is rooted in a social contract whereby men constitute themselves as citizens by virtue of their strength in arms, while women define themselves as private, apolitical, and familial subjects.[6] In Albanian/Kosovar public discourse, however, the assumptions of these gender roles acquire specific meanings, shaped by the ethnic/national dimension of the conflict and designed to emphasize, via the suffering of women, the element of victimization in nationalist thinking. This perspective acknowledges women's claims to the experience of suffering, which is a strong element in female identity construction, but it also interprets that experience as secondary to masculine identity, since it results from the sacrifices of their sons, husbands, and fathers on the battlefield.

Indeed, such sacrifices are a central theme in the women's narratives, which are thus permeated by the logic of the public discourse. The story of sacrifice and loss is, of course, especially powerful and painful for those women who directly experienced it. Edlira lost both her husband and her son, who were killed by Serbian paramilitary fighters before the entire family left Kosovo to seek refuge in Albania.[7] In her recollections, the deaths of the two male family members acquire the characteristics of an immolation that bestows heroic status on the dead and acknowledges the spirit of sacrifice on the part of the survivors:

> It was 28 March, a religious feast day that we call the day of the little Bajram. According to tradition, every year we cut the throat or sacrifice the biggest ram of the herd on that day. My husband and my son sacrificed themselves for the liberation of Kosovo on that day. We who survived gave them with all of our hearts.

Edlira takes credit for the culmination of the sacrifice, the burial rites, describing it as part of the destiny shared by all Albanian mothers:

> It was my fate to be the one to bury my husband and my son, who were shot before my very eyes. . . . I felt terrible seeing their bodies. I gathered all of my strength so that I could comfort [the other] children, so that they wouldn't feel alone. We have to be patient. . . . What happened to me, as a mother, happened to all the mothers and women of Kosovo. Maybe it was written in our destiny.[8]

On the one hand, the allusion to the sorrowful fate of Albanian mothers is consistent with the symbols and imagery that often appear in women's stories about war, evoking the "powerful and primordial" and "strong and enduring" qualities of motherhood. On the other hand, these references also invoke the identification of the common destiny of the victims based on their ethnic/national membership, and the social role attributed to women in a context where the biological reproduction of the nation and the numerical strength of the community have become an obsession.[9]

The ardor with which the heroics of men are observed is reinforced by references to other historical figures who sacrificed themselves for the nation. Drita, in recalling the character of her father, who had been killed by Serbian paramilitary soldiers, remembers how he sought to emulate two figures from the previous century: "He was a history teacher. Many tributes were made to him. He always spoke about Bajram Curri and Isa Boletini, and said that he would fight as they did in their time."[10] Memory's transformation of these deaths into martyrdoms probably imparts meaning and sense to the losses, and thus can help the wives, mothers, and daughters withstand the sorrow associated with them. Teuta buried her father and her brother, both militants in the KLA. At the end of her narrative, in which she recounts the events of the war and highlights the suffering provoked by the bereavement, she concludes: "We must live for the love of those who fought and died for us, because when they picked up their weapons, they did a great thing."[11] In some cases, however, the pain caused by the loss of the men of the family seems to lead to a suffering that renders life meaningless. Shemsije, interviewed with her daughter, recalls the death of her husband and two sons and affirms: "We are also dead. We [the women of the family] lost our men, and so we are dead too. We lost everything."[12]

Insofar as it is an expression of collective victimization, the suffering these women endure acquires a socially recognized value of the highest esteem, which precludes the emergence of other experiences that might complicate or compromise that suffering. We can see this in the story of Sofije. Sofije was widowed during the war and lives with her husband's family and her infant daughter. She suffers from recurrent psychological disturbances that both she and her in-laws attribute to her profound grief. Her account of the events also reveals the underlying causes of her emotional turmoil, which manifests itself as insomnia, a refusal to eat, and fainting spells. Sofije wishes to return to her own parents' home, but because of local customs that maintain the historical priority given to the male line, she would have to leave her child behind if she did so. Consequently, taking refuge in a more protective environment where she could more easily deal with her grief would leave her mourning not only the loss of her husband, but also that of her baby daughter. Sofije's narrative and those of her husband's family seem to replicate the process of selective suffering allowed by public discourse as shaped by nationalistic thinking, which emphasizes the role of the war while setting everything else aside—in this case the painful consequences of a strictly patrilineal and patrilocal system that still governs family life in Albanian communities, especially in rural areas.

The forms of self-representation that emerge in the women's painful narratives seem to follow the public discourse of the Albanian community, and the elaboration of the collective memory of the conflict that is a fundamental part of that discourse.[13] However, the narratives of violence that were endured by the female population—as we will see in the next section—also open the way for the expression of the multiplicity of experiences lived by women during the war. While these experiences do not completely depart from the "suffering victim" model, they fragment and complicate it.

Female Suffering

The suffering produced by the conflict is usually attributed to the bereavement, forced separations, and upheaval that have tragically disrupted the lives of many women in Kosovo. Other circumstances, however, frequently exacerbate this suffering, piling one hardship on top of another. This is the case for Mirdita, a refugee living with her younger sister in a village in Tetovo, a Macedonian region mainly populated by Albanians. Their departure from Kosovo marked the end of long days of terror endured in the regional capital, Pristina,[14] far from their family. They arrived in Macedonia after an exhausting journey and were placed in one of the many refugee camps. A few days later, they were moved to the house of a family in the village. This move was above all desired by their older brother, who had previously emigrated to Germany and had been contacted through the International Red Cross. Their brother was personally acquainted with the head of the household offering the accommodation, and the relocation was meant to guarantee them safer arrangements. "We were two women, alone, without any man. This might have caused some problems in finding us a place with strangers: it was an understandable concern for the man of the family," explains Mirdita. While the new arrangement clearly offered better conditions, it also became the source of unexpected suffering:

> They were very old-fashioned and religious, and so the women were extremely oppressed. They had to stay in the house and they couldn't go out unless they were accompanied by an adult man. They treated us the same way. We didn't have any choice; we had to get used to it. Sometimes we did try to resist their old-fashioned ways. But mostly we had to sacrifice our freedom and stay closed inside because we didn't know where our family was. And they wouldn't let us do as we pleased, anyway, because we were women.

Mirdita recalls the restrictions on their freedom of movement not only as an exacerbation of the turmoil they were already experiencing as a result of their forced exile, but also as the denial of a right that was only possible because of their vulnerability as refugees. Being cloistered within the walls of the household meant that they could not get information about their own family and increased their anguish at being separated from their loved ones.

> During that time we were miserable with sadness and boredom, and from a psychological point of view we were in very bad shape . . . our morale had reached rock bottom. We kept getting bad news about our village, which was being attacked from every direction. Everyone told us that there were a lot of victims, that there had been full-scale massacres, and in the meantime we hadn't heard anything about our family. We wanted to find out, somehow, but you can't get information if you have

to stay closed in the house all the time. . . . I was very upset; above all, I felt offended when I saw the women go to town escorted by the men.[15]

This deep sense of indignation permeates the rest of Mirdita's testimony, in which she recalls in great detail a number of episodes when her sense of resentment was especially acute. Her account describes a suffering caused not only by mistreatment of and separation from her family, but also by the violence inflicted by the rigidly patriarchal rules of the household. Interestingly, this violence is directly attributed to their "Albanian brothers," who, in most war narratives, are lauded for their loyal hospitality to refugees, or else noted as important reference points for the mythic Albanian national identity that remains split by the political borders of various states (Albania, Kosovo, Macedonia). Mirdita's recollections are consistent with the widespread awareness of the sociocultural differences among Albanians living in different countries, which are more or less explicitly cited as exacerbating factors in the narrators' difficult adjustment to the hard life of refugees. Mirdita's account reveals an experience that complicates the discourse of national identity by introducing the dimension of gender.

Everyday Heroics

The women's accounts of the war are filled with references to the dangers they encountered during their dramatic flight from Kosovo, the efforts they made to protect their children, and the moral and material hardships associated with being a refugee. In recounting their experiences, however, it appeared that these women wished to reclaim their suffering and project it through their own lens of female subjectivity. Thus refracted, the memories of the war assumed aspects and meanings different from those proposed in the public discourse for women—that is, the passive role of the suffering victim. Prompted by the occasion of the interview, their memories produced accounts that usually remained governed by the dominant narrative but also in some ways departed from it, though not to the point of outright contradiction. These co-narratives reveal an impulse for reappropriation. Here the pathos of the wives, mothers, and sisters, which is usually portrayed in terms of passive female endurance apparently confined to the domestic sphere, acquires the characteristics of an *active* resistance. Nazife, for example, emphasizes, and not without a hint of pride, her ability to provide for her family during the NATO bombings in Gjakova, when she had few resources at her disposal:

When the war broke out, I was in very difficult circumstances. I didn't have any money, and there was no food. Leonora [Nazife's closest friend, who was present during the interview] gave me a loan . . . we only had 600 German marks in all. I supported my family and myself on this very small amount for three months— 600 marks for three months and I still had 200 when the war was over. . . . I fed everyone with just one piece of chicken! There was only the thigh for my husband, my brother-in-law, and myself. . . . I made lunch with only one piece of meat and . . . it was super![16]

Drita speaks about her efforts to provide for her children during their escape to Macedonia, and the persistent note of pride in her voice colors the dramatic tone of her testimony:

> It was very difficult to find food, and even water. So we, like everyone else, left our house, we left everything behind. All of the villages were burned. But I always managed to come up with something for the children, I always managed to take care of them.[17]

Violeta supported her brother so that he wouldn't have to leave the house: for him, as for all men in the city, the streets of Pristina had become too dangerous:

> The situation there had become very difficult for the men. My brother, for example—he is twenty-one and I am twenty-two—for him it was dangerous to go out to shop, because the Serbs were capturing all the young men, they were kidnapping them. So my uncle said, "Oh, you're a girl, maybe it isn't so dangerous for you," but I wasn't sure. But I was never afraid, never, because for me living or dying was the same thing. . . . I wasn't afraid, I never thought, "If I go out in the street now they will kill me"; for me it was the same, being alive today and dead tomorrow.[18]

In the complex symbolic construct that is part of the war event and that draws upon a society's value systems, expressive codes, and its forms of memory and collective identity, the roles of the defender and the defended are usually masculine and feminine, respectively. Violeta's account, however, is not unique in stories of contemporary conflict, where the distinction between the battlefield and the domestic front (and hence between combatants and noncombatants) is increasingly blurred. Here these traditional roles may be reversed. In this particular case, the reversal also represents women's reappropriation of public space, an extraordinary event in the Albanian/Kosovar context, where the division between masculine space and feminine space is still quite rigid, with women mostly limited to the domestic sphere. Violeta's account is also significant because it recalls and appropriates that kind of heroism—typically considered an attribute of men—that disdains life itself. The protective role played by this sister in procuring food for her brother, her peer, took her heroics out of the private familial sphere and marked them as a contribution to the defense of the community.

On the other hand, Sonja, a Catholic, and one of the few Albanians who remained in the northern zone of Mitrovica after the end of the war, protected no one but herself and the house where she was born and raised, and where she found herself alone after the death of her parents.[19] Recalling the days of the NATO bombardments, she relives the pain of the past in the light of a present still filled with violence and peril.[20] Her account reveals not only the distress of her loneliness and suffering, but also her courage, resisting and relying on her own strength, cleverness, and ingenuity. In the evenings after dark, she would hide in the corner of the house from which she could best observe the door while listening to the Italian news; by day she cultivated her relationship with her Serbian neighbor, for fear that one day a negative word to the Serbian paramilitary soldiers would bring them to her door—as had happened to many other Albanians in the neighborhood. In Sonja's story, the ability to resist does not result only from an instinct for self-defense, but also from a desire "not to give in to the Serbs." She acts in the name of the Albanian community of Mitrovica and thus as part of the collective struggle:

> I was capable of anything to make sure they didn't touch me. I pretended to be stupid, an idiot, as if I didn't know anything. That I was someone who . . . someone who you should be kind to. And she [the neighbor] played along with it. She helped too, because thanks to her. . . . I can't say a word, she helped us, she acted like she was my cousin. She brought me things to eat, she would call me, "Come, come now, come, you have to eat something," and I would force myself to eat, because everything stuck in my throat, I didn't feel like eating.
>
> Because during the war I played the idiot; you could have said that I was a real imbecile, that I didn't understand anything. I was a real actress. She really thought that I didn't understand anything, and so she would tell me all of the news. I could have been a spy, but I didn't have anyone to tell things to! I only spoke with her, only with these neighbors of mine. . . . They would all go down to the cellar, everyone would go down. "There are eleven of us and we are afraid"—they

were afraid of the airplanes—"how can you stand it being by your-self?" In the end she would come to listen to the BBC in English to find out what was happening, because she didn't have a satellite dish. I pretended that I couldn't understand anything in English. "What did they say? What did they say?" I would go in and out of the room to leave her alone to listen. In the last days she came every day. I babysat her daughter. Everything was okay as long as they couldn't touch me. I would ask her—even if I had a better idea than her, because I always listened to the news in Italian—"What are they saying? What are they saying?"[21]

Sonja's "playing the idiot" is one more example of the daily heroism re-called in the women's narratives. These narratives not only tell us about the strategies they used, the skills they exploited, and the resources they employed; they also project an image of new spaces for action and new forms of respon-sibility that were produced by the war, its consequences, and the rapid changes that swept through the Albanian/Kosovar community after its end. These im-ages suggest a partial thaw in the identities, including gender identities, that are usually employed to characterize the war experience, but that can be rene-gotiated at the end of the war, or at least given different meanings in the new social and cultural context produced by the war.[22]

The Defense of Traditions

In the public nationalistic discourse, the preservation of tradition is usually en-trusted to women, and it is seen as one of the constitutive elements of their membership in the community.[23] In recalling the heartbreak and loss inflicted by the war, the women often refer to tradition and make significant use of it in describing their own suffering and the sacrifice of their loved ones. Edlira is worried about her little grandson, who lost his father and his grandfather. Thinking about the future of this infant boy, she affirms:

> I will be the one who raises this baby. It was my husband's last wish. As women, we are bound to fulfill the last wishes of the dead. This is how we honor our loved ones after they have gone. This is how we respect tradition, and honor the dead.

In Edlira's account, respect for tradition and reverence for the dead, duties recognized as specifically feminine, comes to resemble a tribute to Albanian national identity, much like the deaths of her husband and son (although her actions are still seen as subordinate to theirs). The specific meaning attached to respect for the customs and traditions of the community also emerges in the women's repeated references to fulfilling their obligations to raise their children "according to tradition," and the lengths they have gone to—even during the conflict—to make sure that traditional ceremonies, such as weddings, were still observed. Nevertheless, the emergency conditions imposed by the war also led to frequent departures from some specifically gendered customs. In her description of how the experience of war altered certain practices, Naim, a young university professor, chooses the symbolic image of a woman opening the front door of the house. Usually, especially in the countryside, visitors are met on the threshold by one of the men of the family. During the war, however, the constant fear that "the enemy" would come knocking meant that wives, mothers, and sisters had to answer the door while their husbands, sons, and brothers hid themselves.[24]

Even women who had less traumatic war experiences or who had escaped the loss of family members demonstrated a particular sensitivity about maintaining traditions, and were concerned that the war had made it more difficult to carry out those duties. For example, Leonora and Nazife, two friends living in Pristina who are just over thirty years old and are married with children, identify the welcoming and entertaining of guests, usually visiting relatives, as one of the specific duties tradition has assigned to women.[25] Exchanging courtesy visits and entertaining guests became more difficult for women because of the extreme disruption in daily life that characterized Kosovo after the war. In that period, women had to find ways to reconcile old habits with new necessities: "Now," they emphasize, "we work more than we did before the war, and we don't have time to exchange visits." Nazife works full-time in one of the many foreign nongovernmental organizations (NGOs) that initiated cooperative projects in Kosovo after the NATO bombings, and Leonora works at home as a hairdresser but also attends English language and computer classes to improve her chances of finding a better job.

While traditional Albanian principles regard women's employment with disfavor, the consequences of the war, which produced new needs and new opportunities in both rural and urban contexts, have begun to bring about systematic changes in the position of women with respect to employment outside the home. Many of the participants in the interviews emphasize that prices continued to rise after the end of the war and that it was difficult to make ends meet because of their extremely limited household incomes. These women are adamant in their assertion that wives and mothers—and not just those who have lost their husbands and sons—have a greater need than ever to find work so that they can adequately provide for their families. A woman working in a female crafts workshop created by an Italian NGO in Mitrovica affirms this point, in complete agreement with her colleagues:

> Now women are more active, they look for jobs much more than they did in the past. Before the war . . . our financial situation was much better. Now we have to find work because life is harder. We had more money before than we do now, even though before there were more Serbs than Albanians who worked.[26]

As the conversation continues, however, the women employed in the workshop admit that even if they could return to their earlier circumstances (a comfortable home, an employed husband), they would still rather maintain their extra-domestic jobs. "The best scenario," one says, "would be to have our houses back as they were, but to still have our jobs. Now we can't give it [work] up." Indeed, the women attribute more than financial benefits to the work they do outside the household. For example, they mention how their jobs have allowed them to develop reciprocal relations of solidarity and exchange with individuals beyond the borders of their kinship networks, which usually limit such interaction. Nevertheless, the women still identify economic necessity as the main motive for seeking paid work. This emphasis clearly reflects a new and genuine sense of urgency, but it also echoes the victimization expressed in the public discourse, providing a justification for the lack of observance of traditional customs that discourage women from working outside of the household. Yet the women do finally express their perception of work outside the house as a source of personal satisfaction and a chance to develop new and wider forms of social life—which, moreover, they see as a means of support and comfort in their daily struggle with the difficulties of life in postwar Kosovo.

Main Narrative—Multiple Memories

The accounts Albanian women provided of their experiences during and after the war seem to be articulated along a double narrative track. In one sense, these narratives propose nationalistic motifs and are constructed according to the registry of a collective memory that seeks to be the expression of a monolithic national identity. The coherence of this identity becomes one of the motives for the vindication of the right to political independence, one of the original reasons for the war. In another sense, however, the narratives also make room for a multiplicity of voices. They suggest different trajectories; they complicate nationalistic justifications and contradict the one-dimensional image of womanhood it proposes; and they shatter from within the appearance of a homogeneous and coherent community identity. Instead, the narratives introduce a sophisticated chorus of diverse individual memories. In the context of the research conducted by the Archives of Memory, therefore, the interpretation of testimonials from a gender perspective has made a significant contribution to documenting how in postwar Kosovo the public discourse crystallized around a past inspired by nationalism while at the same time coexisted, often in a contradictory and ambiguous manner, with the enduring stories of individuals—stories that sometimes adopted that discourse and sometimes manipulated it or deviated from it. The diffusion of the results of this research through publications and seminars conducted in Kosovo and in the context of projects undertaken by the International Organization for Migration[27] has above all sought to restore the sense of contradictory coexistence revealed in the narratives in order to call attention to the urgent need for a collective discourse that is able to accommodate a diversity of narratives. Clearly, this need is especially acute in a region devastated by a war that has violently separated the various ethnic and national groups and reinforced the construction of separate and opposed memories. In this context, making room for the multiplicity of memories constitutes a first step toward acknowledging difference and dialogue both within a community and beyond its boundaries.

NOTES

1. See Natale Losi, ed., *Psychosocial and Trauma Response in War-Torn Societies: The Case of Kosovo* (Geneva: International Organization for Migration, 2000).

2. The interviews, in both tape and transcript form, are archived at the Psychosocial Unit at the IOM office in Rome.

3. For studies see Silvia Salvatici, "Memory Telling: Individual and Collective Identities in Post-War Kosovo: The Archives of Memory," in Natale Losi, Luisa Passerini, and Silvia Salvatici, eds., *Archives of Memory: Supporting Traumatized Communities through Narration and Remembrance* (Geneva: International Organization for Migration, 2001), 15–52 and bibliography cited there. Here and subsequently, "Albanian community" refers to the Albanian community in Kosovo. On victimization, see Ger Duijzings, *Religion and the Politics of Identity in Kosovo* (London: Hurst & Company, 2000) and bibliography cited there.

4. Organization for Security and Co-operation in Europe (OSCE), "Kosovo/Kosova, As Seen, As Told: An Analysis of the Human Rights Findings of the Osce Kosovo Verification Mission October 1998 to June 1999" (OSCE, 2000), 121.

5. Jean Bethke Elshtain, *Women and War* (New York: Basic Books, 1995); Joanna Bourke, *An Intimate History of Killing: Face-to-Face Killing in Twentieth Century Warfare* (New York: Basic Books, 1999).

6. Carole Pateman, *The Sexual Contract* (Stanford: Stanford University Press, 1988).

7. This and all subsequent names are pseudonyms.

8. This interview was conducted in March 1999 in Tirana as part of the research project on Memory and Culture in the Life Histories of Kosovar Women, promoted by the Centro di

Documentazione delle Donne of Bologna, the Robert Schuman Centre of the European University Institute, and the Women's World Center of New York. The project was directed by Luisa Passerini, and the part concerning the Albanian Kosovar community was conducted by the author. "Little Bajram" (*Bajram I vogel*) is the feast that marks the end of the Ramadan fast; see Robert Elsie, *A Dictionary of Albanian Religion, Mythology, and Folk Culture* (London: Hurst and Company, 2000), 160.

9. For more on the general role attributed to women as the biological reproducers of the nation, see Nira Yuval-Davis, *Gender and Nation* (London: Sage, 1997), 26–38. For more on the particularities of Eastern and Central European and Balkan nationalisms, see Wendy Bracewell, "Women, Motherhood, and Contemporary Serbian Nationalism," *Women's Studies International Forum* 19 (1996): 25–33; Katherine Verdery, "From Parent-State to Family Patriarchs: Gender and Nation in Contemporary Eastern Europe," *East European Politics and Societies* 8 (1994): 223–55.

10. Interview conducted on 23 January 2000 in Pristina, within the context of the International Organization for Migration (IOM) project on Psychosocial and Trauma Response in Kosovo (PTR), directed by Natale Losi; the Archives of Memory section was coordinated by the author. Isa Boletini and Bajram Curri are both remembered as heroic figures in the struggle against the Serbs in Ottoman Kosovo between the end of the 1800s and the beginning of the 1900s.

11. Interview for the IOM's PTR project, Pristina, 14 December 1999. On the different relationships that men and women have with grief and loss, see Alessandro Portelli, *The Order Has Been Carried Out: History, Memory, and Meaning of a Nazi Massacre in Rome* (New York: Palgrave Macmillan, 2004).

12. Interview for the IOM's PTR project, Pristina, 13 January 2000.

13. Salvatici, "Memory Telling."

14. For place names, I use either Serbian or Albanian nomenclature, depending on the context; the international literature generally employs the Serbian name.

15. Interview for the IOM's PTR project, Pristina, 9 June 2000.

16. Interview for the IOM's PTR project, Pristina, 1 July 2000.

17. Interview for the IOM's PTR project, Pristina, 14 December 1999.

18. Interview for the IOM's PTR project, Pristina, 22 March 2000.

19. Catholics are a minority (4 percent) of the Albanian population, which is for the most part Muslim. After the end of the war Mitrovica was divided into two areas split by the river that crosses the city. The northern zone is mainly populated by Serbs: in September 2000 only about 2,000 of the 14,000 residents living there were Albanian.

20. The Albanian minority living in North Mitrovica is under continuous attack, much like Albanians in other places in the region with Serbian enclaves. Some families have been forced to leave their homes and settle in the southern part of the city: UNHCR-OSCE, *Assessment of the Situation of Ethnic Minorities in Kosovo (Period Covering June through September 2000)*, pdf available online through the website of the United Nations High Commissioner for Refugees: http://www.unhcr.org/cgi-bin/texis/vtx/home.

21. Interview for the IOM's PTR project, Mitrovica, 7 July 2000.

22. For this process in earlier conflicts see Margaret R. Higonnet et al., eds., *Behind the Lines: Gender and the Two World Wars* (New Haven: Yale University Press, 1987).

23. For more on women as the guardians of the "cultural borders" constructed by nations, see Yuval-Davis, *Gender and Nation;* and Tricia Cusack, "Janus and Gender: Women and the Nation's Backward Look," *Nations and Nationalism* 6 (2000): 541–61.

24. Interview conducted by the author, Pristina, March 2001. See note 8.

25. Interview for the IOM's PTR project, Pristina, 1 July 2000.

26. Interview for the IOM's PTR project, Pristina, 30 June 2000.

27. Cf. for example Guglielmo Schininà, "Arts and the Theatre: A Circle of Barters and Encounters—A Training Module on Community Needs," in Michele Losi, Steven Reisner, and Silvia Salvatici, eds., *Psychosocial and Trauma Response in War-Torn Societies: Supporting Traumatized Communities through Theatre and the Arts* (Geneva: International Organization for Migration, 2002), 67–104.

14

SEEING THE PAST, VISIONS OF THE FUTURE: MEMORY WORKSHOPS WITH INTERNALLY DISPLACED PERSONS IN COLOMBIA

~

Pilar Riaño-Alcalá

While conducting research in Colombia, I have often been confronted by the question of how best to bridge the distance between academic research activity and the lives of potential research participants who face widespread violence. In this chapter I look at memory workshops as a research method that partially addresses the methodological and ethical challenges of studying the often-brutal effects of violence without dehumanizing the subjects themselves. Drawing from a rich tradition of participatory action research, oral history, popular education, and ethnographic research on the verbal and visual arts,[1] these workshops use an interactive, participatory, and process-oriented format that combines the practice of oral history with memory-work.[2] In a memory workshop, participants join in a series of activities that elicit individual and group remembering. They share memories, listen to oral testimonies, create visual displays through media such as maps, paper quilts, and visual biographies, negotiate understandings of experiences, and reflect on the stories shared. The researcher in these workshops is often, but not necessarily, the facilitator of the session.

The workshops I discuss here took place in Colombia, a country that suffers from a forty-year internal armed conflict among leftist guerrillas, paramilitaries, the army, and drug traffickers. Currently, Colombia faces the worst humanitarian crisis in the continent, with close to three million people having fled their homes and over 260,000 living as refugees in neighboring and more distant countries.[3] In 1996 I designed a series of workshops in consultation with local researchers and community workers from Medellín, a city where ntersecting forms of organized, political, and drug-related crime and everyday violence have profoundly affected daily life over the last twenty years. I have conducted and co-facilitated many of these sessions in both urban and rural regions of Colombia with groups of youth, women, men, internally displaced persons, teachers, students, community leaders, and workers. Discussions on method and process in these workshops highlighted their potential to validate indigenous/local knowledge and the voices and stories of marginalized groups. Participants also considered the challenge of documenting oral histories in an environment of threatened memory and the social responsibility that researchers/facilitators must assume in response to the pain, grief, and expressions of anger and despair that may emerge in the workshop.

This chapter draws from these exchanges and presents my observations on what takes place when a group of internally displaced individuals gather together in a memory workshop. I focus on the *social* and *dialogic* outcomes of the workshop interaction (rather than on a discussion of the validity of the research method) and explore the processes through which participants make meaning of past experiences, negotiate collective narratives of events such as war and displacement, and reconstruct a sense of purpose as members of a community or of several communities. I argue that the production of oral testimonies in a group context facilitates community reconstruction and is a practice that makes public the silenced voices of the victims of war and displacement. This repositioning of silenced stories into a collective place of witnessing has a particular significance in a society like that of Colombia. Currently, the country is polarized by disputes over memory and reparation raised by a peace process involving paramilitary groups, where issues of truth, justice, and reparation appear to be compromised by a focus on forgiveness and national reconciliation.[4]

Contextualizing War and Humanitarian Crises in Colombia

Over the last century Colombia has experienced different phases and forms of violence. The armed conflict between the guerrillas and the army has its roots in the early 1960s, when the Revolutionary Armed Forces of Colombia (FARC) and the National Liberation Army (ELN) emerged.[5] In the 1980s, the Colombian illegal drug economy developed into one of the most powerful in the world, controlling the management and distribution of cocaine as well as playing an important role in the processing of the alkaloid.[6] In these years, paramilitary organizations consolidated their power in the countryside with support from wealthy landowners, cattle ranchers, and the drug cartels. By the late 1990s, paramilitary organizations had expanded throughout the country and had more than 15,000 members. Both the guerrillas and the paramilitary groups finance some of their operations with drug money. The third main player in the violence is the Colombian army, which has a record of human rights abuses; there are also documented links between some of its members and paramilitary activities and violence.[7]

In 1999 the United States increased its military presence in Colombia through the approval and implementation of a five-year aid package known as "Plan Colombia," worth $1.3 billion, and later through the Andean Regional Initiative. These initiatives make Colombia the third-largest recipient of U.S. military aid in the world. In October 2002 the U.S. government authorized the use of aid granted under Plan Colombia (initially for the purposes of a "war on drugs") to finance the state's "war on terror." This has resulted in increased military aid,[8] the doubling of the number of Colombian army personnel trained in the United States (15,000 Colombian military and police officers since 2002), and the further involvement, in quantity and scope, of both U.S. armed forces and private contractors (mercenaries) in training and military actions.[9]

Between 1998 and 2002 an average of 300,000 people per year were internally displaced because of worsening internal conflict, the attempts of armed groups (paramilitary, guerrilla, and armed forces) to establish control over their territories (strategic trade and circulation routes or areas rich in natural and mineral resources), and the state's incapacity to protect the human rights of the population.[10] The internally displaced represent the greatest number of victims of the conflict, making the country the principal source of forced migration in the Americas.[11]

The use of popular gathering places such as the plaza, soccer pitch, and streets as the sites for massacres, executions, and rapes by the various armed factions fragments the basic social referents that nourish community life. The chaos and confusion generated by acts of terror and intimidation corrode the foundations of social cohesion, eroding trust in the community and exacerbating fears.[12] Basic social relations are also undermined as a result of the physical destruction, the loss of lives, and the destabilizing effects brought upon individuals, families, and communities by the armed groups' practices of threatening and "pointing the finger."[13] Forced displacement is a threshold experience that includes multiple losses—one's home, life, and material goods. A precipitous and forced exit from a place of residence causes a series of ruptures and discontinuities in the lives of individuals, families, and communities.[14]

The humanitarian crisis arising out of forced displacement is evidence of the difficult relationship that Colombian society maintains with its violent past and the scars in its collective memory. The oral histories of today's displaced reveal profound links with the silenced histories of those displaced by the violence of the 1950s and 1960s,[15] in the same way that the socioeconomic and ethnic profile of today's displaced resembles that of the peasants, women, children, Afro-Colombians, and indigenous peoples who were displaced in previous wars.[16] The undeclared civil war of the 1950s represented a humiliation for these groups, who, having been trapped in a political confrontation that did not belong to them, were held responsible for the atrocities of this conflict.[17] When the warring Liberal and Conservative parties negotiated a peace agreement, the pain, losses, and humiliations were covered with a veil of oblivion and a call for national reconciliation. For the majority of the people who had suffered the loss of lives, who had lost their land, and who had been forcibly displaced, this imposed forgetting weighed heavily. The intensification of the armed conflict in the last two decades of the twentieth century and the current peace negotiations with the paramilitary forces (where the voices of the victims of paramilitary violence are absent) have marked new losses and reopened old social wounds in the public memory.

Within this historical context, the practice of oral history and questions about memory—from its most public forms to the most private and intimate ones—are attended to with a feeling of urgency. The *forced* oblivion of the atrocities and humiliations of the past, moreover, precedes the formation of a public memory that seeks to confront the past, while continuing to inform the "new" wars and the very course of national life. What type of memory can allow a society to distance itself from collective oblivion? How can the silenced voices and memories of marginalized groups find a just place in the collective memory? How should the memories of the victims and marginalized groups enter the country's historical record of violence and war? As a Colombian-Canadian anthropologist with over twenty-five years of ethnographic research, popular education, and community practice in the region, I recognize that my work is informed by these questions and by an awareness and first-hand experience of the effects of violence on human lives. My tasks of research, writing, and community work are also shaped by the historical events discussed and by a critical exploration of the connections between a society's efforts to remember, mourn, and confront a violent past and a vision of sustainable peace processes.

Labors of Memory: The Workshops

A memory workshop consists of a series of guided and facilitated activities in a group format. A question is posed to the entire group, seeking to activate participants' memories of a specific event, place, or time in their lives. Each participant narrates his or her memory, and then the group reflects on what they have heard. When the method used for the activity involves the elaboration of images, graphs, or maps (for example, mental maps, paper quilts, photo albums, visual biographies, social network mapping), participants first work individually on the elaboration of their images, and then each one shares his or her memories and images with the group. Activities are designed to produce a collective artifact: all images are gathered together on the same piece of paper or, in the case of the maps, the places are located in reference to a common landmark identified by the group.

The individual act of selecting a memory and the sharing of those memories constitute the critical moments of the workshop method; individual memories enter into a group register where listening, dialogue, tensions, and negotiation of meanings take place. This process occurs during the spontaneous comments and interjections that often accompany an individual's telling of his or her story, and also when participants are invited to reflect on what they have heard or seen. The dynamic is one of a "workshop," in the sense that the memory-work is carried out within an interactive group format where relationships are formed during the time the group stays together (anywhere from four hours to two days). Similar to the methods used in focus groups or group interviews, the collective format of the workshop makes the participants' knowledge, histories, and viewpoints visible.[18]

During the memory workshops, several methods are applied, inspired by the work of oral historians and researchers of the verbal and visual arts. The term "verbal arts" stresses the aesthetic feature of forms of expression such as folktales, proverbs, legends, riddles, songs, and poems, as well as verbal processes such as naming and rhetoric.[19] "Visual arts" describes plastic and visual expressions such as drawings, maps, photographs, and quilts. Crucial elements of the observation and reflection that occur in the workshops are the performance aspects of storytelling and the ways in which telling and remembering are physical and sensory practices. Although the memories shared in a workshop are often of a biographical nature (rather than cultural stories or folktales), the act of remembering that takes place is not organized within the temporal and causal frames of a life history or autobiography.[20] *Discrete memories* are collected, shorter, event-based, accounting for specific moments in the life of a person.[21]

From a popular education standpoint, the workshop embraces praxis as a method (learning by doing) and as an epistemological point of departure (knowledge starts from the experience of participants), which encourages critical thinking directed toward social change.[22] The workshop is understood as an instance of problematizing experience and sharing different types of knowledge through a multiplicity of "doings": seeing, speaking, remembering, reflecting, discussing, performing, and analyzing.[23] The tacit agreement that participants are together for the duration of the workshop facilitates the construction of a temporary community of knowledge and praxis[24] and activates multiple forms of encounter and communication among participants and re-searchers: between participants sitting beside or across from each other, among the group as a whole, and between participants and the facilitator. The interweaving of multiple lines of communication and relationships among participants unsettles the distance between researcher and participants, locates the researcher in a social milieu where "the freedom of the researcher is limited by the group boundaries,"[25] and allows the researcher to observe and partici-pate in a collective human interaction that resembles but does not reproduce the ways in which individuals negotiate meanings and interact in daily life.[26]

Expertise in facilitation and popular education methods has been crucial in my experience, as these sessions require knowledge of group dynamics, con-flict resolution skills, and a deep awareness of the researcher's power to control the group. As with any other research method, the dialogic and reflective po-tential of the memory workshop is mediated by the social and cultural context and by the researcher's skills and ability to use the method. It is also mediated by the presence of power relations within the workshop that, given the group setup and the context of violence, pose challenges in ensuring that everyone is heard and that potential negative reactions to what is said and shared are con-trolled. Power dynamics include the asymmetrical relationships that originate in the authority of the facilitator, questions about the use of the material gath-ered during the workshop, the various relationships among participants, and the influences upon group members of gender, ethnicity, class, or generational differences.

One of the goals of the memory workshop is the creation of a temporary nonviolent space of listening and respect where mourning, reflection, and a degree of conflict are all possible. This requires the establishment of previous contacts and relationships with each participant;[27] the development at the be-ginning of each session of basic agreements that guide participation, respectful listening, and interaction; a careful design of the workshop process; and a sen-sitive facilitation and observation of the group process. The following sections illustrate this process and present some observations on what takes place. The narratives and reflections included here are based on four five-hour work-shops conducted in Medellín in 2003.[28] Participants were men, women, and youths (two of the workshops were with men and two with women) who were forcibly displaced from various regions in the province of Antioquia[29] and were subsequently living in two of the fifty townships of displaced people that span the mountainsides of Medellín. The majority of the participants had ar-rived in Medellín within the past five years. There were two facilitators in each session and one other person whose main task was to observe the group pro-cess and individual reactions.

Remembering the Past and Reconstructing Meaning:
Workshops with Internally Displaced Persons in Medellín

Although violence and armed conflict have been present for more than four decades in many Colombian communities, forced displacement ruptures even the few remaining elements that maintained a sense of social cohesion and an appearance of normality. Because it undermines the very basis from which individuals make sense of their experiences, forced displacement profoundly affects individuals' attempts to reconstruct their lives. In this section, I discuss the ways in which remembering, storytelling, listening, and the multiple forms of interaction in the workshop facilitate the work of constructing meaning out of past experiences and making sense of current situations.

William is a youth who lives with his family in one of the townships of displaced people in the central eastern zone of Medellín.[30] He and his family are part of a circus that traditionally traveled from town to town and now goes from barrio to barrio with their tricks, pirouettes, and animals. The family was forced to migrate when "the armed forces arrived and started inviting us all, all of us young guys [to join them]. So some of us, we didn't want to go, but they said, 'Ah, we'll come for you later.'" Under the threat of forced recruitment, the family fled their town. William told the following story in a memory workshop with eleven other men who were displaced from various towns in the region of Urabá and from the northwest and east of the department of Antioquia. All are currently residents in a settlement of displaced people:

> Because wherever you were, how were you going to tell those people, "No, get out of my house" or to kick one of them out, you'd be in big trouble, so what you had to do was to shut up and because of that, you turned into a . . . nothing more, since when those people walked by your house, your life was already in danger, *by the eyes of everyone else.* So what could you do? Stay put . . . if the paramilitaries go by, stay quiet, if it was the guerrilla, stay quiet, because if you kick those people out, they kill you, if you don't kick them out, *the others will be watching you for collaborating with them,* they tell you; so there you are . . . your life is . . . is . . . like they say in the Bible, the ones . . . as the end nears for the . . . the people from the countryside will die by firearms and the ones from the city will die of hunger; so we're already in that situation that . . . that we are already finishing ourselves off; because I see that . . . that God doesn't have anything to do with this; it's among ourselves that we're finishing ourselves off. [Emphasis added]

The controls that armed groups exercise on the population (including restricted movement, "unofficial" martial law, and strict norms of social behavior), as well as their threats, demand a change in the ways individuals organize their daily lives.[31] As William's story suggests, these pressures require a shift in the ways of looking at and relating to the environment, a shift that demands a strategic-survival gaze that sometimes looks but does not tell, a looking in order to survive, blend in, hide.

In a similar manner, Doña Rosa, a displaced woman from rural eastern Antioquia, shared her experience with a group of women who are residents of another township in the central eastern zone of Medellín. The townspeople suffered three consecutive incursions from the paramilitaries and guerrillas, during which Doña Rosa's house was destroyed, several of the townspeople were massacred, and many fled. From the very first paramilitary incursion, they were pressured to leave, but Rosa refused. After the paramilitary incursion, the military arrived to *darles moral* (pick up their spirits), but they did not stay, and that very week the guerrillas came:

> We were hiding in a little house, at a girlfriend's house, in a house made of palm, because we knew the next one was for us.... We cry, we pray, we smoke, we chitchat, we did everything to calm the nerves, right? And explosions here and there, bombs here and there, grenades here and there, and we listen ... and us *there* in the house, what we did was, we opened the doors, because if they found a closed door, it was *run, run* machine gun blast, they opened it right away, ... so we opened the doors, we threw ourselves on the ground under a bed, hearing gun blasts, hearing grenades, I heard everything going by our house ... at about 9 A.M. ... so then the woman told me, "I'm going to go out to have a look ..."

When terror and violence dominate daily life, *vision*—the act or power of seeing but also the power of the imagination—is shattered and displaced to the areas where one hides; it becomes the gaze from below, from the cracks and margins. Doña Rosa, her neighbors, and William participate in an economy of looking, rationing and administering their gazes with caution. This allows Rosa to survive the second and third siege of the town and to escape hidden in a truck carrying the dead.

When Rosa and William shared their stories, a series of exchanges and reflections were sparked off among participants. William told his story in dialogue with those of other men who described fleeing from their towns because of guerrilla or paramilitary violence, which included forced recruitment. Cesar, another participant, noted that the most common aspect of their experiences was that all of them had to escape because of threats from an armed group: "In all the cases it's the same, the common denominator," he concluded. William spoke afterward and provided a vivid description of the dilemmas faced in a daily life controlled by illegally armed actors, with some social commentary on the moral and ethical implications of living as civilians in the middle of the conflict.

This kind of sharing can facilitate changes in how individuals *look* at their past experiences: how their stories relate to the experiences of others and how they can link what happened in the past to what is happening in the present.[32] The process of making sense of the past is activated when the individual—through storytelling and listening to others' stories—identifies the shared nature of his or her experience of displacement. This dialogue with others also enables the individual to see the past with some critical distance from the tragic events and allows him or her to recognize those events as a shared experience of social suffering. It is in this way that meaning can be reconstructed.

The stories about participants' arrival in Medellín and the exchanges they triggered further illustrate how individuals can invest their experiences with new meanings. In all four workshops, participants spoke of their sense of disorientation and fear upon arriving in the large city:

Liliana (young woman): I studied in Angostura; my mom worked with her ex-husband, and got a house here by Acevedo. When I finished school I went to her place. I pictured Medellín like the town, all small without any cars, with lots of trees, but when I got to Medellín I saw lots of cars and I was all scared . . .

Martha (adult woman): I came from Salgar, Antioquia, with my five sons; we arrived at the Popular No. 1 [a township in Medellín] to a sister-in-law's house, I had to, well, I arrived very disoriented, seeing a lot of vice; well, there was a lot of gunfire in that barrio, and I was doing really bad . . .

Fredy (adult man): Well, I arrived at the Popular No. 2, well . . . it hasn't gone too bad for me around here, because I already had family in Medellín and well, the family always helps you out, and I find some work . . . construction, but it's always a problem, because you don't know the city very well, and you get lost. They found me a job the same week that I arrived and every day I would lose myself downtown. Until finally I learned to walk by myself downtown . . .

Juan (young man): Well, when I got here, I came directly to . . . well, of course I was lost when I arrived, but not lost in downtown, but . . . when

I left, my mother lived in a house, outside of the Pacific [a township] and . . . well, I left and I didn't tell anyone I was coming, I didn't even know where I was going. . . . When I came, I arrived at the terminal at two in the morning, eh, . . . I went to look for my mom at her house and she had sold her house so I went to one of my brothers. When I arrived at my brother's house, it seemed that the gully had taken his house; so there I was at three o'clock in the morning, totally disoriented, I didn't know where to go, with . . . I had a bundle of leftovers, I had to leave it lying around, when my mom found me, when I went back for the bundle of leftovers, they had already stolen it.

In the city, as Fredy explains, one has to learn how to orient oneself; for this, it is necessary to redirect one's vision with an outlook toward survival, local integration, and learning to circulate. Here, the newly arrived face the challenge of adjusting their vision in a way that can give meaning to a new environment where disorientation, the unknown, suspicion, and an overload of new information permeate perception.[33] Fredy and Juan shared their stories in a workshop with men from one of the settlements. After several of them had recalled events surrounding their arrival, Don Gallo noted that his experience had been "the same thing . . . you'd lose yourself around there," and as he said this, another participant interjected, "When you don't know, you say to yourself, 'I'll get lost, but I'll get to know more.'" Here, the narrative thread of "getting lost in the city" is linked to an act of discovery, while feelings of disorientation are reframed as learning. These short reflective interventions frame each other's experiences in a manner that highlights their positive and proactive aspects and provide ways to make sense of them.

Encountering memories within a collective setting has the potential to construct a common space that allows for the articulation of participants' histories and experiences. During one of the workshops with a group of women, Maria Eugenia spoke of her younger son's fears of going to bed. "When he goes to bed at night, you wish him a good night, but then he says no, how is he supposed to have a good night if he sees the *barranco* that is going to come and is going to come right for him." Following her, another participant elaborated on this fear: "Speaking of, yeah, that you feel a lot of fear over there because of that case of the hill over there that's 'spose to filter the water from below . . . so they say it's really dangerous because if it rains a lot, well, 'sposedly the whole hill is going to come down." Their remarks triggered new stories and commentaries about their greatest fear in Medellín, a fear that Nelly had articulated earlier on as "[the fear of] what would happen to us in case of a second displacement." The township where they live is located in an area with a high risk of avalanches, and the threat of a mudslide that would destroy their fragile houses is all too real. For these women, the fear of a "second displacement" is also associated with the shootings, forced recruitment, rapes, and drug addiction that are part of the daily life of the barrio. The sharing of individual stories and fears in an environment marked by respect and listening created for these women a testimonial space that acknowledges what has happened to them and also, in this case, what could happen.

The reconstruction of the past, of people's trajectories, and of individual biographies is noted as a basic condition for emotional healing and for the reconstruction of life projects within displaced communities.[34] The key is not only to open the doors to a creative process of finding meaning and significance, but also to confront and recognize feelings and emotions (fear, pain, rage, desolation, impotence) and the mechanisms that keep them internalized.[35] In the workshop described, the women were able to pinpoint how natural and social threats pose a risk to their residence in the township and how they and their children live in a continuous state of fear. From identifying the social nature of their fears, they moved into a discussion of the various threats they suffer in the settlement where they now live (for example, forced recruitment of their children, sexual abuse, and rape) and how to respond to them. The discussion led them to recognize their collective fear and the feelings of impotence that accompany their fears, and to examine some ways in which they might confront tangible threats within their neighborhood. Recounting past experiences and addressing their present and future concerns establishes a common ground of recognition between those doing the telling and those listening. It is in this recognition that telling becomes a testimony and a communal act.[36]

Reconstructing Communities through Storytelling, the Visual Arts, and Witnessing

The power of oral history practiced within community settings is linked to its potential to maintain "a living memory of the past" and a sense of community.[37] The experience of forced migration has been characterized as deeply cultural, given that it requires refugees or the internally displaced, who are at once individual and collective victims *and* survivors of mass chaos, to solve the problem of meaning and ultimately to affirm the coherence of experience.[38] The processes of reconstructing their life projects and the struggle to reestablish their rights as social and legal subjects are consequently closely linked to the challenge of making sense of the past. During the memory workshops, the diverse strategies used for eliciting memories open up a transitional space for communication and interaction that makes possible a *remembering* of the past and potentially a reconstruction of a sense of purpose as members of a community or communities.

One of these workshops was attended by thirteen women who were displaced from rural sectors in Urabá and from the northeastern and western sectors of the Department of Antioquia. These women shared their memories of their arrival in Medellín:

Maria (thirty-five years old): We came to Moravía [another township], we don't have very much, we got to Moravía, what? around 8 P.M., not knowin' where to go, and we got to the house of a relative of the girl's father, and you know, it was very hard because I lived there for one or two months, and after two months they kicked us out, we had to live under a bridge, under the . . . what? What was it called? A bridge that's over there in Moravía ["The monkey bridge," says another woman], no, closer to here ["Acevedo or the monkey bridge, so the bridge that goes to the terminal," answers another woman], okay, . . . two bridges over there, I don't know, we had to sleep in the bridge because they had kicked us out of the house, *that* woman kicked us out around 7 P.M. I had to go out with the kids and a very kind woman let us store some stuff, and let the kids sleep.

Griselda (thirty-six): I, we came from Carepa [a town in the region of Urabá, north of Medellín]. We came at 1 A.M. and arrived at the station at 5:30. We went downtown, I didn't know anything because I didn't know anything here in Medellín, I couldn't tell anything apart, and we woke up on a sidewalk with all the girls, I was pregnant and due in about 15 days . . . [She cries; after a pause, she continues.] So we got to Medellín, eh, well, there downtown . . . well, we woke up downtown, we had just finished waking up, and then a lady, where we woke up on that sidewalk, she told us: 'Why are you waking up on this sidewalk, you guys with so many kids?' Oh, well, we came, well, the thing is that we had to come, displaced from down below, and we don't have anywhere to stay, so then she said, "I will give you 5,000 pesos and tomorrow you can go to a traffic light in El Poblado [an upper-class neighborhood], and you can go sell stuff there, something that the kids can sell, to give them food." The lady made food for us, gave us some, and then we went to El Poblado to sell stuff.

One after the other they shared their stories while placing an image that recalled their moment of arrival on the large piece of paper on the wall. Some meticulously detailed the events that precipitated their departure, while others provided more detail about their arrival in the township where they now live and how they built their houses out of garbage, cardboard, plastic, and metal sheets; some spoke uninterrupted for over fifteen minutes, while others spoke for less than five. The last participant to share her story concluded with this statement: "Well, thanks to God, we've, like she says, come out ahead and, relatively speaking, if we really look at things, we don't have anything compared to others, but relative to others we have a lot." Another offered a reflection on the stories told:

> Amparo (twenty-seven): I think it depends on each person, how they're received [by the city dwellers], because if there are people that are received or rejected because of what you lived, because of what happened to you, well, you feel bad like an *arrimado* [an unwelcome guest, freeloader], there are people that give you a helping hand and share with you what you've lived through.

Their stories evoked an oral history built around individual and collective tragedies, as well as struggles for survival and local integration. The multiple lines of communication and forms of expression created in the workshop offered those participants a safe space for remembering and for noticing the similarities and differences in each other's stories. Amparo's comment initiated the following dialogue:

> Rosa (forty-five): No, and sorry but you also find . . . everybody, I think everyone without differentiating here, I think all of us have found somebody who gave them a hand, that gave them a voice, an encouraging word . . .

> Eugenia (forty): See with that part I would say yes, what Doña Rosa says is true because, you see, when I got here. . . . And I got here and I threw my things there where the other woman was, and I was in so much anguish with everything, I cried, and so one night this young woman, Dora's sister, came out on a Saturday night and we were all piled up there, and since I was new, well, I, one still did not have to do everything, so when that young woman got there at midnight and said, "Oh man, this sucks" [that the woman's family was there], this is the truth. . . . "Look at this horrible displacement," that's what she said, and it made me so sad, and I started to cry, for real, so during those days, in those days came, oh, Doña María was there, and I would tell her my . . . my situation to her, and so whatever they gave her she would share with me . . .

Added to the previous stories, this dialogue suggests the ways in which the arrival in the city constitutes a liminal situation of chaos/creativity. In the process of telling and sharing, these women recognize themselves as agents of change who can creatively use and adapt their existing resources as they also realize what their resources are and identify the individuals who have supported them. The sharing of stories provides the basis from which the women negotiate an understanding of their situation and situate themselves as resourceful, internally displaced individuals in the city. The selection of stories, the narrative forms used, the interruptions of others, and their moral reflections slowly construct a consensus about the meaning of their experience. This building of a common understanding makes visible individual and group resources and potentially strengthens the fabric of social relations. On other occasions during the workshops, debates and disagreements arose, prompting different and contradictory interpretations. This process of collective conversation and negotiation is at the core of how social memories are shared by groups of people in their daily lives and how meaning is created in everyday social interactions.[39] Not all of the participants lived through the same experiences, and remembering reveals facets of experience and relations previously unknown. These instances of negotiation, disagreement, and consensus make the reconstruction and resignification of experience and the elaboration of meaning possible.[40]

Visualizing Stories: Seeing the Past
and Envisioning the Future

The previous examples of narratives and interactions have illustrated the types of verbal exchanges and negotiations that take place in the workshop. Visual arts provide a further means for exploring the sensory dimension of memories. They permit an emotional reconstruction and elaboration of lived experiences as well as create a visual referent for *seeing* memories and observing commonalities and differences among them. Figure 14.1 presents the paper quilt that a group of men created during their workshop. In this activity each man remembered a significant event or period of change in his life. They worked individually on their images, using paper cutouts of many colors and constructing them on a square piece of paper. They placed the finished images in a quilt-like pattern on a large piece of paper and then presented their stories. I highlight two of the images and stories told on this occasion to illustrate how making and sharing images provide a further means of expressing emotions and memories that can be difficult to express in solely narrative or oral forms.

William (bottom row, third image): My drawing represents a circus. As you all know, almost all of my life has been next to a circus . . .'cause

Fig 14.1   Paper quilt illustrating significant life events, developed by memory workshop participants, 2004. *(Photograph by Pilar Riaño-Alcalá.)*

here where you see me I'm a soldier, I have a license to kill, but to kill people with laughter [laughter in audience], and I wish there were more people like me, that make people laugh and not make people cry. Yes, because I go from town to town making people laugh, I don't go from town to town killing people or taking away the little they have, or anything like that. . . . We, on the other hand, go from town to town and the only thing we want is to be able to sustain ourselves, we don't do any harm to anyone, the only thing we do is to steal smiles, I don't think there is anything wrong with that; so, yeah . . . what does this have to do with violence? Well, it has a lot to do with it, because I'm the kind of guy that wherever I arrive, where nobody knows me, or is around . . . do you understand? Nobody knows me and they don't know where this dude's come from, so . . . they already have you checked out: "No, this guy is awfully nosy, and such and such thing . . ." We were showing a good art, I believe it's good, an art that makes people laugh, stealing a little smile from the children.

Jorge (early thirties): All right . . . you were asking me about something that happened to me . . . something important, well, for me the most important . . . this red signifies blood, I'm referring to the fact that my dad was killed, I saw him get killed, well, it's not like it happened to you but . . . for me the most important is that, except that, well, this one is like sharing with you all . . . I don't know . . .

William and Jorge remembered a critical moment in their lives from different perspectives. William presents a colorful and descriptive image that represents a crucial referent of place and memory in his life: the circus. The accompanying narrative does not recall a specific time or event but rather moves into a more discursive level. He talks about the significance of his work in the circus by using and subverting the meanings of key words of war and violence—"I'm a soldier, I have a licence to kill, but to kill people with laughter"—to stress the social function of laughter. Jorge's image contrasts with William's because it is primarily symbolic: he filled the square with one single stain of red to represent death through its most dramatic symbol—blood. In further contrast, the memory is very specific, and it refers to what he considers the most critical event in his life: witnessing his father's assassination.

Through the creation of images, participants explore ways to communicate and represent their histories and experiences of violence, suffering, and pain. Through these acts of representation and seeing, they leave further testimonials to the past. In the paper quilts, or on the walls, the images stand as mnemonic artifacts that record past events and retain a sense of the past.[41] William's and Jorge's images give testimony to the very personal ways in which violence has marked their lives and, in William's case, to his response to violence through the definition of his work as teaching people the art of laughter. Elaboration of images during the workshop involves participants in the crucial task of re-presentation; they use signs, symbols, and drawings to expose their emotions and experiences. Through image construction, individuals not only negotiate narrative threads and common understandings to frame their experiences but also find ways to represent their experience. Jorge's image assumes the task of representation through one single but powerful visual effect. He makes use of the strong cultural and religious symbolism behind the color red not only as a frame for his story but also as a sign or code for violence and suffering.

At the end of the memory quilt activity, when the group looks at the paper quilt as a whole, the comments reflect on the scope of their social suffering and the commonality of their experiences. For some of the workshop participants, sharing their stories is practically impossible; in some cases these experiences of terror and displacement, where doubt and the unpredictable predominate, can erode even the most fundamental operations by which individuals give meaning to their daily lives.[42] The weight of a traumatic past, moreover, blocks narrative expression. The workshops, and their use of various media of expression, create a realm where narrative expression can be explored and also allow reflection and a reconstruction of the past by means of listening and, importantly, image-making. Research on violence and subjectivity has demonstrated how trust and "the ordinary" as a site for the "taken-for-granted" seem to disappear in the face of terror and terrible tragedy.[43] In my view, one of the most important tasks in the engagement of a collective process of mourning is the recovery of the everyday context as a site of trust and of face-to-face relationships. The use of various verbal and visual media for expressing and sharing memories in a respectful group context can contribute to this task.

Hearing other people's stories of displacement, suffering, and violence allows for a re-evaluation of one's own traumatic experiences. It also allows for the identification—even when one's story is not told—of common suffering and for the discovery of different resources and strategies for survival. Listening, then, allows the individual to come to a new understanding of his or her situation. Recognizing one's personal history within the history of others is directly linked to the task of rebuilding trust; this rebuilding of trust, moreover, is a fundamental condition for re-establishing a sense of purpose as members of a community and regaining a sense of control over the anxieties created by an unpredictable environment.[44] The exchanges that take place when individuals come together to remember and share stories make momentary inroads into this long and complex process of reconstruction and mourning.

In the workshops with internally displaced individuals in Medellín, I have learned that the determination to forge ahead and to continue living is a clear option for these women and men. Their willingness to participate in a memory workshop and to share their stories is in itself an act of breaking the silence and secrecy that they have had to adopt in order to protect their lives.[45] Comments made at the end of one of the women's workshops reveal that a fundamental dimension in the reconstruction of experience and emotional re-establishment is the recognition of the social suffering that holds their individual stories together:

Mariana (adult woman): I learned other things from some women that, well, there were different things . . . and that, yeah, that we all have like the same pain, and that we're united by the same cause.

The task of giving meaning to experience during the collective exercise of remembering in turn enriches the meanings with which each individual imbues her or his experience. This task of resignification is mediated by the individual's repertoire of cultural practices (rituals, beliefs, value systems), her or his life stories, and the collection of individual and social resources that the subject relies upon.[46] This process activates a recognition mechanism that creates a temporary "we" among those who share their stories and memories.[47] Recognizing a common foundation of emotions and experiences transforms the way individuals *see*. This transformation leads toward a *vision* that bestows meaning on the experience because it establishes relationships between the present and the past, between what is remembered, told, and heard, and between the intimate and individual and the collective suffering. The establishment of such relationships allows subjects to position themselves as *surviving witnesses* whose acts of storytelling give testimony to "what happened."

Making Silenced Memories Public: Producing History

The collective context of the workshops allows for a movement between remembering and reflection. In this movement, connections are made between the personal, subjective dimension of the experiences of loss and displacement and the collective dimension of exodus as the human manifestation of the impact of war and violence. Similarly, there is a movement in seeing—a repositioning of vision from the absurd to the meaningful—which positions the subjects as *surviving witnesses* of the drama. This understanding situates individuals and social groups as witnesses of a violent and atrocity-laden past and compels them to confront their past through testimony, recognition of pain, and dialogue.[48] The value and transforming potential of remembering as a group resides in this *displacement* of vision, which situates subjects as social agents and witnesses. Memory-work and narratives are dynamic communication media that allow individuals to recognize social suffering and that encourage collective mourning. Moreover, they are elements of a *collective act of historical production* that addresses the need to *work with*—not avoid or deny—suffering and mourning. These collective acts of historical production situate personal history within a broader social frame of collective suffering and help trigger subjects' ability to rebuild their life projects and engage in collective action.

This projection of memory-work and oral history as a social practice of history production has particular implications for a society like Colombia, where oblivion and suppression permeate official history. The narratives of the internally displaced population are testimonials to the violence in Colombia, to critical social fractures, and to the broader historical and contextual forces that shape the most serious conflict in the Western hemisphere. These narratives expose the horrors and dehumanizing paths of the war and the deep social wounds affecting Colombian society because of its unresolved relationship with its past. The voices and first-hand experiences of these women and men *must* enter the historical record if the society is going to seriously confront its relationship with its past atrocities and with the current task of negotiating a resolution to the present conflict—and, importantly, if it is going to respond appropriately to demands for justice and reparation. Reflection on the communication that takes place in the memory workshops suggests some of the ways in which we may begin the task of exploring individual and collective memories while contributing to a more inclusive social history. They may also help us build a different relationship with the past and to alternative forms of public memory: forms that, in the words of Nadia Seremetakis, are "the moment when the buried, the discarded, and the forgotten escape to the social surface of awareness like life-supporting oxygen. It is the moment of exit from historical dust."[49]

NOTES

1. For participatory action research see Orlando Fals-Borda, *Conocimiento y poder popular* (Bogotá: Siglo XXI Editores, 1984); and the same author's "Participación popular: retos del futuro," paper presented at the Registro del Congreso Mundial de Convergencia en Investigación Participativa 97 (Bogotá: ICFES, IEPRI, Colciencias, 1997), and "Participatory (Action) Research in Social Theory: Origins and Challenges," in P. Reason and H. Bradbury, eds., *Handbook of Action Research: Participative Inquiry and Practice* (London: Sage Publications, 2001), 27–37; Francisco Ibañez-Carrasco, "Desire and Betrayal in Community-Based Research," in F. Ibañez-Carrasco and E. Meiners, eds., *Public Acts: Disruptive Readings on Making Curriculum Public—Re-engaging the Public Sphere* (New York: Routledge, 2004): 211–36; P. Maguire, *Doing Participatory Research: A Feminist Approach* (Amherst, MA: Center for International Education, 1987); "Uneven Ground: Feminisms and Action Research," in Reason and Bradbury, *Handbook of Action Research*, 59–70; Pilar Riaño, *Descifrando la cultura popular: Investigación participativa en los barrios*, Controversia 166 (Bogotá: Editorial CINEP, 1991). For oral history see David W. Cohen, *The Combing of History* (Chicago: University of Chicago Press, 1994); Sherna Gluck and Daphne Patai, eds., *Women's Words: The Feminist Practice of Oral History* (New York: Routledge, 1991); Hugo Slim and Paul Thompson, eds., *Listening for a Change: Oral Testimony and Community Development* (Gabriola Island: New Society, 1995). For popular education see Alfredo Ghiso, "Acercamientos: El taller en procesos investigativos interactivos," *Estudios sobre las Culturas Contemporaneas* 5:9 (1999): 141–53; Augusto Boal, *Games for Actors and Non Actors* (London: Routledge, 1994); Denise Nadeau, *Counting Our Victories: Popular Education and Organizing—A Training Guide on Popular Education and Organizing* (Vancouver: Repeal the Deal Productions, 1996); Pilar Riaño, "Paths and Movements in Popular Education," *Aquelarre Magazine* 20/21 (1996): 26–30. For the verbal and visual arts, see Julie Cruikshank, *Life*

Lived Like a Story: Life Stories of Three Yukon Native Elders (Vancouver: University of British Columbia Press, 1991); Julie Cruikshank, *The Social Life of Stories: Narrative and Knowledge in the Yukon Territory* (Vancouver: University of British Columbia Press, 1998); Ruth Finnegan, *Oral Traditions and the Verbal Arts: A Guide to Research Practices* (London: Routledge, 1992).

2. Memory-work is a research methodology and field of practice that addresses issues of power by bridging the gap between researcher and research subjects, as well as by using personal memories and experience as a basis for social knowledge; see Frigga Haug, *Female Sexualization: A Collective Work of Memory,* trans. Erica Carter (London: Verso, 1986); Michael Schratz, Rob Walker, and Barbara Schratz-Hadwich, "Collective Memory-work: The Self as a Re/source for Re/search," in *Research as Social Change* (London: Routledge, 1995). According to Adrienne Hyle and her collaborators, memory-work explores the "ways in which the discursive practices of a community influence the ways of being that we experience." See Adrienne Hyle, Judy Kaufman, Margaret Ewing, and Diane Montgomery, "Philosophy and Overview of Memory Work," manuscript (2004), 2. Of particular relevance for memory workshops is their differentiation between the type of narratives that are created by autobiographical and testimonial research methods and the "discrete memories" that are generated by memory-work—stand-alone memories that highlight "the moments of a life" of a person and that indicate the "ways in which individuals construct themselves into existing relations": Haug, *Female Sexualization,* 34.

3. ACNUR (Alto Comisionado de las Naciones Unidas para los Refugiados), "Balance a la política de atención al desplazamiento interno forzado en Colombia, 1999–2000," available at www.acnur.org; Consultoría para los Derechos y el Desplazamiento (CODHES), "Desplazamiento: implicaciones y retos para la gobernabilidad, la democracia, y los derechos humanos," *II Seminario Internacional,* available at www.codhes.org; U.S. Committee for Refugees, *World Refugee Survey 2004, Warehousing Issue* (Washington, DC: Immigration and Refugee Services of America, 2004).

4. Maria T. Uribe, "Memorias, historias, y ciudad," paper presented at the seminar on Medellín y Buenos Aires se Miran y Encuentran, City of Medellín, 8–15 October 2004.

5. FARC is the oldest and most powerful guerrilla group in the country, with 17,000 active members and a presence in more than 60 percent of the national territory; see Marco Palacios, *Por una agenda de paz* (Bogotá: Departamento Nacional de Planeación, 1997). The ELN was inspired by the Cuban revolution and is the second-largest guerrilla group; see Charles Bergquist, Ricardo Peñaranda, and Gonzalo Sánchez, eds., *Violence in Colombia: The Contemporary Crisis in Historical Perspective* (Wilmington, DE: Scholarly Resources, 1992).

6. Alonso Salazar, *La cola del lagarto: Drogas y narcotráfico en la sociedad colombiana* (Medellín: Corporación Región, 1998).

7. Cynthia Arnson, ed., *The Peace Process in Colombia with the Autodefensas Unidas de Colombia-AUC* (Washington, DC: Woodrow Wilson International Center for Scholars, Latin American Program, 2005), available at http://www.wilsoncenter.org/topics/pubs/PeaceProcColAUC.pdf; Mauricio Romero, *Paramilitares y autodefensas, 1982–2003* (Bogotá: Editorial Planeta, 2003).

8. Between 2000 and 2004, the U.S. government granted $3.3 billion in assistance: Arnson, *The Peace Process in Colombia.*

9. Adam Isacson, Joy Olson, and Lisa Haugaard, "Blurring the Lines: Trends in US Military Programs in Latin America," Latin American Working Group Education Fund, the Center for International Policy and the Washington Office on Latin America, 2004, available

at http://ciponline.org/facts/0410btl.pdf; United States Institute of Peace, "Civil Society Under Siege in Colombia," Special Report 114 (2004), available at http://www.usip.org/pubs/specialreports/sr114.html.

10. Jorge Rojas R., "Una sociedad en medio del colapso," *Hechos y Análisis*, cited 14 November 2002, available at www.codhes.org. In 2002, paramilitary groups were responsible for 52 percent of the displacements and guerrilla groups were responsible for 43 percent: see ibid. In the majority of cases, Colombians flee from their homes because of general threats, clashes between armed groups, and targeted threats from armed groups. Forced displacement is part of wider migratory forces and historic dynamics that reveal the close association between the increase of armed violence, massive displacements of the rural population, and a concentration of resources—particularly land ownership. Dario Fajardo notes how these processes of territorial concentration have been characterized by three factors since the 1980s: the permanent agricultural crisis, the development of the drug trade, and the growing influence and presence of transnational capital: Dario Fajardo M., "Migraciones internas, desplazamientos forzados y estructuras regionales," *Palimpsesto: Revista de la Facultad de Ciencias Humanas Universidad Nacional de Colombia* (2002): 69.

11. ACNUR, "Balance a la política de atención al desplazamiento interno forzado en Colombia, 1999–2000"; U.S. Committee for Refugees, *World Refugee Survey 2004, Warehousing Issue*.

12. Alejandro Castillejo, *Poética de lo otro: Antropología de la guerra, la soledad, y el exilio interno en Colombia* (Bogotá: Instituto Colombiano de Antropología e Historia, Colciencias, 2000); Valentine Daniel and John Knudsen, eds., "Introduction," *Mistrusting Refugees* (Berkeley: University of California Press, 1995), 1–12; Ana María Jaramillo, Marta I. Villa, and Luz Amparo Sánchez, *Miedo y desplazamiento* (Medellín: Corporación Región, 2004).

13. Jaramillo, Villa, and Sánchez, *Miedo y desplazamiento*.

14. Fernando J. Arias and Sandra Ruiz, "Construyendo caminos con familias y comunidades afectadas por la situación de desplazamiento en Colombia," in Martha N. Bello, Elena Martin C., and Fernando J. Arias, eds., *Efectos psicosociales y culturales del desplazamiento* (Bogotá: Universidad Nacional de Colombia, 2002), 41–62; Martha N. Bello, "Identidad, dignidad, y desplazamiento forzado: Una lectura psicosocial," in CODHES, *Desplazamiento forzado interno en Colombia: Conflicto, paz, y desarrollo* (Bogotá: CODHES, 2001), 299–318; Gloria A. Camilo, "Impacto psicológico del desplazamiento forzoso: Estrategia de intervención," in Bello et al., *Efectos psicosociales y culturales del desplazamiento*, 27–40; Donny Meertens, "Encrucijadas urbanas: Población desplazada en Bogota y Soacha—Una mirada diferenciada por genero, edad, y etnia" (Bogota: ACNUR, 2003); Flor E. Osorio, *La violencia del silencio, desplazados del campo a la ciudad* (Bogota: CODHES, Universidad Javeriana, 1993).

15. The war known as "La Violencia" lasted from 1946 to 1965, claiming the lives of 200,000 Colombians and affecting extensive areas of the country. It was ostensibly waged between the Liberal and Conservative parties over the control of the government, but the stakes included social and economic issues, such as the struggle for land and resources, the emergence of new elites, the control of the lower social classes, and the search for social mobility. See Catherine LeGrand, "Comentario al estudio de la historiografía sobre la violencia," in Bernando Tovar, ed., *La historia al final del milenio: Ensayos de historiografía Colombiana y Latinoaméricana* (Bogotá: Editorial Universidad Nacional, 1994), 425–32; Mary Roldán, *Blood and Fire: La Violencia in Antioquia, Colombia, 1946–1953* (Durham: Duke University Press, 2002).

16. Roldán, *Blood and Fire.*

17. Daniel Pecaut, "The Loss of Rights, the Meaning of Experience, and Social Connection: A Consideration of the Internally Displaced in Colombia," *International Journal of Politics, Culture, and Society* 14:1 (2000): 89–106.

18. Ester Madriz, "Focus Groups in Feminist Research," in N. Denzin and Y. Lincoln, eds., *Collecting and Interpreting Qualitative Materials,* 2nd ed. (Thousand Oaks, CA: Sage Publications, 2003), 363–88; Clemencia Rodríguez, "Guía para la primera fase de la evaluación de experiencias de medios ciudadanos y comunitarios," manuscript (2005).

19. Finnegan, *Oral Traditions and the Verbal Arts.*

20. Hyle et al., "Philosophy and Overview of Memory Work."

21. Ibid.

22. Ghiso, "Acercamientos"; Pilar Riaño, "Recuerdos metodológicos: El taller y la investigación etnográfica," *Estudios sobre las Culturas Contemporáneas* 5:10 (2000): 143–68.

23. Néstor García-Canclini and Ana Rosas M., "Las múltiples ciudades de los viajeros," in Néstor García Canclini, Alejandro Castellanos, and Ana Rosas Mantecón, eds., *La ciudad de los viajeros: Travesía e imaginarios urbanos: México, 1940–2000* (México: Universidad Autónoma Metropolitana, 1996), 61–106; Ghiso, "Acercamientos."

24. Jean Lave and Etienne Wenger, *Situated Learning: Legitimate Peripheral Participation* (Cambridge: Cambridge University Press, 1991); Riaño, "Recuerdos metodológicos."

25. Jesús Ibañez, "Como se realiza una investigación mediante grupos de discusión," in Francisco Alvira, Jesús Ibañez, and Manuel García Ferrando, eds., *El Análisis de la realidad social* (Madrid: Alianza Editorial, 1989), 569–81.

26. García Canclini et al., *La ciudad de los viajeros;* Madriz, "Focus Groups in Feminist Research"; Rossana Reguillo, "La memoria debate: El grupo de discusión y los mitos urbanos," paper presented at the second International Seminar on Oral History, Jalisco, México, 1–6 November 1996.

27. In most cases I developed the workshops in coordination with a local community group to ensure not only previous contact but also follow-up after the workshop.

28. I am currently working with researchers from Colombia, Ecuador, and Canada on a project involving the forced migration of Colombians. This research examines this growing problem through a comparative study of two types of forced migration: forced displacement *within* Colombia and that of Colombian refugees *living abroad* in Ecuador and Canada. In this research, we use memory workshops to collect qualitative information on the ways that fear, historical memory, and public representations of internally displaced persons and refugees affect their processes of settlement and integration into a new society. We see these workshops as part of a process of documenting the histories of internally displaced persons and refugees and constructing a humanistic and respectful account of their experiences of upheaval and arrival in a new society. One of the first stages of this research on the theme of "Fear and Displacement" was developed by an interdisciplinary team from Corporación Región in Colombia and was funded by the Colombian Institute of Science and Technology, Colciencias. In this chapter I use material compiled during this first phase. The researchers involved in this study are Marta I. Villa, Ana María Jaramillo, and Luz Amparo Sánchez. I have benefited greatly from our ongoing exchange of ideas and from their excellent analyses.

29. The northwestern province of Antioquia, the region in which the research will be conducted, shows the highest rates of displacement in terms of both expelled and incoming population. Between 1995 and March of 2004, 238,844 people were forced to flee. Medellín, the capital of the province, received the largest number of IDPs. See Secretariado Nacional

de Pastoral Social, *Desplazamiento forzado en Antioquia, 1985–1998* (Bogotá: Secretariado Nacional de Pastoral Social, 2001); ; Jaramillo, Villa, and Sánchez, *Miedo y desplazamiento.*

30. All names are pseudonyms.

31. As Daniel and Knudsen write, the decision to flee and the events that surround these moments of terror and chaos create a disjunction between "this person's familiar *way-of-being* in the world and a new reality of the socio-political circumstances that not only threatens that *way-of-being* but also forces one to *see* the world differently": "Introduction," i (emphasis added).

32. Ibid.

33. Meertens, "Encrucijadas urbanas"; Castillejo, *Poética de lo otro.*

34. Bello, "Identidad, dignidad, y desplazamiento forzado"; Meertens, "Encrucijadas urbanas"; Antonius Robben, "The Assault on Basic Trust: Disappearance, Protest, and Reburial in Argentina," in Antonius Robben and Marcelo Suárez-Orozco, eds., *Cultures under Siege: Collective Violence and Trauma* (Cambridge: Cambridge University Press, 2000), 70–101; Robben and Suàrez-Orozco note that for the individual who has lost her or his home, goods, and life, this reconstruction of the past is the foundation upon which a new and meaningful relationship to the world can be built.

35. The invitation to remember significant moments in one's life can provoke a series of critical experiences of violence and accompanying emotions. During those moments, a series of possibilities opens up: the elaboration of grief, catharsis, silence, the expression of pain, critical reflection. Some professionals have questioned the consequences of reviving the memory of traumatic events and the ability of a group and a facilitator to respond to the unchaining of emotions and the revival of trauma, as well as the limitations of the social and cultural context of a memory workshop. Although it is important to recognize that trauma has psychological repercussions for the individual, it is also necessary to locate trauma in its particular social, political, and cultural contexts. The risk of such a "professional" stance is that it personifies and individualizes trauma, and thereby converts collective experiences of suffering into individual experience, and social and political problems into medical pathologies and psychosocial problems that can only be dealt with by professionalized bodies. The memory workshop utilizes the idea that communities have always had social spaces, cultural rituals, and practices that provide spaces for mourning and ways of collectively dealing with loss and pain.

36. George Yúdice defines testimony as a narrative, told by a witness who is moved to narrate by the urgency of a situation (for example, war, oppression, revolution). The narrator/witness describes his or her own experience, and this narrative is considered representative of a collective memory and identity. Testimonial literature has framed the acts of witnessing and telling as part of communal traditions that aim at making individual histories public and the individual history representative of the exploited conditions of larger social groups. See George Yúdice, "Testimonio and Postmodernism," *Latin American Perspectives* 18:3 (Summer 1991): 15–31; George Gugelberger, ed., *The Real Thing: Testimonial Discourse and Latin America* (Durham, NC: Duke University Press, 1996).

37. Slim and Thompson, *Listening for a Change*, 11.

38. Daniel and Knudsen, "Introduction."

39. Some of the literature on focus groups questions the artificial nature of the interaction and raises questions about the controlled nature of the setting. The same could be said for the workshops, which are based on a similar group format. The potential with the focus groups and workshops, however, is that participants soon establish relationships and contacts beyond the structured format of a facilitated group meeting. As workshop participants

move from one activity to another, take breaks, and talk to each other, all types of group dynamics emerge. Through this social interaction, research also becomes a social event. See García Canclini et al., *La ciudad de los viajeros.*

40. In my article on methodological memories ("Recuerdos metodológicos"), I note that when a group collectively explores its past through sharing stories, the practices of memory often cover a continuum between description, sensory experience, and analytical reflection. This allows individuals to construct meaning and to strengthen social bonds. Remembering as an individual within a group where the majority of other participants have lived through similar situations creates a temporary community of shared feelings and emotions. See Alessandro Portelli, *The Death of Luigi Trastulli and Other Stories: Form and Meaning in Oral History* (Albany: State University of New York Press, 1991).

41. Michael Roth and Charles Salas, eds., *Disturbing Remains: Memory, History, and Crisis in the Twentieth Century—Issues and Debates* (Los Angeles: Getty Research Institute, 2001).

42. Daniel and Knudsen, "Introduction."

43. Robben, "The Assault on Basic Trust"; Marcelo Suárez-Orozco and Antonius Robben, "Interdisciplinary Perspectives on Violence and Trauma," in Robben and Suárez-Orozco, *Cultures under Siege,* 1–42. This transformed quality of everyday life is seen as a loss of context, according to Veena Das, Arthur Kleinman, Margaret Lock, Mamphela Ramphele, and Pamela Reynolds, eds., *Remaking a World: Violence, Social Suffering, and Recovery* (Berkeley: University of California Press, 2001).

44. Robben, "The Assault on Basic Trust"; Marcelo Suárez-Orozco and Antonius Robben, "Interdisciplinary Perspectives on Violence and Trauma."

45. Osorio, *La violencia del silencio, desplazados del campo a la ciudad.*

46. Bello, "Identidad, dignidad, y desplazamiento forzado."

47. I describe this mechanism as the means to activate a "community of memory"; the consolidation of a temporary "we" that grounds itself as a community of listening and speaking and that constitutes itself in the acts of remembering. See Pilar Riaño, "La memoria viva de las muertes: Lugares e identidades juveniles en Medellín," *Análisis Político* 41 (2000): 23–39; Pilar Riaño, *Dwellers of Memory: Youth and Violence in Medellín, Colombia* (New Brunswick: Transaction Publishers, 2006).

48. Michael Humphrey, *The Politics of Atrocity and Reconciliation: From Terror to Trauma* (London: Routledge, 2002).

49. Nadia Seremetakis, ed., *The Senses Still: Perception and Memory as Material Culture in Modernity* (Chicago: University of Chicago Press, 1994), 12.

Contributors

Kevin Blackburn teaches history at the National Institute of Education, Nanyang Technological University, Singapore, where he also coordinates the oral history program for training social studies teachers. He has conducted research, including oral history interviews, on the Japanese occupation of Singapore; his articles appear in *Oral History* and *Journal of Chinese Overseas*. He is also coauthor with Karl Hack of *Did Singapore Have to Fall?* (2004).

Senka Božić-Vrbančić is McArthur Research Fellow at the University of Melbourne, Australia, and senior lecturer at the University of Zadar, Croatia. She completed her doctoral thesis on Maori-Croatian relationships in 2004 at the University of Auckland, New Zealand. Her scholarly interests range from indigenous to migrant identity formations, the politics of representation, visual culture, diaspora, nationalisms, and multiculturalisms, and her work addresses questions of globalization, home, belonging, community, and transnational connections. She has recently completed a book based on her research: *Tarara: The Cultural Politics of Croat and Maori Identity in New Zealand* (2008). Her work has appeared in the *Journal of the Polynesian Society, History and Anthropology, Ethnography,* and *Quarterly Sociological Review*.

Işıl Cerem Cenker is a doctoral student in the Political Science Department at Sabanci University, Istanbul. Her research interests include social network analysis, policy networks of development, institutions, social capital, and trust. She holds masters degrees from the Central European University in Hungary and from the European Institute of the London School of Economics, where she studied EU policy making. She has published an award-winning article on the oral history project at Seddülbahir in *Toplumsal Tarih* [Social History], a monthly journal published by the Economic and Social History Foundation of Turkey.

Gail Lee Dubrow is vice provost and dean of the Graduate School at University of Minnesota, where she is a professor in both the College of Architecture and Landscape Architecture, Hubert H. Humphrey Institute of Public Affairs, and the Department of History in the College of Liberal Arts. She has published two award-winning books: *Sento at Sixth and Main*, with Donna Graves (2004), and *Restoring Women's History through Historic Preservation*, edited with Jennifer Goodman (2003).

Sean Field is senior lecturer in the Historical Studies Department and director of the Centre for Popular Memory, a training, research, and archival center committed to the dissemination of marginalized people's stories, at the University of Cape Town, South Africa. After early study at the University of Cape Town, he completed a doctorate in social history at the University of Essex in 1996. He is the author of several publications on memory, life stories, and identity dynamics within urban communities. Current research interests include the traumatic and emotional aspects of popular memories of the apartheid era in South Africa and the genocide in Rwanda.

Paula Hamilton is associate professor of history at the University of Technology, Sydney, Australia, where she has taught oral and public history for several years. She has worked in a range of projects with community groups, museums, heritage agencies, and local councils, and since 1992 has been co-editor of the *Public History Review*. She has written a number of essays on public memory and historical consciousness in Australia; recently completed a book based on oral histories: *Cracking Awaba: Stories of Mosman and Northern Beaches during the Depression* (2005); and is completing, with Paul Ashton, *History in Australia Today: Australians and the Past*, a study of how Australians use the past in their everyday lives.

Robert F. Jefferson is associate professor of African American studies and U.S. history at Xavier University in Ohio. His articles on African American GIs and their communities during World War II have appeared in the *Journal of Family History*, *Quaderni Storici* (Bologna), *Contours: A Journal of the African Diaspora*, and *The Historian*. He is the author of *Fighting for Hope: African Americans of the Ninety-third Infantry Division in World War II and Postwar America* (2008) and is currently working on a book-length study, *The American Society of African Culture and the Pan-African Imaginary from 1957 to 1968*.

Daniel Kerr is an assistant professor in the History Department at James Madison University in Virginia. Since 1992 he has focused, as both activist and researcher, on housing, homelessness, and contingent labor and has published his research in the *Oral History Review*. He played a significant role in the movement to organize day laborers in Cleveland, Ohio, was a founding member of the Day Laborers' Organizing Committee and the Cleveland Community Hiring Hall, and helped found the Cleveland chapter of Food Not Bombs. He received his Ph.D. in history from Case Western Reserve University in 2005.

David Neufeld has worked as the Yukon and Western Arctic historian for Parks Canada since 1986. Much of his career has been devoted to questions arising from collaborative research with northern Aboriginal communities and tensions between national government mandate and First Nation sovereignty. In addition to extensive fieldwork, recent publications include "The Commemoration of Northern Aboriginal Peoples by the Canadian Government" in the *George Wright Forum* (2002) and "Ethics in the Practice of Public History with Aboriginal Communities" in the *Public Historian* (2006), completed while a visiting scholar at the Scott Polar Research Institute, Cambridge University.

Maria Nugent is a research fellow in the Centre for Historical Research at the National Museum of Australia. She is co-author with Denis Byrne of *Mapping Attachment: A Spatial Approach to Aboriginal Post-contact Heritage* (2004) and author of *Botany Bay: Where Histories Meet* (2005). She was an Australian Research Council Postdoctoral Fellow in the School of Historical Studies, Monash University, Melbourne, and has had extensive experience as a public and oral historian primarily with Aboriginal communities in New South Wales.

Horacio N. Roque Ramírez, a Salvadoran immigrant to the United States, teaches LGBT/queer studies, Central American migrations, and oral history theories and methods in the Department of Chicana and Chicano Studies at the University of California, Santa Barbara. He earned his Ph.D. in comparative ethnic studies at the University of California, Berkeley, and has contributed to *CENTRO: Journal of the Center for Puerto Rican Studies*, the *Oral History Review*, the *Journal of the History of Sexuality*, and the anthologies *Queer Migrations: Sexuality, U.S. Citizenship, and Border Crossings* (2005) and *Archive Stories: Facts, Fictions, and the Writing of History* (2005). He is currently completing a study of queer Latino history and culture in the San Francisco Bay area from the 1960s through the 1990s.

Pilar Riaño-Alcalá is an assistant professor in the School of Social Work, University of British Columbia Canada. She is the editor of *Women in Grassroots Communications: Furthering Social Change* (1994); the special issue of the *Journal of Latin American Anthropology*, "Memory, Representation and Narratives: Rethinking Violence in Colombia" (2002); and the books *Memoria, arte público y violencia en la ciudad* [Memory, Public Art and Violence in the City] (2003) and *Dwellers of Memory: Youth and Violence in Medellín, Colombia* (2006). She received her Ph.D. in anthropology from the University of British Columbia.

Silvia Salvatici is a lecturer in modern history at the University of Teramo, Italy, where she teaches women's and gender history. She is currently working on gendered forced migration in the twentieth century. She is the editor, with Natale Losi and Luisa Passerini, of "The Archives of Memory: Supporting Traumatised Communities through Narration and Remembrance," *Psychosocial Notebook* 2 (2001), and of "Profughe" [Women Refugees], a special issue of *Genesis: Rivista della Società italiana delle Storiche* III (2004).

Linda Shopes retired from her position as historian at the Pennsylvania Historical and Museum Commission in Harrisburg, Pennsylvania, in 2007 and now works as a freelance developmental editor and also consults in oral and public history. She has written widely on oral and public history and is co-editor of *The Baltimore Book: New Views of Local History* (1991). She currently co-edits Palgrave's series *Studies in Oral History* and has served as contributing editor for oral history for the *Journal of American History* and as book review editor for the *Oral History Review*. She is a past president of the U.S. Oral History Association.

Selma Thomas is a U.S.-based filmmaker who produces documentary films as well as media installations for museum exhibitions. Much of her work for museums and documentaries relies on oral history. She is the media editor of *Curator: The Museum Journal* and co-editor of *The Virtual and the Real: Media in the Museum* (1998).

Lucienne Thys-Şenocak is assistant professor in the Department of Archaeology and History of Art at Koç University, Istanbul, and coordinator of its graduate program in Anatolian civilizations and cultural heritage management. She is the author of *Ottoman Women Builders: Hadice Turhan Sultan* (2006) and currently co-directs a restoration project for the Ottoman fortress of Seddülbahir on the Gallipoli peninsula. She received her Ph.D. in the history of art from the University of Pennsylvania.

Riki Van Boeschoten teaches social anthropology and oral history in the Department of History, Archaeology and Social Anthropology at the University of Thessaly in Greece. She directs the Laboratory of Social Anthropology and the department's oral history archive and supervises a research project on gender and migration. She is the author of four books and many articles on modern Balkan history and anthropology. The main focus of her work is on social memory and interdisciplinarity.

INDEX

Page numbers followed by *n* denote endnotes. Page number in *italics* denote illustrations.